Life Skills

>> Making tough choices

What happens when your personal values appear to directly conflict with those of your employer? Three options are open to you: (1) Leave and find another job (not as easy as it sounds); (2) keep your head down, do what you have been asked to do, and hold onto the job; and (3) talk to someone in the company about how uncomfortable the situation is making you feel and see if you can change things. All three options represent a tough choice that you may face at some point in your career. The factors that you will have to consider in making that choice will also change as you move through your working life. Making a job change on the basis of an ethical principle may seem much less challenging to a single person with fewer responsibilities than to a midlevel manager with a family and greater financial obligations.

The important point to remember here is that while an ethical dilemma may put you in a tough situation in the present, the consequences of the choice you make may remain with you far into the future. For that reason, make the choice as objectively and unemotionally as you can. Use the checklists and other tools that are available to you in this book to work through the exact nature of the issue so that you can resolve it in a manner that you can live with.

<< **Life Skills** apply et[...] that might affect stu[...] personal, and academic lives.

PROGRESS ✓ QUESTIONS

1. Explain the term *business ethics*.
2. Explain the difference between a descriptive and prescriptive approach to business ethics.
3. Identify six stakeholders of an organization.
4. Give four examples of how stakeholders could be negatively impacted by unethical corporate behavior.

∧ **Progress Check Questions** provide assessments of comprehension throughout each chapter.

ONE AND THE SAME

Real World Applications

You are a sales executive for a national equipment manufacturer. You joined the company straight out of college and have always been proud to work for the organization. Lately, however, you have become increasingly concerned about the office politics that have been going on at the corporate headquarters. Several senior executives have left, some very suddenly, and a lot of the changes can be traced back to the appointment of the CEO, Guy Ashley. Yesterday it was announced that Jack Lamborn, the chairman of the company (and the grandson of the founder) would be retiring at the end of the month (only two weeks away). The e-mail announcement also clarified that Guy Ashley would be assuming the position of chairman in addition to his role as CEO. You think back to your college ethics course and wonder whether this is really a good thing for the company as a whole. Would combining both roles raise any concerns for stakeholders over effective corporate governance? Why or why not?

<< **Real World Applications** prompt students to reflect further on workplace dilemmas.

Thinking Critically 5.3

>> HEALTHSOUTH

HealthSouth is America's largest provider of outpatient surgery and rehabilitation services. It owns or operates over 1,800 facilities across the country and serves 70 percent of the rehabilitation market. It was founded in 1984 by Richard Scrushy, a former respiratory therapist who believed that efficient one-stop shopping could be applied to the health care industry. From the time it went public in 1986, the Birmingham, Alabama, firm exceeded Wall Street expectations, a pattern that would continue for the next 15 years. In 1992 Scrushy aggressively began to acquire other clinics, and HealthSouth stock soared 31 percent annually between 1987 and 1997.

Scrushy cut a charismatic figure; the headquarters housed a museum dedicated to his achievements. He flew his own jet, mingled with celebrities, and sang with a band. For his third wedding in 1997 he chartered a plane to fly 150 guests to Jamaica. His workers knew him as King Richard.

His management style impressed many analysts. *Fortune* magazine described him in 1999 as executing his ideas brilliantly and said he was a taskmaster and a micromanager. Scrushy honed his technique, centralizing every piece of data imaginable. Every Friday a stack of printouts detailing the performance of each facility landed on his desk; when any one of them had a problem, Scrushy pounced. HealthSouth managed everything out of Birmingham: construction, purchasing, billing, even personnel. While this kind of top-down management may sound impossibly bureaucratic, Scrushy's troops made it work efficiently. Needed supplies and authorizations arrived within 30 days. Administrators who couldn't hit their budget targets were fired. Says Scrushy, "We can call 'em and tell 'em, 'Jump through hoops! Stand on your head!'"

However, behind the scenes was a pattern of institutionalized fraud. By the third quarter of 2002, the $8 billion company had overstated its assets by $800 million. According to testimony, the fraud began shortly after the company went public when Scrushy wanted to impress Wall Street. If the results were not what he expected, Scrushy would allegedly tell his staff to "fix it." They would then convene in what came to be known as a "family meeting" to adjust the figures, a process they called "filling the gap." The internal accountants kept two sets of books—one with the true figures and one that they presented to the outside world.

HealthSouth was able to keep up the deception in a number of ingenious ways that systematically fooled outside auditors. One scheme involved what are known as contractual adjustments. Sometimes the government or insurer would not fully reimburse a facility for the amount charged to a patient. This amount would be subtracted from gross revenues. In typical double-entry accounting, any loss of revenue has to be balanced by an increase in liabilities. HealthSouth simply failed to enter the liability amount. Its accountants also posted regular expenses as long-term capital expenditures and billed group therapies as single-person sessions. They routinely inflated the value of their assets. The practices were pervasive but individually so small that they rarely met the threshold levels that would trigger review by an outside auditor. The inside accountants were careful to make sure the adjustments were uneven and dispersed around the country so they appeared realistic.

Five HealthSouth accounting employees have been convicted of fraud. Four did not receive prison sentences, though. Their lawyers argued that they were obeying orders, subject to constant intimidation, and relatively low on the organizational chart. The judge declared at sentencing that although three held the rank of vice president, "These four were essentially data entry clerks, regardless of their job titles."

Scrushy was fired by the board on March 31, 2003. On November 4, 2003, Scrushy was indicted for securities fraud, money laundering, and other charges. He had maintained throughout that he was unaware of the illegal accounting practices. He was secretly recorded saying that he was worried about signing "fixed up" financials.

CONTINUED >>

Thinking Critically exercises appear at the end of every chapter. These detailed case studies, featuring well-known companies, present ethical situations that encourage students to focus on the impact of decisions they may face someday.

BusinessEthicsNow

Vice president/Editor in chief *Elizabeth Haefele*
Vice president/Director of marketing *Alice Harra*
Sponsoring editor *Barbara Owca*
Developmental editor *Danielle McCumber*
Executive marketing manager *Keari Green*
Lead digital product manager *Damian Moshak*
Digital development editor *Kevin White*
Director, Editing/Design/Production *Jess Ann Kosic*
Project manager *Kathryn D. Wright*
Senior buyer *Michael R. McCormick*
Senior designer *Anna Kinigakis*
Senior photo research coordinator *Keri Johnson*
Photo researcher *Allison Grimes*

Manager, Digital production *Janean A. Utley*
Interior design *Jessica M. Lazar*
Typeface *11/13 Minion Pro*
Compositor *Laserwords Private Limited*
Printer *Quad/Graphics*
Cover credit *Computer Mouse Padlock: ©TS Photography/ GettyImages; Lightbulb: ©gilles lougassi/iStockphoto; Bull: ©EightFish/GettyImages*
Credits *The credits section for this book begins on page 233 and is considered an extension of the copyright page.*

BUSINESS Ethics NOW

Published by McGraw-Hill, a business unit of The McGraw-Hill Companies, Inc., 1221 Avenue of the Americas, New York, NY, 10020. Copyright © 2012 by The McGraw-Hill Companies, Inc. All rights reserved. Previous editions © 2008 and 2010. No part of this publication may be reproduced or distributed in any form or by any means, or stored in a database or retrieval system, without the prior written consent of The McGraw-Hill Companies, Inc., including, but not limited to, in any network or other electronic storage or transmission, or broadcast for distance learning.

Some ancillaries, including electronic and print components, may not be available to customers outside the United States.

This book is printed on acid-free paper.

3 4 5 6 7 8 9 0 DOW/DOW 1 0 9 8 7 6 5 4 3

ISBN   978-0-07-352469-6
MHID   0-07-352469-7

Library of Congress Cataloging in Publication Data

Library of Congress Control Number: 2011920252

The Internet addresses listed in the text were accurate at the time of publication. The inclusion of a Web site does not indicate an endorsement by the authors or McGraw-Hill, and McGraw-Hill does not guarantee the accuracy of the information presented at these sites.

www.mhhe.com

Dedication

To my father, Norman Ghillyer

About the [AUTHOR]

Dr. Andrew Ghillyer is an Associate Professor at Argosy University in Tampa, Florida. His operational management experience spans over 30 years across a wide range of industries, including Chief Operating Officer (COO) of a civil engineering software company and Director of International Business Relations for a global training organization. Dr. Ghillyer is a Certified Compliance and Ethics Professional (CCEP), and he also served on the Board of Examiners for the Malcolm Baldrige National Quality Award for the 2007 award year. He received his doctorate in Management Studies from the University of Surrey in the United Kingdom. His first McGraw-Hill textbook, *Business Ethics: A Real World Approach*, was published in January 2007.

Ch. 1
DEFINING BUSINESS ETHICS

BusinessEthicsNow
BRIEF TABLE OF CONTENTS

Ch. 3
THE PRACTICE OF BUSINESS ETHICS

Ch. 4
CORPORATE SOCIAL RESPONSIBILITY

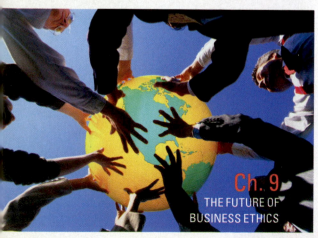

Ch. 9
THE FUTURE OF BUSINESS ETHICS

Table of Contents

PART 2 The Practice of Business Ethics

6 > The Role of Government

7 > Blowing the Whistle

8 > Ethics and Technology

PART 3 The Future of Business Ethics

9 > Ethics and Globalization

10 > Making It Stick: Doing What's Right in a Competitive Market

Welcome to
BusinessEthicsNow

WHAT'S NEW

Throughout the book:

Modified *Learning Outcomes* meet student and instructor needs.

For Review section at the end of each chapter revisits and discusses the Learning Outcomes.

Real World Applications element in each chapter highlights situations students may face in their own life.

New, up-to-the-moment ethical examples include the BP oil spill and WikiLeaks.

1 Understanding Ethics

NEW *ETHICAL DILEMMA* TOPIC   Sexting

NEW *INTERNET EXERCISE* TOPIC   Taking ethics pledges

2 Defining Business Ethics

NEW *ETHICAL DILEMMA* TOPIC   The AIG collapse

NEW *THINKING CRITICALLY*   The Phoenix Consortium

3 Organizational Ethics

NEW *ETHICAL DILEMMA* TOPIC   Mortgage modification programs

NEW *INTERNET EXERCISES* TOPIC   Codes of ethics and product recalls

NEW *THINKING CRITICALLY*   Bank of America

4 Corporate Social Responsibility

NEW *ETHICAL DILEMMA*   Global Oil

NEW *REVIEW EXERCISE*   Pangea Green Energy Philippines, Inc.

PART 1

DEFINING BUSINESS ETHICS

1 Understanding Ethics

2 Defining Business Ethics

We begin by exploring how people live their lives according to a standard of "right" or "wrong" behavior. Where do people look for guidance in deciding what is right or wrong or good or bad? Once they have developed a personal set of moral standards or ethical principles, how do people then interact with other members of their community or society as a whole who may or may not share the same ethical principles?

With a basic understanding of ethics, we can then examine the concept of business ethics, where employees face the dilemma of balancing their own moral standards with those of the company they work for and the supervisor or manager to whom they report on a daily basis. We examine the question of whether the business world should be viewed as an artificial environment where the rules by which you choose to live your own life don't necessarily apply.

CHAPTER 1

UNDERSTANDING ETHICS

LEARNING OUTCOMES

After studying this chapter, you should be able to:

1 Define *ethics*.

2 Explain the role of values in ethical decision making.

3 Understand opposing ethical theories and their limitations.

4 Discuss ethical relativism.

5 Explain an ethical dilemma and apply a process to resolve it.

FRONTLINE FOCUS
Doing the Right Thing

Megan is a rental agent for the Oxford Lake apartment complex. The work is fairly boring, but she's going to school in the evening, so the quiet periods give her time to catch up on her studies, plus the discounted rent is a great help to her budget. Business has been slow since two other apartment complexes opened up, and their vacancies are starting to run a little high.

The company recently appointed a new regional director to "inject some energy and creativity" into their local campaigns and generate some new rental leases. Her name is Kate Jones, and based on first impressions, Megan thinks Kate would rent her grandmother an apartment as long as she could raise the rent first.

Kate's first event is an open house, complete with free hot dogs and cokes and a clown making balloon animals for the kids. They run ads in the paper and on the radio and manage to attract a good crowd of people.

Their first applicants are Michael and Tania Wilson, an African-American couple with one young son, Tyler. Megan takes their application. They're a nice couple with a stable work history, more than enough income to cover the rent, and good references from their previous landlord. Megan advises them that they will do a background check as a standard procedure and that things "look very good" for their application.

After they leave, Kate stops by the rental office. "How did that couple look? Any issues with their application?"

"None at all," answers Megan. "I think they'll be a perfect addition to our community."

"Don't rush their application through too quickly," replies Kate. "We have time to find some more applicants, and, in my experience, those people usually end up breaking their lease or skipping town with unpaid rent."

QUESTIONS
1. What would be "the right thing" to do here? How would the "Golden Rule" on page **6** relate to Megan's decision?
2. How would you resolve this ethical dilemma? Review the three-step process on page **9** for more details.
3. What should Megan do now?

Ethics is about how we meet the challenge of doing the right thing when that will cost more than we want to pay.

The Josephson Institute of Ethics

>> What Is Ethics?

The field of **ethics** is the study of how we try to live our lives according to a standard of "right" or "wrong" behavior—in both how we think and behave toward others and how we would like them to think and behave toward us. For some, it is a conscious choice to follow a set of moral standards or ethical principles that provide guidance on how they should conduct themselves in their daily lives. For others, where the choice is not so clear, they look to the behavior of others to determine what is an acceptable standard of right and wrong or good and bad behavior. How they arrive at the definition of what's right or wrong is a result of many factors, including how they were raised, their religion, and the traditions and beliefs of their **society.**

Ethics The manner by which we try to live our lives according to a standard of "right" or "wrong" behavior—in both how we think and behave toward others and how we would like them to think and behave toward us.

Society A structured community of people bound together by similar traditions and customs.

Culture A particular set of attitudes, beliefs, and practices that characterize a group of individuals.

Value System A set of personal principles formalized into a code of behavior.

Intrinsic Value The quality by which a value is a good thing in itself and is pursued for its own sake, whether anything comes from that pursuit or not.

collection of all these influences as they are built up over your lifetime. A strict family upbringing or religious education would obviously have a direct impact on your personal moral standards. These standards would then provide a moral compass (a sense of personal direction) to guide you in the choices you make in your life.

HOW SHOULD I LIVE?

You do not acquire your personal moral standards in the same way that you learn the alphabet. Standards of ethical behavior are absorbed by osmosis as you observe the examples (both positive and negative) set by everyone around you—parents, family members, friends, peers, and neighbors. Your adoption of those standards is ultimately unique to you as an individual. For example, you may be influenced by the teachings of your family's religious beliefs and grow to believe that behaving ethically toward others represents a demonstration of religious devotion. However, that devotion may just as easily be motivated by either fear of a divine punishment in the afterlife or anticipation of a reward for living a virtuous life.

Alternatively, you may choose to reject religious morality and instead base your ethical behavior on your experience of human existence rather than any abstract concepts of right and wrong as determined by a religious doctrine.

When individuals share similar standards in a community, we can use the terms *values* and *value system.* The terms *morals* and *values* are often used to mean the same thing—a set of personal principles by which you aim to live your life. When you try to formalize those principles into a code of behavior, then you are seen to be adopting a **value system.**

>> Understanding Right and Wrong

Moral standards are principles based on religious, **cultural,** or philosophical beliefs by which judgments are made about good or bad behavior. These beliefs can come from many different sources:

- Friends
- Family
- Ethnic background
- Religion
- School
- The media—television, radio, newspapers, magazines, the Internet
- Personal role models and mentors

Your personal set of morals—your *morality*—represents a

THE VALUE OF A VALUE

Just as the word *value* is used to denote the worth of an item, a person's values can be said to have a specific "worth" for them. That worth can be expressed in two ways:

1. An **intrinsic value**—by which a value is a good thing in itself and is pursued for its own sake, whether anything good comes from that pursuit or not. For example, happiness, health,

and self-respect can all be said to have intrinsic value.

2. An **instrumental value**—by which the pursuit of one value is a good way to reach another value. For example, money is valued for what it can buy rather than for itself.

VALUE CONFLICTS

The impact of a person's or a group's value system can be seen in the extent to which their daily lives are influenced by those values. However, the greatest test of any personal value system comes when you are presented with a situation that places those values in direct conflict with an action. For example:

1. *Lying is wrong*—but what if you were lying to protect the life of a loved one?
2. *Stealing is wrong*—but what if you were stealing food for a starving child?
3. *Killing is wrong*—but what if you had to kill someone in self-defense to protect your own life?

How do you resolve such conflicts? Are there exceptions to these rules? Can you justify those actions based on special circumstances? Should you then start clarifying the exceptions to your value system? If so, can you really plan for every possible exception?

It is this gray area that makes the study of ethics so complex. We would like to believe that there are clearly defined rules of right and wrong and that you can live your life in direct observance of those rules. However, it is more likely that situations will arise that will require exceptions to those rules. It is how you choose to respond to those situations and the specific choices you make that really define your personal value system.

DOING THE RIGHT THING

If you asked your friends and family what ethics means to them, you would probably arrive at a list of four basic categories:

1. Simple truth—right and wrong or good and bad.
2. A question of someone's personal character—his or her integrity.
3. Rules of appropriate individual behavior.

4. Rules of appropriate behavior for a community or society.

The first category—*a simple truth*—also may be expressed as simply *doing the right thing*. It is something that most people can understand and support. It is this basic simplicity that can lead you to take ethical behavior for granted—you assume that everyone is committed to doing the right thing, and it's not until you are exposed to unethical behavior that you are reminded that, unfortunately, not all people share your interpretation of what "the right thing" is, and even if they did, they may not share your commitment to doing it.

The second category—*personal integrity,* demonstrated by someone's behavior—looks at ethics from an external rather than an internal viewpoint. All our classic comic-book heroes—Superman, Spider-Man, Batman, and Wonder Woman, to name just a few—represent the ideal of personal integrity where a person lives a life that is true to his or her moral standards, often at the cost of considerable personal sacrifice.

Rules of appropriate individual behavior represent the idea that the moral standards we develop for ourselves impact our lives on a daily basis in our behavior and the other types of decisions we make.

Rules of appropriate behavior for a community or society remind us that we must eventually bring our personal value system into a world that is shared with people who will probably have both similar and very different value systems. Establishing an ethical ideal for a community or society allows that group of people to live with the confidence that comes from knowing they share a common standard.

Each category represents a different feature of ethics. On one level, the study of ethics seeks to understand how people make the choices they make—how they develop their own set of moral standards, how they live their lives on the basis of those standards, and how they judge the behavior of others in relation to those standards. On a second level, we then try to use that understanding to develop a set of ideals or principles by which a group of ethical individuals can combine as a community with a common understanding of how they "ought" to behave.

Instrumental Value The quality by which the pursuit of one value is a good way to reach another value. For example, money is valued for what it can buy rather than for itself.

Superman has become a fictional representation of personal integrity. Can you find examples of individuals with personal integrity in your own life?

PROGRESS ✓ QUESTIONS

1. What is the definition of *ethics*?
2. What is a moral compass, and how would you apply it?
3. Explain the difference between intrinsic and instrumental values.
4. List the four basic categories of ethics.

THE GOLDEN RULE

For some, the goal of living an ethical life is expressed by the **Golden Rule:** *Do unto others as you would have them do unto you,* or *treat others as you would like to be treated.* This simple and very clear rule is shared by many different religions in the world:

- Buddhism: "Hurt not others in ways that you yourself would find hurtful."—*Udana-Varga* 5:18
- Christianity: "Therefore all things whatsoever ye would that men should do to you, do ye even so to them."—*Matthew* 7:12
- Hinduism: "This is the sum of duty: do naught unto others which would cause you pain if done to you."—*Mahabharata* 5:1517

The Golden Rule Do unto others as you would have them do unto you.

Virtue Ethics A concept of living your life according to a commitment to the achievement of a clear ideal— *what sort of person would I like to become, and how do I go about becoming that person?*

Utilitarianism Ethical choices that offer the greatest good for the greatest number of people.

Universal Ethics Actions that are taken out of *duty* and *obligation* to a purely moral ideal rather than based on the needs of the situation, since the universal principles are seen to apply to everyone, everywhere, all the time.

Of course, the danger with the Golden Rule is that not everyone thinks like you, acts like you, or believes in the same principles that you do, so to live your life on the assumption that your pursuit of an ethical ideal will match others' ethical ideals could get you into trouble. For example, if you were the type of person who values honesty in your personal value system, and you found a wallet on the sidewalk, you would try to return it to its rightful owner. However, if you lost your wallet, could you automatically expect that the person who found it would make the same effort to return it to you?

>> Ethical Theories

The subject of ethics has been a matter of philosophical debate for over 2,500 years—as far back as the Greek philosopher Socrates. Over time and with considerable debate, different schools of thought have developed as to how we should go about living an ethical life.

Ethical theories can be divided into three categories: virtue ethics, ethics for the greater good, and universal ethics.

VIRTUE ETHICS

The Greek philosopher Aristotle's belief in individual character and integrity established a concept of living your life according to a commitment to the achievement of a clear ideal— *what sort of person would I like to become, and how do I go about becoming that person?*

The problem with **virtue ethics** is that societies can place different emphasis on different virtues. For example, Greek society at the time of Aristotle valued wisdom, courage, and justice. By contrast, Christian societies value faith, hope, and charity. So if the virtues you hope to achieve aren't a direct reflection of the values of the society in which you live, there is a real danger of value conflict.

ETHICS FOR THE GREATER GOOD

As the name implies, *ethics for the greater good* is more focused on the outcome of your actions rather than the apparent virtue of the actions themselves— that is, a focus on the greatest good for the greatest number of people. Originally proposed by a Scottish philosopher named David Hume, this approach to ethics is also referred to as **utilitarianism.**

The problem with this approach to ethics is the idea that the ends justify the means. If all you focus on is doing the greatest good for the greatest number of people, no one is accountable for the actions that are taken to achieve that outcome. The 20th century witnessed one of the most extreme examples of this when Adolf Hitler and his Nazi party launched a national genocide against Jews and "defective" people on the utilitarian grounds of restoring the Aryan race.

UNIVERSAL ETHICS

Originally attributed to a German philosopher named Immanuel Kant, **universal ethics** argues that there are certain and universal principles that should apply to all ethical judgments. Actions are taken out

>> What do you stand for, or what will you stand against?

Your personal value system will guide you throughout your life, both in personal and professional matters. How often you will decide to stand by those values or deviate from them will be a matter of personal choice, but each one of those choices will contribute to the ongoing development of your values. As the work of Lawrence Kohlberg (page **11**) points out, your understanding of moral complexities and ethical dilemmas grows as your life experience and education grow. For that reason, you will measure every choice you make against the value system you developed as a child from your parents, friends, society, and often your religious upbringing. The cumulative effect of all those choices is a value system that is unique to you. Of course, you will share many of the same values as your family and friends, but some of your choices will differ from theirs because your values differ.

The great benefit of having such a guide to turn to when faced with a difficult decision is that you can both step away from the emotion and pressure of a situation and, at the same time, turn to a system that truly represents who you are as a person—someone with integrity who can be counted on to make a reasoned and thoughtful choice.

of *duty* and *obligation* to a purely moral ideal rather than based on the needs of the situation, since the universal principles are seen to apply to everyone, everywhere, all the time.

The problem with this approach is the reverse of the weakness in ethics for the greater good. If all you focus on is abiding by a universal principle, no one is accountable for the consequences of the actions taken to abide by those principles. Consider, for example, the current debate over the use of stem cells in researching a cure for Parkinson's disease. If you recognize the value of human life above all else as a universal ethical principle, how do you justify the use of a human embryo in the harvesting of stem cells? Does the potential for curing many major illnesses—Parkinson's, cancer, heart disease, and kidney disease—make stem cell research ethically justifiable? If not, how do you explain that to the families who lose loved ones waiting unsuccessfully for organ transplants?

> **Ethical Relativism** Concept that the traditions of your society, your personal opinions, and the circumstances of the present moment define your ethical principles.

>> Ethical Relativism

When the limitations of each of these theories are reviewed, it becomes clear that there is no truly comprehensive theory of ethics, only a choice that is made based on your personal value system. In this context, it is easier to understand why, when faced with the requirement to select a model of how we ought to live our lives, many people choose the idea of **ethical relativism,** whereby the traditions of their society, their personal opinions, and the circumstances of the present moment define their ethical principles.

The idea of relativism implies some degree of flexibility as opposed to strict

PROGRESS ✓ QUESTIONS

5. What is the Golden Rule?

6. List the three basic ethical theories.

7. Identify the limitations of each theory.

8. Provide an example of each theory in practice.

Why is the issue of accountability relevant in considering alternate ethical theories?

Study Alert

Applied Ethics The study of how ethical theories are put into practice.

Ethical Dilemma A situation in which there is no obvious right or wrong decision, but rather a right or right answer.

black-and-white rules. It also offers the comfort of being a part of the ethical majority in your community or society instead of standing by your individual beliefs as an outsider from the group. In our current society, when we talk about peer pressure among groups, we are acknowledging that the expectations of this majority can sometimes have negative consequences.

>> Ethical Dilemmas

Up to now we have been concerned with the notion of ethical theory—how we conduct ourselves as individuals and as a community in order to live a good and moral life. However, this ethical theory represents only half of the school of philosophy we recognize as ethics. At some point, these theories have to be put into practice, and we then move into the area of **applied ethics.**

The basic assumption of ethical theory is that you as an individual or community are in control of all the factors that influence the choices that you make. In reality, your ethical principles are most likely to be tested when you face a situation in which there is no obvious right or wrong decision but rather a right or right answer. Such situations are referred to as **ethical dilemmas.**

As we saw earlier in our review of value systems and value conflicts, any idealized set of principles or standards inevitably faces some form of challenge. For ethical theories, that challenge takes the form of

PEER PRESSURE

In the days before the dominance of technology in the lives of teenagers and young adults, concerns over *peer pressure* (stress exerted by friends and classmates) focused on bullying, criminal behavior, drug use, and sexual activity. The arrival of "smart phones" and the ability to send text messages to a wide audience and post short videos on the Internet have brought a new element to concerns over peer pressure at school. A 2008 survey by the National Campaign to Prevent Teen and Unplanned Pregnancy found that 20 percent of teens ages 13 to 19 said they have electronically sent or posted online nude or seminude pictures or video of themselves. Nearly 50 percent of the teen girls surveyed said "pressure from guys" was the reason they shared sexually explicit photos or messages, and boys cited "pressure from friends."

Incidents of "sexting" have increased so quickly that local communities and law enforcement agencies have been caught unprepared. While many consider the incidents to be examples of negligent behavior on the part of the teens involved, the viewing and distribution of such materials could result in charges of felony child pornography and a listing on a sex offender registry for decades to come. In one case, 18-year-old Philip Alpert was convicted of child pornography after distributing a revealing photo of his 16-year-old girlfriend after they got into an argument. He will be labeled a "sex offender" until he is 43 years old.

Unfortunately, the dramatic increase in the number of incidents of sexting has brought about tragic consequences. Cincinnati teen Jessie Logan killed herself after nude pictures she had sent to her boyfriend were sent to

hundreds of students. Even though only five teens were involved in sending the pictures, their unlimited access to technology allowed them to reach several hundred students in four school districts before the incident was stopped. At the time of writing this case, 15 states are now considering laws to deter teens from sexting without charging them as adult sex offenders.

QUESTIONS

1. In what ways does giving in to peer pressure constitute ethical relativism?
2. How could you use your personal value system to fight back against peer pressure?

3. How would you communicate the risks of sexting to students who are struggling to deal with peer pressure?

4. Is a change in the law the best option for addressing this problem? Why or why not?

Sources: Satta Sarmah, " 'Sexting' on the Rise among Teens," http://rye.patch .com, May 21, 2010; "Sexting Bill Introduced at Statehouse," www.onntv.com, May 13, 2010; and "Sex and Tech: Results from a Survey of Teens and Young Adults," www.thenationalcampaign.org/sextech/PDF/SexTech_Summary .pdf, October 20, 2010.

a dilemma in which the decision you must make requires you to make a right choice knowing full well that you are:

- Leaving an equally right choice undone.
- Likely to suffer something bad as a result of that choice.
- Contradicting a personal ethical principle in making that choice.
- Abandoning an ethical value of your community or society in making that choice.

RESOLVING ETHICAL DILEMMAS

By its very definition, an ethical dilemma cannot really be resolved in the sense that a resolution of the problem implies a satisfactory answer to the problem. Since, in reality, the "answer" to an ethical dilemma is often the lesser of two evils, it is questionable to assume that there will always be an acceptable answer—it's more a question of whether or not you can arrive at an outcome you can live with.

Joseph L. Badaracco Jr.'s book *Defining Moments* captures this notion of living with an outcome in a discussion of "sleep-test ethics":[1]

The sleep test . . . is supposed to tell people whether or not they have made a morally sound decision. In its literal version, a person who has made the right choice can sleep soundly afterward; someone who has made the wrong choice cannot. . . . Defined less literally and more broadly, sleep-test ethics rests on a single, fundamental belief: that we should rely on our personal insights, feelings, and instincts when we face a difficult problem. Defined this way, sleep-test ethics is the ethics of intuition. It advises us to follow our hearts, particularly when our minds are confused. It says that, if something continues to gnaw at us, it probably should.

When we review the ethical theories covered in this chapter, we can identify two distinct approaches to handling ethical dilemmas. One is to focus on the practical consequences of what we choose to do, and the other focuses on the actions themselves and the degree to which they were the right actions to take. The first school of thought argues that the ends justify the means and that if there is no harm, there is no foul. The second claims that some actions are simply wrong in and of themselves.

So what should you do? Consider this three-step process for solving an ethical problem:[2]

Step 1. *Analyze the consequences.* Who will be helped by what you do? Who will be harmed? What kind of benefits and harm are we talking about? (Some are more valuable or more harmful than others: good health, someone's trust, and a clean environment are very valuable benefits, more so than a faster remote control device.) How does all of this look over the long run as well as the short run?

Step 2. *Analyze the actions.* Consider all the options from a different perspective, without thinking about the consequences. How do the actions measure up against moral principles like honesty, fairness, equality, respecting the dignity of others, and people's rights? (Consider the common good.) Are any of the actions at odds with those standards? If there's a conflict between principles or between the rights of different people involved, is there a way to see one principle as more important than the others? Which option offers actions that are least problematic?

Step 3. *Make a decision.* Take both parts of your analysis into account, and make a decision. This strategy at least gives you some basic steps you can follow.

PROGRESS ✓ QUESTIONS

9. Define *ethical relativism.*
10. Define *applied ethics.*
11. What is an ethical dilemma?
12. Explain the three-step process for resolving an ethical dilemma.

Ethical Reasoning Looking at the information available to us in resolving an ethical dilemma, and drawing conclusions based on that information in relation to our own ethical standards.

If a three-step model seems too simple, Arthur Dobrin identified eight questions you should consider when resolving an ethical dilemma:[3]

1. *What are the facts?* Know the facts as best you can. If your facts are wrong, you're liable to make a bad choice.
2. *What can you guess about the facts you don't know?* Since it is impossible to know all the facts, make reasonable assumptions about the missing pieces of information.
3. *What do the facts mean?* Facts by themselves have no meaning. You need to interpret the information in light of the values that are important to you.
4. *What does the problem look like through the eyes of the people involved?* The ability to walk in another's shoes is essential. Understanding the problem through a variety of perspectives increases the possibility that you will choose wisely.

> **Study Alert**
>
> Apply Dobrin's eight questions to an ethical dilemma you have faced in the past. Would applying this process have changed your decision? Why or why not?

5. *What will happen if you choose one thing rather than another?* All actions have consequences. Make a reasonable guess as to what will happen if you follow a particular course of action. Decide whether you think more good or harm will come of your action.
6. *What do your feelings tell you?* Feelings are facts too. Your feelings about ethical issues may give you a clue as to parts of your decision that your rational mind may overlook.
7. *What will you think of yourself if you decide one thing or another?* Some call this your conscience. It is a form of self-appraisal. It helps you decide whether you are the kind of person you would like to be. It helps you live with yourself.
8. *Can you explain and justify your decision to others?* Your behavior shouldn't be based on a whim. Neither should it be self-centered. Ethics involves you in the life of the world around you. For this reason you must be able to justify your moral decisions in ways that seem reasonable to reasonable people. Ethical reasons can't be private reasons.

The application of these steps is based on some key assumptions: first, that there is sufficient time for the degree of contemplation that such questions require; second, that there is enough information available for you to answer the questions; and third, that the dilemma presents alternative resolutions for you to select from. Without alternatives, your analysis becomes a question of finding a palatable resolution that you can live with—much like Badaracco's sleep test—rather than the most appropriate solution.

ETHICAL REASONING

When we are attempting to resolve an ethical dilemma, we follow a process of **ethical reasoning.** We look at the information available to us and draw conclusions based on that information in relation to our own ethical standards. Lawrence Kohlberg developed a framework (see Figure 1.1) that presents the argu-

Level	Stage	Social Orientation
Preconventional	1	Obedience and Punishment
	2	Individualism, instrumentalism, and exchange
Conventional	3	"Good boy/nice girl"
	4	Law and order
Postconventional	5	Social contract
	6	Principled conscience

Figure 1.1 • Lawrence Kohlberg's Stages of Ethical Reasoning

THE OVERCROWDED LIFEBOAT

In 1842, a ship struck an iceberg, and more than 30 survivors were crowded into a lifeboat intended to hold 7. As a storm threatened, it became obvious that the lifeboat would have to be lightened if anyone were to survive. The captain reasoned that the right thing to do in this situation was to force some individuals to go over the side and drown. Such an action, he reasoned, was not unjust to those thrown overboard, for they would have drowned anyway. If he did nothing, however, he would be responsible for the deaths of those whom he could have saved. Some people opposed the captain's decision. They claimed that if nothing were done and everyone died as a result, no one would be responsible for these deaths. On the other hand, if the captain attempted to save some, he could do so only by killing others and their deaths would be his responsibility; this would be worse than doing nothing and letting all die. The captain rejected this reasoning. Since the only possibility for rescue required great efforts of rowing, the captain decided that the weakest would have to be sacrificed. In this situation it would be absurd, he thought, to decide by drawing lots who should be thrown overboard. As it turned out, after days of hard rowing, the survivors were rescued and the captain was tried for his action.

QUESTIONS

1. Did the captain make the right decision? Why or why not?
2. What other choices could the captain have made?
3. If you had been on the jury, how would you have decided? Why?
4. Which ethical theory or theories could be applied here?

Source: Adapted from www.friesian.com/valley/dilemmas.htm.

---

ment that we develop a reasoning process over time, moving through six distinct stages (classified into three levels of moral development) as we are exposed to major influences in our lives.[4]

Level 1: Preconventional. At this lowest level of moral development, a person's response to a perception of right and wrong is initially directly linked to the expectation of punishment or reward.

- *Stage 1: Obedience and punishment orientation.* A person is focused on avoidance of punishment and deference to power and authority—that is, something is right or wrong because a recognized authority figure says it is.
- *Stage 2: Individualism, instrumentalism, and exchange.* As a more organized and advanced form of stage 1, a person is focused on satisfying his or her own needs—that is, something is right or wrong because it helps the person get what he or she wants or needs.

Level 2: Conventional. At this level, a person continues to become aware of broader influences outside of the family.

- *Stage 3: "Good boy/nice girl" orientation.* At this stage, a person is focused on meeting the expectations of family members—that is, something is right or wrong because it pleases those family members. Stereotypical behavior is recognized, and conformity to that behavior develops.
- *Stage 4: Law-and-order orientation.* At this stage, a person is increasingly aware of his or her membership in a society and the existence of codes of behavior—that is, something is right or wrong because codes of legal, religious, or social behavior dictate it.

Level 3: Postconventional. At this highest level of ethical reasoning, a person makes a clear effort to define principles and moral values that reflect an individual value system rather than simply reflecting the group position.

- *Stage 5: Social contract legalistic orientation.* At this stage, a person is focused on individual rights and the development of standards based on critical examination—that is, something is right or wrong because it has withstood scrutiny by the society in which the principle is accepted.

- *Stage 6: Universal ethical principle orientation.* At this stage, a person is focused on self-chosen ethical principles that are found to be comprehensive and consistent—that is, something is right or wrong because it reflects that person's individual value system and the conscious choices he or she makes in life. While Kohlberg always believed in the existence of stage 6, he was never able to find enough research subjects to prove the long-term stability of this stage.

Kohlberg's framework offers us a clearer view into the process of ethical reasoning—that is, that someone can arrive at a decision, in this case the resolution of an ethical dilemma—on the basis of a moral rationale that is built on the cumulative experience of his or her life.

Kohlberg also believed that a person could not move or jump beyond the next stage of his or her six stages. It would be impossible, he argued, for a person to comprehend the moral issues and dilemmas at a level so far beyond his or her life experience and education.

Real World Applications

Michelle Lopane takes her managerial role very seriously. Sometimes managers are called on to make tough decisions—firing nonperformers and letting people go when cost cuts have to be made. She has always found a way to come to terms with the tough decisions: "As long as I can sleep at night, then I know I have made the best decision I can under the circumstances." Lately, however, the material in her business ethics class has made her reconsider some of her previous decisions. "Am I really making the best decision or just the decision I can live with?" How do you think most managers would answer that question?

PROGRESS ✓ QUESTIONS

13. What are the eight questions you should consider in resolving an ethical dilemma?
14. What assumptions are we making in the resolution of a dilemma? What should you do if you can't answer these eight questions for the dilemma you are looking to resolve?
15. What are Kohlberg's three levels of moral development?
16. What are the six stages of development in those three levels?

>> Conclusion

Now that we have reviewed the processes by which we arrive at our personal ethical principles, let's consider what happens when we take the study of ethics into the business world. What happens when the decision that is expected of you by your supervisor or manager goes against your personal value system? Consider these situations:

- As a salesperson, you work on a monthly quota. Your sales training outlines several techniques to "up sell" each customer—that is, to add additional features, benefits, or warranties to your product that the average customer doesn't really need. Your sales manager draws a very clear picture for you: If you don't make your quota, you don't have a job. So if your personal value system requires that you sell customers only what they really need, are you willing to make more smaller sales to hit your quota, or do you do what the top performers do and "up sell like crazy" and make every sale count?

- You are a tech-support specialist for a small computer software manufacturer. Your supervisor informs you that a bug has been found in the software that will take several weeks to fix. You are instructed to handle all calls without admitting the existence of the bug. Specific examples are provided to divert customers' concerns with suggestions of user error, hardware issues, and conflicts with other software packages. The bug, you are told, will be fixed in a scheduled version upgrade without any admission of its existence. Could you do that?

How organizations reach a point in their growth where such behavior can become the norm, and how employees of those organizations find a way to work in such environments, is what the field of business ethics is all about.

FRONTLINE FOCUS
Doing the Right Thing—Megan Makes a Decision

Kate was right; they did receive several more applications at the open house, but each one was less attractive as a potential tenant than the Wilsons. Some had credit problems, others couldn't provide references because they had been "living with a family member," and others had short work histories or were brand new to the area.

This left Megan with a tough choice. The Wilsons were the best applicants, but Kate had made her feelings about them very clear, so Megan's options were fairly obvious—she could follow Kate's instructions and bury the Wilsons' application in favor of another couple, or she could give the apartment to the best tenants and run the risk of making an enemy of her new boss.

The more Megan thought about the situation, the angrier she became. Not giving the apartment to the Wilsons was discriminatory and would expose all of them to legal action if the Wilsons ever found out—plus it was just plain wrong. There was nothing in their application that suggested that they would be anything other than model tenants, and just because Kate had experienced bad tenants like "those people" in the past, there was no reason to group the Wilsons with that group.

Megan picked up the phone and started dialing. "Mrs. Wilson? Hi, this is Megan with Oxford Lake Apartments. I have some wonderful news."

QUESTIONS

1. Did Megan make the right choice here?
2. What do you think Kate's reaction will be?
3. What would have been the risks for Oxford Lake if Megan had decided not to rent the apartment to the Wilsons?

[For Review]

1. **Define *ethics*.**

   Ethics is the study of how we try to live our lives according to a standard of "right" or "wrong" behavior—in both how we think and behave toward others and how we would like them to think and behave toward us. For some, it is a conscious choice to follow a set of moral standards or ethical principles that provide guidance on how they should conduct themselves in their daily lives. For others, where the choice is not so clear, they look to the behavior of others to determine what is an acceptable standard of right and wrong or good and bad behavior.

2. **Explain the role of values in ethical decision making.**

   Values represent a set of personal principles by which you aim to live your life. Those principles are most often based on religious, cultural, or philosophical beliefs that you have developed over time as a collection of influences from family, friends, school, religion, ethnic background, the media, and your personal mentors and role models. When you try to formalize these principles into a code of behavior, then you are seen to be adopting a value system which becomes your benchmark in deciding which choices and behaviors meet the standard of "doing the right thing."

3. **Understand opposing ethical theories and their limitations.**

   Ethical theories can be divided into three categories: virtue ethics (focusing on individual character and integrity); ethics for the greater good, also referred to as utilitarianism (focusing on the choices that offer the greatest good for the greatest number of people); and universal ethics (focusing on universal principles that should apply to all ethical judgments, irrespective of the outcome). Each category is limited by the absence of a clear sense of accountability for the choices being made. As we have seen in this chapter, individual character and integrity can depend on many influences and are therefore unlikely to be a consistent standard. Utilitarianism only focuses on the outcome of the choice without any real concern for the virtue of the actions themselves, and human history has produced many atrocities that have been committed in the name of the "end justifying the means." At the other end of the scale, staying true to morally pure ethical principles without considering the outcome of that choice is equally problematic.

4. **Discuss "ethical relativism."**

   In the absence of a truly comprehensive theory of ethics and a corresponding model or checklist to guide them, many people choose to approach ethical decisions by pursuing the comfort of an ethical majority that reflects a combination of the traditions of their society, their personal opinions, and the circumstances of the present moment. This relativist approach offers more flexibility than the pursuit of definitive black-and-white rules. However, the pursuit of an ethical majority in a peer pressure situation can sometimes have negative consequences.

5. **Explain an ethical dilemma, and apply a process to resolve it.**

   An ethical dilemma is a situation in which there is no obvious right or wrong decision, but rather a right or right answer. In such cases you are required to make a choice even though you are probably leaving an equally valid choice unmade and contradicting a personal or societal ethical value in making that choice. There is no definitive checklist for ethical dilemmas because the issues are often situational in nature. Therefore the best hope for a "right" choice can often fall to the "lesser of two evils" and an outcome you can live with. Arthur Dobrin offers eight questions that should be asked to ensure that you have as much relevant information available as possible (in addition to a clear sense of what you don't know) as to the available choices, the actions needed for each choice, and the anticipated consequences of each choice.

[Key Terms]

Applied Ethics **8**

Culture **4**

Ethical Dilemma **8**

Ethical Reasoning **10**

Ethical Relativism **7**

Ethics **4**

The Golden Rule **6**

Instrumental Value **5**

Intrinsic Value **4**

Society **4**

Universal Ethics **6**

Utilitarianism **6**

Value System **4**

Virtue Ethics **6**

[Review Questions]

1. Why do we study ethics?

2. Why should we be concerned about doing "the right thing"?

3. If each of us has a unique set of influences and values that contribute to our personal value system, how can that be applied to a community as a whole?

4. Is it unrealistic to expect others to live by the Golden Rule?

5. Consider how you have resolved ethical dilemmas in the past. What would you do differently now?

6. What would you do if your resolution of an ethical dilemma turned out to be the wrong approach and it actually made things worse?

[Review Exercises]

How would you act in the following situations? Why? How is your personal value system reflected in your choice?

1. You buy a candy bar at the store and pay the cashier with a $5 bill. You are mistakenly given change for a $20 bill. What do you do?

2. You are riding in a taxicab and notice a $20 bill that has obviously fallen from someone's wallet or pocketbook. What do you do?

3. You live in a small midwestern town and have just lost your job at the local bookstore. The best-paying job you can find is at the local meatpacking plant, but you are a vegetarian and feel strongly that killing animals for food is unjust. What do you do?

4. You are having a romantic dinner with your spouse to celebrate your wedding anniversary. Suddenly, at a nearby table, a man starts yelling at the young woman he is dining with and becomes so verbally abusive that she starts to cry. What do you do?

5. You are shopping in a department store and observe a young man taking a watch from a display stand on the jewelry counter and slipping it into his pocket. What do you do?

6. You are the manager of a nonprofit orphanage. At the end of the year, a local car dealer approaches you with a proposition. He will give you a two-year-old van worth $10,000 that he has just taken as a trade-in on a new vehicle if you will provide him with a tax-deductible donation receipt for a new van worth $30,000. Your current transportation is in very bad shape, and the children really enjoy the field trips they take. Do you accept his proposition?

[Internet Exercises]

1. Visit the My Code of Ethics Project (MCOE) at www.mycodeofethics.org.
   a. What is the purpose of MCOE?
   b. What is the organization's pledge?
   c. Record three different codes/pledges/oaths from those listed on the site.
   d. Write your own pledge on a topic that is important to you (a maximum of two paragraphs).

2. In these days of increasing evidence of questionable ethical practices, many organizations, communities, and business schools are committing to ethics pledges as a means of underscoring the importance of ethical standards of behavior in today's society. Using Internet research, find two examples of such pledges and answer the following questions:
   a. Why did you select these two examples specifically?
   b. Why did each entity choose to make an ethical pledge?
   c. In what ways are the pledges similar and different?
   d. If you proposed the idea of an ethics pledge at your school or job, what do you think the reaction would be?

[Team Exercises]

1. ***Take me out to the cheap seats.***
   Divide into two groups, and prepare arguments *for* and *against* the following behavior: *My dad takes me to a lot of baseball games and always buys the cheapest tickets in the park. When the game starts, he moves to better, unoccupied seats, dragging me along. It embarrasses me. Is it OK for us to sit in seats we didn't pay for?*

2. **Umbrella exchange.**
   Divide into two groups, and prepare arguments *for* and *against* the following behavior: *One rainy evening I wandered into a shop, where I left my name-brand umbrella in a basket near the door. When I was ready to leave, my umbrella was gone. There were several others in the basket, and I decided to take another name-brand umbrella. Should I have taken it, or taken a lesser-quality model, or just gotten wet?*

3. **A gift out of the blue.**
   Divide into two groups, and prepare arguments *for* and *against* the following behavior: *I'm a regular customer of a men's clothing mail-order company, and it sends me new catalogs about six times a year. I usually order something because the clothes are good quality with a money-back guarantee, and if the item doesn't fit or doesn't look as good on me as it did in the catalog, the return process is very easy. Last month I ordered a couple of new shirts. When the package arrived, there were three shirts in the box, all in my size, in the three colors available for that shirt. There was no note or card, and the receipt showed that my credit card had been charged for two shirts. I just assumed that someone in the shipping department was recognizing me as a valuable customer—what a nice gesture, don't you think?"*

4. **Renting a dress?**
   Divide into two groups, and prepare arguments *for* and *against* the following behavior: *My friend works for a company that manages fund-raising events for nonprofit organizations—mostly gala benefits and auctions. Since these events all take place in the same city, she often crosses paths with the same people from one event to the other. The job doesn't pay a lot, but the dress code is usually very formal. To stretch her budget and ensure that she's not wearing the same dress at every event, she buys dresses, wears them once, has them professionally dry-cleaned, reattaches the label using her own label gun, and returns them to the store, claiming that they were the wrong color or not a good fit. She argues that the dry-cleaning bill is just like a rental charge, and she always returns them for store credit, not cash. The dress shop may have made a sale, but is this fair?*

Source: Exercises 1 and 2 adapted from Randy Cohen, *The Good, the Bad, and the Difference: How to Tell Right from Wrong in Everyday Situations* (New York: Doubleday, 2002), pp. 194–201.

Thinking Critically

>> ALL THE NEWS THAT'S FIT TO PRINT

In May 2003 an investigation by journalists from *The New York Times* found that one of its staff reporters, Jayson Blair, had committed several acts of journalistic fraud in reporting on key events for the newspaper over a period of four years with the company. The investigation revealed that at least 36 of the last 73 articles he wrote contained significant errors. Of the around 600 articles he wrote during his four years of service with the company, many contained fabricated quotes from key individuals connected with the event being reported, invented scenes that were created to build emotional intensity for the article, and material copied directly from other newspapers or news services. In addition, Blair used photographic evidence of events to write articles as if he had been there in person or interviewed people at the scene, when he had actually remained at his desk in New York.

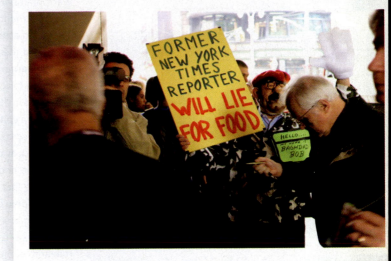

When the extent of his unprofessional behavior was uncovered, Blair elected to resign from his position. *The New York Times* published a four-page apology to its readers, including a public commitment to better journalistic integrity, and asked those readers for help in identifying any other incorrect material yet to be identified in Blair's extensive body of work. As a direct result of this fraudulent behavior, the executive editor of the paper, Howell Raines, and the managing editor, Gerald Boyd, resigned. Jayson Blair went on to publish a memoir of his four years at *The Times,* called *Burning Down My Master's House.*

In her 2008 book *This Land Is Their Land*, author and columnist Barbara Ehrenreich comments that technology and the constant push for cost control in regional newspapers and news sites has prompted editors to apparently view the Jayson Blair case from a slightly different angle. Referencing the news Web site www.pasadenanow.com, Ehrenreich comments:

> The Web site's editor points out that he can get two Indian reporters for a mere $20,800 a year—and, no they won't be commuting from New Delhi. Since Pasadena's city council meetings can be observed on the Web, the Indian reporters will be able to cover local politics from half the planet away. And if they ever feel a need to see the potholes of Pasadena, there's always Google Earth.

So it would seem that if there is money to be saved, editors can be flexible about the location of their reporters after all. No word from Ehrenreich on whether the location of the reporters will be disclosed in the stories featured on the Web site.

QUESTIONS

1. What do Blair's actions suggest about his personal and professional ethics?

2. Blair's issues with accuracy and corrections were well known to his supervisors, prompting one of his editors to send out an e-mail reminding all the journalists that "accuracy is all we have . . . it's what we are and what we sell." What steps should they have taken to address Blair's behavior?

3. Should we expect journalists to uphold a higher level of professional ethics than businesspeople? Why or why not?

4. Since the editors of pasadenanow.com are choosing to hire reporters they know for certain will be at a considerable distance from the stories they will be covering, does that change the ethics of the situation in comparison to the Blair story?

5. Should pasadenanow.com disclose the overseas location of its reporters? Why or why not?

6. Blair has since joined the "speaker circuit," lecturing on ethics under the title "Lessons Learned." Is it ethical to make money from lecturing on your own unethical behavior? Why or why not?

Sources: B. Ehrenreich, *This Land Is Their Land: Reports from a Divided Nation* (New York: Metropolitan Books, Henry Holt & Co., 2008); D. Barry, D. Barstow, J. Glater, A. Liptak, and J. Steinberg, "Times Report Who Resigned Leaves Long Trail of Deception," *The New York Times,* May 11, 2003; and B. Calame, "Preventing a Second Jason Blair," *The New York Times,* June 18, 2006.

>> THE MAN WHO SHOCKED THE WORLD

In July 1961, a psychologist at Yale University, Dr. Stanley Milgram, a 28-year-old Harvard graduate with a PhD in social psychology, began a series of experiments that were destined to shock the psychological community and reveal some disturbing insights into the capacity of the human race to inflict harm on one another. Participants in the experiments

were members of the general public who had responded to a newspaper advertisement for volunteers in an experiment on punishment and learning.

The "teacher" in the experiment (one of Milgram's team of researchers) instructed the participants to inflict increasingly powerful electric shocks on a test "learner" every time the learner gave an incorrect answer to a word-matching task. The shocks started, in theory, at the low level of 15 volts and increased in 15-volt increments up to a potentially fatal shock of 450 volts. In reality, the voltage machine was an elaborate stage prop, and the learner was an actor screaming and imitating physical suffering as the voltage level of each shock appeared to increase. The participants were told about the deception at the end of the experience, but during the experiment they were led to believe that the voltage and the pain being inflicted were real. The teacher used no force or intimidation in the experiment other than maintaining an air of academic seriousness.

The experiment was repeated more than 20 times using hundreds of research subjects. In every case the majority of the subjects failed to stop shocking the learners, even when they believed they were inflicting a potentially fatal voltage and the learner had apparently stopped screaming with pain. Some did plead to stop the test, and others argued with the teacher that the experiment was going wrong, but in the end, the majority of them obeyed the instructions of the teacher to the letter.

It's important to remind ourselves that these research participants were not criminals or psychopaths with a documented history of sadistic behavior. They were average Americans who responded to an ad and came in off the street to take part. What Milgram's research appears to tell us is that people are capable of suspending their own individual morality to someone in authority—even killing someone just because they were instructed to do it.

Milgram's research shocked the academic world and generated heated debate about the ethical conduct of the study and the value of the results in comparison to the harm inflicted on the research participants who were led to believe that it was all really happening. That debate continues to this day, even though subsequent repetitions of the study in various formats have validated Milgram's original findings. Almost 50 years later, we are faced with research data that suggest ordinary human beings are capable of performing destructive and inhumane acts without any physical threat of harm to themselves. As Thomas Bass commented, "While we would like to believe that when confronted with a moral dilemma we will act as our conscience dictates, Milgram's obedience experiments teach us that in a concrete situation with powerful social constraints, our moral senses can easily be trampled."

QUESTIONS

1. Critics of Milgram's research have argued that the physical separation between the participant and the teacher in one room and the learner in the other made it easier for the participant to inflict the shocks. Do you think that made a difference? Why or why not?

2. The treatment of the participants in the study raised as much criticism as the results the study generated. Was it ethical to mislead them into believing that they were really inflicting pain on the learners? Why?

3. The participants were introduced to the learners as equal participants in the study—that is, volunteers just like them. Do you think that made a difference in the decision to keep increasing the voltage? Why?

4. What do you think Milgram's research tells us about our individual ethical standards?

5. Would you have agreed to participate in this study? Why or why not?

6. Do you think if the study were repeated today we would get the same kind of results? Why?

Sources: A. Cohen, "Four Decades after Milgram, We're Still Willing to Inflict Pain," *The New York Times,* December 29, 2008; and A. Altman, "Why We're OK with Hurting Strangers," www.time.com, December 19, 2008.

Thinking Critically

>> LIFE AND DEATH • Elder Suicide or Dignified Exit? A Letter from Ohio

I'm 80. I've had a good life—mostly pretty happy, though certainly with its ups and downs. My wife died seven years ago. My children are healthy and happy, busy with their kids, careers, friends. But I know they worry about me; they feel increasingly burdened with thoughts about how to care for me when I can no longer care for myself, which—let's not kid ourselves—is coming all too soon. I live four states away from them so either they will have to uproot me and move me close to them or I'll have to go live in a nursing home. I don't relish either option. This town has been my home for nearly my whole adult life, and I don't fancy leaving. On the other hand, I do not want to live among strangers and be cared for by those who are paid minimum wage to wash urine-soaked sheets and force-feed pudding to old people.

I'm in decent health—for the moment. But things are slipping. I have prostrate cancer, like just about every other man my age. It probably won't kill me . . . but having to get up and pee four or five times a night, standing over the bowl for long minutes just hoping something will come out, this might do me in. My joints are stiff, so it doesn't really feel good to walk. I've got bits and pieces of skin cancer here and there that need to be removed. These things are all treatable, or so they say (there are pills to take and procedures to have done). But it seems to me a waste of money. Why not pass my small savings on to my grandkids, to give them a jump on college tuition?

What I don't understand is why people think that it is wrong for someone like me to just call it a day, throw in the towel. How can it be possible that I don't have a right to end my own life, when I'm ready? (But apparently I don't.)

I'm tired and I'm ready to be done with life. I'd so much rather just quietly die in my garage with the car running than eke out these last few compromised years. (Even better would be a quick shot or a small dose of powerful pills—but, alas, these are not at my disposal.)

But if I do myself in, I will be called a suicide. My death will be added to the statistics: another "elder suicide." How sad! (Doesn't the fact that so many elderly people commit suicide—and with much greater rates of success, I must say, than any other demographic group—tell you something?) Why can't this society just come up with a humane, acceptable plan for those of us ready to be finished? Why can't we old folks go to city hall and pick up our End-of-Life Packet, with the financial and legal forms to bring things into order for our children, with assistance on how to recycle all our unneeded furniture and clothes, and with a neat little pack of white pills: When ready, take all 10 pills at once, with plenty of water. Lie down quietly in a comfortable place, close your eyes, and wait.

How can choosing my own end at my own time be considered anything other than a most dignified final exit?

— Anonymous. June, 2003

QUESTIONS

1. Should people have the moral right to end their lives if they so please?
2. Does being near the end of one's life make the decision to end it justified?
3. What might the phrase "right to die" mean?
4. Do people have the right to seek assistance in dying?
5. Do people have the right to give assistance in dying?
6. What kind of restrictions, if any, should there be on assisted suicide?

Source: Jessica Pierce, *Morality Play: Case Studies in Ethics* (New York: McGraw-Hill, 2005).

DEFINING BUSINESS ETHICS

After studying this chapter, you should be able to:

1 Define the term *business ethics.*

2 Identify an organization's stakeholders.

3 Discuss the position that business ethics is an oxymoron.

4 Summarize the history of business ethics.

5 Identify and propose a resolution for an ethical dilemma in your work environment.

6 Explain how executives and employees seek to justify unethical behavior.

FRONTLINE FOCUS
The Customer Is Always Right

Nancy Marr was the shift leader at a local fast-food restaurant. She first started working there as a summer job for gas money for that old Honda Civic she used to drive. That was more years ago than she cared to remember, and she had managed to upgrade her car to something far more reliable these days. She enjoyed working for this company. The job was hard on her feet, but when she hit the breakfast, lunch, or dinner rush, she was usually too busy to notice.

Today was an important day. Rick Fritzinger, the store manager, had called an "all staff meeting" to discuss the new healthy menu that the company had launched in response to public pressure for healthier lunch choices—lots of salads and new options for their side items. It was going to take a lot of work to get her staff up to speed, and Nancy expected that a lot of the customers would need extra time to work through all the new options, but overall she liked the new menu. She thought that the new lower-priced items would bring in a lot of new customers who were looking for something more than burgers and fries.

The company had sent a detailed information kit on the new menu, and Rick covered the material very thoroughly. As he finished the last PowerPoint slide, he asked if anyone had any questions. Since they had been in the meeting for over an hour, her team was very conscious of all the work that wasn't getting done for the lunch rush, so no one asked any questions.

As a last comment Rick said: "This new menu should hopefully bring in some new customers, but let's not forget what we're doing here. We're here to make money for our shareholders, and to do that, we have to make a profit. So we're only going to make a limited number of these new items. If they run out, offer customers something from the regular menu and don't forget to push the "up-size" menu options and ice creams for dessert—those are still our most profitable items. And if someone wants one of these new healthy salads, make sure you offer them an ice cream or shake to go with it."

Nancy was amazed. The company was making a big push for this new menu and spending a ton of money on advertising, and here was Rick planning to sabotage it just because he was afraid that these lower-priced items would hurt his sales (and his bonus!).

QUESTIONS

1. Look at Figures 2.1 and 2.2, and identify which stakeholders would be directly impacted by Rick's plan to sabotage the new healthy menu.
2. Describe the ethical dilemma that Nancy is facing here.
3. What should Nancy do now?

A large company was hiring a new CEO. The four leading candidates worked inside the company so the board decided to ask each candidate a very basic question. The comptroller was brought in. "How much is 2 plus 2?" "This must be a trick question, but the answer is 4. It will always be 4." They brought in the head of research and development, an engineer by training. "How much is 2 plus 2?" "That depends on whether it is a positive 2 or a negative 2. It could be 4, zero, or minus 4." They brought in the head of marketing. "The way I figure it, 2 plus 2 is 22." Finally, they brought in legal counsel. "How much is 2 plus 2?" they asked. He looked furtively at each board member. "How much do you want it to be?"

Tom Selleck, Commencement Speech, Pepperdine University, 2000

>> Defining Business Ethics

Business ethics involves the application of standards of moral behavior to business situations. Just as we saw in our review of the basic ethical concepts of right and wrong in Chapter 1, students of business ethics can approach the topic from two distinct perspectives:

1. A *descriptive* summation of the customs, attitudes, and rules that are observed within a business. As such, we are simply documenting what is happening.

2. A *normative* (or *prescriptive*) evaluation of the degree to which the observed customs, attitudes, and rules can be said to be ethical. Here we are more interested in recommending what should be happening.

Business Ethics The application of ethical standards to business behavior.

Stakeholder Someone with a share or interest in a business enterprise.

In either case, business ethics should not be applied as a separate set of moral standards or ethical concepts from general ethics. Ethical behavior, it is argued, should be the same both inside and outside a business situation. By recognizing the challenging environment of business, we are acknowledging the identity of the key players impacted by any potentially unethical behavior—the stakeholders. In addition, we can identify the troubling situation where your personal values may be placed in direct conflict with the standards of behavior you feel are expected of you by your employer.

>> Who Are the Stakeholders?

Figure 2.1 maps out the relevant **stakeholders** for any organization and their respective interests in the ethical operation of that organization. Not every stakeholder will be relevant in every business situation—not all companies use wholesalers to deliver their products or services to their customers, and customers would not be involved in payroll decisions between the organization and its employees.

Of greater concern is the involvement of these stakeholders with the actions of the organization and the extent to which they would be impacted by unethical behavior. As Figure 2.2 illustrates, the decision of an organization such as WorldCom to hide the extensive debt and losses it was accumulating in its aggressive pursuit of growth and market share can be seen to have impacted all of its stakeholders in different ways.

FIG. 2.1 Stakeholder Interests

Stakeholders	Interest in the Organization
Stockholders or shareholders	• Growth in the value of company stock • Dividend income
Employees	• Stable employment at a fair rate of pay • A safe and comfortable working environment
Customers	• "Fair exchange"—a product or service of acceptable value and quality for the money spent • Safe and reliable products
Suppliers/vendor partners	• Prompt payment for delivered goods • Regular orders with an acceptable profit margin
Retailers/wholesalers	• Accurate deliveries of quality products on time and at a reasonable cost • Safe and reliable products
Federal government	• Tax revenue • Operation in compliance with all relevant legislation
Creditors	• Principal and interest payments • Repayment of debt according to the agreed schedule
Community	• Employment of local residents • Economic growth • Protection of the local environment

FIG. 2.2 Stakeholder Impact from Unethical Behavior

Stakeholders	Interest in the Organization
Stockholders or shareholders	• False and misleading financial information on which to base investment decisions • Loss of stock value • Cancellation of dividends
Employees	• Loss of employment • Not enough money to pay severance packages or meet pension obligations
Customers	• Poor service quality (as WorldCom struggled to combine the different operating and billing systems of each company they acquired, for example)
Suppliers/vendor partners	• Delayed payment for delivered goods and services • Unpaid invoices when the company declared bankruptcy
Federal government	• Loss of tax revenue • Failure to comply with all relevant legislation
Creditors	• Loss of principal and interest payments • Failure to repay debt according to the agreed schedule
Community	• Unemployment of local residents • Economic decline

PROGRESS ✓ QUESTIONS

1. Explain the term *business ethics*.
2. Explain the difference between a descriptive and prescriptive approach to business ethics.
3. Identify six stakeholders of an organization.
4. Give four examples of how stakeholders could be negatively impacted by unethical corporate behavior.

>> An Ethical Crisis: Is Business Ethics an Oxymoron?

Our objective in identifying the types of unethical concerns that can arise in the business environment and the impact that such unethical behavior can have on the stakeholders of an organization is to develop the ability to anticipate such events and ultimately to put the appropriate policies and procedures in place to prevent such behavior from happening at all.

Unfortunately, over the last two decades, the ethical track record of many organizations would lead us to believe that no such policies or procedures have been in place. The standard of **corporate governance,** the extent to which the officers of a corporation are fulfilling the

duties and responsibilities of their offices to the relevant stakeholders, appears to be at the lowest level in business history:

Corporate Governance The system by which business corporations are directed and controlled.

- Several prominent organizations (all former "Wall Street darlings")—Enron, WorldCom, Lehman Brothers, Bear Stearns—have been found to have hidden the true state of their precarious finances from their stakeholders.
- Others—Adelphia Cable, Tyco, Merrill Lynch—have been found to have senior officers who appeared to regard the organization's funds as their personal bank accounts.
- Financial reports are released that are then restated at a later date.
- Products are rushed to market that have to be recalled due to safety problems at a later date (Toyota).
- Organizations are being sued for monopolistic practices (Microsoft), race and gender discrimination (Walmart, Texaco, Denny's), and environmental contamination (GE).
- CEO salary increases far exceed those of the employees they lead.
- CEO salaries have increased while shareholder returns have fallen. *Fast Company* magazine prints a regular column titled "CEO See-Ya" that targets CEOs who have failed to deliver at least average shareholder returns while earning lucrative compensation packages.

- CEOs continue to receive bonuses while the stocks of their companies underperform the market average (as indicated by the documented performance of the Standard & Poor's 500 Index) and thousands of employees are being laid off.

It is understandable, therefore, that many observers would believe that the business world lacks any sense of ethical behavior whatsoever. Some would even argue that the two words are as incompatible as "government efficiency," Central Intelligence Agency, or "authentic reproduction," but is "business ethics" really an **oxymoron?**

It would be unfair to brand every organization as fundamentally unethical in its business dealings. There's no doubt that numerous prominent organizations that were previously held as models of aggressive business management (e.g., Enron, Global Crossing, HealthSouth, IMClone, Tyco, and WorldCom) have later been proved to be fundamentally flawed in their ethical practices. This has succeeded in bringing the issue to the forefront of public awareness. However, the positive outcome from this has been increased attention to the need for third-party guarantees of ethical conduct and active commitments from the rest of the business world. Institutions such as the Ethics and Compliance Officer Association, the Ethics Resource Center, and the Society of Corporate Compliance and Ethics, among others, now offer organizations clear guidance and training in making explicit commitments to ethical business practices.[1]

So while these may not be the best of times for business ethics, it could be argued that the recent negative publicity has served as a wake-up call for many organizations to take a more active role in establishing standards of ethical conduct in their daily operations. One of the key indicators in this process has been the increased prominence of a formal **code of ethics** in an organization's public statements. The Ethics Resource Center (ERC) defines a code of ethics as:[2]

> A central guide to support day-to-day decision making at work. It clarifies the cornerstones of your organization—its mission, values and principles— helping your managers, employees and stakeholders

Oxymoron The combination of two contradictory terms, such as "deafening silence" or "jumbo shrimp."

Code of Ethics A company's written standards of ethical behavior that are designed to guide managers and employees in making the decisions and choices they face every day.

How do conversations regarding ethics change when your business is closely linked to human well-being? Should ethical standards be different for a hospital or day care center?

understand how these cornerstones translate into everyday decisions, behaviors and actions. While some may believe codes are designed to limit one's actions, the best codes are actually structured to liberate and empower people to make more effective decisions with greater confidence.

PROGRESS ✓ QUESTIONS

5. Define the term *oxymoron* and provide three examples.
6. Is the term *business ethics* an oxymoron? Explain your answer.
7. Define the term *corporate governance*.
8. Explain the term *code of ethics*.

So the code of ethics can be seen to serve a dual function. As a message to the organization's stakeholders, the code should represent a clear corporate commitment to the highest standards of ethical behavior. As an internal document, the code should represent a clear guide to managers and employees in making the decisions and choices they face every day. Unfortunately, as you will see in many of the case studies and discussion exercises in this book, a code of ethics can be easily sidestepped or ignored by any organization.

Study Alert!

Does your company have a code of ethics? Where is it published? How frequently does the company promote it?

THE FORD PINTO

Thirty years after its production, the Ford Pinto is still remembered as a dangerous firetrap.

In the late 1960s, the baby boom generation was starting to attend college. With increasing affluence in America, demand for affordable transportation increased, and foreign carmakers captured the market with models like the Volkswagen Beetle and Toyota Corolla. Ford needed a competitive vehicle, and Lee Iacocca authorized production of the Pinto. It was to be small and inexpensive— under 2,000 pounds and under $2,000. The production schedule had it in dealers' lots in the 1971 model year, which meant that it went from planning to production in under two years. At the time, it was typical to make a prototype vehicle first and then gear up production. In this case, Ford built the machines that created the shell of the vehicle at the same time as it was designing the first model. This concurrent development shortened production time but made modifications harder.

The compact design called for a so-called saddlebag gas tank, which straddled the rear axle. In tests, rear impacts over 30 mph sometimes caused the tank to rupture in such a way that it sprayed gas particles into the passenger compartment, somewhat like an aerosol. Canadian regulations demanded a greater safety factor, and models for export were modified with an extra buffer layer. However, the Pinto met all U.S. federal standards at the time it was made.

Ford actively campaigned against stricter safety standards throughout the production of the Pinto. The government actively embraced cost-benefit analysis, and Ford's argument against further regulations hinged on the purported benefits. Under pressure, the National Highway Traffic Safety Administration came up with a figure that

put a value of just over $200,000 on a human life. Using this figure, and projecting some 180 burn deaths a year, Ford argued that retrofitting the Pinto would be overly problematic.

At one point, over 2 million Pintos were on the road, so it is not surprising that they were involved in a number of crashes. However, data began to indicate that some kinds of crashes, particularly rear-end and rollover crashes, were more likely to produce fires in the Pinto than in comparable vehicles. A dramatic article in *Mother Jones* drew on internal Ford memos to show that the company was aware of the safety issue and indicted the company for selling cars "in which it knew hundreds of people would needlessly burn to death." It also claimed that installing a barrier between the tank and the passenger compartment was an inexpensive fix (less than $20). In 1978, in an almost unprecedented case in Goshen, Indiana, the state charged the company itself with the criminal reckless homicide of

CONTINUED >>

three young women. The company was acquitted, largely because the judge confined the evidence to the particular facts—the car was stalled and rammed at high speed by a pickup truck—but Ford was faced with hundreds of lawsuits and a severely tarnished reputation.

Under government pressure, and just before new standards were enacted, Ford recalled 1.5 million Pintos in 1978. The model was discontinued in 1980.

Lee Iacocca said that his company did not deliberately make an unsafe vehicle, that the proportion of deadly accidents was not unusually high for the model, and that the controversy was essentially a legal and public relations issue.

QUESTIONS

1. Should a manufacturer go beyond government standards if it feels there may be a potential safety hazard with its product?

2. Once the safety issue became apparent, should Ford have recalled the vehicle and paid for the retrofit? Should it have invited owners to pay for the new barrier if they so chose? If only half the owners responded to the recall, what would the company's obligation be?

3. Is there a difference for a consumer between being able to make a conscious decision about upgrading safety features (such as side airbags) and relying on the manufacturer to determine features such as the tensile strength of the gas tank?

4. Once Pintos had a poor reputation, they were often sold at a discount. Do private sellers have the same obligations as Ford if they sell a car they know may have design defects? Does the discount price absolve sellers from any responsibility for the product?

Source: K. Gibson, *Business Ethics: People, Profits, and the Planet* (New York: McGraw-Hill, 2006), pp. 630–32.

>> The History of Business Ethics

Figure 2.3 documents a brief history of business ethics. It illustrates several dramatic changes that have taken place in the business environment over the last four decades:

- The increased presence of an employee voice has made individual employees feel more comfortable speaking out against actions of their employers that they feel to be irresponsible or unethical. They are also more willing to seek legal resolution for such issues as unsafe working conditions, harassment, discrimination, and invasion of privacy.
- The issue of corporate social responsibility has advanced from an abstract debate to a core performance-assessment issue with clearly established legal liabilities.
- Corporate ethics has moved from the domain of legal and human resource departments into the organizational mainstream with the appointment of corporate ethics officers with clear mandates.
- Codes of ethics have matured from cosmetic public relations documents into performance-measurement documents that an increasing number of organizations are now committing to share with all their stakeholders.
- The 2002 Sarbanes-Oxley Act has introduced greater accountability for chief executive officers and boards of directors in signing off on the financial performance records of the organizations they represent.

PROGRESS ✔ QUESTIONS

9. Identify a major ethical dilemma in each of the last four decades.
10. Identify a key development in business ethics in each of the last four decades.
11. Which decade saw the most development in business ethics? Why?
12. Which decade saw the most ethical dilemmas? Why?

>> Resolving Ethical Dilemmas

So what does all this mean for the individual employee on the front lines of the organization, dealing with stakeholders on a daily basis? In most cases, the code of ethics that is displayed so prominently for all stakeholders to see (and, presumably, be reassured by) offers very little guidance when employees face ethical conflicts in the daily performance

FIG. 2.3 A Brief History of Business Ethics

Decade	Ethical Climate	Major Ethical Dilemmas	Business Ethics Developments
1960s	Social unrest. Antiwar sentiment. Employees have an adversarial relationship with management. Values shift away from loyalty to an employer to loyalty to ideas. Old values are cast aside.	• Environmental issues. • Increased employee-employer tension. • Civil rights issues dominate. • Honesty. • The work ethic changes. • Drug use escalates.	• Companies begin establishing codes of conduct and values statements. • Birth of social responsibility movement. • Corporations address ethics issues through legal or personnel departments.
1970s	Defense contractors and other major industries riddled by scandal. The economy suffers through recession. Unemployment escalates. There are heightened environmental concerns. The public pushes to make businesses accountable for ethical shortcomings.	• Employee militancy (employee versus management mentality). • Human rights issues surface (forced labor, substandard wages, unsafe practices). • Some firms choose to cover rather than correct dilemmas.	• Ethics Resource Center (ERC) founded (1977). • Compliance with laws highlighted. • Federal Corrupt Practices Act passed in 1977. • Values movement begins to move ethics away from compliance orientation to being "values centered."
1980s	The social contract between employers and employees is redefined. Defense contractors are required to conform to stringent rules. Corporations downsize and employees' attitudes about loyalty to the employer are eroded. Health care ethics are emphasized.	• Bribes and illegal contracting practices. • Influence peddling. • Deceptive advertising. • Financial fraud (savings and loan scandal). • Transparency issues arise.	• ERC develops the U.S. Code of Ethics for Government Service (1980). • ERC forms first business ethics office at General Dynamics (1985). • Defense Industry Initiative established. • Some companies create ombudsman positions in addition to ethics officer roles. • False Claims Act (government contracting).
1990s	Global expansion brings new ethical challenges. There are major concerns about child labor, facilitation payments (bribes), and environmental issues. The emergence of the Internet challenges cultural borders. What was forbidden becomes common.	• Unsafe work practices in Third World countries. • Increased corporate liability for personal damage (cigarette companies, Dow Chemical, etc.). • Financial mismanagement and fraud.	• Federal Sentencing Guidelines (1991). • Class action lawsuits. • Global Sullivan Principles (1999). • *In re Caremark* (Delaware Chancery Court ruling regarding board responsibility for ethics). • IGs requiring voluntary disclosure. • ERC establishes international business ethics centers. • Royal Dutch/Shell International begins issuing annual reports on its ethical performance.
2000s		• Cyber crime. • Increased corporate liability. • Privacy issues (data mining). • Financial mismanagement. • International corruption. • Loss of privacy—employees versus employers. • Intellectual property theft.	• Business regulations mandate stronger ethical safeguards (Federal Sentencing Guidelines for Organizations; Sarbanes-Oxley Act of 2002). • Anticorruption efforts grow. • Shift to emphasis on corporate social responsibility and integrity management. • Formation of International ethics centers to serve the needs of global business. • OECD Convention on Bribery (1997–2000).

Source: Adapted from Ethics Resource Center, "Business Ethics Timeline." Copyright © 2002, Ethics Resource Center.

of their work responsibilities. When employees observe unethical behavior (for example, fraud, theft of company property, or incentives being paid under the table to suppliers or vendor partners) or are asked to do something that conflicts with their own personal values (selling customers products or services they don't need or that don't fill their needs), the extent of the guidance available to them is often nothing more than a series of clichés:

- Consult the company code of ethics.
- Do what's right for the organization's stakeholders.
- Do what's legal.
- Do what you think is best ("use your best judgment").
- Do the right thing.

However, in many cases, the scenario the employee faces is not a clear-cut case of right and wrong, but a case of right versus right. In this scenario, the **ethical dilemma** involves a situation that requires selecting between conflicting values that are important to the employee or the organization. For example:[3]

> **Ethical Dilemma** A situation in which there is no obvious right or wrong decision, but rather a right or right answer.

- You have worked at the same company with your best friend for the last 10 years—in fact, he told you about the job and got you the interview. He works in the marketing department and is up for a promotion to marketing director—a position he has been wanting for a long time. You work in sales, and on your weekly conference call, the new marketing director—someone recruited from outside the company—joins you. Your boss explains that although the formal announcement hasn't been made yet, the company felt it was important to get the new director up to speed as quickly as possible. He will be joining the company in two weeks, after completing his two weeks' notice with his current employer. Should you tell your friend what happened?
- You work in a small custom metal fabrication company that is a wholly owned subsidiary of a larger conglomerate. Your parent company has announced cost-cutting initiatives that include a freeze on pay increases, citing "current market difficulties." At the same time, the CEO trades in the old company plane for a brand-new Gulfstream jet. Your colleagues are planning to strike over the unfair treatment—a strike that will cause considerable hardship for many of your customers who have come to rely on your company as a quality supplier. Do you go on strike with them?

- At a picnic given by your employer for all of the company's employees, you observe that your supervisor—who is also a friend—has had a bit too much to drink. As you're walking home after the party, she stops her car and asks if you'd like a ride home. Do you refuse her offer, perhaps jeopardizing the friendship, or take a chance on not getting home safely?

RESOLUTION

Resolution of an ethical dilemma can be achieved by first recognizing the type of conflict you are dealing with:

- *Truth versus loyalty.* Do you tell the truth or remain loyal to the person or organization that is asking you not to reveal that truth?
- *Short term versus long term.* Does your decision have a short-term consequence or a longer-term consequence?
- *Justice versus mercy.* Do you perceive this issue as a question of dispensing justice or mercy? (Which one are you more comfortable with?)
- *Individual versus community.* Will your choice affect one individual or a wider group or community?

In the examples used above, both sides are right to some extent, but since you can't take both actions, you are required to select the better or higher right based on your own resolution process. In the first example, the two rights you are facing are:

- It is right, on the one hand, to tell your friend the truth about not getting the promotion. After all, you know the truth, and what kind of world would this be if people did not honor the truth? Perhaps your friend would prefer to hear the truth from you and would be grateful for time to adjust to the idea.

It is right, on the other hand, not to say anything to your friend because the person who told you in the first place asked you to keep it secret and you must be loyal to your promises. Also, your friend may prefer to hear the news from his supervisor and may be unhappy with you if you tell.

In this example you are faced with a truth versus loyalty conflict: Do you tell your friend the truth or remain loyal to the person who swore you to secrecy?

Once you have reached a decision as to the type of conflict you are facing, three resolution principles are available to you:

- *Ends-based*. Which decision would provide the greatest good for the greatest number of people?
- *Rules-based*. What would happen if everyone made the same decision as you?
- *The Golden Rule*. Do unto others as you would have them do unto you.

None of these principles can be said to offer a perfect solution or resolution to the problem since you cannot possibly predict the reactions of the other people involved in the scenario. However, the process of resolution at least offers something more meaningful than "going with your gut feeling" or "doing what's right."

Life Skills

>> Making tough choices

What happens when your personal values appear to directly conflict with those of your employer? Three options are open to you: (1) Leave and find another job (not as easy as it sounds); (2) keep your head down, do what you have been asked to do, and hold onto the job; and (3) talk to someone in the company about how uncomfortable the situation is making you feel and see if you can change things. All three options represent a tough choice that you may face at some point in your career. The factors that you will have to consider in making that choice will also change as you move through your working life. Making a job change on the basis of an ethical principle may seem much less challenging to a single person with fewer responsibilities than to a midlevel manager with a family and greater financial obligations.

The important point to remember here is that while an ethical dilemma may put you in a tough situation in the present, the consequences of the choice you make may remain with you far into the future. For that reason, make the choice as objectively and unemotionally as you can. Use the checklists and other tools that are available to you in this book to work through the exact nature of the issue so that you can resolve it in a manner that you can live with.

>> Justifying Unethical Behavior

So how do supposedly intelligent, and presumably experienced, executives and employees manage to commit acts that end up inflicting such harm on their companies, colleagues, customers, and vendor partners? Saul Gellerman identified "four commonly held rationalizations that can lead to misconduct":[4]

1. *A belief that the activity is within reasonable ethical and legal limits—that is, that it is not "really" illegal or immoral.* Andrew Young is quoted as having said, "Nothing is illegal if a hundred businessmen decide to do it." The notion that anything that isn't specifically labeled as wrong must be OK is an open invitation for the ethically challenged employer and employee—especially if there are explicit rewards for such creativity within those newly expanded ethical limits. The Porsches and Jaguars that became the vehicles of choice for Enron's young and aggressive employees were all the incentives needed for newly hired employees to adjust their viewpoint on the company's creative practices.

2. *A belief that the activity is in the individual's or the corporation's best interests—that the individual would somehow be expected to undertake the activity.* In a highly competitive environment, working on short-term targets, it can be easy to find justification for any act as being "in the company's best interest." If landing that big sale or beating your competitor to market with the latest product upgrades can be seen to ensure large profits, strong public relations, a healthy stock price, job security for hundreds if not thousands of employees, not to mention a healthy bonus and promotion for you, the issue of doing whatever it takes becomes a much more complex, increasingly gray ethical area.

3. *A belief that the activity is safe because it will never be found out or publicized—the classic crime-and-punishment issue of discovery.* Every unethical act that goes undiscovered reinforces this belief. Companies that rely on the deterrents of audits and spot checks make some headway in discouraging

TOO BIG TO FAIL?

Your employer, American International Group (AIG), received almost $180 billion in federal bailout dollars in the belief that the collapse of AIG would have a catastrophic effect on the U.S. financial markets—the company was "too big to fail." Poor management choices had led the company to depend heavily on revenue from insuring investors against defaults on financial bonds backed by risky subprime mortgages (up to trillions of dollars of policy coverage). With the collapse of the housing market, investors filed claims on those insurance policies with AIG, and the company quickly discovered that it had insufficient financial resources to meet all those claims.

1. You are responsible for signing off on bonuses for AIG executives in the amount of $165 million, with the top seven executives of the company each receiving more than $4 million. News of the bonuses creates a public outcry over the payment of millions of dollars to executives who had driven the company into near bankruptcy. Supporters of the bonus structure at AIG argue that failure to pay the bonuses would result in the departure of senior executives to AIG's competitors. Is this a valid defense? Why or why not?

2. The AIG collapse was blamed on one division of the company—the credit default swap department. Executives in the other departments that contributed positive revenue to AIG's bottom line feel strongly that they have earned their bonuses. Do they have a case?

3. Your boss encourages you to try and convince the executives to forgo their bonuses "for the good of

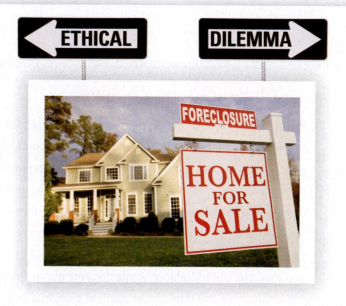

the company and its reputation." How would you go about doing that?

4. Is it possible to resolve this issue to the satisfaction of both the taxpayers who bailed out AIG and the senior executives? Why or why not?

Sources: Gretchen Morgenson, "Behind Insurer's Crisis, Blind Eye to a Web of Risk," *The New York Times*, September 28, 2008; Sharona Coutts, "AIG Bonus Scandal," *ProPublica*, March 18, 2009; and Op-Ed contributor, "Dear AIG: I Quit!" *The New York Times*, March 25, 2009.

Real World Applications

Mei Lynn D'Allesandro enjoyed her job as an human resource generalist—helping to recruit and hire new employees and seeing those employees succeed in the organization was very rewarding. Occasionally an employee performed below expectations and would be asked to leave the company. Today was one of those days. Steve had been caught falsifying sales reports to make sure he hit his monthly quota, and Mei Lynn had been asked to sit in on the meeting in which Steve's manager confronted him with the news. What amazed Mei Lynn was Steve's response: "Everybody does it in some form or another. As far as this company is concerned, you're only as good as your last quarter, and sometimes you have to bend the rules a little to meet that expectation." Is Steve's statement a valid defense? Why or why not?

unethical behavior (or at least prompting people to think twice about it). Gellerman argues, "A trespass detected should not be dealt with discreetly. Managers should announce the misconduct and how the individuals involved were punished. Since the main deterrent to illegal or unethical behavior is the perceived probability of detection, managers should make an example of people who are detected."

4. *A belief that because the activity helps the company, the company will condone it and even protect the person who engages in it.* This belief suggests some confusion over the loyalty being demonstrated here. Companies engaged in unethical behavior—willingly or otherwise—may protect the identity of the personnel involved but only for as long as it is in the company's best interests to do so. Once that transgression is made public and regulatory bodies get involved, most cases would seem to suggest that the situation rapidly becomes one of every man for himself. As we saw with the Enron case, once the extent of the fraud became public, everyone involved suddenly became eager to distance him- or herself from both the activity and any key personnel in direct contact with that activity.

Study Alert!

Which of the four rationalizations for unethical behavior do you think gets used the most? Why?

>> Conclusion

It is unfortunate that the media have been given so much material on unethical corporate behavior over the last decade. Unethical CEOs have become household names to the extent that the term *business ethics* seems to be more of an oxymoron now than ever before. In such a negative environment, it is easy to forget that businesses can and do operate in an ethical manner and that the majority of employees really are committed to doing the right thing in their time at work. The organizations that build an ethical culture based on that fundamental belief can be seen to succeed in exactly the same manner as their more "creative" counterparts, with increased revenue, profits, and market share. In the following chapters we examine how they attempt to do just that.

However, as we will see in the following chapters, the challenge of building and operating an ethical business requires a great deal more than simply doing the right thing. The organization must devote time to the development of a detailed code of ethics that offers "guidance with traction" as opposed to traditional general platitudes that are designed to cover a multitude of scenarios with a healthy mix of inspiration and motivation.

Of greater concern is the support offered to employees when they are faced with an ethical dilemma. This involves not only the appointment of a designated corporate ethics officer with all the appropriate policies and procedures for bringing an issue to his/her attention but also the creation and ongoing maintenance of a corporate culture of *trust*.

FRONTLINE FOCUS
The Customer Is Always Right—Nancy Makes a Decision

Adam Boyle, one of Nancy's brightest team members, identified the problem that Rick had created for them right away: "So we have a new menu that's supposed to bring in new customers, but we're only going to make a few healthy items to ensure that we sell lots of our unhealthy but more profitable items—is that it?"

"Looks like it," said Nancy.

"Well, I hope I'm not working the drive-thru window when we start to run out of the new items," said Adam. "Can you say 'bait and switch'?"

Fortunately, the new menu items wouldn't start until next week, so Nancy had time to work on this potential disaster. She couldn't believe that Rick was being so shortsighted here. She understood his concern about sales, but healthier menu items would bring in new customers, not reduce his sales to existing ones. Sure, some might switch from their Jumbo Burger to a salad once in a while, but the new sales would more than make up for that. Plus, advertising items and then deliberately running out just wasn't right. She'd run out of things before—if there had been a run on a particular item or Rick had messed up the supply order—but she had never deliberately not made items just to push customers toward more profitable items before, and she didn't plan to start now.

For the first week of the new menu choices, Nancy worked harder than she had done in a long time. She covered the drive-thru window through the breakfast, lunch, and dinner rushes, and when Rick made his trips to the bank for change or to their suppliers when he forgot something in the supply order, she ran in the back and made extra portions to make sure they never ran out. It was a close call once or twice when she was making things to order, but the customers were never kept waiting.

At the end of the week, she had all the information she needed. Sales were up—way up—the new items were a big hit. She had been able to sell everything she had made without affecting the sales of their traditional items. Now all she had to do was confess to Rick.

QUESTIONS

1. Did Nancy make the right choice here?
2. What do you think Rick's reaction will be?
3. What would the risk have been for the restaurant if they had implemented Rick's plan and deliberately run out of the new items?

[For Review]

1. **Define the term *business ethics*.**

   Business ethics involves the application of standards of moral behavior to business situations. The subject can be approached from a *descriptive* perspective (documenting what is happening) or a *prescriptive* perspective (recommending what should be happening). In either case, the expectation is that business ethics should not be a separate set of standards from general ethics. Ethical behavior, it is argued, should be the same both inside and outside a business situation.

2. **Identify an organization's stakeholders.**

   An organization's stakeholders are any companies, institutions, or individuals that have a connection with or vested interest in the efficient and ethical operations of that organization. Depending on the market or industry in which the organization conducts business, those stakeholders can include shareholders, employees, customers, suppliers, wholesalers, creditors, community organizations, and the federal government.

3. **Discuss the position that business ethics is an oxymoron.**

   It would be unfair to brand every organization as fundamentally unethical in its business dealings. There's no doubt that numerous prominent organizations that were previously held as models of aggressive business management (Enron, Global Crossing, HealthSouth, IMClone, Tyco, and WorldCom) have later been proved to be fundamentally flawed in their ethical practices. This has

   succeeded in bringing the issue to the forefront of public awareness. However, the positive outcome from this has been increased attention to the need for third-party guarantees of ethical conduct and active commitments from the rest of the business world.

4. **Summarize the history of business ethics.**

   Several dramatic changes have taken place in the business environment over the last four decades:

   - The increased presence of an employee voice has made individual employees feel more comfortable speaking out against actions of their employers that they feel to be irresponsible or unethical. They are also more willing to seek legal resolution for such issues as unsafe working conditions, harassment, discrimination, and invasion of privacy.

   - The issue of corporate social responsibility has advanced from an abstract debate to a core performance-assessment issue with clearly established legal liabilities.

   - Corporate ethics has moved from the domain of legal and human resource departments into the organizational mainstream with the appointment of corporate ethics officers with clear mandates.

   - Codes of ethics have matured from cosmetic public relations documents into performance-measurement documents that an increasing number of organizations are now committing to share with all their stakeholders.

- The 2002 Sarbanes-Oxley Act has introduced greater accountability for chief executive officers and boards of directors in signing off on the financial performance records of the organizations they represent.

5. **Identify and propose a resolution for an ethical dilemma in your work environment.**

Resolution of an ethical dilemma can be approached in two stages: recognizing the type of conflict you are dealing with and then selecting a resolution principle based on that conflict type. Conflict types can be grouped into four categories:

- *Truth versus loyalty.* Do you tell the truth or remain loyal to the person or organization that is asking you not to reveal that truth?

- *Short term versus long term.* Does your decision have a short-term consequence or a longer-term consequence?

- *Justice versus mercy.* Do you perceive this issue as a question of dispensing justice or mercy? (Which one are you more comfortable with?)

- *Individual versus community.* Will your choice impact one individual or a wider group or community?

Three resolution principles can then be considered:

- *Ends-based.* Which decision would provide the greatest good for the greatest number of people?
- *Rules-based.* What would happen if everyone made the same decision as you?
- *The Golden Rule.* Do unto others as you would have them do unto you.

6. **Explain how executives and employees seek to justify unethical behavior.**

When their conduct or decisions are questioned as being unethical, most executives and employees seek to rationalize their behavior with four common justifications:

- A belief that the activity is within reasonable ethical and legal limits—that is, that it is not "really" illegal or immoral.

- A belief that the activity is in the individual's or the corporation's best interests—that the individual would somehow be expected to undertake the activity.

- A belief that the activity is safe because it will never be found out or publicized—the classic crime-and-punishment issue of discovery.

- A belief that because the activity helps the company, the company will condone it and even protect the person who engages in it.

[Key Terms]

Business Ethics **22**

Code of Ethics **24**

Corporate Governance **23**

Ethical Dilemma **28**

Oxymoron **24**

Stakeholder **22**

[Review Questions]

1. Based on the history of business ethics reviewed in this chapter, do you think the business world is becoming more or less ethical? Explain your answer.

2. How would you propose the resolution of an ethical dilemma using the Golden Rule?

3. Why should a short-term or long-term consequence make a difference in resolving an ethical dilemma?

4. Of the four commonly held rationalizations for unethical behavior proposed by Saul Gellerman, which one do you think gets used most often? Why?

5. Is it ever acceptable to justify unethical behavior? Why or why not?

6. Explain what "doing the right thing" in a business environment means to you.

[Review Exercises]

You are returning from a business trip. As you wait in the departure lounge for your flight to begin boarding, the gate personnel announce that the flight has been significantly overbooked and that they are offering incentives for passengers to take later flights. After several minutes, the offer is raised to a free round-trip ticket anywhere in the continental United States plus meal vouchers for dinner while you wait for your later flight. You give the offer serious consideration and realize that even though you'll get home several hours later than planned, the inconvenience will be minimal, so you give up your seat and take the free ticket and meal vouchers.

1. Since you are traveling on company time, does the free ticket belong to you or your company? Defend your choice.

2. If the later flight was actually the next day (and the airline offered you an accommodation voucher along with the meal vouchers) and you would be late getting into work, would you make the same choice? Explain your answer.

3. What if the offer only reached a $100 discount coupon on another ticket—would you still take it? If so, would you hold the same opinion about whether the coupon belonged to you or your company?

4. Should your company offer a clearly stated policy on this issue, or should it trust its employees to "do the right thing"? Explain your answer.

[Internet Exercises]

1. Locate the Web site for the Ethics and Compliance Officer Association (ECOA). The ECOA makes a public commitment to three key values. What are they? How does the mission of the ECOA differ from that of the ERC?

2. Locate the Web site for the Center for Business Ethics (BCE). Find the Research Publications page, and identify the most recent research report released by the CBE. Briefly summarize the ethical issue discussed in the report. Do you agree or disagree with the conclusions reached in the report? Explain your answer.

[Team Exercises]

1. **Thanks for the training!**

   Divide into two groups, and prepare arguments *for* and *against* the following behavior: *You work in the IT department of a large international company. At your annual performance review, you were asked about your goals and objectives for the coming year, and you stated that you would like to become a Microsoft Certified Systems Engineer (MCSE). You didn't get much of a pay raise (yet another cost-cutting initiative!), but your boss told you there was money in the training budget for the MCSE course—you're attending the training next week. However, after receiving the poor pay raise, you had polished your résumé and applied for some other positions. You received an attractive job offer from another company for more money, and, in the last interview, your potential new boss commented that it was a shame you didn't have your MCSE certification because that would qualify you for a higher pay grade. The new company doesn't have the training budget to put you through the MCSE training for at least two years. You tell the interviewer that you will complete the MCSE training prior to starting the new position in order to qualify for the higher pay grade. You choose not to qualify that statement with any additional information on who will be paying for the training. You successfully gain the MCSE certification and then give your two weeks' notice. You start with your new company at the higher pay grade. Is that ethical?*

2. **What you do in your free time . . .**

   Divide into two groups, and prepare arguments *for* and *against* the following behavior: *You are attending an employee team-building retreat at a local resort. During one of the free periods in the busy agenda, you observe one of your colleagues in a passionate embrace with a young woman from another department. Since you work in HR and processed the hiring paperwork on both of them, you know that neither one of them is married, but your benefit plan provides coverage for "life partners," and both of them purchased health coverage for life partners. As you consider this revelation further, you are reminded that even if they have both ended their relationships with their respective partners, the company has a policy that expressly forbids employees from dating other employees in the company. Both you and the colleague you observed have applied for the same promotion—a promotion that carries a significant salary increase. What is your obligation here? Should you report him to your boss?*

3. **Treatment or prevention?**

   Divide into two groups, and prepare arguments for *treatment* (Group A) and *prevention* (Group B) in the following situation: *You work in your city for a local nonprofit organization that is struggling to raise funds for its programs in a very competitive grant market. Many nonprofits in your city are chasing grant funds, donations, and volunteer hours for their respective missions—homelessness, cancer awareness and treatment, orphaned children, and many more. Your organization's mission is to work with HIV/AIDS patients in your community to provide increased awareness of the condition for those at risk and also to provide treatment options for those who have already been diagnosed. Unfortunately, with such a tough financial situation, the board of directors of the nonprofit organization has determined that a more focused mission is needed. Rather than serving both the prevention and treatment goals, the organization can only do one. The debate at the last board meeting, which was open to all employees and volunteers, was very heated. Many felt that the treatment programs offered immediate relief to those in need, and therefore represented the best use of funds. Others felt that the prevention programs needed much more time to be effective and that the funds were spread over a much bigger population who might be at risk. A decision has to be reached. What do you think?*

4. **Time to raise prices . . .**

   Divide into two groups, and prepare arguments *for* and *against* the following behavior: *You are a senior manager at a pharmaceutical company that is facing financial difficulties after failing to receive FDA approval for a new experimental drug for the treatment of Alzheimer's disease. After reviewing your test data, the FDA examiners decided that further testing was needed. Your company is now in dire financial straits. The drug has the potential to revolutionize the treatment of Alzheimer's, but the testing delay could put you out of business. The leadership team meets behind closed doors and decides the only way to keep the company afloat long enough to bring the new drug to market is to raise the prices of its existing range of drug products. However, given the financial difficulties your company is facing, some of those price increases will exceed 1,000 percent. When questions are raised about the size of the proposed increases, the chief executive officer defends the move with the following response: "Look, our drugs are still a cheaper option than surgery, even at these higher prices; the insurance companies can afford to pick up the tab; and, worst case scenario, they'll raise a few premiums to cover the increase. What choice do we have? We have to bring this new drug to market if we are going to be a player in this industry."*

>> PHOENIX OR VULTURE?

After acquiring the Rover Group from British Aerospace in 1994, German automaker BMW set about carving up the assets of the group: The Land Rover division was sold to Ford Motor Company in the United States, and the reborn Mini business was established as a subsidiary of BMW based in the UK. The remaining assets were sold as MG Rover in 2000 after continued losses and declining market share. Having recouped some of its purchase price with the Land Rover sale to Ford for $1.8 billion, and with an expected contribution of positive revenue from the Mini subsidiary, the assets of MG Rover were sold for a nominal £10 ($20) in May 2000 to a group of businessmen led by ex-Rover Chief Executive John Towers. Called the "Phoenix Consortium," Towers and his partners (John Edwards, Nick Stephenson, and Peter Beale) received an interest-free loan of £427 million from BMW and

the backing of the British government and automobile trade unions as they committed to turning around the last domestically owned mass-production car company in Britain.

Critics argued (and were later vindicated) that the project was doomed from the start. Despite having purchased a large stock of unsold inventory from BMW for only £10, the new consortium lacked the financial resources to design and develop new cars that could match its global competitors. Even with aggressive cost-cutting measures (including cutting 3,000 jobs), MG Rover continued to lose money for the next four years. In June 2004, the company signed a development agreement with the Shanghai Automotive Industry Corporation (SAIC) to a joint venture of new car models and automobile technologies with SAIC contributing £1 billion for a 70 percent share in MG Rover. A competing offer from India's Tata Motors was disclosed in December 2004, but by then MG Rover was out of money and desperately negotiating with the British government for a £120 million loan to keep the company alive until one of the deals could be completed. In April 2005, MG Rover confirmed that it had received a £6.5 million "stop-gap" loan from the British government, but the funds proved insufficient to maintain the company as a viable operation, and it ceased trading on May 20, 2005, with debts of £1.3 billion and a further 6,000 jobs lost.

The closure of MG Rover marked the end of British mass production of automobiles, but the story of MG Rover was about to take a dramatic turn. With suspicions of poor financial management at the company, the British government commissioned a report by the National Audit Office (NAO) into the collapse of the company. That report, issued in March 2006, revealed that the senior executives of the "Phoenix Consortium" (soon to be referred to as the "Phoenix Four"), had, along with Chief Executive Kevin Howe, received total compensation in the amount of £42 million over the five years in which the group operated MG Rover. While the compensation (around $80 million) may be small by American bailout standards, the Phoenix Consortium had been welcomed as saviors of MG Rover and had negotiated aggressive cost cuts based on its popularity and its commitment to rescuing Britain's last volume carmaker.

The NAO report prompted an investigation by the Serious Fraud Office (SFO) over misuse of taxpayer funds (for the £6.5 million loan from the government). The investigation took four years to complete and cost the British taxpayers another £16 million on top of the £6.5 million loan that was now worthless. The SFO report concluded that the Phoenix Four had done a much better job of structuring their compensation and pension plans than they had of running the company, but found insufficient grounds for criminal prosecution. The Phoenix Four maintained their innocence throughout the investigation and condemned the SFO report as "a witch hunt against us and a whitewash for the government."

1. Why would BMW sell millions of pounds of assets for £10 and lend the buyer an additional £427 million?

2. Why would SAIC want to buy 70 percent of a company that was losing money for £1 billion?

3. With compensation packages already locked in, do you think the executives were committed to making the SAIC's or Tata Motors' deals work?

4. If MG Rover had been successful in winning a £120 million loan from the government rather than a £6.5 million loan, would the outcome of the SFO investigation have been any different?

5. The Phoenix Four maintain they did nothing wrong. How would you defend their conduct from a business ethics perspective?

6. What do you think the outcome should have been for the Phoenix Four?

Sources: "A Death Revisited," *The Economist*, July 9, 2009; Jonathan Guthrie, "War of Words over MG Rover Collapse," *Financial Times*, September 11, 2009; "Phoenix Four's Statement over Rover Report," *The Daily Telegraph*, September 11, 2009; and Graham Ruddick, "SFO Rules Out MG Rover Investigation," *The Daily Telegraph*, August 11, 2009.

Thinking Critically   2.2

>> UNEQUIVOCAL DEDICATION TO BUSINESS ETHICS?

At a time of increasing skepticism that businesses can be both successful and ethical, one group of companies, who between them account for almost a billion dollars in global sales, have come together as the charter members of the Business Ethics Leadership Alliance (BELA). Formed in December 2008, the founding membership consisted of 17 companies from a wide range of industries, including retail, airlines, financial services, and computers. Some of the names may be familiar to you:

- Accenture
- Avaya
- CACI International
- Crawford
- Dell
- Dun & Bradstreet
- Ecolab
- Fluor
- General Electric
- Jones Lang
- Lasalle
- NYK Line
- PepsiCo
- Sempra Energy
- Southern Company
- The Hartford
- United Airlines
- Walmart

Working with the Ethisphere Institute, an international think tank that dedicates itself to "the creation, advancement and sharing of best practices in business ethics, corporate social responsibility, anti-corruption and sustainability," BELA appears to take a very clear position and invites public and private companies to join it in making an explicit pledge to four core values: (1) legal compliance, (2) transparency, (3) identification of conflicts of interest, and (4) accountability.

Responding to a situation where "through the cacophony of media stories, political finger pointing, infuriating reports of greed, and compelling stories of hardship, the business community as a whole has been characterized as a barrel full of bad apples that has the ability to spoil the global economy," the alliance members

CONTINUED >>

present themselves as "a growing quorum made up of some of the world's most recognizable companies joining together to affirm an unequivocal dedication to business ethics." In addition, they see it as their responsibility to "reestablish ethics as the foundation of everyday business practices."

Response to the new alliance has been mixed. Optimists appear to see this new organization as a step in the right direction, arguing that "a public so badly burned by ethical shortcomings in so many American companies will be cynical for years to come, but BELA is to be applauded for trying to turn the situation around." There are certainly some large companies getting involved here—Walmart, GE, Dell, and Pepsi—and they appear to be committing to specific changes in their business practices that directly correlate to many of the ethical problems identified at companies such as Enron, WorldCom, Tyco, and many others.

However, many cynics see this as just a public relations exercise for companies that have had their own business practices brought into question in the past and are now seeking redemption through a commitment to a new ethical philosophy. For example, Walmart paid $11 million to the Department of Justice in settlement of a case involving the hiring of illegal immigrants by its cleaning contractors in 2005. Other class action suits are pending against the world's largest retailer. In 2006, Sempra Energy agreed to pay more than $377 million in response to allegations of manipulation of the price of natural gas during the 2001 California energy crisis.

For such a young alliance, much appears to be promised, including audits every two years and the requirement of strict compliance to the four core values, with the threat of removal from the alliance for failure to comply. It remains to be seen, however, whether such a public commitment by such well-known organizations can truly make a dent in a growing global conviction that businesses cannot really be trusted to perform in an ethical manner.

QUESTIONS

1. Visit the Web site for BELA at www.ethisphere.com/bela. Define the four core values in detail, and explain which one you think will be the hardest for members to achieve and why.

2. Do you think it was a good idea to welcome founding members with such widely publicized ethical transgressions in their past? Why or why not?

3. BELA is a U.S.-driven initiative at the moment. Do you think it will achieve a wider global acceptance over time? Why or why not?

4. Are the four core values—legal compliance, transparency, identification of conflicts of interest, and accountability—enough to establish a credible reputation as an ethical company? What other values would you consider adding and why?

5. Cynics could argue that this is simply a public relations exercise for companies that have performed unethical business practices in the past. Optimists could argue that this is, at the very least, a step in the right direction of restoring the ethical reputation of business as a whole. What do you think?

6. According to the rules of BELA, members will be audited every two years to make sure they are in compliance with BELA standards, and can face removal from the alliance should that audit provide evidence of failure to comply. Do you think the threat of removal from the alliance will keep members in line? Why or why not?

Sources: F. Guerrera and J. Birchall, "U.S. Groups in Ethical Standards Push," *Financial Times*, December 8, 2008; P. Faur, "17 U.S. Companies Form Business Ethics Leadership Alliance," www.communitelligence.com, December 10, 2008; "Business Ethics Leadership Alliance Forms to Affirm Core Business Ethics Principles, Supply and Demand Chain Executive," www.sdcexec.com/online, December 12, 2008; and C. MacDonald, "Business Ethics Leadership Alliance: What's in a Promise?" http://businessethicsblog.com/2008/12/12/business-ethics-leadership-alliance-whats-in-a-promise/; and www.ethisphere.com/bela/.

Thinking Critically

Watch Video

>> TEACHING OR SELLING? • Drugmakers Worried ab[out] of Interest Modify Their Approach to Sponsorship of Conti[nuing] Education

In response to increasing criticism over its sponsorship of physician-education courses (and the suggestion of undue influence on doctors' prescriptions and procedures), the drugmaker Pfizer announced in July 2008 that it would no longer pay marketing communications companies to arrange continuing medical education (CME) courses, which doctors must take to maintain their licenses. Pfizer said it would support medical education only when it was put on by hospitals and professional medical associations. Zimmer Holdings, a medical device manufacturer that manufactures hip, knee, and elbow implants, suspended funding of all CME activity. The company said it will restrict the way it funds courses in the future by identifying an independent third party, such as a professional society, to organize educational programs.

"We understand that even the appearance of conflicts in CME is damaging, and we are determined to take actions that are in the best interests of patients and physicians," Dr. Joseph M. Feczko, Pfizer's chief medical officer, said in a press release.

Industry support for CME has quadrupled since 1998, to $1.2 billion a year, according to the Accreditation Council for Continuing Medical Education (ACCME), an organization in Chicago that approves CME providers. More than half of that is funneled to marketers, with the rest going to hospitals, medical associations, and other nonprofit entities.

As industry money for continuing education proliferates, so do worries that many of the courses have become at least partly aimed at promoting products. The industry and its outside marketers say they ensure that the courses remain free of commercial influence. But some medical experts argue that when employees of communications firms are beholden to pharmaceutical and device companies, they will produce CME courses that are slanted in favor of their sponsors, even if they don't realize what they are doing. "There's not only a perception of bias, there's a reality," says Dave Davis, a vice president of the Association of American Medical Colleges.

In January 2010, Pfizer appeared to modify its 2008 position by announcing a $3 million grant to Stanford University to create continuing medical education courses that the company claims will come with "no conditions, and the company will not be involved in developing the curriculum." However, critics have argued that the curriculum will most likely focus on at least two areas in which Pfizer has major product lines: smoking cessation and heart disease.

QUESTIONS

1. Where is the conflict of interest in this CME relationship?
2. Do you think doctors are likely to be influenced by such promotional tactics? Why or why not?
3. If the pharmaceutical company is paying for the event, shouldn't it have the right to promote its products at the event? Why or why not?
4. Pfizer stated in 2008 that it would only support medical education put on by hospitals and professional medical associations. How can it then justify the Stanford grant?
5. Has Pfizer simply replaced one conflict of interest with another? Why or why not?
6. Propose an alternative approach to ensure that CME is provided without a conflict of interest.

Sources: Arlene Weintraub, "Teaching Doctors or Selling to Them," *BusinessWeek*, July 31, 2008; Duff Wilson, "Using a Pfizer Grant, Courses Aim to Avoid Bias," *The New York Times*, January 11, 2010; and Jacob Goldstein, "Stanford's Continuing Medical Ed., Brought to You by Pfizer," *The Wall Street Journal*, January 11, 2010.

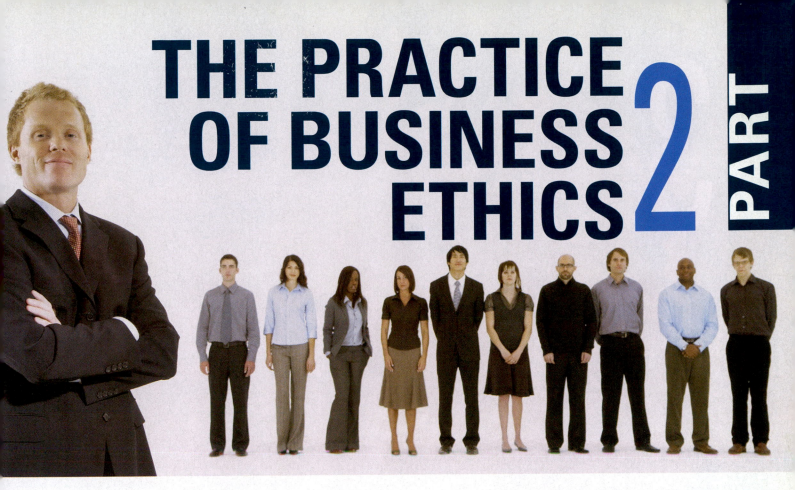

THE PRACTICE OF BUSINESS ETHICS

PART 2

With a clearer understanding of the issues relating to business ethics and the key players involved, we can now examine how the practice of business ethics affects an organization on a daily basis.

Chapter 3 examines how each functional department within an organization manages the challenge of building and maintaining an ethical culture.

Chapter 4 examines the topic of corporate social responsibility (CSR) where we change the internal perspective of the organization to an external one and look at how an organization should interact with its stakeholders in an ethical manner.

Chapter 5 examines the challenges in maintaining an ethical culture within an organization. What policies and procedures should be put into place to ensure that the company conducts itself in an ethical manner, and what should be the consequences when evidence of unethical conduct is found?

Chapter 6 steps outside the organizational framework and examines the legislation the government has put into place to enforce ethical conduct.

Chapter 7 examines how employees who find evidence of unethical conduct in their companies go about bringing that information to the attention of the companies' senior management or the appropriate regulatory authorities.

Chapter 8 examines the ethical debate over employee surveillance and the extent to which technology not only facilitates the prevention of unethical behavior but also jeopardizes the rights of individual employees.

ORGANIZATIONAL ETHICS

After studying this chapter, you should be able to:

1 Define *organizational ethics.*

2 Explain the respective ethical challenges facing the functional departments of an organization.

3 Discuss the position that a human resource (HR) department should be at the center of any corporate code of ethics.

4 Explain the potential ethical challenges presented by generally accepted accounting principles (GAAP).

5 Determine potential conflicts of interest within any organizational function.

FRONTLINE FOCUS
Just Sign the Forms

Matt, a new employee at TransWorld Industries (TWI), showed up bright and early for his first day of orientation. He was very excited. He had applied for several jobs in the area, but TWI was the one he really wanted. He had friends there, and they had told him that the company seemed to be growing very quickly with lots of new products coming online. To Matt, growth meant new opportunities, and he was looking forward to applying to the management-training program as soon as he finished his 90-day probationary period.

Steve Phillips, Matt's new boss, was waiting for him as soon as he reached the factory floor. "Hey, Matt, very punctual; I like that," said Steve, looking at this watch.

"Listen kid, I know HR gave you a list of things to be checked off today—payroll paperwork, training videos, parking pass, ID, and all that stuff—but we could really use an extra pair of hands around here. Your position was vacant for quite a while, and we've built a nasty backlog of work that needs to get caught up ASAP.

"We could really use your help on the Morton6000—you've worked with one of those before, right?"

Matt nodded, not quite sure where this was going.

"Well, here's the deal," said Steve. "The way I see it, all those videos are going to do is tell you not to harass any of the young babes around here (which won't be difficult since none of them are young or babes), not to insult anyone's race, and not to do anything unethical, which you weren't going to do anyway, right?"

Matt nodded again, still not sure where this was going.

"So I think all that time spent watching TV would be put to better use on that backlog of work on the Morton6000. We can book the shipments, get paid by the customers that have been waiting very patiently, and you can make a good impression on your first day—sound good to you, kid?"

"But what about the videos?" asked Matt.

"Oh, don't worry about them," said Steve. "We keep them here in the office. You just sign the forms saying you watched the videos and take them up to HR after lunch when you do all your other paperwork, OK?"

QUESTIONS

1. HR requires that these training videos be viewed for a reason. What risks is Steve taking here? Review the four reasons on page **50** why HR should be directly involved in any code of ethics.
2. Do you think Steve's argument for skipping the training videos is justified?
3. What should Matt do now?

I very much doubt that the Enron executives came to work one morning and said, "Let's see what sort of illegal scheme we can cook up to rip off the shareholders today." More likely, they began by setting extremely high goals for their firm . . . and for a time exceeded them. In so doing they built a reputation for themselves and a demanding expectation among their investors. Eventually, the latter could no longer be sustained. Confronting the usual judgmental decisions which one presented to executives virtually every day, and not wanting to face reality, they gradually began to lean more and more towards extreme interpretations of established accounting principles. The next thing they knew they had fallen off the bottom of the ski jump.

Norman R. Augustine, Retired Chairman of Lockheed Martin Corporation, in his 2004 acceptance of the Ethics Resource Center's Stanley C. Pace Leadership in Ethics Award

>> Defining Organizational Ethics

In Chapter 2, we proposed business ethics as an area of study separate from the general subject of ethics because of two distinct issues:

1. Other parties (the stakeholders) have a vested interest in the ethical performance of an organization.
2. In a work environment, you may be placed in a situation where your personal value system may clash with the ethical standards of the organization's operating culture.

Organizational Culture The values, beliefs, and norms that all the employees of that organization share.

Value Chain The key functional inputs that an organization provides in the transformation of raw materials into a delivered product or service.

Study Alert

How would your describe the culture of your company? What "values, beliefs, and norms" do your employees share?

Organizational culture can be defined as the values, beliefs, and norms shared by all the employees of that organization. The culture represents the sum of all the policies and procedures—both written and informal—from each of the functional departments in the organization in addition to the policies and procedures that are established for the organization as a whole.

In this chapter, we can begin to examine individual departments within an organization and the ethical dilemmas that members of those departments face each day. To simplify this examination, we consider an organization in terms of its functional areas within a value chain (see Figure 3.1).

A **value chain** is composed of the key functional inputs that an organization provides in the transformation of raw materials into a delivered product or service. Traditionally, these key functions are identified as:

- Research and development (R&D), which develops and creates new product designs
- Manufacturing, which sources the components and builds the product
- Marketing (and advertising)
- Sales
- Customer service

Supporting each of these functional areas are the line functions:

- Human resource management (HRM), which coordinates the recruitment, training, and development of personnel for all aspects of the organization.
- Finance, which can include internal accounting personnel, external accounting personnel, and external auditors who are called upon to certify the accuracy of a company's financial statements.
- Information systems (IS or IT), which maintain the technology backbone of the organization—data transfer and security, e-mail communications, internal and external Web sites, as well as the individual hardware and software needs that are specific to the organization and its line of business.

FIG.3.1 A Representative Company Value Chain

Sources: Adapted with permission of the Free Press, a division of Simon & Schuster Adult Publishing Group, from *Competitive Advantage: Creating and Sustaining Superior Performance,* by Michael Porter. Copyright © 1995, 1998 by Michael E. Porter. All rights reserved; and from A. A. Thompson Jr. and A. I. Strickland III, *Crafting & Executing Strategy: The Quest for Competitive Advantage: Concepts and Cases,* 14th ed. (New York: Irwin McGraw-Hill, 2005), p. 99.

- Management, the supervisory role that oversees all operational functions.

Each of these functional line areas can represent a significant commitment of resources—personnel, dollars, and technology. From an ethical perspective, employees in each area can face ethical challenges and dilemmas that can be both unique to their departmental responsibilities and common to the organization as a whole.

The functional areas of sales, customer service, information technology, and management typically have operational policies that reflect the overall ethical culture of the organization. They will be addressed in subsequent chapters in this text. In this chapter, we focus on five specific organizational areas: R&D, manufacturing, marketing (including advertising), human resources (HR), and finance (including accounting and auditing).

PROGRESS ✓ QUESTIONS

1. Explain the term *organizational culture*.
2. Define the term *value chain*.
3. List the five key functional areas within an organization.
4. List the four primary line functions.

>> Ethical Challenges by Organizational Function

THE ETHICS OF RESEARCH AND DEVELOPMENT

R&D professionals carry the responsibility for the future growth of the organization. Without new products to sell, organizations can lose their customers to competitors who are offering better, faster, and/or cheaper products. R&D teams incorporate customer feedback from market research, competitive feedback from closely monitoring their competition, and strategic input from the organization's senior management team to develop a product design that, hopefully, will allow the organization to capture and maintain a leading position in its market.

However, alongside this responsibility comes an equally critical commitment to the consumer in the provision of a product that is of the highest quality, safety, and reliability. Defective products not only put consumers at risk but also generate negative press coverage (damaging the organization's reputation) and very expensive lawsuits that can put the organization at risk of bankruptcy.

When we consider these opposing objectives, the potential for ethical dilemmas is considerable. As

A FIRM PRODUCTION DATE

Scott Kelly, XYZ's marketing vice president, was shouting on the telephone to Tom Evers, director of new product development in XYZ's R&D laboratories: "We're going to kick off a major ad campaign timed to make people want your new model appliance, just before we start delivering them to dealers, and I want to be sure your production date is firm and not one of those best estimates you've stuck us with in the past." Taking a quick breath, he continued: "You people in R&D don't have much credibility with marketing! You don't tell us what you're up to until it's too late for us to advise you or interact in any way. I still remember the money you spent on that water purifier we didn't want. And it didn't help your credibility when you tried to keep the project alive after we told you to kill it!"

Tom assured Scott that the schedule for starting production was absolutely firm. "We've run extensive tests, including life tests, and everything definitely indicates 'go'! We're going to do a small pilot production run and test those pilot units in employee homes. That's a purely routine confirmation, so I can assure you that the production date is locked in. Go

CONTINUED >>

ahead with your ad campaign—we're giving you a sure winner this time."

But Tom was wrong. A glitch appeared near the end of the pilot test and very close to the production date. In a hastily called engineering meeting, to which marketing was not invited, a quick-fix design change was approved. Another short pilot production run would be made, and the revised units would again be tested in employee homes. A delay of one to two months, perhaps longer, for start of production was indicated. With this schedule set, Tom arranged a meeting to apprise marketing of the problem and the new production schedule.

Scott exploded as soon as Tom began his account of the production delay. "You gave me a firm production date! We've got a major ad campaign under way, and its timing is critical. We'll have customers asking for these new models, and the dealers won't have them. We'll look silly to our customers, and our dealers will be upset."

"Now wait," Tom interrupted, "I didn't give you the production date as absolutely firm. I remember cautioning you that a problem could develop in the pilot run and suggested you allow for it in kicking off the ad campaign. I told you

we'd do our best to make the date but that there's always an element of chance with a new machine. We're better off having customers asking dealers where the new models are than being out there with a big quality problem."

QUESTIONS

1. Tom was obviously overconfident in the final stages of the testing process, but was his behavior unethical? Why or why not?
2. Given Scott's concerns over R&D's credibility, should he have taken Tom's production date as being absolutely firm?
3. In fact, Scott was so skeptical of Tom's production date that he recorded their original conversation without Tom's knowledge and then produced the recording when Tom denied giving a firm production date. Tom responded: "You taped my conversation without telling me! That's unethical." Was it?
4. Has Scott's behavior damaged future relations between marketing and R&D? In what way? How could this situation have been avoided?

Source: Adapted from W. Gale Cutler, "When R&D Talks, Marketing Listens—on Tape," *Research Technology Management* 37, no. 4 (July–August 1994), p. 56.

---

professionals in their respective fields of science, engineering, and design, R&D teams are tasked with making a complex set of risk assessments and technical judgments in order to deliver a product design. However, if the delivery of that design does not match the manufacturing cost figures that are needed to sell the product at a required profit margin, then some tough decisions have to be made.

If "better, cheaper, faster" is the ideal, then compromises have to be made in functionality or manufacturing to meet a targeted cost figure. If too many features are taken out, marketing and advertising won't have a story to tell, and the salespeople will face difficulties in selling the product against stiff competition. If too few changes are made, the company won't be able to generate a profit on each unit and meet its obligations to shareholders who expect the company to be run efficiently and to grow over the long term.

For the R&D team, the real ethical dilemmas come when decisions are made about product quality. Do we use the best materials available or the second best to save some money? Do we run a full battery of tests or convince ourselves that the computer simulations will give us all the information we need?

ETHICS IN MANUFACTURING

The relationship between R&D and manufacturing is often a challenging one. Managers complain about

designs being thrown "over the wall" to manufacturing with the implication that the product design may meet all the required specifications, but now it falls to the manufacturing team to actually get the thing built.

The pressures here are very similar to those in the R&D function as manufacturers face the ethical question, "Do you want it built fast, or do you want it built right?" Obviously, from an organizational perspective, you want both, especially if you know that your biggest competitor also is racing to put a new product on the market (and if it gets there before you do, all your sales projections for your product will be worthless).

Here again, you face the ethical challenges inherent in arriving at a compromise—which corners can be cut and by how much. You want to build the product to the precise design specifications, but what if there is a supply problem? Do you wait and hold up delivery, or do you go with an alternative (and less reliable) supplier? Can you be sure of the quality that alternative supplier will give you?

ETHICS IN MARKETING

Once the manufacturing department delivers a finished product, it must be sold. The marketing process (which includes advertising, public relations, and sales) is responsible for ensuring that the product reaches the hands of a satisfied customer. If the marketers did their research correctly and communicated the data to the R&D team accurately, and assuming the finished product meets the original design specifications and the competition hasn't beaten you to market with their new product, this should be a slam dunk, but with all these assumptions, a great deal can go wrong.

Opinions on the marketing process vary greatly in relation to how close you are to the process itself. Marketers see themselves as providing products (or services) to customers who have already expressed a need for and a desire to purchase those products. In this respect, marketers are simply communicating information to their customers about the functionality and availability of the product, and then communicating back to the organization the feedback they receive from those customers.

Critics of marketing tend to see it as a more manipulative process whereby unsuspecting customers are induced by slick and entertaining commercials and advertisements in several different media—magazines, radio, television, the Internet, and so forth—to buy products they don't really need and could quite easily live without.

From an ethical standpoint, these opposing arguments can be seen to line up with distinct ethical theories. Marketers emphasize customer service and argue that since their customers are satisfied, the good outcome justifies the methods used to achieve that outcome no matter how misleading the message or how unnecessary the product sold. As we reviewed in Chapter 1, this represents a view of ethics called **utilitarianism.** Critics argue that the process itself is wrong irrespective of the outcome achieved—that is, how can you be proud of an outcome when the customer never needed that product to begin with and was manipulated, or at the very least influenced, by a slick ad campaign into feelings of envy, inadequacy, or inequality if he or she didn't rush out and buy it? On this side of the debate we are considering **universal ethics.**

Utilitarianism Ethical choices that offer the greatest good for the greatest number of people.

Universal Ethics Actions that are taken out of *duty* and *obligation* to a purely moral ideal, rather than based on the needs of the situation, since the universal principles are seen to apply to everyone, everywhere, all the time.

What role does marketing play in the perception that coffee brewed at Starbucks is superior to coffee brewed at home?

Real World Applications

From his first marketing course at college, Mike Ambrosino always believed that marketers had the responsibility of accurately describing the features and benefits of their product or service to their customers. If those features and benefits didn't meet the needs of those customers, Mike always assumed that survey data would be fed back to the designers to fix that. After only a year in the industry, Mike's viewpoint has completely changed. The job of the marketing department is to support the sales team with messages, brochures, and ads that help convince prospective customers that buying our product or service is the right choice. Whether it really is the right choice for them, or whether they need that product or service at all, never comes up for discussion. What happened?

These opposing positions become more complex when you consider the responsibility of a corporation to generate profits for its stockholders. Long-term profits come from sales growth, which means selling more of what you have or bringing new products or services to the market to increase your overall sales revenue. To do that, you must find ways to sell more to your existing customer base and, ideally, find more customers for your products and services. Unless you are selling a basic commodity in a developing country that has a desperate need for your product, at some point you reach a place where customers can survive without your product or service, and marketing must now move from informing customers and prospects about the product or service to persuading or influencing them that their lives will be better with this product or service and, more importantly, they will be better with your company's version.

Marketing professionals abide by a code of ethics adapted by the American Marketing Association (AMA). That code speaks eloquently about doing no harm, fostering trust, and improving "customer confidence in the integrity of the marketing exchange system," and establishes clear ethical values of honesty, responsibility, fairness, respect, openness, and citizenship. These are all honorable standards for any profession, but the question remains as to whether or not encouraging people to buy things they don't need is truly an ethical process.

Philip Kotler explored this debate further in his classic article, "Is Marketing Ethics an Oxymoron?"[1] His concern over the pressures of expanding consumption (the constant growth we discussed earlier in this section) was further complicated by the issue of reducing the side effects of that consumption, specifically in products that are perceived as harmful to the body—cigarettes, alcohol, junk food—as well as to the environment—nonrecyclable packaging or products that leach chemicals into landfills such as batteries or electrical equipment.

In response to these pressures, Kotler makes the following observation:

> As professional marketers, we are hired by . . . companies to use our marketing toolkit to help them sell more of their products and services. Through our research, we can discover which consumer groups are the most susceptible to increasing their consumption. We can use the research to assemble the best 30-second TV commercials, print ads, and sales incentives to persuade them that these products will deliver great satisfaction. And we can create price discounts to tempt them to consume even more of the product than would normally be healthy or safe to consume. But, as professional marketers, we should have the same ambivalence as nuclear scientists who help build nuclear bombs or pilots who spray DDT over crops from the airplane. Some of us, in fact, are independent enough to tell these clients that we will not work for them to find ways to sell more of what hurts people. We can tell them that we're willing to use our marketing toolkit to help them build new businesses around substitute products that are much healthier and safer. But, even if these companies moved toward these healthier and safer products, they'll probably continue to push their current cash cows. At that point, marketers will have to decide whether to work for these companies, help them reshape their offerings, avoid these companies altogether, or even work to oppose these company offerings.

5. Identify the three functional components of the marketing process.

6. Explain why marketers feel that their involvement in the production and delivery of goods and services is an ethical one.

7. Explain the opposing argument that marketing is an unethical process.

8. Which argument do you support? Provide an example to explain your answer.

>> Ethics in Human Resources

The human resources function within an organization should ideally be directly involved in the relationship between the company and the employee throughout that employee's contract with the company:

- The creation of the job description for the position.
- The recruitment and selection of the right candidate for the position.
- The orientation of the newly hired employee.
- The efficient management of payroll and benefits for the (hopefully) happy and productive employee.

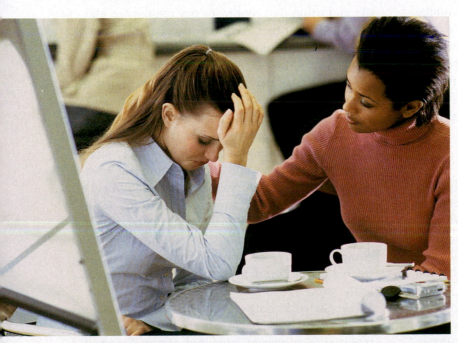

What ethical issues might arise for a human resource professional when privy to an employee's personal and professional history?

- The documentation of periodic performance reviews.
- The documentation of disciplinary behavior and remedial training, if needed.
- The creation of a career development program for the employee.

Finally, if the employee and the company eventually part ways, the HR department should coordinate the final paperwork, including any severance benefits, and should host an exit interview to ensure that anything that the organization can learn from the departure of this employee is fed back into the company's strategic plan for future growth and development.

Every step of the life cycle of that company-employee contract has the potential for ethical transgressions. Most HR professionals see their direct involvement in this contract as acting as the conscience of the organization in many ways. If the right people are hired in the first place, it is believed, many other problems are avoided down the road. It's when organizations fail to plan ahead for vacancies and promotions that the pressure to hire someone who was needed yesterday can lead to the gradual relaxation of what may be clearly established codes of ethics.

Consider the following ethical transgressions:[2]

- You are behind schedule on a building project, and your boss decides to hire some illegal immigrants to help get the project back on track. They are paid in cash "under the table," and your boss justifies the decision as being "a 'one-off'—besides, the INS [Immigration and Naturalization Service] has bigger fish to fry than a few undocumented workers on a building site! If we get caught, we'll pay the fine—it will be less than the penalty we would owe our client for missing our deadline on the project."

- Your company has hired a new regional vice president. As the HR specialist for her region, you are asked to process her payroll and benefits paperwork. Your boss instructs you to waive the standard one-year waiting period for benefits entitlement and enroll the new VP in the retirement and employee bonus plan immediately. When you raise the concern that this is illegal, your boss informs you that this new VP is a close friend of the company president and advises you that, in the interests of your job security, you should "just do it and don't ask questions!"

- On your first day as the new HR specialist, you mention to your boss that the

Accounting Function The function that keeps track of all the company's financial transactions by documenting the money coming in (credits) and money going out (debits) and balancing the accounts at the end of the period (daily, weekly, monthly, quarterly, annually).

company appears to be out of employee handbooks and both the minimum wage and Occupational Safety and Health Administration (OSHA) posters that are legally required to be posted in the employee break room. Your boss laughs and says, "We've been meaning to get around to that for years—trust me, there will always be some other crisis to take priority over all that administrative stuff."

In each of these scenarios, accountability for the transgression would ultimately end with the HR department as the corporate function that is legally responsible for ensuring that such things don't happen.

For this reason, many advocates of ethical business conduct argue that HR should be at the center of any corporate code of ethics—not as the sole creator of the code, since it is a document that should represent the entire organization, but certainly as the voice of reason in ensuring that all the critical areas are addressed:[3]

1. *HR professionals must help ensure that ethics is a top organizational priority.* The recent business scandals have shown that simply relying on the presence of an ethical monitor will not prevent unethical behavior. HR should be the ethical champion in the organization, including hiring a formal ethics officer if necessary.

2. *HR must ensure that the leadership selection and development processes include an ethics component.* The terrible metaphor of a fish rotting from the head is relevant here. HR must be involved in hiring leaders who not only endorse and support but also model the ethical standards needed to keep the company out of danger. The biggest challenge here is convincing the leadership team that it's not just the rank-and-file employees who should be put through ethics training.

3. *HR is responsible for ensuring that the right programs and policies are in place.* As we will learn in future chapters in this book, financial penalties for unethical behavior are now directly connected to evidence of efforts to actively prevent unethical conduct. The absence of appropriate policies and training programs can increase the fines that are levied for unethical behavior.

4. *HR must stay abreast of ethics issues (and in particular the changing legislation and sentencing guidelines for unethical conduct).* Response to recent corporate scandals has been swift and frustratingly bureaucratic. Organizations now face reams of documentation that are designed to regulate ethical behavior in the face of overwhelming evidence that organizations cannot, it would seem, be trusted to do it on their own.

PROGRESS ✓ QUESTIONS

9. Explain why HR personnel might consider themselves to be the conscience of the organization.

10. Select one of the ethical transgressions listed in the HR sections, and document how you would respond to that situation as the employee.

11. Why is HR's involvement in the selection of the leaders of the company so important to ethical business conduct?

12. Why have ethics policies and ethics training suddenly become so important?

>> Ethics in Finance

The finance function of an organization can be divided into three distinct areas: financial transactions, accounting, and auditing:

1. The financial transactions—the process by which the flow of money through an organization is handled—involve receiving money from customers and using that money to pay employees, suppliers, and all other creditors (taxes and the like), with hopefully enough left over to create a profit that can be either reinvested back into the business or paid out to owners/shareholders. Part of this function may be outsourced to specialists such as Paychex or ADP, for example.

2. The accounting function keeps track of all those financial transactions by documenting the money coming in (credits) and money going out (debits) and balancing the accounts at the end of the period (daily, weekly, monthly, quarterly, annually). The accounting function can be handled by accounting professionals that are hired by the company, outside accounting firms that are contracted by the company, or usually a combination of the two.

3. When an organization's financial statements, or books, have been balanced, they must then be reported to numerous interested parties. For small businesses, the most important customers are government agencies—state income and sales taxes and

federal taxes the IRS collects on the profits generated by the business. In addition, lenders and creditors will want to see financial statements that have been certified as accurate by an impartial third-party professional. That certification is offered by the **auditing function**—typically handled by certified professional accountants and/or auditing specialists.

As an organization grows and eventually goes public by selling stock in the organization on a public stock exchange, the need for certified financial documents becomes even greater. Existing and potential investors will make the decision to invest in the shares of that organization based on the information presented in those certified financial statements—specifically, the profit and loss statement and the balance sheet. Investors look to those documents for evidence of financial stability, operational efficiency, and the potential for future growth. Many organizations are large enough to maintain their own internal auditors to monitor the accuracy of their financial functions.

ALL IN A DAY'S WORK: INTERNAL AUDITORS' ROLES

According to the Institute of Internal Auditors:[4]

Internal auditors are grounded in professionalism, integrity, and efficiency. They make objective assessments of operations and share ideas for best practices; provide counsel for improving controls, processes and procedures, performance, and risk management; suggest ways for reducing costs, enhancing revenues, and improving profits; and deliver competent consulting, assurance, and facilitation services.

Auditing Function The certification of an organization's financial statements, or "books," as being accurate by an impartial third-party professional. An organization can be large enough to have internal auditors on staff as well as using external professionals—typically certified professional accountants and/or auditing specialists.

Internal auditors are well disciplined in their craft and subscribe to a professional code of ethics. They are diverse and innovative. They are committed to growing and enhancing their skills. They are continually on the lookout for emerging risks and trends in the profession. They are good thinkers. And to effectively fulfill all their roles, internal auditors must be excellent communicators who listen attentively, speak effectively, and write clearly.

Sitting on the right side of management, modern-day internal auditors are consulted on all aspects of the organization and must be prepared for just about anything. They are coaches, internal and external stakeholder advocates, risk managers, controls experts, efficiency specialists, and problem-solving partners. They are the organization's safety net.

It's certainly not easy, but for these skilled and competent professionals, it's all in a day's work.

A DIFFERENT PERSPECTIVE

You work for a mortgage servicing company—making sure that mortgage payments get processed accurately and the funds forwarded to the mortgage holder. Lately your company has been dealing with as many foreclosure notices as payments, and the market is starting to turn in an interesting direction. Customers whose houses are worth 30 or 40 percent less than they paid for them just a couple of years ago are starting to question whether it makes sense to continue to pay for an asset (their home) that may remain "upside down" for many years to come. They can still afford the mortgage payment they are currently making, but since the house is worth so much less than what they paid for it, they are starting to feel that they are throwing good money after bad.

The company's growing concern over this new phenomenon was the topic of an all-staff meeting earlier this week. Senior leaders reminded everyone that mortgages are a legal contract and that homeowners have a legal obligation to make the payments to which they agreed. After the meeting, however, several of your colleagues shared some of the case histories they are currently working on.

CONTINUED >>

Several common issues are starting to come up with these cases:

- Because of multibillion dollar bailouts for banks, many people see themselves as victims of predatory lending practices with no apparent willingness on the part of the banks that received those bailout funds to help the individual homeowners.
- Media coverage of mortgage modification programs is reporting that banks are unwilling or unable to help, so what's the point in even trying?
- Because pools of mortgages have been sliced and diced into complicated financial derivatives, no one is even sure who the mortgage holder is anymore.
- The foreclosure process is so backed up in many cities that it can take as long as two years—that's a lot of time to live rent-free while you are saving up funds to move somewhere else—and with so many homes in foreclosure, rental property is attractively cheap these days.

You recall from your business ethics course in college that the elements of trust and consumer confidence in business are built on the belief that each party to a financial transaction has an ethical as well as a legal obligation to fulfill its part of the transaction, but it's clear that people are starting to feel that predatory lending practices now give them an excuse to ignore that ethical obligation.

QUESTIONS

1. Which ethics theories are being applied here?
2. If homeowners made poor financial decisions—taking too much equity out of their houses or buying at the wrong time—do the predatory lending practices of the banks and mortgage companies justify walking away from those mortgages?
3. Are homeowners really "throwing good money after bad" in making payments on mortgages for homes that are worth much less than the mortgage?
4. Would you walk away from your mortgage in this situation? How would you justify that decision?

Sources: Roger Lowenstein, "Walk Away from Your Mortgage," *The New York Times,* January 10, 2010; Glenn Setzer, "Stop Paying Your Mortgage and Walk Away?" www.mortgagenewsdaily.com, March 11, 2008; and David Streitfeld, "Owners Stop Paying Mortgages, and Stop Fretting," *The New York Times,* May 31, 2010.

>> Ethical Challenges

For internal employees in the finance, accounting, and auditing departments, the ethical obligations are no different from those of any other employee of the organization. As such, they are expected to maintain the reputation of the organization and abide by the code of ethics. Within their specific job tasks, this would include not falsifying documents, stealing money from the organization, or undertaking any other form of fraudulent activity related to the management of the organization's finances.

However, once we involve third-party professionals who are contracted to work for the company, the potential for ethical challenges and dilemmas increases dramatically.

GAAP

The accounting profession is governed not by a set of laws and established legal precedents but by a set of generally accepted accounting principles, typically referred to as **GAAP** (pronounced *gap*). These principles are accepted as standard operating procedures within the industry, but, like any operating standard, they are open to interpretation and abuse. The taxation rates that Uncle Sam expects you to pay on generated profits may be very clear, but the exact process by which you arrive at that profit figure is far from clear and places considerable pressure on accountants to manage the expectations of their clients.

> **GAAP** The generally accepted accounting principles that govern the accounting profession—not a set of laws and established legal precedents but a set of standard operating procedures within the profession.

CREATIVE BOOKKEEPING TECHNIQUES

Corporations try to manage their expansion at a steady rate of growth. If they grow too slowly or too erratically from year to year, investors may see them as unstable or in danger of falling behind their competition. If they grow too quickly, investors may develop unrealistic expectations of their future growth. This inflated outlook can have a devastating effect on your stock price when you miss your quarterly numbers for the first time. Investors have shown a pattern of overreacting to bad news and dumping their stock.

It is legal to defer receipts from one quarter to the next to manage your tax liability. However, accountants face ethical challenges when requests are made for far more illegal practices, such as falsifying accounts, underreporting income, overvaluing assets, and taking questionable deductions.

These pressures are further compounded by competitive tension as accounting firms compete for client business in a cutthroat market. Unrealistic delivery deadlines, reduced fees, and fees that are contingent on providing numbers that are satisfactory to the client are just some examples of the ethical challenges modern accounting firms face.

A set of accurate financial statements that present an organization as financially stable, operationally efficient, and positioned for strong future growth can do a great deal to enhance the reputation and goodwill of an organization. The fact that those statements have been certified by an objective third party to be "clean" only adds to that. However, that certification is meant to be for the public's benefit rather than the corporation's. This presents a very clear ethical predicament. The accounting/auditing firm is paid by the corporation, but it really serves the general public, who are in search of an impartial and objective review.

The situation can become even more complex when the accounting firm has a separate consulting relationship with the client—as was the case with Arthur Andersen and its infamous client Enron. Andersen's consulting business generated millions of dollars in fees from Enron alone. If the auditing side of its business chose to stand up to Enron's requests for creative bookkeeping policies, those millions of dollars of consulting fees, as well as additional millions of dollars in auditing fees, would have been placed in serious jeopardy. As we now know, the senior partners on the Enron account chose not to stand up to

Enron, and their decision eventually sank Arthur Andersen entirely.

With so many ethical pressures facing the accounting profession, and a guidebook of operating standards that is open to such abuse, the last resort for ethical guidance and leadership is the Code of Conduct issued by the American Institute of Certified Public Accountants (AICPA).

PROGRESS ✓ QUESTIONS

13. List the three primary areas of the finance function in an organization.
14. Explain how the accounting profession is governed by GAAP.
15. Why would audited accounts be regarded as being "clean"?
16. What key decision brought about the demise of Arthur Andersen?

Life Skills

>> Being ethically responsible

Review the company value chain in Figure 3.1. Consider the company you currently work for, or one that you hope to work for in the future. The department in which you work holds a specific place and function in that value chain, and the extent to which you interact with the other departments on that chain in a professional and ethical manner has a great deal to do with the long-term growth and success of the organization.

Of course, that's easy to say but a lot harder to do. Balancing departmental goals and objectives (to which you are held accountable) with larger company performance targets can be a challenge when resources are tight and you are balancing fierce competition in a tough economy. In that kind of environment, an organization's commitment to ethical conduct can be tested as the pressure to close deals and hit sales targets increases. Ethical dilemmas develop here when business decisions have to be made that will negatively affect one department or another. In addition, you may face your own dilemmas when you are tasked with obligations or responsibilities that conflict with your own value system.

In those situations, remain aware of the bigger picture and consider the results for all the stakeholders involved in the decision—whether it's your colleagues at work or your family members and friends. You may be the one making the decision, but others will share the consequences.

>> Conflicts of Interest

The obligation that an auditing firm has to a paying client while owing an objective, third-party assessment of that client's financial stability to stakeholders and potential investors represents a potentially significant **conflict of interest.** We examine the government's response to this conflict of interest in more detail in Chapter 6 when we review the Sarbanes-Oxley Act of 2002 and the impact that legislation has attempted to have on the legal enforcement of ethical business practices.

> **Conflict of Interest** A situation in which one relationship or obligation places you in direct conflict with an existing relationship or obligation.

However, as the value chain model we reviewed at the beginning of this chapter shows us, the potential for conflicts of interest within an organization can go far beyond the finance department:

- At the most basic level, simply meeting the needs of your organization's stakeholders can present conflicts of interest when you consider the possibility that what is best for your shareholders (increased profits) may not be best for your employees and the community if the most efficient means to achieve those increased profits is to close your factory and move production overseas.
- Selling a product that has the potential to be harmful to your customers represents an equally significant conflict of interest. The convenience of fast food carries with it the negative consequences of far more calories than you need to consume in an average day. McDonald's, for example, has responded with increased menu choices to include salads and alternatives to french fries and soda—but the Big Mac continues to be one of its best-selling items.
- Selling a product that has the potential to be harmful to the environment also carries a conflict of interest. Computer manufacturers such as Dell and Hewlett-Packard now offer plans to recycle your old computer equipment rather than throwing it into a landfill. Fast-food companies like McDonald's have changed their packaging to move away from clamshell boxes for their burgers. Beverage companies such as Nestlé are producing bottles for their bottled water that use less plastic to minimize the impact on landfills.

These attempts to address conflicts of interest all have one thing in common. Whether they were prompted by internal strategic policy decisions or aggressive campaigns by customers and special interest groups, the decisions had to come from the top of the organization. Changing the way an organization does business can sometimes begin with a groundswell of support from the front line of the organization (where employees interact with customers), but eventually the key decisions on corporate policy and (where appropriate) capital expenditure have to come from the senior leadership of the organization. Without that endorsement, any attempts to make significant changes tend to remain as departmental projects rather than organization-wide initiatives.

Conflicts of interest do not just happen in large corporations. What are the potential conflicts that arise by this employee informing her friend that a sale next week will save her 30 percent, but not informing other customers?

>> Conclusion

The Ethics Resource Center (ERC), a nonprofit U.S. organization devoted to the advancement of organizational ethics, surveyed more than 3,000 American workers in its 2005 National Business Ethics Survey (NBES). The findings showed that more than half of U.S. employees had observed at least one example of workplace ethical misconduct in the past year and 36 percent had observed two or more. This represents a slight increase from the results of the 2003 survey. During the same period, willingness to report observed misconduct at work to management declined to 55 percent, a decrease of 10 percentage points since 2003. Types of misconduct employees observed most include:[5]

- Abusive or intimidating behavior toward employees (21 percent).
- Lying to employees, customers, vendors, or the public (19 percent).
- Situations that placed employee interests over organizational interests (18 percent).
- Violations of safety regulations (16 percent).
- Misreporting of actual time worked (16 percent).

Behavior such as the Ethics Resource Center documented in the NBES represents the real organizational culture more than any corporate statements or policy manuals. Employees learn very quickly about "the rules of the game" in any work environment and make the choice to "go with the flow" or, if the rules are unacceptable to their personal value systems, to look for employment elsewhere.

Of greater importance for the organization as a whole is the fact that any unethical behavior is allowed to persist for the long term. Explanations for the behavior (or for the failure to address the behavior) are plentiful:

- "That's common practice in this industry."
- "It's a tough market out there, and you have to be willing to bend the rules."
- "They're not in my department."
- "I don't have time to watch their every move—head office gives me too much to do to babysit my people."

- "If I fire them for a policy violation, the union rep would be on my back in a heartbeat."
- "If I fire them for a policy violation, I'd be one short—do you know how long it would take me to find a replacement and train him?"
- "The bosses know they do it—if they turn a blind eye, why shouldn't I?"
- "They don't pay me to be a company spy—I've got my own work to do."

So if bending the rules, stretching the truth, breaking the rules, and even blatantly lying have become a depressingly regular occurrence in your workplace, the question must be asked as to where the pressure or performance expectation comes from to make this behavior necessary. The answer can be captured in one word: *profit*.

This doesn't mean that nonprofit organizations don't also face problems with unethical behavior or that the pursuit of profit is unethical. What it means is that the obligation to deliver profits to owners or shareholders has created a convenient "get out of jail free" card, where all kinds of behavior can be justified in the name of meeting your obligations to your shareholders. You, as an individual, wouldn't normally do this, but you have a deadline or quota or sales target to meet, and your boss isn't the type to listen to explanations or excuses, so maybe just this once if you *(insert ethical transgression here)*, you can get over this hurdle—just this once. Unfortunately, that's how it started for the folks at Enron, and that's how it could start for you. They fudged the numbers for one quarter and managed to get away with it, but all that did was raise investor expectations for the next quarter, and they found themselves on a train they couldn't get off.

As we shall see in the next chapters, if the organization doesn't set the ethical standard, employees will perform to the ethical standards of the person who controls their continued employment with the company—their boss.

How well companies set ethical standards can be measured by the extensive legislation that now exists to legally enforce (or at least attempt to enforce) ethical behavior in business.

FRONTLINE FOCUS
Just Sign the Forms—Matt Makes a Decision

Matt really wanted this job, and he really wanted to make a good first impression with Steve. Plus, Steve was right; he wasn't going to harass anyone or insult others based on their race, and he certainly wasn't going to risk his chances at the management-training program by doing anything unethical. What was the worst that could happen? If anyone from HR ever found out that he didn't watch the training videos, he could show how the company had benefited from his making up the backlog on the Morton6000, and he was sure that Steve would back him up.

Matt signed the forms and got to work.

Three months later, Matt finished his probationary period and met with the HR director to review his performance and, Matt hoped, discuss his application for the management-training program. The HR director was very friendly and complimentary about Matt's performance over the last 90 days. But he had one question for Matt: "The production log for the Morton6000 shows that you made a big dent in our backlog on your first morning here. I'm curious how you managed to do that when your paperwork shows that you spent three hours watching training videos as part of your new employee orientation."

QUESTIONS

1. What should Matt tell the HR director?
2. What do you think the HR director's reaction will be?
3. What are Matt's chances of joining the management-training program now?

[For Review]

1. **Define *organizational ethics*.**

   Organizational ethics can be considered as an area of study separate from the general subject of ethics because of two distinct issues:

   - Other parties (the stakeholders) have a vested interest in the ethical performance of an organization.

     In a work environment, you may be placed in a situation where your personal value system may clash with the ethical standards of the organization's operating culture (the values, beliefs, and norms shared by all the employees of that organization).

2. **Explain the respective ethical challenges facing the functional departments of an organization.**

   The functional line areas of an organization—R&D, manufacturing, marketing, HR, and finance—face operational and budgetary pressures that present ethical challenges over what they should do as opposed to what the company may be asking them to do:

   - Research and development (R&D) carries the burden of developing products or services that are sufficiently better, faster, or cheaper than the competition to give the company a leading position in the market. However, market pressures often prompt instructions from senior management to lower costs and/or escalate deadlines that can prevent the designers and engineers from doing all the quality testing they would normally want to do.

   - People in manufacturing share the same challenge: Do we build the best-quality product and price it accordingly, or do we build a product that meets a price point that is lower than our competition, even if it means using poorer-quality materials?

   - The marketing challenge is more directly aligned to the debate between universal ethics and utilitarianism. Do you build a product that customers really need and focus your marketing message on showing customers how that product meets their needs (universal), or do you build a product that you think you can sell at a healthy profit and offer gainful employment to your workers and then focus your marketing message on convincing customers to buy a product they may not need (utilitarianism).

   - For HR, there is a potential ethical dilemma at every step of the life cycle of an employee's contract with an organization. From recruitment and hiring to eventual departure from the company (either voluntarily or involuntarily), HR carries the responsibility of corporate compliance to all prevailing employment legislation. Any evidence of discrimination, harassment, poor working conditions, or failure to offer equal employment opportunities presents a significant risk for the company, and HR must combat managers willing to bend the rules to meet their department goals in keeping the company in compliance.

   - Whether it is fraudulent financial transactions, poor accounting practices, or insufficient auditing procedures, poor financial management has featured in every major financial scandal over the last fifty years. Investors trust companies to use their invested capital wisely and to generate a reasonable return. Checks and balances are stipulated under GAAP (generally accepted accounting principles) to ensure that corporate funds are managed correctly, but as cases such as Enron have shown, those checks and balances are often modified, overruled, or ignored completely.

3. **Discuss the position that a human resource (HR) department should be at the center of any corporate code of ethics.**

   Most HR professionals see their direct involvement in every aspect of an employee-employer relationship as acting as the corporate conscience of the organization in many ways. If the right people are hired in the first place, then, it is believed, many other problems are avoided down the road. It's when organizations fail to plan ahead for vacancies and promotions that the pressure to hire someone who was needed yesterday can lead to the gradual relaxation of what may be clearly established codes of ethics.

4. **Explain the potential ethical challenges presented by generally accepted accounting principles (GAAP).**

The accounting profession is governed not by a set of laws and established legal precedents but by a set of generally accepted accounting principles, typically referred to as GAAP (pronounced *gap*). These principles are accepted as standard operating procedures within the industry, but, like any operating standard, they are open to interpretation and abuse. The taxation rates that Uncle Sam expects you to pay on generated profits may be very clear, but the exact process by which you arrive at that profit figure is far from clear and places considerable pressure on accountants to manage the expectations of their clients.

5. **Determine potential conflicts of interest within any organizational function.**

Any situation in which one relationship or obligation places you in direct opposition with an existing relationship or obligation presents a conflict of interest. Selling the product with the highest profit margin for the company rather than the product that best meets the customer's need is one example. McDonald's promotion of a new, healthier menu while continuing to sell its most unhealthy but best-selling Big Mac places it in a conflict of interest. Hiring someone who has the minimum qualifications but is available now as opposed to waiting for a better-qualified applicant who won't be available for another month is another example.

[Key Terms]

[Review Questions]

1. Consider the functional departments we have reviewed in this chapter. Which department do you think faces the greatest number of ethical challenges? Why?

2. Provide three examples of unethical behavior that you have observed at the company you work for (or a company you have worked for in the past). What were the outcomes of this behavior?

3. Philip Kotler argues that professional marketers "should have the same ambivalence as nuclear scientists who help build nuclear bombs." Is that a valid argument? Why or why not?

4. Should the HR department be the ethics champion in the organization? Why or why not?

5. What are "creative bookkeeping techniques"? Provide three examples.

6. Would you leave your position with a company if you saw evidence of unethical business practices? Why or why not? What factors would you consider in making that decision?

[Review Exercises]

Ambush Marketing. As billboards, radio commercials, print ads, and 30- or 60-second TV spots become increasingly lost in the blurred onslaught of advertising, the larger advertising companies are increasingly turning to more creative means to get the name of their product or service in front of the increasingly overloaded attention span of Joe Public.

Consider the following:

- Imagine you're at [the Washington Monument] when a young couple with a camera approaches and kindly asks if you'll take their picture. They seem nice enough, so you agree to take a photo of them. As you're lining up the shot, the gentleman explains it's the newest model, he got it for only $400 and it does this, that and the other. Cool. You take the picture and walk away. It's nice to help people.

- The New York bar is crowded, with a line of people three deep. Just as you manage to flag the bartender's attention, a neighboring patron tries to latch on to your good luck. "Say, buddy, I see you're about to order a couple of drinks," your neighbor says. "If I give you a ten-spot, could you get me a Peach Royale?" The request seems harmless. Why not?

- A colorful cardboard box plastered with a well-known logo of a certain computer maker sits in the lobby of your building for several days. Not only does the trademark get noticed, but residents may also assume a neighbor has made the purchase. So the computer company gets a warm association in the minds of certain consumers.

All perfectly reasonable and innocent everyday occurrences, right? But how would you feel if the couple at the Washington Monument raving about their new camera was really a pair of actors planted in targeted locations to praise the virtues of digital cameras to an unsuspecting public? Your innocent neighbor in the bar was actually performing a "lean-over"—a paid commercial for Peach Royale; and the computer box was left in the lobby of your building deliberately at the minimal cost of a "contribution" to the building's doorman.

So now you get really paranoid. You've heard of product placement, where movies offer lingering shots on specific products (funny how the actors always drink Coke or Heineken beer; and didn't Halle Berry look great in that coral-colored Ford Thunderbird in the James Bond movie *Die Another Day*—did you know you could buy a Thunderbird in that exact color?). But what if that group of commuters on your morning train discussing a new movie or TV show or book was planted there deliberately? What if the friendly woman with the cute six-year-old at the playground who was talking about how her son loves his new video game was also an actress?

Such tactics take the concept of target marketing to a whole new level. Advertisers plant seemingly average folks in the middle of a demographically desirable crowd and begin to sing the praises of a new product or service while conveniently failing to mention that they have been hired to do so, and may have never even heard of the product or service before they took the gig.

1. Is this unethical marketing? Explain why or why not.

2. Critics argue that such campaigns "blur the lines between consumerism and con artistry." Is that a fair assessment? Why or why not?

3. How would you feel if you were involved in such an ambush?

4. If the majority of consumers are already skeptical about most advertising they are exposed to, how do you think the general public would feel about such marketing campaigns?

5. Supporters of these campaigns argue that our economy is built on consumerism and that if you don't find more effective ways to reach consumers, the entire economy will suffer. Does that make the practice OK? Should we just accept it as a nuisance and a necessary evil like solicitation calls during dinner?

6. Would your opinion change if the advertisers were more obvious in their campaigns—such as admitting after each skit that the raving fans were really actors?

Sources: First and second items are adapted from Neil McOstrich, "Crossing the Line," *Marketing Magazine* 107, no. 45 (November 11, 2002), p. 24; and the third from Brian Steinberg, "Undercover Marketing Is Gaining Ground—Some Promoters Are Doing It—Others Question Its Ethics," *The Wall Street Journal* (eastern edition), December 18, 2000, p. B17D.

[Internet Exercises]

1. Visit the U.S. government recall Web site www.recalls.gov, select a product recall event from the past three years, and answer the following questions:

   a. What information would you consider to be evidence of an ethical transgression in this product recall?

   b. Other than recalling the product, what other actions did the company take to address the situation?

   c. What steps would you suggest that the company should have taken to restore that reputation?

   d. Locate the Web sites for the American Marketing Association (AMA) and the American Institute of Certified Public Accountants (AICPA). One has a "Professional Code of Conduct," and the other has a "Statement of Ethics." Does the terminology make a difference? Why or why not?

   e. Compare and contrast the components of each approach.

   f. Since the AMA offers certification as a "Professional Certified Marketer," would the organization benefit from promoting a professional code of conduct like the AICPA? Why or why not?

[Team Exercises]

1. **Is it ethical to ambush?**
   Divide into two teams. One team must prepare a presentation advocating the use of the ambush marketing tactics described in the Review Exercise. The other team must prepare a presentation explaining the ethical dilemmas those tactics present.

2. **In search of an ethical department.**
   Divide into groups of three or four. Each group must select one of the organizational departments featured in this chapter (HR, R&D, marketing, sales, and finance) and document the potential areas for unethical behavior in that department. Prepare a presentation outlining an example of an ethical dilemma in that department and proposing a solution for resolving it.

3. **An isolated incident?**
   Divide into two groups, and prepare arguments *for* and *against* the following behavior: *You are the regional production manager for a tire company that has invested many millions of dollars in a new retreading process that will allow you to purchase used tires, replace the tread, and sell them at a significantly lower cost (with a very healthy profit margin for your company). Initial product testing has gone well, and expectations for this very lucrative new project are very high. Promotion prospects for those managers associated with the project are also very good. The company chose to go with a "soft" launch of the new tires, introducing them into the Malaysian market with little marketing or advertising to draw attention to the new product line. Once demand and supply are thoroughly tested, the plan is to launch the new line worldwide with a big media blitz. Sales so far have been very strong based on the low price. However, this morning, your local contact in Malaysia sent news of a bus accident in which two schoolchildren were killed. The cause of the accident was the front left tire on the bus, which lost its tread at high speed and caused the bus to roll over. You are only three days away from your next progress report meeting and only two weeks from the big worldwide launch. You decide to categorize the accident as an isolated incident and move forward with your plans for the introduction of your discount retread tires to the world market.*

4. **The sole remaining supplier.**
   Divide into two groups, and prepare arguments *for* and *against* the following behavior: *Back in the mid-1970s heart pacemakers ran on transistors before advances in technology replaced them with the silicon computer chips we are all familiar with today. Your company has found itself in a situation where it is the last remaining supplier of a particular transistor for the current models of heart pacemakers on the market. Your competitors have all chosen to get out of the business, claiming that the risks of lawsuits related to malfunctioning pacemakers was simply too great to make the business worthwhile. Your management team has now arrived at the same conclusion. The chief executive officer defends the decision by arguing that as a business-to-business supplier to other manufacturers, you have no say in how the transistors are used, so why should the fact that they are used in life-saving equipment factor into the decision? Your responsibility is to your shareholders, not to the patients who depend on these pacemakers. You are not responsible for all the other manufacturers getting out of the business.*

>> BOOSTING YOUR RÉSUMÉ

"Everybody has stretched the truth a little on their résumés at one time or another, right?" That's the question that people who are about to give their own résumés a little boost ask themselves as a way of dealing with the twinge of guilt they are probably feeling as they adjust their job title or make that six months of unemployment magically disappear by claiming a consulting project. In the harsh light of day, résumé inflation is not only unethical, but if you transfer those untruths onto a job application form, which is a legal document, then the act becomes illegal. Consider the outcomes for these former occupants of high-ranking (and high-paying) positions:

Former Notre Dame football coach George O'Leary

- Marilee Jones, dean of admissions for the Massachusetts Institute of Technology (MIT), claimed to hold degrees in biology from Rensselaer Polytechnic Institute and Albany Medical College and to hold a doctorate degree. She resigned in April 2007 after officials at MIT discovered the truth.
- George O'Leary resigned just five days after being hired as Notre Dame's football coach in 2001 when it was revealed that he did not hold a master's degree in education from "NYU–Stony Brook" (a nonexistent institution), nor had he lettered three times as a football player for the University of New Hampshire (both of which he had claimed on his résumé).
- Ronald Zarrella, former CEO of Bausch & Lomb, the eye care company, was required to give up $1.1 million of a planned $1.65 million bonus when it was discovered that although he had attended New York University's Stern School of Business, he had never earned the MBA that he claimed to have on his résumé. Interestingly, the board of directors of Bausch & Lomb, a company recognized by Standard & Poor's as an example of good corporate governance, chose not to fire Zarrella, claiming that he brought too much value to the company and its shareholders to dismiss him.

So if the risks are so high, why do people continue to embellish the details on a document that is supposed to accurately reflect their skills and work experience? Pressure! Getting hired by a company is a competitive process, and you need to make the best sales pitch you can to attract the attention of the HR person assigned to screen the applications for a particular position (or, at least, the applications that make it through the software program that screens résumés for keywords related to the open position). In such a pressured environment, justifying an action on the basis of an assumption that everyone else is probably doing it starts to make sense. So changing dates, job titles, responsibilities, certifications, and/or academic degrees can now be classified as "little white lies"; but as you can see from our three examples in this case, those little white lies can come back to haunt you.

1. Does the competitive pressure to get hired justify the decision to boost your résumé? Why?
2. Do you think the board of directors of Bausch & Lomb made the right decision in choosing not to fire Zarrella? Why or why not?
3. What steps should companies take during the hiring process to ensure that such bad hires do not happen?
4. Can you polish your résumé without resorting to little white lies? Provide some examples of how you might do that.
5. Your friend has been unemployed for two years. She decides to boost her résumé by claiming to have been a consultant for those two years in order to compete in a very tough job market. She explains that a colleague of hers did the same thing to cover a six-month period of unemployment. Does the longer period of unemployment make the decision any less unethical? Why or why not?
6. If you discovered that a colleague at work had lied on her résumé, what would you do?

Sources: J. Stroud, "Six People Who Were Caught Lying on Their Résumés," www.therecruiterslounge, October 11, 2007; and R. Weiss, "By George It's Blarney," *New York Daily News,* December 15, 2001.

Thinking Critically

>> BANK OF AMERICA'S MOST TOXIC ASSET

In December 2008, Ken Lewis, chairman and chief executive officer of Bank of America (BoA), was named as *American Banker*'s "banker of the year" for the second time in six years. Lewis was found worthy of this recognition for his back-to-back acquisitions of Countrywide Financial for $4 billion and Merrill Lynch for $50 billion in Bank of America stock. The deals were applauded as much for their strategic value as their supposedly hard-bargained prices.

By the first week of January 2009, Lewis's world appeared to be collapsing around him. Both deals had proved to be career-enders. Both Countrywide and Merrill Lynch were virtually bankrupt, with assets on their balance sheets that set a new standard for toxicity in an imploding financial market. Some $45 billion in bailout dollars in addition to insurance on $118 billion of toxic securities kept BoA afloat but at the cost of welcoming U.S. taxpayers as the company's largest shareholder.

By mid-February, BoA stock was down 65 percent and almost 90 percent over the preceding 52 weeks. The Obama administration had introduced a $500,000 salary cap for all executives of banks receiving bailout dollars, and the banking sector was anticipating a mass exodus of personnel to foreign banks that were, so far at least, untouched by the financial meltdown. In April 2009, BoA shareholders made a strong statement of their frustration with Lewis by removing him as chairman while allowing him to remain as CEO—a clear message that he was living on borrowed time.

The highly questionable lending practices at Countrywide Financial that became apparent after the financial meltdown raised serious questions about the extent of due diligence performed before the acquisition. This deal alone could have caused great embarrassment for a "banker of the year," but when compared to the travesty of the Merrill Lynch acquisition, Countrywide seemed like a rounding error. Not only did BoA seriously overpay for Merrill (when compared to Jamie Dimon's deal for JPMorgan Chase to purchase the assets of Bear Stearns for only $10 a share), but the deal was also allowed to proceed in the face of clear evidence of financial mismanagement within Merrill Lynch. Weeks before the merger was announced in September 2008, BoA approved a $5.8 billion bonus pool for Merrill employees, including $40 million for soon-to-be-ex-CEO John Thain. Once the true nature of Merrill's financial difficulties became know, any hope of Thain's bonus being paid soon evaporated, with Thain making one final proposal of a $10 million bonus before he was fired in December 2008 in response to leaked media reports that he spent $1.2 million redecorating his executive office suite at Merrill Lynch, including $87,784 on a rug, $28,091 on curtains, and $18,468 on an antique George IV chair.

Once the full extent of the damage at Merrill Lynch was known, and the questions were raised about the due diligence performed by BoA before the deal was completed, Ken Lewis faced additional scrutiny for his failure to exercise the "material adverse event" clause that would have allowed the bank to walk away from the deal. His response? He was pressured (including an implied threat to his tenure as CEO) by federal officials including Ben Bernanke, the chairman of the Federal Reserve, and former secretary of the Treasury Henry M. Paulson Jr. The government, Lewis argued, felt that the completion of the deal would bring an element of stability to an increasingly unstable financial market. The federal officials vehemently denied Lewis's claims, but the question remains as to why else a deal that was so full of holes and so clearly based on assets that would soon have no marketable value would be allowed to proceed.

CONTINUED >>

1. Why would a $500,000 salary cap prompt personnel to leave for other banks?

2. Was the stripping of Lewis's chairmanship a significant move on the part of BoA shareholders?

3. How could John Thain justify spending $1.2 million on his office when Merrill Lynch was on the verge of bankruptcy?

4. What did Ken Lewis hope to gain by claiming that he was "pressured" into completing the Merrill Lynch deal?

5. Of all the decisions made by Ken Lewis in this case study, which one do you think did the most damage to his reputation? Why?

6. What should Lewis have done?

Sources: William Cohan, "The Tattered Strategy of the Banker of the Year," *Financial Times,* January 20, 2009; Maria Bartiromo, "Ken Lewis: Bank of America's CEO Answers His Critics," *BusinessWeek,* February 12, 2009; "Changing Course," *The Economist,* April 30, 2009; and Louise Story and Julie Creswell, "For Bank of America and Merrill, Love Was Blind," *The New York Times,* February 8, 2009.

Thinking Critically `3.3`

>> JOHNSON & JOHNSON AND THE TYLENOL POISONINGS

A bottle of Tylenol is a common feature of any medicine cabinet as a safe and reliable painkiller, but in the fall of 1982, this household brand was driven to the point of near extinction along with the fortunes of parent company Johnson & Johnson as a result of a product-tampering case that has never been solved. On September 29, 1982, seven people in the Chicago area died after taking Extra-Strength Tylenol capsules that had been laced with cyanide. Investigators later determined that the bottles of Tylenol had been purchased or shoplifted from seven or eight drugstores and supermarkets and then replaced on shelves after the capsules in the bottle had been removed, emptied of their acetaminophen powder, and filled with cyanide.

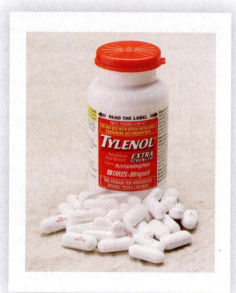

The motive for the killings was never established, although a grudge against Johnson & Johnson or the retail chains selling the brand was suspected. A man called James Lewis attempted to profit from the event by sending an extortion letter to Johnson & Johnson, presumably inspired by the $100,000 reward the company had posted, but the police dismissed him as a serious suspect. He was jailed for 13 years for the extortion but never charged with the murders.

The response of Johnson & Johnson to the potential destruction of its most profitable product line has since become business legend and is taught today as a classic case study in crisis management at universities all over the world.

Company chairman James E. Burke and other senior executives were initially advised to only pull bottles from the Midwest region surrounding the Chicago area where the deaths had occurred. The decision they made was to order the immediate removal and destruction of more than 31 million bottles of the product nationwide, at an estimated cost to the company of more than $100 million. At the time, Tylenol held a 35 percent share of the painkiller market. This attack on the brand quickly reduced that share to less than 7 percent.

Why would the company make such an expensive decision when there were cheaper and more acceptable options open to it? To answer that question, we need to look at the company's Credo—the corporate philosophy statement that has guided the company since its founder, General Robert Wood Johnson, wrote the first version in 1943.

The opening line of the Credo explains why the decision to incur such a large cost in responding to the Tylenol deaths was such an obvious one for the company to make: "We believe our first responsibility is to the doctors, nurses and patients, to mothers and fathers, and all others who use our products and services." That responsibility prompted the company to invest millions in developing tamper-proof bottles for their number-one brand and a further $100 million to win back the confidence of their customers.

The actions appeared to pay off. In less than a year, Tylenol had regained a market share of more than 28 percent. Whether that dramatic recovery was due to savvy marketing or the selfless response of company executives in attempting to do "the right thing" for their customers remains a topic of debate over a quarter of a century later.

QUESTIONS

1. Although Johnson & Johnson took a massive short-term loss as a result of its actions, it was cushioned by the relative wealth of the company. Should it have acted the same way if the survival of the firm were at stake?

2. James E. Burke reportedly said that he felt that there was no other decision he could have made. Do you agree? Could he, for example, have recalled Tylenol only in the Midwest? Was there a moral imperative to recall all Tylenol?

3. What was the moral minimum required of the company in this case? Would it favor some stakeholders more than others? How would you defend balancing the interests of some stakeholders more than others?

4. Imagine that a third-world country volunteers to take the recalled product. Its representatives make assurances that all the tablets will be visually inspected and random samples taken before distribution. Would that be appropriate in these circumstances? Would it have been a better solution than destroying all remaining Tylenol capsules?

5. Apparently no relatives of any of the victims sued Johnson & Johnson. Would they have had a moral case if they had? Should the company have foreseen a risk and done something about it?

6. How well do you think a general credo works in guiding action? Would you prefer a typical mission statement or a clear set of policy outlines, for example? Do you see any way in which the Johnson & Johnson Credo could be improved or modified?

Sources: S. Tifft and L. Griggs, "Poison Madness in the Midwest," www.Time.com, October 11, 1982; I. Molotsky, "Tylenol Maker Hopeful on Solving Poisoning Case," *The New York Times*, February 20, 1986; B. Rudolph, "Coping with Catastrophe," www.Time.com, February 24, 1986; and Johnson & Johnson Credo, www.jnj.com/connect/about-jnj/jnj-credo/.

>> Corporate Social Responsibility

Consider that age-old icon of childhood endeavors: the lemonade stand. Within a corporate social responsibility context, it's as if today's thirsty public wants much more than a cool, refreshing drink for a quarter. They're demanding said beverage be made of juice squeezed from lemons not sprayed with insecticides toxic to the environment and prepared by persons of appropriate age in kitchen conditions which pose no hazard to those workers. It must be offered in biodegradable paper cups and sold at a price which generates a fair, livable wage to the workers—who, some might argue, are far too young to be toiling away making lemonade for profit anyway. It's enough to drive young entrepreneurs . . . straight back to the sandbox.[1]

Corporate social responsibility (CSR)—also referred to as *corporate citizenship* or *corporate conscience*—may be defined as the actions of an organization that are targeted toward achieving a social benefit over and above maximizing profits for its shareholders and meeting all its legal obligations.

> **Corporate Social Responsibility (CSR)** The actions of an organization that are targeted toward achieving a social benefit over and above maximizing profits for its shareholders and meeting all its legal obligations. Also known as *corporate citizenship* and *corporate conscience*.

This definition assumes that the corporation is operating in a competitive environment and that the managers of the corporation are committed to an aggressive growth strategy while complying with all federal, state, and local legal obligations. These obligations include payment of all taxes related to the profitable operation of the business, payment of all employer contributions for its workforce, and compliance with all legal industry standards in operating a safe working environment for its employees and delivering safe products to its customers.

However, the definition only scratches the surface of a complex and often elusive topic that has gained increased attention in the aftermath of corporate scandals that have presented many organizations as being the image of unchecked greed. While CSR may be growing in prominence, much of that prominence has come at the expense of organizations that found themselves facing boycotts and focused media attention on issues that previously were not considered as part of a traditional strategic plan. As Porter and Kramer point out:[2]

Many companies awoke to [CSR] only after being surprised by public responses to issues they had not previously thought were part of their business responsibilities. Nike, for example, faced an extensive consumer boycott after *The New York Times* and other media outlets reported abusive labor practices at some of its Indonesian suppliers in the early 1990s. Shell Oil's decision to sink the Brent Spar, an obsolete oil rig, in the North Sea led to Greenpeace protests in 1995 and to international headlines. Pharmaceutical companies discovered that they were expected to respond to the AIDS pandemic in Africa even though it was far removed from their primary product lines and markets. Fast-food and packaged food companies are now being held responsible for obesity and poor nutrition.

Activists of all kinds . . . have grown much more aggressive and effective in bringing public pressure to bear on corporations. Activists may target the most visible or successful companies merely to draw attention to an issue, even if those corporations actually have had little impact on the problem at hand. Nestlé, for example, the world's largest purveyor of bottled water, has become a major target in the global debate about access to fresh water, despite the fact that Nestlé's bottled water sales consume just 0.0008% of the world's fresh water supply. The inefficiency of agricultural irrigation, which uses 70% of the world's supply annually, is a far more pressing issue, but it offers no equally convenient multinational corporation to target.

Whether the organization's discovery of the significance of CSR was intentional or as a result of unexpected media attention, once CSR becomes part of its strategic plan, choices have to be made as to how the company will address this new element of corporate management.

PROGRESS ✓ QUESTIONS

1. Define *corporate social responsibility*.
2. Name two other terms that may be used for socially aware corporate behavior.
3. Give four examples of a corporation's legal obligations.
4. Do investors always invest money in companies to make a profit?

>> Management without Conscience

Many take an **instrumental approach** to CSR and argue that the only obligation of a corporation is to make profits for its shareholders in providing goods and services that meet the needs of its customers. The most famous advocate of this "classical" model is the Nobel Prize–winning economist Milton Friedman, who argued that:[3]

> The view has been gaining widespread acceptance that corporate officials . . . have a social responsibility that goes beyond serving the interests of their stockholders. . . . This view shows a fundamental misconception of the character and nature of a free economy. In such an economy, there is one and only one social responsibility of business—to use its resources and engage in activities designed to increase its profits so long as it stays within the rules of the game, which is to say, engages in open and free competition, without deception or fraud. . . . Few trends could so thoroughly undermine the very foundations of our free society as the acceptance by corporate officials of a social responsibility other than to make as much money for their stockholders as possible.

From an ethical perspective, Friedman argues that it would be unethical for a corporation to do anything other than deliver the profits for which its investors have entrusted it with their funds in the purchase of shares in the corporation. He also stipulates that those profits should be earned "without deception or fraud." In addition, Friedman argues that, as an employee of the corporation, the manager has an ethical obligation to fulfill his role in delivering on the expectations of his employers:[4]

> In a free-enterprise, private-property system, a corporate executive is an employee of the owners of the business. He has direct responsibility to his employers. That responsibility is to conduct the business in accordance with their desires, which generally will be to make as much money as possible while conforming to the basic rules of the society, both those embodied in law and those embodied in ethical custom. . . . The key point is that, in his capacity as a corporate executive, the manager is the agent of the individuals who own the corporation . . . and his primary responsibility is to them.

Is McDonald's more culpable for childhood obesity than a local burger joint since it sells to a much wider audience? Should your local restaurants be held to similar standards?

Friedman's view of the corporate world supports the rights of individuals to make money with their investments (provided it is done honestly), and it recognizes the clear legality of the employment contract—as a manager, you work for me, the owner (or us, the shareholders), and you are expected to make as much profit as possible to make our investment in the company a success. This position does not prevent the organization from demonstrating some form of social conscience—donating to local charities or sponsoring a local Little League team, for example—but it restricts such charitable acts to the discretion of the owners (presumably in good times rather than bad), rather than recognizing any formal obligation on the part of the corporation and its management team.

This very simplistic model focuses on the internal world of the corporation itself and assumes that there are no external consequences to the actions of the

> **Instrumental Approach** The perspective that the only obligation of a corporation is to maximize profits for its shareholders in providing goods and services that meet the needs of its customers.

Social Contract Approach The perspective that a corporation has an obligation to society over and above the expectations of its shareholders.

corporation and its managers. Once we acknowledge that there is a world outside that is affected by the actions of the corporation, we can consider the **social contract approach** to corporate management.

In recent years, the notion of a social contract between corporations and society has undergone a subtle shift. Originally, the primary focus of the social contract was an economic one, assuming that continued economic growth would bring an equal advancement in quality of life. However, the rapid growth of U.S. businesses in size and power in the 1960s, 1970s, and 1980s changed that focus. Continued corporate growth was not matched by an improved quality of life. Growth at the expense of rising costs, wages growing at a lower rate than inflation, and the increasing presence of substantial layoffs to control costs were seen as evidence that the old social contract was no longer working.

The growing realization that corporate actions had the potential to impact tens of thousands of citizens led to a clear opinion shift. Fueled by special interest groups including environmentalists and consumer advocates, consumers began to question some fundamental corporate assumptions: Do we really need 200 types of breakfast cereal or 50 types of laundry soap just so we can deliver aggressive earnings growth to investors? What is this constant growth really costing us?

> ### Study Alert
>
> How does your company approach the issue of corporate social responsibility? Does it take an instrumental or social contract approach? Provide an example to support your answer.

The modern social contract approach argues that since the corporation depends on society for its existence and continued growth, there is an obligation for the corporation to meet the demands of that society rather than just the demands of a targeted group of customers. As such, corporations should be recognized as social institutions as well as economic enterprises. By recognizing all their stakeholders (customers, employees, shareholders, vendor partners, and their community partners) rather than just their shareholders, corporations, it is argued, must maintain a longer-term perspective than just the delivery of quarterly earnings numbers.

PROGRESS ✔ QUESTIONS

5. What is the instrumental model of corporate management?

6. What is the social contract model of corporate management?

7. Read Friedman's article (see chapter reference #3 on page 231)—what are the assumptions of his argument?

8. Do you agree or disagree with the social contract model? Why?

>> Management by Inclusion

Corporations do not operate in an isolated environment. As far back as 1969, Henry Ford II recognized that fact:[5]

> The terms of the contract between industry and society are changing. . . . Now we are being asked to serve a wider range of human values and to accept an obligation to members of the public with whom we have no commercial transactions.

Their actions impact their customers, their employees, their suppliers, and the communities in which they produce and deliver their goods and services. Depending on the actions taken by the corporation, some of these groups will be positively affected and others will be negatively affected. For example, if a corporation is operating unprofitably in a very competitive market, it is unlikely that it could raise prices to increase profits. Therefore, the logical choice would be to lower costs—most commonly by laying off its employees, since giving an employee a pink slip takes him or her off the payroll immediately.

While those laid-off employees are obviously hardest hit by this decision, it also has other far-reaching consequences. The communities in which those employees reside have now lost the spending power of those employees, who, presumably, no longer have as much money to spend in the local market until they find alternative employment. If the corporation chooses to shut down an entire factory, the community also loses property tax revenue from that factory, which negatively impacts the services it can provide to its residents—schools, roads, police force, and so forth. In addition, those local suppliers who made deliveries to that factory also have lost business and may have to make their own tough choices as a result.

What about the corporation's customers and shareholders? Presumably the layoffs will help the corporation remain competitive and continue to offer low prices to its customers, and the more cost-effective operation will hopefully improve the profitability of the corporation. So there are, at least on paper, winners and losers in such situations.

Recognizing the interrelationship of all these groups leads us far beyond the world of the almighty bottom line, and those organizations that do demonstrate a "conscience" that goes beyond generating profit inevitably attract a lot of attention. As Jim Roberts, professor of marketing at the Hankamer School of Business, points out:[6]

> I like to think of corporate social responsibility as doing well by doing good. Doing what's in the best long-term interest of the customer is ultimately doing what's best for the company. Doing good for the customer is just good business.

Look at the tobacco industry. Serving only the short-term desires of its customers has led to government intervention and a multibillion dollar lawsuit against the industry because of the industry's denial of the consequences of smoking. On the other hand, alcohol manufacturers realized that by at least showing an interest in their consumers' well-being ("Don't drink and drive," "Drink responsibly," "Choose a designated driver"), they have been able to escape much of the wrath felt by the tobacco industry. It pays to take a long-term perspective.

"Doing well by doing good" seems, on the face of it, to be an easy policy to adopt, and many organizations have started down that road by making charitable donations, underwriting projects in their local communities, sponsoring local events, and engaging in productive conversations with special interest groups about earth-friendly packaging materials and the use of more recyclable materials. However, mistrust and cynicism remain among their customers

WARNING:
CIGARETTES CAUSE LUNG CANCER

85% of lung cancers are caused by smoking. 80% of lung cancer victims die within 3 years.

Health Canada

In Canada, cigarette packaging is required to have a graphic label that details the potential health risks of smoking. The same requirement will soon be introduced in the United States. How do you think American consumers will respond to the government's decision?

Real World Applications

Theresa Taggart works the drive-through station at her local fast-food restaurant. Lately the company has been aggressively promoting its "healthy options" kids menu that includes apple slices instead of french fries and chocolate or plain milk instead of sodas. For the first couple of weeks, Theresa is instructed to clarify with each customer whether the person wanted fries or apple slices and soda or milk. However, her manager quickly realizes that the extra questions increased the average order time and contributed to longer lines at the drive-through. Now she has been told to assume that the order is regular (fries and a soda) unless the customer specifies otherwise. What responsibility (CSR) does the fast-food restaurant have to the consumer in this situation? What would you do if you were Theresa?

and citizens of their local communities. Many still see these initiatives as public relations exercises with no real evidence of dramatic changes in the core operating philosophies of these companies.

>> The Driving Forces behind Corporate Social Responsibility

Joseph F. Keefe of NewCircle Communications asserts that there are five major trends behind the CSR phenomenon:[7]

1. *Transparency:* We live in an information-driven economy where business practices have become increasingly transparent. Companies can no longer sweep things under the rug—whatever they do (for good or ill) will be known, almost immediately, around the world.

In the past five years, as part of its strategic resource development program, Global Oil Inc. had made strategic capital investments in African countries with historically unstable government regimes and highly sensitive tribal relationships in order to tie up future oil reserves. With each investment, Global Oil placed considerable emphasis (and PR attention) on its role as a "partner" or "good neighbor" in each region, making very public donations to local infrastructure projects, schools, and health care initiatives.

Jon Bennett had risen through the ranks in his 15-year career with Global Oil to the position of director of Corporate Social Responsibility for the African Region. In this role, Bennett's responsibilities could be summarized in one phrase: Keep the locals happy at each one of Global's project sites. With enough funds in the CSR budget to support a few strategically placed projects, this goal had been easy to achieve, and Bennett had received his fair share of coverage in the local media as he promoted all of Global's community projects. However, in the last nine months, one particular area had begun to show up on Bennett's daily incident reports with increasing regularity.

The Odone people were the first to admit that Global's presence on their land (and the few community projects it funded) had brought some improvement to the welfare of their citizens—there was some preventive health care now, an improved water supply, a couple of schools for the children, and regular work for an increasing number of men drawn away from their traditional farming work to the higher-paying oil crew jobs. However, with all those benefits had come substantial profits for Global Oil and many negatives for the Odone people: Global had experienced several oil spills that damaged the coastal waters of the region, and there were increasing reports of accidents and threats to any employees who considered discussing Global's business activities with local journalists. The frequent positive press coverage of Global's good neighbor programs in the region provided a constant reminder of the disparity between perception and reality.

The Odone's discontent started to express itself through picketing outside the refinery gates and small acts of property damage. Slowly their case began to gather a higher media profile until it reached the attention of an environmental and human rights organization that began to spread the Odone story to its worldwide membership. With this higher profile came an increase in momentum. The picketing became more vocal, and the property damage more expensive. It was obvious that tempers were beginning to rise.

Two weeks later, one of the leading members of the human rights organization was found badly beaten in a remote area of Odone land. He never recovered from his injuries and died a week later. The media response was immediate and extremely negative, accusing Global Oil (without any proof) of either direct or indirect involvement depending on the angle of the story.

Suddenly Jon Bennett's reputation in the region came under extreme scrutiny. The good neighbor was

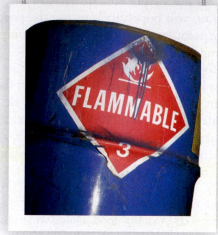

suddenly the corporate bully, and the environmental and human rights organizations quickly built support for boycotts of Global products and any Global customers or suppliers. Bennett's bosses at Global Oil headquarters wanted answers and action—quickly!

Bennett stuck with what he knew best—his media contacts. Responding to the obvious urgency of the situation, he launched a new initiative—"A Plan of Action for the Odone People"—in which he pledged, as a corporate officer of Global Oil, to clean up all the oil spills, address any threats to local employees, and further increase Global's community projects in the area. In short, Bennett committed to addressing all the complaints on the Odone's list of grievances, though in true corporate fashion, the pledges came without specific performance deadlines. In the interests of saving time and getting the greatest PR bang for his buck, Bennett announced his new initiative at a press conference from Global's regional headquarters. No one from the Odone was informed of the new initiative before the press conference, nor was anyone from the Odone people invited to attend.

The environmental and human rights activists claimed an immediate victory and switched their attentions to other corporate wrongdoers elsewhere in the world. Bennett kept his job. But the next morning, the picket line outside the refinery was larger and louder than ever.

QUESTIONS

1. Did Global Oil commit any ethical violations here? Why or why not?
2. Did Bennett's response reinforce Global's public commitment to CSR?
3. Why did "the good neighbor" suddenly become "the corporate bully"?
4. How could Global Oil have handled things differently?

Source: Adapted from David Wheeler, Heike Fabig, and Richard Boele, "Paradoxes and Dilemmas for Stakeholder Responsive Firms in the Extractive Sector: Lessons from the Case of Shell and the Ogoni," *Journal of Business Ethics* 39, no. 3 (September 2002), p. 297.

2. *Knowledge:* The transition to an information-based economy also means that consumers and investors have more information at their disposal than at any time in history. They can be more discerning, and can wield more influence. Consumers visiting a clothing store can now choose one brand over another based upon those companies' respective environmental records or involvement in sweatshop practices overseas.

3. *Sustainability:* The earth's natural systems are in serious and accelerating decline, while global population is rising precipitously. In the last 30 years alone, one-third of the planet's resources—the earth's "natural wealth"—have been consumed. . . . We are fast approaching or have already crossed the sustainable yield thresholds of many natural systems (fresh water, oceanic fisheries, forests, rangelands), which cannot keep pace with projected population growth. . . . As a result, corporations are under increasing pressure from diverse stakeholder constituencies to demonstrate that business plans and strategies are environmentally sound and contribute to sustainable development.

4. *Globalization:* The greatest periods of reform in U.S. history . . . produced child labor laws, the minimum wage, the eight-hour day, workers' compensation laws, unemployment insurance, antitrust and securities regulations, Social Security, Medicare, the Community Reinvestment Act, the Clean Air Act, Clean Water Act, Environmental Protection Agency, and so forth. All of these reforms constituted governmental efforts to intervene in the economy in order to [improve] the worst excesses of market capitalism. Globalization represents a new stage of capitalist development, this time without . . . public institutions [in place] to protect society by balancing private corporate interests against broader public interests.

5. *The Failure of the Public Sector:* Many if not most developing countries are governed by dysfunctional regimes ranging from the [unfortunate] and disorganized to the brutal and corrupt. Yet it is not developing countries alone that suffer from [dilapidated] public sectors. In the United States and other developed nations, citizens arguably expect less of government than they used to, having lost confidence in the public sector as the best or most appropriate venue for addressing a growing list of social problems.

Even with these major trends driving CSR, many organizations have found it difficult to make the transition from CSR as a theoretical concept to CSR as an operational policy. Ironically, it's not the ethical action itself that causes the problem; it's how to promote those acts to your stakeholders as proof of your new corporate conscience without appearing to be manipulative or scheming to generate press coverage for policies that could easily be dismissed as feel-good initiatives that are simply chasing customer favor.

In addition, many CSR initiatives do not generate immediate financial gains to the organization. Cynical customers may decide to wait and see if this is real or just a temporary project to win new customers in a tough economic climate. This delayed response tests the commitment of those organizations that are inclined to dispense with experimental initiatives when the going gets tough.

Corporations that choose to experiment with CSR initiatives run the risk of creating adverse results and ending up worse off than when they started:

- Employees feel that they are working for an insincere, uncaring organization.
- The public sees little more than a token action concerned with publicity rather than community.
- The organization does not perceive much benefit from CSR and so sees no need to develop the concept.

PROGRESS ✓ QUESTIONS

9. List the five major trends driving CSR.
10. Which one do you think is the most important? Why?
11. Explain why organizations are struggling to adopt CSR initiatives.
12. Why would customers be cynical of CSR initiatives?

In 1999, following a campaign by a student group known as Students Organizing for Labor and Economic Equality (SOLE), the University of Michigan instituted a Vendor Code of Conduct that specified key performance criteria from all university vendors. The code included the following:

General Principles

The University of Michigan has a longstanding commitment to sound, ethical, and socially responsible practices. In aligning its purchasing policies with its core values and practices, the University seeks to recognize and promote basic human rights, appropriate labor standards for employees, and a safe, healthful, and sustainable environment for workers and the general public. . . . In addition, the University shall make every reasonable effort to contract only with vendors meeting the primary standards prescribed by this Code of Conduct.

Primary Standards

- Nondiscrimination
- Affirmative Action
- Freedom of Association and Collective Bargaining
- Labor Standards: Wages, Hours, Leaves, and Child Labor
- Health and Safety
- Forced Labor
- Harassment or Abuse

Preferential Standards

- Living Wage
- International Human Rights
- Environmental Protection
- Foreign Law

Compliance Procedures

University-Vendor Partnership. The ideal University-vendor relationship is in the nature of a partnership, seeking mutually agreeable and important goals. Recognizing our mutual interdependence, it is in the best interest of the University to find a resolution when responding to charges or questions about a vendor's compliance with the provisions of the Code.

On November 30, 2004, SOLE submitted formal complaints against one specific university vendor—the Coca-Cola Company—with which the university held 12 direct and indirect contracts totaling just under $1.3 million in fiscal year 2004. The complaints against Coke were as follows:

- Biosolid waste disposal in India. The complaint alleged that bottling plant sludge containing cadmium and other contaminants has been distributed to local farmers as fertilizer.
- Use of groundwater in India. The complaint alleged that Coca-Cola is drawing down the water table/aquifer by using deep-bore wells; water quality has declined; shallow wells used by local farmers have gone

dry; and poor crop harvests near bottling plants have resulted from lack of sufficient irrigation water.

- Pesticides in the product in India. Studies have found that pesticides have been detected in Coca-Cola products in India that are in excess of local and international standards.
- Labor practices in Colombia. Data showing a steep decline in SIALTRAINAL, a Colombian bottler's union (from approximately 2,300 to 650 members in the past decade); SOLE claims repeated incidents with paramilitary groups threatening and harming union leaders and potential members, including allegations of kidnapping and murder. SOLE is also concerned about working conditions within the bottling plants.

The Vendor Code of Conduct Dispute Review Board met in June 2005 to review the complaints and recommended that Coca-Cola agree in writing no later than September 30, 2005, to a third-party independent audit to review the complaints. An independent auditor satisfactory to both parties had to be selected by December 31, 2005. The audit had to be completed by March 2006, with the findings to be received by the university no later than April 30, 2006. Coca-Cola would then be expected to put a corrective action plan in place by May 31, 2006. Since one of the 12 contracts was scheduled to expire on June 30, 2005, with another 7 expiring between July and November 2005, Coca-Cola was formally placed on probation until August 2006 pending further investigation of the SOLE complaints. The board also recommended that the university not enter into new contracts or renew any expiring contracts during this period and that it agree only to short-term conditional extensions with reassessment at each of the established deadlines to determine if Coca-Cola has made satisfactory progress toward demonstrating its compliance with the Vendor Code of Conduct.

The situation got progressively worse for Coca-Cola. By December 2005, at least a dozen institutions worldwide had divested from the Coca-Cola Company on the grounds of alleged human rights violations in Asia and South America. On December 8, New York University began pulling all Coke products from its campus after

Coke refused to submit to an independent investigation by that day's deadline.

On December 30, 2005, the University of Michigan suspended sales of Coke products on its three campuses beginning January 1, 2006, affecting vending machines, residence halls, cafeterias, and campus restaurants. Kari Bjorhus, a spokesperson for the Coca-Cola Company, told the *Detroit News,* "The University of Michigan is an important school, and I respect the way they worked with us on this issue. We are continuing to try hard to work with the university to address concerns and assure them about our business practices."

QUESTIONS

1. Which ethical standards are being violated here?
2. Is the university being unreasonable in the high standards demanded in its Vendor Code of Conduct?
3. Do you think the university would have developed the Vendor Code of Conduct without the aggressive campaign put forward by SOLE?
4. How should Coca-Cola respond in order to keep the University of Michigan contracts?

Sources: University of Michigan, www.umich.edu; Associated Press, December 30, 2005; *The Michigan Daily,* September 29, 2005; and University of Michigan News Service, June 17, 2005.

>> The Triple Bottom Line

Organizations pursue operational efficiency through detailed monitoring of their bottom line—that is, how much money is left over after all the bills have been paid from the revenue generated from the sale of their product or service. As a testament to how seriously companies are now taking CSR, many have adapted their annual reports to reflect a triple bottom-line approach, for which they provide social and environmental updates alongside their primary bottom-line financial performance. The phrase has been attributed to John Elkington, cofounder of the business consultancy SustainAbility, in his 1998 book *Cannibals with Forks: The Triple Bottom Line of 21st Century Business.* As further evidence that this notion has hit the business mainstream, there is a trendy acronym, *3BL,* for you to use to prove, supposedly, that you are on the "cutting edge" of this new trend. (For a more detailed critique of 3BL, please review the 2003 article by Wayne Norman and Chris MacDonald in Appendix B.)

To some degree, 3BL is like the children's story, "The Emperor's New Clothes." While it may be easy to support the idea of organizations pursuing social and environmental goals in addition to their financial goals, there has been no real evidence of how to measure such achievements, and no one has yet volunteered to play the part of the little boy who tells the emperor he is naked. If you subscribe to the old management saying that "if you can't measure it, you can't manage it," the challenges of delivering on any 3BL goals become apparent. Wayne and MacDonald present the following scenario:[8]

Imagine a firm reporting that:

(a) 20 percent of its directors were women,
(b) 7 percent of its senior management were members of "visible" minorities,
(c) It donated 1.2 percent of its profits to charity,
(d) The annual turnover rate among its hourly workers was 4%, and
(e) It had been fined twice this year for toxic emissions.

Now, out of context (e.g., without knowing how large the firm is, where it is operating, and what the averages are in its industrial sector) it is difficult to say how good or bad these figures are. Of course, in the case of each indicator we often have a sense of whether a higher or lower number would generally be better, from the perspective of social/ethical performance. The conceptual point, however, is that these are quite simply not the sort of data that can be fed into an income-statement-like calculation to produce a final net sum.

So if you can't measure it, can you really arrive at a "bottom line" for it? It would appear that many organizations are taking a fairly opportunistic approach in adopting the terminology without following through on the delivery of a consistent methodology. Could the feel-good terminology associated with 3BL help you make a convincing case if you are seeking to make amends for prior transgressions? Consider the following from Coca-Cola's "2004 Citizenship Report":[9]

> Our Company has always endeavored to conduct business responsibly and ethically. We have long been committed to enriching the workplace, preserving and protecting the environment, and strengthening the communities where we operate. These objectives are all consistent with—indeed essential to—our principal goal of refreshing the marketplace with high-quality beverages.

If we compare this commitment to the accusations made by students at the University of Michigan in the ethical dilemma "Banning the Real Thing," on page **72**, we can see how challenging CSR can be. It may be easy to make a public commitment to CSR, but actually delivering on that commitment to the satisfaction of your customers can be much harder to achieve.

JUMPING ON THE CSR BANDWAGON

Just as we have a triple bottom line, organizations have jumped on the CSR bandwagon by adopting three distinct types of CSR—ethical, altruistic, and strategic—for their own purposes.

Ethical CSR Purest or most legitmate type of CSR in which organizations pursue a clearly defined sense of social conscience in managing their financial responsibilities to shareholders, their legal responsibilities to their local community and society as a whole, and their ethical responsibilities to do the right thing for all their stakeholders.

Altruistic CSR Philanthropic approach to CSR in which organizations underwrite specific initiatives to give back to the company's local community or to designated national or international programs.

Ethical CSR represents the purest or most legitimate type of CSR in which organizations pursue a clearly defined sense of social conscience in managing their financial responsibilities to shareholders, their legal responsibilities to their local community and society as a whole, and their ethical responsibilities to do the right thing for all their stakeholders.

Organizations in this category have typically incorporated their beliefs into their core operating philosophies. Companies such as The Body Shop, Ben & Jerry's Homemade Ice Cream, and Tom's of Maine were founded on the belief that the relationship between companies and their consumers did not have to be an adversarial one and that corporations should honor a social contract with the communities in which they operate and the citizens they serve.

Altruistic CSR takes a philanthropic approach by underwriting specific initiatives to give back to the company's local community or to designated national or international programs. In ethical terms, this giving back is done with funds that rightly belong to shareholders (but it is unlikely that McDonald's shareholders, for example, would file a motion at the next annual general meeting for the return of the funds that McDonald's gives to the support of its Ronald McDonald Houses).

Of greater concern is that the choice of charitable giving is at the discretion of the corporation, which places the individual shareholders in the awkward position of unwittingly supporting causes they may not support on their own, such as the pro-life and gun control movements. Critics have argued that, from an ethical perspective, this type of CSR is immoral since it represents a violation of shareholder rights if they are not given the opportunity to vote on the initiatives launched in the name of corporate social responsibility.

The relative legitimacy of altruistic CSR is based on the argument that the philanthropic initiatives are authorized without concern for the corporation's overall profitability. Arguing in *utilitarian* terms, corporations are merely doing the greatest good for the greatest number.

Examples of altruistic CSR often occur during crises or situations of widespread need. Consider the following:

- In the 1980s, Richard Branson's Virgin Group launched Mates Condoms in response to growing concern over the spread of HIV/AIDS. The company operated on the philosophy that the need for the availability of the product far outweighed the need to make a profit.
- Southwest Airlines supports the Ronald McDonald Houses with donations of both dollars and employee-donated volunteer hours. The company considers giving back to the communities in which it operates an appropriate part of its mission.
- Shell Oil Corporation responded to the devastation of the tsunami disaster in Asia in December 2004 with donations of fuel for transportation rescue and water tanks for relief aid, in addition to financial commitments of several million dollars for disaster relief. Shell employees matched many of the company's donations.
- In September 2005, the home improvement retail giant Home Depot announced a direct cash donation of $1.5 million to support the relief and rebuilding efforts in areas devastated by Hurricane

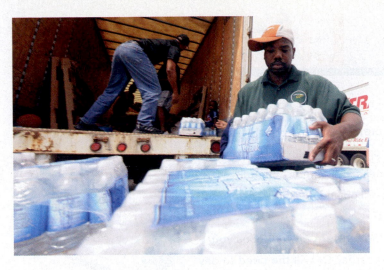
Volunteer work as corporate policy is not limited to major corporations. What are some smaller-scale examples of altruistic efforts that companies can engage in?

Katrina. In addition, the company announced a corporate month of service, donating 300,000 volunteer hours to communities across the country and over $200,000 in materials to support the activities of 90 stores in recovery, cleanup, and rebuilding efforts in their local communities.

Strategic CSR runs the greatest risk of being perceived as self-serving behavior on the part of the organization. This type of philanthropic activity targets programs that will generate the most positive publicity or goodwill for the organization. By supporting these programs, companies achieve the best of both worlds: They can claim to be doing the right thing, and, on the assumption that good publicity brings more sales, they also can meet their fiduciary obligations to their shareholders.

Compared to the alleged immorality of altruistic CSR, critics can argue that strategic CSR is ethically commendable because these initiatives benefit stakeholders while meeting fiduciary obligations to the company's shareholders. However, the question remains: Without a win-win payoff, would such CSR initiatives be authorized?

The danger in this case lies in how actions are perceived. Consider for example, two initiatives launched by the Ford Motor Corporation:

- Ford spent millions on an ad campaign to raise awareness of the need for booster seats for children over 40 pounds and under 4 feet 9 inches (most four- to eight-year-olds) and gave away almost a million seats as part of the campaign.

- During the PR battle with Firestone Tires over who was to blame for the rollover problems with the Ford Explorer, Ford's CEO at the time, Jacques Nasser, made a public commitment to spend up to $3 billion to replace 13 million Firestone Wilderness AT tires for free on Ford Explorers because he saw them as an "unacceptable risk to our customers."

If we attribute motive to each campaign, the booster seat campaign could be interpreted as a way to position Ford as the auto manufacturer that cares about the safety of its passengers as much as its drivers. The tire exchange could be interpreted the same way, but given the design flaws with the Ford Explorer alleged by Firestone, couldn't it also be seen as a diversionary tactic?

One of the newest and increasingly questionable practices in the world of CSR is the notion of making your operations "carbon neutral" in such a way as to offset whatever damage you are doing to the environment through your greenhouse gas emissions by purchasing credits from "carbon positive" projects to balance out your emissions. Initially developed as a solution for those industries that face significant challenges in reducing their emissions (airlines or automobile companies, for example), the concept has quickly spawned a diverse collection of vendors that can assist you in achieving carbon neutrality, along with a few markets in which emissions credits can now be bought and sold.

> **Strategic CSR** Philanthropic approach to CSR in which organizations target programs that will generate the most positive publicity or goodwill for the organization but which runs the greatest risk of being perceived as self-serving behavior on the part of the organization.

Study Alert

Should it matter if a company is being opportunistic in adopting CSR practices? As long as there is a positive outcome, doesn't everyone benefit in the long run? Why or why not?

PROGRESS ✓ QUESTIONS

13. Explain the term *triple bottom line*.
14. Explain the term *ethical CSR*.
15. Explain the term *altruistic CSR*.
16. Explain the term *strategic CSR*.

>> Being socially responsible

Consider how important your beliefs about corporate social responsibility and sustainability are in your daily life. Do you spend your hard-earned money at stores that promote environmental awareness and "green" capitalism? Or does your budget force you to find the best prices and not think about the damage done to achieve the lowest possible cost?

How will those beliefs impact your life choices in the future? Will you focus your employment search on companies with good CSR records? Or will the need to pay the bills outweigh that element and force you to take the highest-paying job you can find? It is important to remember that the paycheck may not be enough to address a poor cultural fit or a direct conflict between your values and those of your employer. It's better to extend your search for a while, if necessary, to find a company that you are proud to work for rather than taking the first opportunity that comes along only to find yourself at odds with many of the company's policies and philosophies.

>> Buying Your Way to CSR

Do you know what your carbon footprint is? At www.carbonfootprint.com/calculator.aspx, you can calculate the carbon dioxide emissions from your home, your car, and any air travel you do, and then calculate your total emissions on an annual basis. The result is your "footprint." You can then purchase credits to offset your emissions and render yourself "carbon neutral." If you have sufficient funds, you can purchase more credits than you need to achieve neutrality and then join the enviable ranks of carbon-positive people who actually take more carbon dioxide out of the cycle than they produce. That, of course, is a technicality since you aren't driving less or driving a hybrid, nor are you being more energy conscious in how you heat or cool your home. You are doing nothing more than buying credits from other projects around the world, such as tree planting in indigenous forests, wind farms, or even outfitting African farmers with energy-efficient stoves, and using those positive emissions to counterbalance your negative ones. Companies such as Dell Computer, British Airways, Expedia Travel, and BP have experimented with programs where customers can pay a fee to offset the emissions spent in manufacturing their products or using their services.

If this sounds just a little strange, consider that this issue of offsetting is serious enough to have been ratified by the Kyoto Protocol—an agreement between 160 countries that became effective in 2005 (and which the United States has yet to sign). The protocol requires developed nations to reduce their greenhouse gas emissions not only by modifying their domestic industries (coal, steel, automobiles, etc.) but also by funding projects in developing countries in return for carbon credits. It didn't take long for an entire infrastructure to develop in order to facilitate the trading of these credits so that organizations with high emissions (and consequently a larger demand for offset credits) could purchase credits in greater volumes than most individual projects would provide. In the first nine months of 2006, the United Nations estimated that over $22 billion of carbon was traded.

As with any frontier (read: unregulated) market, the early results for this new industry have been questionable to say the least. Examples of unethical practices include:

- Inflated market prices for credits—priced per ton of carbon dioxide—varying from $3.50 to $27 a ton, which explains why some traders are able to generate profit margins of 50 percent.
- The sale of credits from projects that don't even exist.

- Selling the same credits from one project over and over again to different buyers who are unable to verify the effectiveness of the project since they are typically set up in remote geographic areas.
- Claiming carbon-offset credits on projects that are profitable in their own right.

As these questionable practices gain more media attention, some of the larger players in this new industry—companies such as JPMorgan Chase and Deutsche Bank, which have multibillion dollar investments in the credit trading arena—are demanding that commonly accepted codes of conduct be established in order to clean up the market and offer greater incentives for customers to trade their credits. In November 2006, Deutsche Bank teamed up with more than a dozen investment banks and five carbon-trading organizations in Europe to create the European Carbon Investors and Services Association (ECIS) to promote the standardization of carbon trading on a global scale. In 2003, the Chicago Climate Exchange (CCX) was launched with 13 charter members and today remains the only trading system for all six greenhouse gases (carbon dioxide, methane, nitrous oxide, hydrofluorocarbons, perfluorocarbons, and sulfur hexafluoride) in North America. In 2005, CCX launched the European Climate Exchange (ECX) and the Chicago Climate Futures Exchange (CCFE), which offers options and futures contracts on emissions credits. Membership of CCX has now reached almost 300 members.

>> Conclusion

So if there is nothing ethically wrong in "doing well by doing good," why isn't everyone doing it? The key concern here must be customer perception. If an organization commits to CSR initiatives, then they must be real commitments rather than short-term experiments. You may be able to gamble on the short-term memory of your customers, but the majority will expect you to deliver on your commitment and to provide progress reports on those initiatives that you publicized so widely.

But what about some of the more well-known CSR players? When we consider Ben & Jerry's Homemade Ice Cream or The Body Shop, for example, both organizations made the concept of a corporate social conscience a part of their core philosophies before CSR was ever anointed as a management buzzword. As such, their good intent garnered vast amounts of goodwill: Investors admired their financial performance, and customers felt good about shopping there. However, if the quality of their products had not lived up to customer expectations, would they have prospered over the long term? Would customers have continued to shop there if they didn't like the products? "Doing well by doing good" will only get you so far.

In this context, it is unfair to accuse companies with CSR initiatives of abandoning their moral responsibilities to their stakeholders. Even if you are leveraging the maximum possible publicity from your efforts, that will only get the people in the door. If the product or service doesn't live up to expectations, they won't be back. Customers will not settle for second-rate service or product quality just because a charitable cause is involved. Therefore, your product or service must meet and ideally exceed the expectations of your customers, and if you continue to do that for the long term (assuming you have a reasonably competent management team), the needs of your stakeholders should be well taken care of.

What remains to be seen, however, is just how broadly or, more specifically, how quickly the notion of 3BL will become part of standard business practice and reach some common terminology that will allow consumers and investors to accurately assess the extent of a company's social responsibility. As long as annual reports simply present glossy pictures of the company's good deeds around the world, it will be difficult for any stakeholder to determine whether a change has taken place in that company's core business philosophy, or whether it's just another example of opportunistic targeted marketing.

Without a doubt, the financial incentive (or threat, depending on how you look at it) is now very real, and has the potential to significantly impact an organization's financial future. Consider these two recent examples:

- In April 2003, the California Public Employees Retirement System (CALPERS), which manages almost $750 million for 1.5 million current and retired employees of California, publicly urged pharmaceutical company GlaxoSmithKline to review its policy of charging for AIDS drugs in developing countries. In March 2008, CALPERS went even further and listed five American companies on its 2008 Focus List to highlight the pension fund's concerns about stock and

CONTINUED >>

financial underperformance and corporate governance practices (which we'll learn more about in Chapter 5). The companies listed were the Cheesecake Factory, Hilb Rogal & Hobbs (an insurance brokerage firm), Ivacare (a health care equipment provider), La-Z-Boy, and Standard Pacific (a homebuilding company).

- In June 2006, the government of Norway, which manages a pension fund from oil revenues for its citizens of over $200 billion notified Walmart and Freeport (a U.S.–based mining company) that they were being excluded as investments for the pension fund on the grounds that the companies have been responsible for either environmental damage or the violation of human rights in their business practices.

With such financial clout now being put behind CSR issues, the question of adoption of some form of social responsibility plan for a corporation should no longer be *if* but *when*.

FRONTLINE FOCUS
A Stocking Error—Jennifer Makes a Decision

Jennifer decides to follow Tony's instructions and leave the shelves stocked with much more of MegaDrug's own brand than the name brands that many customers use exclusively.

As the day progresses, the allergy medicines continue to be a top-selling item because it is the middle of allergy season, and by noon the stocks of name brands are getting low. Now Jennifer has a choice to make. Does she follow Tony's instructions and encourage customers to try MegaDrug's own brand? Or does she simply apologize for the item being out of stock, with the risk that upset customers will ask to speak to the manager?

After a few minutes, Jennifer hits upon a solution—rain checks! She'll work the register for the rest of the day (Tony was only going to have her do paperwork anyway), and anyone who complains about the name brand being out of stock will be issued a rain check with a sincere apology.

By closing time, 24 rain checks have been issued. Jennifer provides Tony with the numbers and suggests that a more even balance of brand-name and own-brand items be placed on the shelves. The good news is that the store would have a new delivery by tomorrow afternoon.

QUESTIONS
1. Did Jennifer do the right thing here?
2. What would the consequences have been for MegaDrug if Jennifer had not done this?
3. What do you think Tony will do when he finds out?

[For Review]

1. **Describe and explain *corporate social responsibility (CSR)*.**

   Corporate social responsibility—also referred to as "corporate citizenship" or "corporate conscience"—may be defined as the actions of an organization that are targeted toward achieving a social benefit over and above maximizing profits for its shareholders and meeting all its legal obligations. Typically, that "benefit" is targeted toward environmental issues, such as reducing pollution levels or recycling materials instead of dumping them in a landfill. For global organizations, CSR can also involve the demonstration of care and concern for local communities and indigenous populations.

2. **Distinguish between *instrumental* and *social contract* approaches to CSR.**

   An instrumental approach to CSR takes the perspective that the only obligation of a corporation is to make profits for its shareholders in providing goods and services that meet the needs of its customers. Corporations argue that they meet their social obligations through the payment of federal and state taxes, and they should not, therefore, be expected to contribute anything beyond that.

   Critics of the instrumental approach argue that it takes a simplistic view of the internal processes of a corporation in isolation, with no reference to the external consequences of the actions of the corporation and its managers. The social contract approach acknowledges that there is a world outside that is impacted by the actions of the corporation, and since the corporation depends on society for its existence and continued growth, there is an obligation for the corporation to meet the demands of that society rather than just the demands of a targeted group of customers.

3. **Explain the business argument for "doing well by doing good."**

   Rather than waiting for the media or their customers to force them into better CSR practices, many organizations are realizing that incorporating the interests of all their stakeholders (customers, employees, shareholders, vendor partners, and their community partners), instead of just their shareholders, can generate positive media coverage, improved revenues, and higher profit margins. "Doing well by doing good" seems, on the face of it, to be an easy policy to adopt, and many organizations have started down that road by making charitable donations, underwriting projects in their local communities, sponsoring local events, and engaging in productive conversations with special interest groups about earth-friendly packaging materials and the use of more recyclable materials.

4. **Summarize the five driving forces behind CSR.**

   Joseph F. Keefe of NewCircle Communications asserts that there are five major trends behind the CSR phenomenon. Each of the trends is linked with the greater availability and dispersal of information via the World Wide Web using Web sites, blogs, and social media mechanisms such as Twitter:

   - *Transparency: Companies can no longer sweep things under the rug—whatever they do (for good or ill) will be known, almost immediately, around the world.*

   - *Knowledge: The transition to an information-based economy also means that consumers and investors have more information at their disposal than at any time in history. They can be more discerning, and can wield more influence. Consumers visiting a clothing store can now choose one brand over another based upon those companies' respective environmental records or involvement in sweatshop practices overseas.*

   - *Sustainability: We are fast approaching or have already crossed the sustainable yield thresholds of many natural systems (fresh water, oceanic fisheries, forests,*

rangelands), which cannot keep pace with projected population growth. . . . As a result, corporations are under increasing pressure from diverse stakeholder constituencies to demonstrate that business plans and strategies are environmentally sound and contribute to sustainable development.

   - *Globalization: Globalization represents a new stage of capitalist development, this time without . . . public institutions [in place] to protect society by balancing private corporate interests against broader public interests.*

   - *The Failure of the Public Sector: In the United States and other developed nations, citizens arguably expect less of government than they used to, having lost confidence in the public sector as the best or most appropriate venue for addressing a growing list of social problems. This, in turn, has increased pressure on corporations to take responsibility for the social impact of their actions rather than expecting the public sector to do so.*

5. **Explain the *triple bottom-line* approach to corporate performance measurement.**

   Documenting corporate performance using a triple bottom-line (3BL) approach involves recording social and environmental performance in addition to the more traditional financial bottom-line performance. As corporations understand the value of promoting their CSR activities, annual reports start to feature community investment projects, recycling initiatives, and pollution reduction commitments. However, while financial reports are standardized according to generally accepted accounting principles (GAAP), social and environmental performance reports currently do not offer the same standardized approach.

6. **Discuss the relative merits of carbon-offset trading.**

   The Kyoto Protocol—an agreement between 160 countries that became effective in 2005 (and which the United States has yet to sign)—required developed nations to reduce their greenhouse gas emissions either by modifying their own domestic industries or funding projects in developing nations in return for "carbon credits." This has spawned a thriving (and currently unregulated) business in trading credits for cold hard cash. On the one hand, those funds can be used to develop infrastructures in poorer communities, but critics argue that the offset credit option allows corporations to buy their way into compliance rather than being forced to change their operational practices.

[Key Terms]

[Review Questions]

1. Would organizations really be paying attention to CSR if customers and federal and state agencies weren't forcing them to? Why or why not?

2. Would the CSR policies of an organization influence your decision to use its products or services? Why or why not?

3. Which is more ethical: altruistic CSR or strategic CSR? Provide examples to explain your answer.

4. How would you measure your carbon footprint?

5. If a carbon-offset project is already profitable, is it ethical to provide credits over and above those profits? Why or why not?

6. Consider the company you currently work for (or one you have worked for in the past). What initiatives could it start to be more socially responsible? How would you propose such changes?

[Review Exercise]

Payatas Power. On July 1, 2000, a mountain of garbage at the Payatas landfill on the outskirts of Quezon City in the Philippines fell on the surrounding slum community killing nearly three hundred people and destroying the homes of hundreds of families who foraged the dump site. In 2007, Pangea Green Energy Philippines Inc. (PGEP) a subsidiary of Italian utility company Pangea Green Energy, announced an ambitious plan to drill 33 gas wells on the landfill to harvest methane gas from the bottom of the waste pile. An initial U.S.$4 million investment built a 200-kilowatt power plant to be fueled by the harvested methane. The power generated makes the landfill self-sufficient and allows excess power to be sold to the city power grid.

However, the real payoff will come from carbon-offset credits. Methane gas is 21 times more polluting that carbon dioxide as a greenhouse gas. Capturing and burning methane releases carbon dioxide and therefore has 21 times less emission impact—a reduction that can be captured as an offset credit. PGEP will arrange trading of those carbon credits in return for a donation of an estimated U.S.$300,000 to the Quezon City community—funds that will be used to develop the local infrastructure and build schools and medical centers for the Payatas community. The landfill has now been renamed "Quezon City Controlled Disposal Facility."

1. The PGEP-Payatas project is being promoted as a win-win project for all parties involved. Is that an accurate assessment? Why or why not?

2. The Payatas project is estimated to generate 100,000 carbon credits per year. At an average market value of U.S.$30 per credit (prices vary according to the source of the credit), PGEP will receive an estimated U.S.$3 million from the project. On those terms, is the U.S.$300,000 donation to the Payatas community a fair one?

3. How could Quezon City officials ensure that there is a more equitable distribution of wealth?

Sources: Melody M. Aguiba, "Payatas: From Waste to Energy," www.newsbreak.com, September 24, 2007; and www.quezoncity.gov.ph.

[Internet Exercises]

1. Review the CSR policies of a Fortune 100 company of your choice. Would you classify its policies as ethical, altruistic, strategic, or a combination of all three? Provide examples to support your answer.

2. Review the annual report of a Fortune 100 company of your choice. What evidence can you find of triple bottom-line reporting in the report? Provide examples to support your answer.

[Team Exercises]

1. **Instrumental or social contract?**

    Divide into two teams. One team must prepare a presentation advocating for the instrumental model of corporate management. The other team must prepare a presentation arguing for the social contract model of corporate management.

2. **Ethical, altruistic, or strategic?**

    Divide into three groups. Each group must select one of the following types of CSR: ethical CSR, altruistic CSR, or strategic CSR. Prepare a presentation arguing for the respective merits of each approach, and offer examples of initiatives that your company could engage in to adopt this strategy.

3. **Closing down a factory.**

    Divide into two groups, and prepare arguments *for* and *against* the following behavior: *Your company is managing to maintain a good profit margin on the computer parts you manufacture in a very tough economy. Recently, an opportunity has come along to move your production capacity overseas. The move will reduce manufacturing costs significantly as a result of tax incentives and lower labor costs, resulting in an anticipated 15 percent increase in profits for the company. However, the costs associated with shutting down your U.S.–based operations would mean that you wouldn't see those increased profits for a minimum of three years. Your U.S. factory is the largest employer in the surrounding town, and shutting it down will result in the loss of over 800 jobs. The loss of those jobs is expected to devastate the economy of the local community.*

4. **A limited campaign.**

    Divide into two groups and prepare arguments *for* and *against* the following behavior: *You work in the marketing department of a large dairy products company. The company has launched a "revolutionary" yogurt product with ingredients that promote healthy digestion. As a promotion to launch the new product, the company is offering to donate 10 cents to the American Heart Association (AHA) for every foil top from the yogurt pots that is returned to the manufacturer. To support this campaign, the company has invested millions of dollars in a broad "media spend" on television, radio, Web, and print outlets, as well as the product packaging itself. In very small print on the packaging and advertising is a clarification sentence that specifies that the maximum donation for the campaign will be $10,000. Your marketing analyst colleagues have forecast that first-year sales of this new product will reach 10 million units, with an anticipated participation of 2 million units in the pot-top return campaign (a potential donation of $200,000 without the $10,000 limit). Focus groups that were tested about the new product indicated clearly that participants in the pot-top return campaign attach positive feelings about their purchase to the added bonus of the donation to the AHA.*

Granted, measuring overall corporate responsibility requires more than just analyzing a company's philanthropic donations. Fair treatment of employees, making or selling safe products, paying taxes, and complying with environmental standards are all ingredients that should be in the social responsibility mix. However important these things are, though, they are not more important than a corporationwide commitment to use an appropriate percentage of a company's pretax resources to address critical issues that affect employees, communities, the nation, and the planet.

Badly needed is a meaningful voluntary commitment by the business community to "ante up" a minimum budget for corporate philanthropy. A reasonable requirement for any company that wants to call itself a good corporate citizen ought to be to spend at least 1 percent of its previous year's pretax profit for philanthropic purposes.

NONFINANCIAL RETURNS

Convincing senior management to increase rather than cut back a company's philanthropy budget may seem a daunting, if not impossible, task, particularly at a time when the overall corporate profit picture has become so fuzzy. But if executives understand that an effectively managed contribution program can deliver strong returns to a corporation, then 1 percent of pretax earnings should take on the look and feel of an investment, not a handout.

Rather than a self-imposed tax, a contribution can actually be managed in a way that makes it a powerful business tool. That happens when, to the extent practicable, company donations are directed to nonprofit groups closely aligned with the interests of the corporation's employees, communities, and business objectives. At the same time, a corporate contribution shouldn't be solely about advancing the interests of the company. If contributions are designed only to bolster the bottom line, if they are used to support pet projects of senior managers or board members, or if they are purely selfish in their intent, we believe they fall short of the definition of what it takes to be considered the proper conduct of a good corporate citizen.

This ante-up proposal is intended to be the bottom rung of the corporate citizenship ladder. Businesses that are "best in class" in the corporate philanthropy field also need to manage contributions strategically that go well beyond the recommended pretax minimum of 1 percent. Some companies are already clearing this higher bar. In Minneapolis–St. Paul, for example, more than 150 companies—including such large corporations as Target and General Mills—are every year donating at least 5 percent of their pretax earnings. (Disclosure: In 1998, the year before Tele-Communications, where I was then CEO, merged into AT&T, TCI contributed a bit more than 1 percent of its operating cash flow to charity. Like our counterparts in the cable industry, TCI in those years had substantial pretax losses because of significant depreciation and amortization.)

To reverse the downward trend in corporate giving, we need a cadre of self-motivated and sensitive CEOs to lead the way. We need men and women who will match actions with words by carrying out combined corporate contributions and community-relations initiatives that are supported by adequate resources and time, rather than by more chest-beating ad campaigns and press releases.

QUESTIONS

1. Why would companies choose to inflate the image of their corporate citizenship?

2. Is it ethical to direct company donations to "nonprofit groups closely aligned with the interests of the corporation's employees, communities, and business objectives"? Why or why not?

3. Is it ethical to direct company donations to support "pet projects of senior managers or board members"? Why or why not?

4. Why would budgeting a fixed percentage of pretax profits for corporate philanthropy be seen as a more convincing commitment to CSR than just funding a variety of projects?

5. The authors of this article claim that "an effectively managed contribution program can deliver strong returns to a corporation." What might those returns be?

6. Does the fact that Target and General Mills donate five times more than the minimum 1 percent make them five times more socially responsible? Why or why not?

Source: Leo Hindery Jr. and Curt Weeden, "Corporate Social Irresponsibility," *BusinessWeek* Viewpoint, July 8, 2008. Hindery is a contributor to the *BusinessWeek* column Outside Shot. He is a managing partner of InterMedia Partners, former CEO of Tele-Communications Inc., its successor AT&T Broadband, and the YES Network. Curt Weeden is president of Business & Nonprofit Strategies, Inc., and former CEO of the Association of Corporate Contributions Professionals. He is the author of *Corporate Social Investing* (Berrett-Koehler, 1998).

>> THE PESTICIDE DDT

In 1939 Paul Muller, a Swiss chemist working for J. R. Geigy, was looking for a way to protect woolens against moths. His quest led him to a white crystalline powder called *dichlorodiphenyltrichloroethane* that had a devastating effect on flies. The powder, subsequently known as DDT, would become the first modern synthetic pesticide and earn Muller the 1948 Nobel Prize for chemistry. In 1942 Geigy sent some of the powder to its New York office. Victor Froelicher, a Geigy chemist in the New York office, translated the document describing the powder and its amazing attributes into English and gave a sample of the powder to the Department of Agriculture.

The U.S. Army had tasked the Department of Agriculture with finding a way to protect its soldiers from insect-borne diseases. In some of the military units, up to 80 percent of the soldiers were out sick with malaria. After testing thousands of compounds, the department's research station in Orlando, Florida, found DDT to be most effective. It was subsequently used by the armed forces in Europe and Asia to battle typhus, malaria, and other diseases that held the potential to devastate the allied fighting forces. It proved extremely effective and is credited with shortening the war.

At that time malaria was common in Asia, the Caribbean, Europe, and the southern part of the United States. Millions of people died from malaria each year. With the effectiveness of the pesticide proven in the war years, DDT became the insecticide of choice around the world. It was effective on a wide range of insect pests, it did not break down rapidly so it did not have to be reapplied often, and it was not water soluble and thus was not washed off when it rained. Farmers and homeowners used DDT to protect crops and kill nuisance insects and pests that spread disease. Countries used it to protect their populations. In 1931–32 more than 22,000 people died from malaria in South Africa's KwaZulu-Natal province. By 1973 the deaths had dropped to 331 for the whole country, and by 1977 there was only one death from malaria in South Africa.

Chemical manufacturers were turning out DDT in record volumes. Montrose Chemical Corporation in Montrose, California, was one of the largest, beginning production in 1942. However, clouds had been building on the horizon. In 1962 Rachel Carson published a book entitled *Silent Spring* that exposed a link between the mass use of DDT and the death of birds and fish. DDT was found to be toxic to fish and indirectly toxic to birds due to its persistence in the environment. It tended to accumulate in fatty tissue, and it became more concentrated as it moved up the food chain. Birds of prey started failing to reproduce because their eggshells became so thin they could not survive the incubation period. DDT began showing up in human breast milk. Some sources claimed DDT causes cancer, but the experts disagree regarding that claim. Concern about the effects of DDT grew until the Environmental Protection Agency banned its use in the United States at the end of 1972, 10 years after the publication of *Silent Spring*. However, DDT could still be produced and sold abroad. Montrose continued to export DDT to Africa, India, and other countries until 1982. DDT was banned in Cuba in 1970, in Poland in 1976, in Canada and Chile in 1985, and in Korea, Liechtenstein, and Switzerland in 1986. The product has also been banned in the European Union, Mexico, Panama, Sri Lanka, Sweden, and Togo, among other countries. The persistence of the chemical is evidenced by traces of it still found in the Great Lakes 30 years after application stopped.

QUESTIONS

1. Did the Montrose Chemical Corporation violate any ethical standards in manufacturing and selling DDT to the public? *lack of social responsibilities*

2. What should it have done differently?

3. Was it ethical to manufacture and sell DDT to other countries after the Environmental Protection Agency (EPA) banned its use in the United States due to its harmful effects?

4. Did the EPA make the right decision when it banned DDT?

5. Should Muller's Nobel Prize be taken away now that DDT has been found to be harmful?

6. Is the ability to save lives worth the risk to the environment?

Sources: Dan Chapman, "A Father & Son Story: Dusting Off DDT's Image/Long-Maligned Pesticide May Be Regaining Favor as Mosquito Menace Grows," *The Atlanta Journal-Constitution,* September 9, 2001, p. D1; Malcolm Gladwell, *The New Yorker,* July 2, 2001, p. 42; P. S. Thampi, "India among Top DDT Users; Need Early Ban," *The Indian Express,* August 10, 1998; Edmund P. Russell III, "The Strange Career of DDT: Experts, Federal Capacity, and Environmentalism in World War II," *Technology and Culture* 40, 4 (October 1999), pp. 770–96; Michael Satchell and Don L. Boroughs, "Rocks and Hard Places DDT: Dangerous Scourge or Last Resort; South Africa," *U.S. News & World Report,* December 11, 2000, p. 64; Deborah Schoch, "Regional Report South Bay: Chemical Reaction Discovery of DDT in the Back Yards of Two Local Homes Has Rekindled Concern and Fear," *The Los Angeles Times,* June 9, 1994, p. 22; and D. J. Fritzsche, *Business Ethics: A Global and Managerial Perspective,* 2nd ed. (New York: McGraw-Hill, 2005), pp. 176–78.

CORPORATE
GOVERNANCE

After studying this chapter, you should be able to:

1 Explain the term *corporate governance.*

2 Understand the responsibilities of the board of directors and the major governance committees.

3 Explain the significance of the "King I" and "King II" reports.

4 Explain the differences between the following two governance methodologies: "comply or explain" and "comply or else."

5 Identify an appropriate corporate governance model for an organization.

FRONTLINE FOCUS
"Incriminating Evidence"

Adam Rooke is a paralegal for a large regional law firm. His company has just landed a new and very important client—Chemco Industries, one of the largest employers in the area.

Adam's prospects with his firm appear to have taken a major leap, as he has been assigned to support one of the senior partners of the law firm, Jim Lewis, as he prepares to defend Chemco in a lawsuit brought by a group of Chemco shareholders.

The lawsuit claims that the senior management of Chemco knew that the firm's financial performance for the second quarter of the year was way below Wall Street expectations. It also knew that the likely reaction to that news would be a dramatic reduction in the price of Chemco shares. In addition, the lawsuit claims that since the stock price would most likely go below the price of the stock options that the board of directors had granted to senior management, those options would be worthless. So rather than let that happen, the Chemco shareholders argued, executives in senior management "massaged the numbers" on the company's true financial performance while selling their own shares in the company, and they kept massaging the numbers until they were able to exercise all their stock options.

Adam is well aware of the significance of this case and is excited at the prospect of working with Jim Lewis. His first assignment is to review all the correspondence relating to stock transactions by senior executives in order to document exactly when they exercised their stock options and sold their stock. The review is expected to take several days of intensive work.

On the third day, Adam comes across a paper copy of an e-mail from Jim Lewis to the CEO of Chemco. Since this would have no relevance to the sale of stock, Adam assumes that the e-mail was misfiled and starts to place the sheet of paper in a separate pile for refiling later. As he does so, one word that is boldface and underlined in the e-mail catches his eye—"problematic." As he reads the e-mail in full, Adam realizes that Jim Lewis is advising the CEO to "ensure that any e-mails or written documentation that could be 'problematic' for their case be removed immediately."

QUESTIONS

1. Which committee would have granted stock options to the senior management of Chemco Industries? Review Figure 5.1 on page **89** for more information on this.
2. The e-mail suggests that the CEO was well aware of what was going on at Chemco Industries. Do you think the board of directors was aware of the activities of senior management? Which committee would be responsible for monitoring ethical practices at Chemco?
3. What should Adam do now?

> ## Earnings can be as pliable as putty when a charlatan heads the company reporting them.
>
> **Warren Buffet**

>> Corporate Governance

The business world has seen an increasing number of scandals in recent years, and numerous organizations have been exposed for poor management practices and fraudulent financial reporting. When we review those scandals, several questions come to mind:

- Who was minding the store?
- How were these senior executives allowed to get away with this?
- Aren't companies supposed to have a system of checks and balances to prevent such behavior?
- When did the CEO of an organization suddenly become answerable to no one?

In seeking answers to these questions, we come to the issue of who really carries the authority in an organization—that is, who has the final say? In other words, are corporations governed in the same manner as our society? And if they're not, are these examples of unethical corporate behavior evidence that they should be?

Corporate governance is the process by which organizations are directed and controlled. However, when we examine who is controlling the corporation, and for whom, the situation gets a little more complicated. Before the development of large corporations, which are separate legal entities, managers and owners of organizations were the same people. As the organizations grew, wealthy owners started to hire professional managers to run the businesses on their behalf, which raised some interesting questions:

- Could the managers be trusted to run the businesses in the best interests of the owners?
- How would they be held accountable for their actions?
- How would absentee owners keep control over these managers?

The development of a separate corporate entity allowed organizations to raise funds from individual shareholders to enlarge their operations. The involvement of individual shareholders diluted the ownership of the original owners and also brought in a new group to which the managers of the business would now be accountable. As the corporations grew in size, and pension funds and other institutional investors purchased larger blocks of shares, the potential impact of the individual shareholder was greatly diminished, and the managers were presented with a far more powerful "owner" to whom they were now accountable.

As we discussed in Chapter 4, in addition to the interests of their owners, some argue that managers are accountable to the public interest—or, more specifically, to their stakeholders: their customers, their vendor partners, state and local entities, and the communities in which they conduct their business operations.

So corporate governance is concerned with how well organizations meet their obligations to all these people. Ideally, mechanisms are in place to hold them accountable for that performance and to introduce corrective action if they fail to live up to that performance expectation.[1]

Corporate governance is about the way in which boards oversee the running of a company by its managers, and how board members are in turn accountable to shareholders and the company. This has implications for company behavior toward employees, shareholders, customers, and banks. Good corporate governance plays a vital role in underpinning the integrity and efficiency of financial markets. Poor corporate governance weakens a company's potential and at worst can pave the way for financial difficulties and even fraud. If companies are well governed, they will usually outperform other companies and will be able to attract investors whose support can finance further growth.

>> What Does Corporate Governance Look Like?

The owners of the corporation (at the top of Figure 5.1) supply equity or risk capital to the company by purchasing shares in the corporation. They are typically a fragmented group, including individual public shareholders, large blocks of private holders, private and public institutional investors, employees, managers, and other companies.

The **board of directors,** in theory, is elected by the owners to represent their interests in the effective running of the corporation. Elections take place at annual shareholders' meetings, and directors are

Corporate Governance The system by which business corporations are directed and controlled.

Board of Directors A group of individuals who oversee governance of an organization. Elected by vote of the shareholders at the annual general meeting (AGM), the true power of the board can vary from institution to institution from a powerful unit that closely monitors the management of the organization to a body that merely rubber-stamps the decisions of the chief executive officer (CEO) and executive team.

appointed to serve for specific periods of time. The board is typically made up of inside and outside members—inside members hold management positions in the company, whereas outside members do not. The term *outside director* can be misleading because some outside members may have direct connections to the company as creditors, suppliers, customers, or professional consultants.

The **audit committee** is staffed by members of the board of directors plus independent or outside directors. The primary responsibilities of the audit committee are to oversee the financial reporting process, monitor internal controls (such as how much spending authority an executive has), monitor the choice of accounting policies and procedures, and oversee the hiring and performance of external auditors in producing the company's financial statements.

The **compensation committee** is also staffed by members of the board of directors plus independent or outside directors. The primary responsibility of the compensation committee is to oversee compensation packages for the senior executives of the corporation (such as salaries, bonuses, stock options, and other benefits such as, in extreme cases, personal use of company jets). Compensation policies for the employees of the corporation are left to the management team to oversee.

Audit Committee An operating committee staffed by members of the board of directors plus independent or outside directors. The committee is responsible for monitoring the financial policies and procedures of the organization—specifically the accounting policies, internal controls, and the hiring of external auditors.

Compensation Committee An operating committee staffed by members of the board of directors plus independent or outside directors. The committee is responsible for setting the compensation for the CEO and other senior executives. Typically, this compensation will consist of a base salary, performance bonus, stock options, and other perks.

FIG.5.1 Governance of the Modern Corporation

Source: Adapted from Fred R. Kaen, *A Blueprint for Corporate Governance* (New York: AMACOM, 2003).

The **corporate governance committee** represents a more public demonstration of the organization's commitment to ethical business practices. The committee (staffed by board members and specialists) monitors the ethical performance of the corporation and oversees compliance with the company's internal code of ethics as well as any federal and state regulations on corporate conduct.

>> In Pursuit of Corporate Governance

While the issue of corporate governance has reached new heights of media attention in the wake of recent corporate scandals, the topic itself has been receiving increasing attention for over a decade.

In 1992 Sir Adrian Cadbury led a committee in Great Britain to address *financial aspects of corporate governance* in response to public concerns over directors' compensation at several high-profile companies in Great Britain. The subsequent financial scandals surrounding the Bank of Credit and Commerce International (BCCI) and the activities of publishing magnate Sir Robert Maxwell generated more attention for the committee's report than was originally anticipated. In the executive summary of the report, Cadbury outlined the committee's position on the newly topical issue of corporate governance:[2]

> At the heart of the Committee's recommendations is a Code of Best Practice designed to achieve the necessary high standards of corporate behaviour.... By adhering to the Code, listed companies will strengthen both their control over their businesses and their public accountability. In so doing they will be striking the right balance between meeting the standards of corporate governance now expected of them and retaining the essential spirit of enterprise.

Two years after the release of the Cadbury report, attention shifted to South Africa, where Mervyn King, a corporate lawyer, former High Court judge, and the current governor of the Bank of England, led a committee that published the "King Report on Corporate Governance" in 1994. In contrast to Cadbury's focus on internal governance, the King report "incorporated a code of corporate practices and conduct that looked beyond the corporation itself, taking into account its impact on the larger community."[3]

"King I," as the 1994 report became known, went beyond the financial and regulatory accountability upon which the Cadbury report had focused and took a more integrated approach to the topic of corporate governance, recognizing the involvement of all the corporation's stakeholders—the shareholders, customers, employees, vendor partners, and the community in which the corporation operates—in the efficient and appropriate operation of the organization.[4]

Even though King I was widely recognized as advocating the highest standards for corporate governance, the committee released a second report eight years later—inevitably referred to as "King II," which formally recognized the need to move the stakeholder model forward and consider a triple bottom line as opposed to the traditional single bottom line of profitability. The triple bottom line recognizes the economic, environmental, and social aspects of a company's activities. In the words of the King II report, companies must "comply or explain" or "comply or else."[5]

Corporate Governance Committee Committee (staffed by board members and specialists) that monitors the ethical performance of the corporation and oversees compliance with the company's internal code of ethics as well as any federal and state regulations on corporate conduct.

Mervyn King

According to King II,

> successful governance in the world in the 21st century requires companies to adopt an inclusive and not exclusive approach. The company must be open to institutional activism and there must be greater emphasis on the sustainable or non-financial aspects of its performance. Boards must apply the test of fairness, accountability, responsibility and transparency to all acts or omissions and be accountable to the company but also responsive and responsible towards the company's identified stakeholders. The correct balance between conformance with governance principles and performance in an entrepreneurial market economy must be found, but this will be specific to each company.[6]

>> Two Governance Methodologies: "Comply or Explain" or "Comply or Else"?

The Cadbury report argued for a guideline of **comply or explain,** which gave companies the flexibility to comply with governance standards or explain why they do not in their corporate documents (annual reports, for example). The vagueness of what would constitute an acceptable explanation for not complying, combined with the ease with which such explanations could be buried in the footnotes of an annual report (if they were even there at all), raised concerns that comply or explain really wouldn't do much for corporate governance.

The string of financial scandals that followed the report led many critics to argue that comply or explain obviously offered no real deterrent to corporations. The answer, they argued, was to move to a more aggressive approach of **comply or else,** where failure to comply results in stiff financial penalties. The Sarbanes-Oxley Act of 2002 (see Chapter 6) incorporates this approach.

PROGRESS ✓ QUESTIONS

5. Which two scandals greatly increased the attention paid to the 1992 Cadbury report?

6. Explain the "right balance" that Cadbury encourages companies to pursue.

7. Explain the difference between the King I and King II reports.

8. Explain the difference between "comply or explain" and "comply or else."

"IN THE KNOW" OR "IN THE DARK"?

With the exception, perhaps, of corporate governance committees, each of the corporations that have faced charges for corporate misconduct in recent years used the governance model shown in Figure 5.1. When questioned, the boards of these corporations all shared similar stories of being "ambushed" or kept in the dark about the massive frauds the senior executives of their corporations allegedly carried out.

What does this mean for investors seeking to put their retirement funds in dependable companies that are well run? What about employees seeking reassurance that those senior corporate officers in the executive suites can be counted on to steer the company to a promising future rather than run it aground?

If all these companies had a governance model in place, where was the oversight? Is it the model that's at fault or the people filling the assigned roles in that model? Consider the different interpretations of just how much authority rests with these official overseers illustrated in the two ethical dilemmas of this chapter, "20/20 Hindsight" (page **92**) and "A Spectacular Downfall" (page **95**).

> **"Comply or Explain"** A set of guidelines that require companies to abide by a set of operating standards or explain why they choose not to.
>
> **"Comply or Else"** A set of guidelines that require companies to abide by a set of operating standards or face stiff financial penalties.

THE CHAIRMAN AND THE CEO

If the model of corporate structure shown at the beginning of this chapter is followed, the stockholders of a corporation should elect members of the board of directors. In turn, that board of directors should elect a chairperson. For the vast majority of corporations, however, the model is typically ignored.

The first step in a policy of disregarding the corporate governance model is the decision to merge the roles of chief executive officer (CEO) and chairperson of the board into one individual. In this situation, the oversight that the board of directors is supposed to provide has been lost, and the operational focus of the company has switched from long term (to the extent that board members serve a two-year contract) to short term, where the CEO is focusing on the numbers for the next quarter.

Study Alert! The King II report stated that successful governance requires an "inclusive" rather than an "exclusive" approach. What would be the difference between those two approaches?

Sir Allen Stanford, a Texas-born citizen of the Caribbean island of Antigua who resided in the U.S. Virgin Islands, seemed to have the life that dreams are made of. As the founder and majority shareholder of the Stanford Financial Group (SFG), based in Houston, Texas, Stanford led a complex network of interlinked financial companies that claimed to manage over $50 billion in assets. He loved the English game of cricket and invested millions of dollars in supporting West Indian teams, including building a cricket ground in Antigua and underwriting the "Stanford Twenty20 tournament" that offered a $20 million winner-take-all prize in a championship of 20 cricket matches.

Stanford's business skills seemed to know no limits. His business interests included two major banks, a trust company, a real estate development company, a newspaper, a cricket ground, two restaurants, and large tracts of land—and that was just in Antigua. The jewel of his portfolio was reputed to be the Stanford International Bank (SIB) of Antigua. As an "offshore bank," SIB operated outside of U.S. banking regulations. With a reputed $8.5 billion in assets, the bank took money from depositors by an unusual route. No loans were ever made by the bank, although it did have a traditional stock and bond trading department. Clients deposited funds by purchasing certificates of deposits (CDs) that offered above average interest rates (at times more than twice as high as prevailing market rates) in return for reduced liquidity—in other words, once deposited with SIB, customer funds took 60 days to be returned. The above average interest rates proved irresistible to U.S. investors—over $3.5 billion was invested in SIB CDs, which inevitably brought the bank to the attention of the Securities and Exchange Commission (SEC).

Stanford's lifestyle has been referenced in the past tense, because at the time of writing, he is in jail charged by U.S. securities regulators over a "massive investment fraud" through SIB. Investigations by SEC personnel uncovered some interesting information about Stanford's operations:

- Over $8 billion of the CD funds invested in SIB were, it is alleged, used to fund Stanford's lavish lifestyle and other investment vehicles in a complex "Ponzi scheme" (refer to Thinking Critically 6.1 on page **128** for more information on Ponzi schemes). The reduced liquidity of the CDs gave Stanford time to move money around if any investors elected to cash in their investments. Some $6 billion is claimed to be "unaccounted for."
- Other companies in SFG claimed investment funds that far exceeded their actual deposits. For example, Stanford Financial Company (SFC), a registered broker and asset management business, had only about $147 million of assets as the wealth management

division of a $50 billion company. Further investigation revealed that SFC served only as an "introductory broker" to other investment companies such as Bear Stearns and, ironically, Bernard Madoff.
- When stock markets around the world began crashing in 2008, SFG reported a year-end loss of only 1.3 percent after a decade of consistent double-digit growth that has been described as "suspiciously smooth."
- Stanford's heavily marketed knighthood came not from the Queen of England, but from the governor general of Antigua.

The biggest red flag of Stanford's operation was the governance structure of his multiple and complex corporations. The chief financial officer (CFO) of SIB, James Davis, was Stanford's college roommate. The chief investment officer of SFG, Laura Pendergest-Holt, had no financial services or securities experience, and claimed to have limited knowledge of "the whereabouts of the vast majority of the bank's multi-billion investment portfolio" according to the SEC. Other senior corporate officers included Stanford family members, friends, and business associates with cattle ranching and car sales companies in Texas. Of the three key individuals, Pendergest-Holt is the only one to have been charged criminally with obstruction of justice. The indictment contends that she misled SEC investigators on several occasions and failed to disclose that she had several preparatory meetings with other SFG executives before meeting with SEC investigators.

Stanford is professing his innocence by claiming that he was wrong to trust the integrity of his CFO, James Davis. "The investment and risk committee reported to Jim Davis, not to me," he said. As for the collapse of his financial empire and the current inability to repay investors, Stanford blames the SEC for the "ripple effect" of its indictment that prompted regulatory agencies around the world to freeze the assets of his multiple investment companies. "I don't think there is any money missing," Stanford said. "There never was a Ponzi scheme, and there never was an attempt to defraud anybody."

QUESTIONS

1. How did SIB's status as an "offshore bank" facilitate Stanford's alleged fraud?
2. Why would investors be willing to sacrifice immediate access to the funds they deposited with SIB?
3. What elements were missing from the governance structure of Stanford Financial Group?
4. What is the basis of Stanford's defense?

Sources: Sam Jones, "Fraud Probe at Labyrinth of SFG Companies," *Financial Times,* February 18, 2009; "Howzat! Shocking Allegations against Stanford Group," *The Economist,* February 19, 2009; Joanna Chung, Tracey Alloway, and Jeremy Lemer, "The Stanford Scandal: Why Were Red Flags Ignored?" *Financial Times,* February 19, 2009; Clifford Krauss, "Chief Investment Officer at Stanford Group Indicted," *The New York Times,* May 13, 2009; and Clifford Krauss, "Stanford Points Fingers in Fraud Case," *The New York Times,* April 21, 2009.

The argument in favor of merging the two roles is one of efficiency—by putting the leadership of the board of directors and the senior management team in the hands of the same person, the potential for conflict is minimized, and, it is argued, the board is given the benefit of leadership from someone who is in touch with the inner workings of the organization rather than an outsider who needs time to get up to speed.

The argument against merging the two roles is an ethical one. Governance of the corporation is now in the hands of one person, which eliminates the checks and balances process that the board was created for in the first place. As time passes, as we have seen with the Stanford example, the CEO slowly populates the board with friends who are less critical of the CEO's policies and more willing to vote larger and larger salary and benefits packages. With a rubber-stamp board in place to authorize every wish, the CEO now becomes a law unto himself or herself. The independence of the board is compromised, and the power of the stockholders is minimized. The CEO can pursue policies that are focused on maintaining a high share price in the short term (to maximize the price he will get when he cashes in all the share options that his friends on the board gave him in the last contract) without any concern for the long-term stability of the organization—after all, there will probably be another CEO by then.

>> Effective Corporate Governance

To be considered effectively governed, organizations must have mechanisms in place that oversee both the long-term strategy of the company and the appointment of those personnel tasked with the responsibility of delivering that strategy. The appointment of those critical personnel inevitably includes their selection, ongoing performance evaluation, and compensation.

Delivering on these responsibilities requires more than just job descriptions and formal bylaws that govern the respective responsibilities and authority of various committees. To be truly effective, boards should follow these six steps:[7]

1. *Create a climate of trust and candor.* The board of directors and the senior executives should be working in partnership toward the successful achievement of organizational goals rather than developing an adversarial relationship where the board is seen as an obstacle to the realization of the CEO's strategic vision.
2. *Foster a culture of open dissent.* Proposals should be open for frank discussion and review rather than subject to the kind of alleged rubber-stamping that came to characterize Michael Eisner's tenure at Disney. Dissent ensures that all aspects of proposals are reviewed and discussed thoroughly.
3. *Mix up roles.* Rotation of assignments can avoid typecasting, and a conscious effort to switch between "good cop" and "bad cop" supporting

PROGRESS ✓ QUESTIONS

9. What is the argument in favor of merging the roles of chairperson and CEO?
10. What is the argument against merging the roles of chairperson and CEO?
11. Explain the difference between a short-term and long-term view in the governance of a corporation.
12. Is it unethical to populate your board of directors with friends and business acquaintances? Why or why not?

and dissenting roles can ensure positive debate of all key proposals brought before the board.

4. *Ensure individual accountability.* Rubber-stamping generates collective indifference—how can you consider yourself accountable if you were only voting with a clearly established majority? If there is significant fallout from a major strategic initiative, all members should consider themselves accountable. This approach would address any pretense of being ambushed or in the dark.

5. *Let the board assess leadership talent.* The board members should actively meet with future leaders in their current positions within the organization rather than simply waiting for them to be presented when a vacancy arises.

6. *Evaluate the board's performance.* Many critics consider board seats as the U.S. equivalent of life peerages in Great Britain—that is, you win the title of "Lord" on the basis of what you have done in your career or whom you know, without any further assessment of your contribution or performance. Effective corporate governance demands superior performance from everyone involved in the process.

22 QUESTIONS FOR DIAGNOSING YOUR BOARD

Walter Salmon, a longtime director with over 30 years of boardroom experience, took this prescriptive approach even further in a 1993 *Harvard Business Review* article by recommending a checklist of 22 questions to assess the quality of your board. If you answer yes to all 22 questions, you have an exemplary board.[8]

1. Are there three or more outside directors for every insider?
2. Are the insiders limited to the CEO, the COO, and the CFO?
3. Do your directors routinely speak to senior managers who are not represented on the board?
4. Is your board the right size (8 to 15 members)?
5. Does your audit committee, not management, have the authority to approve the partner in charge of auditing the company?
6. Does your audit committee routinely review high-exposure areas?
7. Do compensation consultants report to your compensation committee rather than to the company's human resource officers?
8. Has your compensation committee shown the courage to establish formulas for CEO compensation based on long-term results—even if formulas differ from industry norms?
9. Are the activities of your executive committee sufficiently contained to prevent the emergence of a two-tier board?
10. Do outside directors annually review succession plans for senior management?
11. Do outside directors formally evaluate your CEO's strengths, weaknesses, objectives, personal plans, and performance every year?
12. Does your nominating committee rather than the CEO direct the search for new board members and invite candidates to stand for election?

Real World Applications

You are a sales executive for a national equipment manufacturer. You joined the company straight out of college and have always been proud to work for the organization. Lately, however, you have become increasingly concerned about the office politics that have been going on at the corporate headquarters. Several senior executives have left, some very suddenly, and a lot of the changes can be traced back to the appointment of the CEO, Guy Ashley. Yesterday it was announced that Jack Lamborn, the chairman of the company (and the grandson of the founder) would be retiring at the end of the month (only two weeks away). The e-mail announcement also clarified that Guy Ashley would be assuming the position of chairman in addition to his role as CEO. You think back to your college ethics course and wonder whether this is really a good thing for the company as a whole. Would combining both roles raise any concerns for stakeholders over effective corporate governance? Why or why not?

13. Is there a way for outside directors to alter the meeting agenda set by your CEO?

14. Does the company help directors prepare for meetings by sending relevant routine information, as well as analyses of key agendas ahead of time?

15. Is there sufficient meeting time for thoughtful discussion in addition to management monologues?

16. Do the outside directors meet without management on a regular basis?

17. Is your board actively involved in formulating long-range business strategy from the start of the planning cycle?

18. Does your board, rather than the incumbent CEO, select the new chief executive—in fact as well as in theory?

19. Is at least some of the director's pay linked to corporate performance?

20. Is the performance of each of your directors periodically reviewed?

21. Are directors who are no longer pulling their weight discouraged from standing for reelection?

22. Do you take the right measures to build trust among directors?

Even with a board that passes all the tests and meets all the established criteria, ethical misconduct can still come down to the individual personalities involved. Consider the media storm surrounding the compensation package for John Thain, the former chairman and chief executive officer of Merrill Lynch.

A SPECTACULAR DOWNFALL

When John Thain was hired as chairman and CEO of Merrill Lynch in November 2007, he received a hero's welcome. The legendary investment bank, with a global brand and a vast network of brokers known as "the thundering herd," had fallen on hard times after heavy losses in the credit market and a period of controversial leadership by E. Stanley O'Neal. Thain's reputation as "Mr. Fix-it," earned after successful stints at both Goldman Sachs and the New York Stock Exchange (which Thain lead to a successful public offering in 2006), appeared to make him the right man at the right time. A lack of direction and mounting losses seemed to present the perfect environment for a reputed micromanager with an obsession for crunching the numbers. At the time of his hire, Merrill had announced the largest loss of its 93-year history: $8.4 billion.

In the early weeks of his tenure, Thain appeared to live up to the hype of his hiring by making the kind of tough decisions needed to get Merrill back on track: Bad or "toxic" assets were sold at steep discounts to get them off the balance sheet, and good assets were marked down to more accurately reflect their true value. However, within a brief 14 months, Thain's reputation had crumbled to the point of a brief 15-minute meeting with Ken Lewis of Bank of America (BoA) and an immediate announcement of his termination.

There had been some clear signposts on this road to departure. The first had been the strange case of Thain's $1.2 million expenditure on the redesign of his office at Merrill. For a general public still reeling from stories of Dennis

Koslowksi from Tyco spending $6,000 of shareholder's money on a shower curtain, Thain's excess caused embarrassment to both him and his company. Some $87,784 was reportedly spent on a rug, $68,179 on an antique credenza, $28,091 on drapes, and $18,468 on an antique George IV chair—difficult expenses to justify during a period of belt-tightening and cost-cutting at a company that was looking to recover from an $8.4 billion loss.

The second sign came with Thain's negotiation of the sale of Merrill Lynch to BoA for a price of $29 per share

CONTINUED >>

in BoA stock, valuing Merrill at $50 billion. News of the deal seemed to bring positive coverage for Thain. At a time when revered organizations like Bear Stearns (sold in a fire sale to JPMorgan Chase) and Lehman Brothers (collapsed without a buyer) were disappearing from Wall Street, Thain's fans saw the deal as a major coup. He apparently agreed with those fans when he requested a $40 million bonus from BoA's compensation committee for his part in negotiating the deal. To some, he was probably worth it—the deal valued the combined entity of Merrill Lynch and BoA at $176 billion. Six months later, that figure had fallen to only $39 billion. However, as the story of the "shotgun marriage" of Merrill Lynch and Bank of America became public, the restoration of Thain's reputation became increasingly brief.

The wedding took place after a frenetic 48 hours of negotiations. Despite assertions of extensive due diligence and a brief period of cold feet by BoA chief Ken Lewis (who claimed later that he was "strongly encouraged" to complete the deal by federal regulators looking to stabilize an increasingly unstable financial market), Thain got his price of $29 per share. Before the deal closed, Thain made a pitch for bonuses for his senior leadership team (including his $40 million) to be paid earlier than usual. On December 8, 2008, Merrill's board of directors approved $4 billion in bonuses to be paid to employees: a cash portion on December 29, and a portion in BoA stock on January 2, 2009. Thain's bonus was turned down by John D. Finnegan, the head of Merrill's compensation committee as being "ludicrous." Thain reportedly attempted to negotiate a reduced bonus of $5 to $10 million and ultimately settled for no bonus at all.

Within weeks it emerged that Merrill was facing a fourth quarter loss of $15.3 billion, prompting BoA to seek an additional $25 billion bailout from the government (over and above the $25 billion it had received in October) in addition to a guarantee on $118 billion of toxic assets. Thain, who had been on vacation during the revelation of Merrill's fourth quarter implosion, was dismissed less than a week later.

However, it appears that on Wall Street a reputation is a remarkably resilient thing. Despite extensive media coverage of his office redesign budget and outrageous bonus demands during the Merrill-BoA deal, John Thain returned to prominence just over a year later. In February 2010 the CIT group announced that he had been appointed as its new chairman and CEO. After emerging from bankruptcy (during which $10.4 billion of company debt, including $2.3 billion of government bailout money, was erased) with $58 billion in assets, CIT, which lends to small and medium-size businesses, seemed well positioned to benefit from a market recovery. Bankruptcy negotiations had extended significant debt repayment deadlines out to 2013, giving it significant "breathing room" to put its house in order.

The hiring of Thain was actively promoted by CIT executives: "John is a well respected financial services executive and proven leader who is uniquely qualified to lead CIT at this critical stage," said CIT lead director John Ryan in a press release. Investors seemed to agree. CIT shares rose nearly 20 percent in the four weeks following the announcement.

QUESTIONS

1. Which stakeholders were impacted by Thain's leadership at Merrill Lynch?
2. Where were the failures in corporate governance in this case?
3. Is there any evidence of good corporate governance in this case?
4. If you were a shareholder of CIT, how would you feel about the appointment of John Thain as chairman and CEO?

Sources: Mara Der Hovanesian, "John Thain Resigns from Bank of America," *BusinessWeek,* January 22, 2009; "No Gain, No Thain," *The Economist,* January 23, 2009; Greg Farrell, "Lynched at Merrill," *Financial Times,* January 26, 2009; "CIT Names Ex-Merrill CEO Thain as Chairman," *Time,* February 7, 2010; Louise Story and Julie Creswell, "For Bank of America and Merrill, Love Was Blind," *The New York Times,* February 8, 2009; Michael J. de la Merced, "After Turmoil at Merrill, Thain Will Lead the Lender CIT," *The New York Times,* February 8, 2010; and David Henry, "The Importance of Being John Thain," *Bloomberg BusinessWeek,* April 29, 2010.

THE DANGERS OF A CORPORATE GOVERNANCE CHECKLIST

There is more to effective corporate governance than simply maintaining a checklist of items to be monitored on a regular basis. Simply having the mechanisms in place will not, in itself, guarantee good governance. Enron, for example, had all its governance boxes checked:[9]

- Enron separated the roles of chairman (Kenneth Lay) and chief executive officer (Jeffrey Skilling)—at least until Skilling's surprise resignation.
- The company maintained a roster of independent directors with flawless résumés.

- It maintained an audit committee consisting exclusively of nonexecutives.

However, once you scratched beneath the surface of this model exterior, the true picture was a lot less appealing:

- Many of the so-called independent directors were affiliated with organizations that benefited directly from Enron's operations.
- The directors enjoyed substantial "benefits" that continued to grow as Enron's fortunes grew.
- Their role as directors of Enron, a Wall Street darling, guaranteed them positions as directors for

Life Skills

>> Governing your career

In this chapter we review the importance of organizational oversight through a corporate governance structure. Give some thought to the oversight of your career in the future. As you have read, an organization's board of directors is designed to be both an advisory group and a governing body. Do you have a team of people you can count on for advice or guidance? Do you work with a mentor who is willing to share his or her experience and advice with you to help you make important decisions in your life?

Many successful businesspeople acknowledge that developing a dream team of advisers has been critical to their business and personal success in life. Being willing to reach out to others and seek their advice and guidance on a regular basis, they believe, has helped them prepare for important decisions and plan for long-term career choices. Making those decisions is ultimately your responsibility, but the more insight and information you have available to you, the more confident you may be in the final choice that you make.

Why would people agree to serve on your dream team? Perhaps they want to give something back in recognition of the success they have earned or to share in the joy of watching someone they regard as having tremendous potential move on to bigger and better career opportunities. Then, as you progress in your business career, you, in turn, can give something back by agreeing to mentor a young student with strong potential or to serve on the dream team of several promising students to help them succeed in their lives.

---

other companies—a career package that would be jeopardized if they chose to ask too many awkward questions and gain reputations as troublemakers.

A FIDUCIARY RESPONSIBILITY

While media coverage of corporate scandals has tended to concentrate on the personalities involved—Kenneth Lay and Jeffrey Skilling at Enron, Bernard Ebbers at WorldCom, Richard Scrushy at HealthSouth, John Rigas at Adelphia Cable, and Dennis Kozlowski at Tyco—we cannot lose sight of the fact that corporate governance is about managers fulfilling a fiduciary responsibility to the owners of their companies. A *fiduciary responsibility* is ultimately based on trust, which is a difficult trait to test when you are hiring a manager or to enforce once

that manager is in place. Enforcement only becomes an option when that trust has been broken. In the meantime, organizations must depend on oversight and the development of processes and mechanisms to support that oversight—the famous checks and balances.

The payoff for such diligence is that "a commitment to good corporate governance . . . make[s] a company both more attractive to investors and lenders, and more profitable. Simply put, it pays to promote good corporate governance."[10] Consider the following examples:

- A Deutsche Bank study of Standard & Poor 500 firms showed that companies with strong or improving corporate governance outperformed those with poor or deteriorating governance practices by about 19 percent over a two-year period.

- A Harvard-Wharton study showed that if an investor purchased shares in U.S. firms with the strongest shareholder rights and sold shares in the ones with the weakest shareholder rights, the investor would have earned abnormal returns of 8.5 percent per year.
- The same study also found that U.S.-based firms with better governance have faster sales growth and were more profitable than their peers.
- In a 2002 McKinsey survey, institutional investors said they would pay premiums to own well-governed companies. Premiums averaged 30 percent in Eastern Europe and Africa and 22 percent in Asia and Latin America.

PROGRESS ✓ QUESTIONS

13. What are the six steps to effective corporate governance?

14. Select your top six from Walter Salmon's "22 Questions for Diagnosing Your Board," and defend your selection.

15. Provide three examples of how Enron "had its governance boxes checked."

16. Provide three examples of evidence that good corporate governance can pay off for organizations.

>> Conclusion

So, having the right model in place will not take you far if that model is eventually overrun by a corporate culture of greed and success at all costs. Even organizations that have been publicly exposed for their lack of corporate governance still appear to have lessons to learn. Tyco, for example, made a very public commitment to clean house under the direction of Edward Breen, "but it has refused to replace the audit firm that failed to uncover massive abuses by its former chief executive or to give up its Bermuda domicile [formal offshore residence for tax purposes], which insulates it from shareholder litigation and so genuine accountability." In addition, "at WorldCom (now MCI), where Michael Capellas was brought in to clean up the mess left by Bernie Ebbers, the bankruptcy court vetoed his proposed compensation package as "grossly excessive."[11]

No system of corporate governance can completely defend against fraud or incompetence. The test is how far such aberrations can be discouraged and how quickly they can be brought to light. The risks can be reduced by making the participants in the governance process as effectively accountable as possible. The key safeguards are properly constituted boards, separation of the functions of chairperson and of chief executive, audit committees, vigilant shareholders, and financial reporting and auditing systems that provide full and timely disclosure.[12]

FRONTLINE FOCUS
"Incriminating Evidence"—Adam Makes a Decision

Adam broke into a cold sweat as soon as he finished reading the e-mail. He realized that if it were made public, it would mean the end for the CEO of Chemco, the senior managers, Jim Lewis, and probably anyone assigned to the Chemco case. What the heck was he supposed to do now? Tell Jim Lewis? Pretend he hadn't found it and shred it? Should he go public with it or send it anonymously to the lawyers for the Chemco shareholders?

He started imagining the consequences for each of those actions and decided that anything that involved him looking for a new paralegal position wasn't a good choice. He also thought about the Enron case and how long it had taken to get the two senior officers, Ken Lay and Jeff Skilling, into court,

with no money left at the end of it all to return to shareholders who had lost their life savings when the company collapsed.

"It's just not worth it," Adam thought. "And anyway, who would pay attention to a rookie paralegal?" With that, he took the piece of paper and placed it into the shredder.

QUESTIONS

1. What could Adam have done differently here?
2. What do you think will happen now?
3. What will be the consequences for Adam, Jim Lewis, and Chemco Industries?

[For Review]

1. **Explain the term *corporate governance*.**

   Corporate governance is the process by which organizations are directed and controlled. Using a series of boards and committees, corporate governance is designed to oversee the running of a company by its managers and to ensure that the interests of all the stakeholders (customers, employees, vendor partners, state and local entities, and the communities in which the company operates) are fairly represented and treated.

2. **Understand the responsibilities of the board of directors and the major governance committees.**

   A board of directors is a group of senior experienced executives who oversee governance of an organization. Elected by shareholder vote at the annual general meeting (AGM), the true power of the board can vary from a powerful unit that closely monitors the management of the organization, to a body that merely "rubber-stamps" the decisions of the chief executive officer (CEO) and executive team.

   Effective corporate governance models typically include three major oversight committees, staffed by members of the board of directors and appropriately qualified specialists:

   - *The audit committee, which oversees the financial reporting process; monitors internal controls over corporate expenditure; monitors accounting policies and procedures; and oversees the hiring and performance of external auditors in producing the company's financial statements.*

   - *The compensation committee, which oversees compensation packages for the senior executives of the corporation (such as salaries, bonuses, stock options, and other benefits such as, in extreme cases, personal use of company jets). In these days of highly compensated executives (such as John Thain in Case 5.2), such discussions often involve extensive negotiations with a designated "agent" for the executive in question. Compensation policies for the employees of the corporation are usually left to the management team to oversee.*

   - *As corporations come under increasing pressure to publicly demonstrate their commitment to ethical business practices, many are choosing to establish separate corporate governance committees to monitor the ethical performance of the corporation and oversee compliance with the company's*

   internal code of ethics as well as any federal and state regulations on corporate conduct.

3. **Explain the significance of the "King I" and "King II" reports.**

   Published as the "King Report on Corporate Governance" in 1994, Mervyn King's report changed the emphasis on corporate governance from internal governance of corporate operations to practices that looked beyond the corporation itself and included its impact on the community at large. A second report released eight years later ("King II") formally recognized the need to incorporate all stakeholders and consider a triple bottom-line (3BL) approach to corporate performance and profitability.

4. **Explain the differences between the following two governance methodologies: "comply or explain" and "comply or else."**

   The requirement to "comply or explain" demands that organizations must demonstrate that they are abiding by a set of rules or clearly explain why they are choosing not to. By comparison, "comply or else" imposes financial penalties for organizations that choose not to abide by that set of rules.

5. **Identify an appropriate corporate governance model for an organization.**

   To fulfill its objective of effective oversight of an organization's operations, any corporate governance model should follow these six steps:

   - *Create a climate of trust and candor so that the board of directors and senior executives can work in partnership toward the successful achievement of organizational goals.*

   - *Foster a culture of open dissent so that proposals can be discussed thoroughly without fear of retribution by other board members.*

   - *Mix up roles so that positive debate on all proposals can be encouraged.*

   - *Ensure individual accountability from board and committee members so that no one can abstain from key strategic decisions by simply voting with the majority of the board members.*

   - *Involve the board in the selection and recruitment of senior corporate executives, whether those future leaders come from within the organization or are brought in from the outside.*

   - *Evaluate the board's performance, so that a directorship clearly becomes a position that demands effective performance rather than simple entitlement.*

[Key Terms]

Audit Committee **89**

Board of Directors **88**

Compensation Committee **89**

"Comply or Else" **91**

"Comply or Explain" **91**

Corporate Governance **88**

Corporate Governance Committee **90**

[Review Questions]

1. Why do corporations need a board of directors?

2. What is the value of adding "outside directors" to your board?

3. Which is more important to effective corporate governance: an audit committee or a compensation committee? Why?

4. Many experienced senior business executives serve on multiple corporate boards. Is this a good thing? Explain your answer.

5. Many of Enron's "independent" directors were affiliated with organizations that benefited directly from Enron's operations. How would you address this clear conflict of interest?

6. Outline the corporate governance structure of the company you work for (or one you have worked for in the past).

[Review Exercises]

GlobalMutual was, by all accounts, a model insurance company. Profits were strong and had been for several years in a row. The company carried the highest ratings in its industry, and it had recently been voted one of the top 100 companies to work for in the United States in recognition of its very employee-focused work environment. GlobalMutual offered very generous benefits: free lunches in the cafeteria, onsite day care facilities, and even free Starbucks coffee in the employee break rooms. In an industry that was still struggling with the massive claims after a succession of hurricanes in the United States, GlobalMutual was financially stable and positioned to become one of the major insurance companies in the nation.

So, why were the CEO, William Brown; the CFO, Anne Johnson; and the COO, Peter Brooking, all fired on the same day with no explanation other than that the terminations were related to issues of conduct?

1. Who would most likely have intervened to terminate the senior team over issues of conduct?

2. Give some examples of the kind of ethical misconduct that could have led to the termination of the entire senior leadership of GlobalMutual.

3. Was it a good idea to fire them all at the same time with no detailed explanation?

4. How are the stakeholders of GlobalMutual likely to react to this news? Explain your answer.

Source: Adapted from George O'Brien, "A Matter of Ethics," *BusinessWest* 22, no. 4 (June 13, 2005), p. 9.

[Internet Exercises]

1. Review the Web site of the World Council for Corporate Governance (WCFCG) at www.wcfg.net.

   a. Explain the WCFCG's "IDEA" action plan.

   b. How can this organization affect corporate governance in the business world?

   c. The WCFCG has several prominent corporate partners. Select one and summarize what the company might gain from its partnership with the WCFCG.

2. Review the annual report of a Fortune 100 company of your choice. Who serves on the board of directors for the company? Are there any designated "outside" directors? On how many other boards do those outside directors serve? What does the company gain from having these outside directors on the board?

[Team Exercises]

1. **Chairman and/or CEO.**
   Divide into two teams. One team must prepare a presentation advocating for the separation of the roles of chairperson and CEO. The other team must prepare a presentation arguing for the continued practice of allowing one corporate executive to be both chairperson and CEO.

2. **Compensation.**
   You serve on your organization's compensation committee, and you are meeting to negotiate the retirement package for your CEO who is retiring after a very successful 40-year career with your organization—the last 20 as CEO, during which time the company's revenues grew more than fourfold and gross profits increased by over 300 percent. Divide into two teams, arguing *for* and *against* the following compensation package being proposed by the CEO's representative:

   - Unlimited access to the company's New York apartment.
   - Unlimited use of the corporate jet and company limousine service.
   - Courtside tickets to New York Knicks games.
   - Box seats at Yankee Stadium.
   - VIP seats at the French Open, U.S. Open, and Wimbledon tennis tournaments.
   - A lucrative annual consulting contract of $80,000 for the first five days and an additional $17,500 per day thereafter.
   - Reimbursement for all professional services—legal, financial, secretarial, and IT support.
   - Stock options amounting to $200 million.

3. **An appropriate response.**
   You sit on the board of directors of a major airline that just experienced a horrendous customer service event. A severe snowstorm stranded several of your planes and caused a ripple effect throughout your flight schedule, stranding thousands of passengers at airports across the country and keeping dozens of passengers as virtual hostages on planes for several hours as they waited for departure slots at their airport. The press has covered this fiasco at length and is already calling for a passenger bill of rights that will be based primarily on all the things your airline didn't do to take care of its passengers in this situation. Your CEO is the founder of the airline, and he has been featured in many of your commercials raving about the high level of customer service you deliver. The board is meeting to review his continued employment with the company. Divide into two teams and argue the case *for* and *against* terminating his employment as a first step in restoring the reputation of your airline.

4. **Ideal corporate governance.**
   Divide into groups of three or four. Each group must map out its ideal model for corporate governance of an organization—for example, the number of people on the board of directors, separate roles of chairperson and CEO, inside and outside directors, and employee representation on the board. Prepare a presentation arguing for the respective merits of each model and offer evidence of how each model represents the best interests of all the organization's stakeholders.

- Kerviel's profits in 2007 appeared to convince him that he had discovered a new and highly lucrative system for futures trading. Investigators could find no other motive for his actions than simply a desire to increase his remuneration at the bank through a year-end bonus for strong financial performance. They found no evidence of any intent to embezzle funds, and they noted an apparently naive belief in his trading skills.
- While there were changes in personnel in the aftermath of the disastrous trading activities, including the head of the equity futures division and the head of information technology, the board of directors of Soc-Gen refused to accept the resignation of chief executive officer Daniel Bouton, and he, in turn, declined to accept the resignation of Jean-Pierre Mustier, the chief executive of SocGen's corporate and investment banking division.
- Critics of SocGen's leadership team argued that a takeover of the bank would be the inevitable outcome of this event. One analyst was quoted as stating: "The management has lost its credibility and that is the first barrier to any takeover bid. There is likely to be a lot of interest from around Europe."
- Kerviel was arrested at the end of January and charged with breach of trust, falsifying and using falsified documents, and breaching IT control access codes.
- In contrast, Kerviel has also become something of an Internet celebrity, with many French sites hailing him as a modern-day Robin Hood or the Che Guevara of finance. One enterprising Web merchant quickly produced a range of T-shirts in support of Kerviel, including one that reads "Jérôme Kerviel's girlfriend," and another that reads, "Jérôme Kerviel, €4,900,000,000, Respect."
- SocGen's biggest rival in France, BNP Paribas, had tried unsuccessfully to acquire SocGen back in 1999 in a hostile takeover bid. The rival was therefore the most logical choice to come after SocGen in such an obvious moment of defenselessness. However, after considering the option of another takeover bid, BNP chose not to pursue the opportunity. SocGen has been able to avoid the same fate as Barings Bank by raising an $8 billion rescue fund from private equity investors.

SocGen's clear lack of risk management and financial controls inevitably caught the attention of France's finance minister, Christine Lagarde. Her initial report on the incident, produced within eight days of the event while many simultaneous investigations were still ongoing, raised several key questions including the ease with which Kerviel appeared to avoid detection, even though his trades amounted to billions of dollars, the extent to which the losses caused broader market problems, and what needed to be done to ensure the event never happened again. Her report ended with a call on the French government to give more power to punish those who fail to follow established best practices.

On October 5, 2010, a French court found Kerviel guilty of all charges and sentenced him to five years in jail (with two years of the sentence suspended for time already served). Kerviel was also ordered to repay the €4.9 billion ($7 billion) he lost for SocGen. While the company clarified that it had no intention of pursuing Kerviel for the money, the repayment order served a dual purpose—to repudiate Kerviel's defense that SocGen knew about his activities and "looked the other way" as long as those trades were profitable and, more importantly, to strengthen SocGen's defense against future shareholder lawsuits questioning SocGen's governance practices. Kerviel is appealing the court's decision.

1. Who are the stakeholders in this case?
2. What did Kerviel do wrong?
3. What did SocGen do wrong?
4. Identify the ethical violations that occurred in this case.
5. Would the outcome have been different if Kerviel's trades in European futures had worked out?
6. What actions could SocGen have taken to prevent such large losses?

Sources: BBC, "Nick Leeson and Barings Bank," www.bbc.co.uk/crime/caseclosed/nickleeson.shtml; Marcus W. Brauchli, Nicholas Bray, and Michael R. Sesit, "Barings PLC Officials May Have Been Aware of Trader's Position," *The Wall Street Journal,* March 6, 1995, pp. A1, A6; Nicholas Bray and Michael R. Sesit, "Barings Was Warned Controls Were Lax but Didn't Make Reforms in Singapore," *The Wall Street Journal,* March 2, 1995, p. A3; Paula Dwyer, William Glasgall, Dean Foust, and Greg Burns, "The Lessons from Barings' Straits," *BusinessWeek,* March 13, 1995, pp. 30–33; Alexander MacLeod, "Youthful Trader Sinks Britain's Oldest Bank," *The Christian Science Monitor,* February 28, 1995, pp. 1, 8; Peter Thal Larsen, "SocGen Rogue Trade: Six Sleepless Nights Reveal the Full Impact of Scandal," *Financial Times,* January 25, 2008, pp. 16–17; Martin Arnold and Lina Saigol, "Doubts Cast on Bouton's Position," *Financial Times,* January 25, 2008, p. 17; Pan Kwan Luk, "From 'le Rogue' to the Che of Our Times," *Financial Times,* January 31, 2008, p. 19; Peggy Hollinger, "Hard-Hitting Lagarde Points up SocGen's Lack of Control," *Financial Times,* February 5, 2008, p. 6; and "All His Fault," *The Economist,* October 7, 2010.

Thinking Critically

>> HEALTHSOUTH

HealthSouth is America's largest provider of outpatient surgery and rehabilitation services. It owns or operates over 1,800 facilities across the country and serves 70 percent of the rehabilitation market. It was founded in 1984 by Richard Scrushy, a former respiratory therapist who believed that efficient one-stop shopping could be applied to the health care industry. From the time it went public in 1986, the Birmingham, Alabama, firm exceeded Wall Street expectations, a pattern that would continue for the next 15 years. In 1992 Scrushy aggressively began to acquire other clinics, and HealthSouth stock soared 31 percent annually between 1987 and 1997.

Scrushy cut a charismatic figure; the headquarters housed a museum dedicated to his achievements. He flew his own jet, mingled with celebrities, and sang with a band. For his third wedding in 1997 he chartered a plane to fly 150 guests to Jamaica. His workers knew him as King Richard.

His management style impressed many analysts. *Fortune* magazine described him in 1999 as executing his ideas brilliantly and said he was a taskmaster and a micromanager. Scrushy honed his technique, centralizing every piece of data imaginable. Every Friday a stack of printouts detailing the performance of each facility landed on his desk; when any one of them had a problem, Scrushy pounced. HealthSouth managed everything out of Birmingham: construction, purchasing, billing, even personnel. While this kind of top-down management may sound impossibly bureaucratic, Scrushy's troops made it work efficiently. Needed supplies and authorizations arrived within 30 days. Administrators who couldn't hit budget targets were fired. Says Scrushy, "We can call 'em and tell 'em, 'Jump through hoops! Stand on your head!' "

However, behind the scenes was a pattern of institutionalized fraud. By the third quarter of 2002, the $8 billion company had overstated its assets by $800 million. According to testimony, the fraud began shortly after the company went public when Scrushy wanted to impress Wall Street. If the results were not what he expected, Scrushy would allegedly tell his staff to "fix it." They would then convene in what came to be known as a "family meeting" to adjust the figures, a process they called "filling the gap." The internal accountants kept two sets of books—one with the true figures and one that they presented to the outside world.

HealthSouth was able to keep up the deception in a number of ingenious ways that systematically fooled outside auditors. One scheme involved what are known as contractual adjustments. Sometimes the government or insurer would not fully reimburse a facility for the amount charged to a patient. This amount would be subtracted from gross revenues. In typical double-entry accounting, any loss of revenue has to be balanced by an increase in liabilities. HealthSouth simply failed to enter the liability amount. Its accountants also posted regular expenses as long-term capital expenditures and billed group therapies as single-person sessions. They routinely inflated the value of their assets. The practices were pervasive but individually so small that they rarely met the threshold levels that would trigger review by an outside auditor. The inside accountants were careful to make sure the adjustments were uneven and dispersed around the country so they appeared realistic.

Five HealthSouth accounting employees have been convicted of fraud. Four did not receive prison sentences, though. Their lawyers argued that they were obeying orders, subject to constant intimidation, and relatively low on the organizational chart. The judge declared at sentencing that although three held the rank of vice president, "These four were essentially data entry clerks, regardless of their job titles."

Scrushy was fired by the board on March 31, 2003. On November 4, 2003, Scrushy was indicted for securities fraud, money laundering, and other charges. He had maintained throughout that he was unaware of the illegal accounting practices. He was secretly recorded saying that he was worried about signing "fixed up" financials.

CONTINUED >>

As part of the Sarbanes-Oxley Act of 2002, an executive has to certify the company's financial reports. In August of that year, Scrushy signed that he had reviewed and endorsed HealthSouth's 2001 annual report and the second quarter report for 2002. He claimed on CBS's *60 Minutes* program in October 2003 that he had signed because he trusted the five chief financial officers who prepared the figures. In June 2005, an Alabama jury cleared Scrushy of all charges, although the Securities and Exchange Commission (SEC) reached a settlement of $81 million with him in April 2007, consisting of a payback of $52 million of bonuses and interest as a result of an Alabama lawsuit, $17 million in a similar Delaware lawsuit, $1.5 million to settle a lawsuit brought by former HealthSouth employees, and other forfeitures and fines. Scrushy was also prohibited from serving as an officer or director of a publicly traded company for at least five years under the terms of the settlement.

QUESTIONS

1. Is it fair to hold a CEO responsible for any and all actions of a company? Consider that Scrushy was not an accountant and that the outside auditors, Ernst & Young, did not detect the fraud. If he were not involved, should he still be held accountable?

2. Would it have been appropriate for employees to blow the whistle in this case? Was there imminent harm to people? What would be an appropriate motive for whistle-blowing, and how much proof do you believe the employee would have needed to be credible?

3. From your research and reading, what dynamics set the moral tone at HealthSouth? Do you feel that employees were influenced by the corporate culture?

4. There seems to have been a significant amount of wrongdoing at HealthSouth. A number of executives were involved in fraud, but there also appears to have been a great deal of complicity on the part of more rank-and-file workers. How would you assign moral culpability in a case like this?

5. Derek Parfit describes a case called the "Harmless Torturers." He says that in the bad old days, one torturer gave a jolt of 1,000 volts to a victim, but nowadays 1,000 operators each flip a switch carrying 1 volt. Any individual contribution to the overall effect is negligible, and therefore each one believes he or she has not personally done any significant harm. Would the same logic apply in the HealthSouth case? What, if anything, is wrong with the reasoning involved?

6. For a long time, HealthSouth posted profits, and Scrushy was a darling of Wall Street analysts. At what point, if any, should there have been greater regulatory oversight? Do you believe the outside auditors or the board should have acted more like bloodhounds than watchdogs?

Sources: K. Gibson, *Business Ethics: People, Profits, and the Planet* (New York: McGraw-Hill, 2006), pp. 634–36; and *The New York Times*, April 24, 2007.

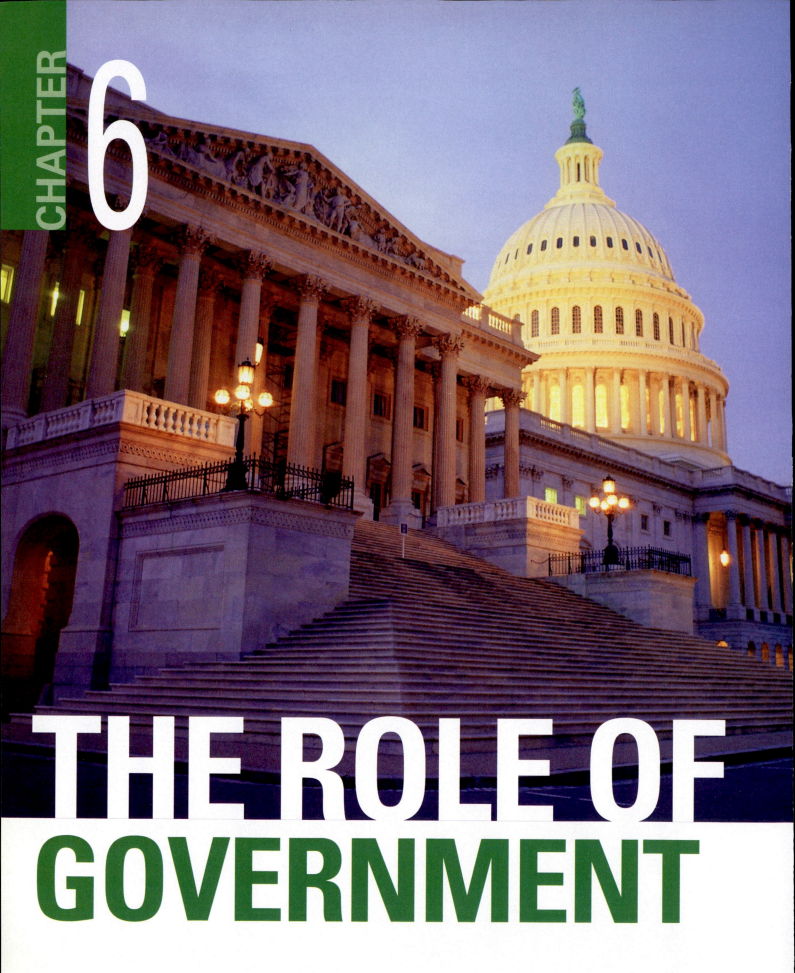

6

THE ROLE OF
GOVERNMENT

After studying this chapter, you should be able to:

1 Identify the five key pieces of U.S. legislation designed to discourage, if not prevent, illegal conduct within organizations.

2 Understand the purpose and significance of the Foreign Corrupt Practices Act (FCPA).

3 Calculate monetary fines under the three-step process of the U.S. Federal Sentencing Guidelines for Organizations (FSGO).

4 Compare and contrast the relative advantages and disadvantages of the Sarbanes-Oxley Act (SOX).

5 Explain the key provisions of the Dodd-Frank Wall Street Reform and Consumer Protection Act.

FRONTLINE FOCUS
Too Much Trouble

Lara Kempton is a junior accounting assistant with one of the largest auditing firms in the Midwest. Since the Enron fraud case and the passing of the Sarbanes-Oxley Act, her company has been very busy—in fact, it has so much business, it is starting to turn clients down.

For Lara, so much business means great opportunities. Each completed audit takes her one step closer to running her own auditing team and finally to leading her own audit. The work is hard and the hours are often long, but Lara loves the attention to detail and the excitement of discovering errors and then getting them corrected. Also, knowing that the clients are releasing financial reports that are clean and accurate makes her feel that she is doing her part to restore the reputation of the financial markets one client at a time.

One morning, her boss, Greg Bartell, comes into her office carrying a thick manila folder. "Hi, Lara, what are you working on right now?" he asks.

"Typical Bartell," Lara thinks. "Straight to the point with no time for small talk."

"We should be finished with the Jones audit by the end of the day. Why?" Lara replied.

"I need a small favor," Bartell continued. "We've had this new small business client show up out of the blue after being dropped by his previous auditor. It really couldn't have happened at a worse time. We've got so many large audits in the pipeline that I can't spare anyone to work on this, but I don't want to start turning business away in case word gets out that we're not keeping up with a growing client base—who knows when the next big fish will come along?"

"I'm not sure I follow you, Greg," answered Lara, confused.

"I don't want to turn this guy away, but we don't want his business either—too small to be a real moneymaker. So just take a quick look at his file, and then quote him a price for our services—and here's where I need the favor. Make the quote high enough that he will want to go somewhere else—can you do that?"

QUESTIONS
1. The Sarbanes-Oxley Act created an oversight board for all auditing firms. Look at the outline of the act on pages **115–117** for more information on the Public Company Accounting Oversight Board (PCAOB). Would the PCAOB endorse trying to dump a prospective client in this manner?
2. Is being too busy with other clients a justification for deliberately driving this customer away?
3. What should Lara do now?

People who enjoy eating sausage and obey the law should not watch either being made.

Otto von Bismarck (1815–1898), Chancellor of Germany

>> Key Legislation

For those organizations that have demonstrated that they are unable to keep their own house in order by maintaining a strong ethical culture, the last line of defense has been a legal and regulatory framework that offers financial incentives to promote ethical behavior and imposes penalties for those that choose not to adopt such behavior. Since the 1970s, there have been several attempts at behavior modification to discourage, if not prevent, illegal conduct within organizations:

- The Foreign Corrupt Practices Act (1977)
- The U.S. Federal Sentencing Guidelines for Organizations (1991)
- The Sarbanes-Oxley Act (2002)
- The Revised Federal Sentencing Guidelines for Organizations (2004)
- The Dodd-Frank Wall Street Reform and Consumer Protection Act (2010)

>> The Foreign Corrupt Practices Act

Foreign Corrupt Practices Act (FCPA) Legislation introduced to control bribery and other less obvious forms of payment to foreign officials and politicians by American publicly traded companies.

Disclosure (FCPA) The FCPA requirement that corporations fully disclose any and all transactions conducted with foreign officials and politicians.

Prohibition (FCPA) The FCPA inclusion of wording from the Bank Secrecy Act and the Mail Fraud Act to prevent the movement of funds overseas for the express purpose of conducting a fraudulent scheme.

Facilitation Payments (FCPA) Payments that are acceptable (legal) provided they expedite or secure the performance of a routine governmental action.

Routine Governmental Action (FCPA) Any regular administrative process or procedure, excluding any action taken by a foreign official in the decision to award new or continuing business.

The **Foreign Corrupt Practices Act (FCPA)** was introduced to more effectively control bribery and other less obvious forms of payment to foreign officials and politicians by American publicly traded companies as they pursued international growth. Prior to the passing of this law, the illegality of this behavior was punishable only through "secondary" sources of legislation:

1. The Securities and Exchange Commission (SEC) could fine companies for failing to disclose such payments under their securities rules.
2. The Bank Secrecy Act also required full disclosure of funds that were taken out of or brought into the United States.

3. The Mail Fraud Act made the use of the U.S. mail or wire communications to transact a fraudulent scheme illegal.

By passing the FCPA, Congress was attempting to send a clear message that the competitiveness of U.S. corporations in overseas markets should be based on price and product quality rather than the extent to which companies had paid off foreign officials and political leaders. To give the legislation some weight, the U.S. Department of Justice (DOJ) and the Securities and Exchange Commission (SEC) jointly enforce the FCPA.

The act encompasses all the secondary measures that were currently in use to prohibit such behavior by focusing on two distinct areas:

- **Disclosure:** The act requires corporations to fully disclose any and all transactions conducted with foreign officials and politicians, in line with the SEC provisions.
- **Prohibition:** The act includes wording from the Bank Secrecy Act and the Mail Fraud Act to prevent the movement of funds overseas for the express purpose of conducting a fraudulent scheme.

A BARK WORSE THAN ITS BITE

Even with the apparent success of consolidating three pieces of secondary legislation into one primary tool for the prohibition of bribery, the FCPA was still criticized for lacking any real teeth because of its formal recognition of **facilitation payments,** which would otherwise be acknowledged as bribes. The FCPA finds these payments acceptable provided they expedite or secure the performance of a **routine governmental action.**

Examples of routine governmental actions include:

- Providing permits, licenses, or other official documents to qualify a person to do business in a foreign country.
- Processing governmental papers, such as visas and work orders.
- Providing police protection, mail pickup and delivery, or scheduling inspections associated with contract performance or inspections related to transit of goods across a country.
- Providing phone service, power, and water supply; loading and unloading cargo; or protecting perishable products or commodities from deterioration.
- Performing actions of a similar nature.

The key distinction in identifying bribes was the exclusion of any action taken by a foreign official in the decision to award new or continuing business. Such decisions, being the primary target of most questionable payments, were not deemed to be routine governmental action.[1]

FCPA IN ACTION

Chiquita Brands International Inc. According to the September 14, 2004, edition of *The Wall Street Journal,* Chiquita Brands International Inc. disclosed to the DOJ and the SEC that its Greek unit made improper payments as part of a local tax audit settlement.[2] Chiquita also disclosed that the payments, totaling $18,021, were similar to payments that its Colombian subsidiary made in 1996 and 1997, which were previously disclosed to the SEC.

ADDITIONAL COMPENSATION

Real World Applications

Enrique is a country manager for a global food company. His plantation is one of the largest employers in an area of political instability. Several local communities depend on employment on his plantation for their economic survival. Yesterday Enrique had a meeting with local officials about purchasing some additional acreage and updating the irrigation system for the plantation. The changes will require several work permits, and the officials made it clear that those permits could be delayed without some "additional compensation." Should Enrique tell his U.S.-based boss or handle the situation locally?

PROGRESS ✓ QUESTIONS

1. What was the primary purpose of the FCPA?
2. What was the maximum fine for a U.S. corporation under the FCPA?
3. Which two distinct areas did the FCPA focus on?
4. List four examples of routine governmental actions.

Monsanto Corporation According to the May 27, 2004, edition of *The Wall Street Journal,* Monsanto Corporation began cooperating with an investigation regarding allegations that it bribed an Indonesian official. The government claimed that in 2002 a senior Monsanto manager based in the United States authorized and directed an Indonesian consulting firm to make an illegal payment of $50,000 to a senior Indonesian Ministry of Environment official in order to repeal an unfavorable decree that could affect the company's operations. However, the decree was not repealed, which highlights the fact that a company can still be found in violation of the FCPA even if a bribe is unsuccessful.

MAKING SENSE OF FCPA

Figure 6.1 summarizes the fine lines between legality and illegality in some of the prohibited behaviors and approved exceptions in the FCPA provisions.

The Department of Justice can enforce criminal penalties of up to $2 million per violation for corporations and other business entities. Officers, directors, stockholders, employees, and agents are subject to a fine of up to $250,000 per violation and imprisonment for up to five years. The SEC may bring a civil fine of up to $10,000 per violation. Penalties under the books and record-keeping provisions can reach up to $5 million and 20 years' imprisonment for individuals and up to $25 million for organizations.

Study Alert !

If you pay money to a government official to expedite the processing of permits, licenses, or other official documents over and above the normal processing time, how is that not a bribe? Is the distinction between "normal operations" and "new or continuing business" a valid one?

FIG.6.1 Illegal versus Legal Behaviors under the FCPA

Illegal	Legal
Bribes: • Payments of money or anything else of value to influence or induce any foreign official to act in a manner that would be in violation of his or her lawful duty. • Payments, authorizations, promises, or offers to any other person if there is knowledge that any portion of the payment is to be passed along to a foreign official or foreign political party, official, or candidate for a prohibited purpose under the act. Note that knowledge is defined very broadly and is present when one knows an event is certain or likely to occur; even purposely failing to take note of an event or being willfully blind can constitute knowledge.	**Grease payments:** • Facilitating payments to foreign officials in order to expedite or secure the performance of a routine governmental action. For example, routine governmental action could include obtaining permits, licenses, or other official documents; expediting lawful customs clearances; obtaining the issuance of entry or exit visas; providing police protection, mail pick-up and delivery, and phone service; and performing actions that are wholly unconnected to the award of new business or the continuation of prior business.
Recordkeeping and accounting provisions: • Books, records, and accounts must be kept in reasonable detail to accurately and fairly reflect transactions and dispositions of assets. • A system of internal accounting controls is devised to provide reasonable assurances that transactions are executed in accordance with management's authorization.	**Marketing expenses:** • Payments to foreign officials made in connection with the promotion or demonstration of company products or services (e.g., demonstration or tour of a pharmaceutical plant) or in connection with the execution of a particular contract with a foreign government.
	Payments lawful under foreign laws: • Payments may (very rarely) be made to foreign officials when the payment is "lawful under the written laws of the foreign country."
	Political contributions: • Unlike in the United States, where foreign nationals are prohibited from making political contributions to U.S. political parties and candidates, it may occasionally be appropriate for a U.S. company's overseas operations to make a political contribution on behalf of the company. Contributions not only include checks to political parties or candidates, but also payments for fundraising dinners and similar events. This would be an example of a payment that could violate the FCPA were it not for written local law. **Donations to foreign charities:** • U.S. companies may make donations to bona fide charitable organizations provided that the donation will not be used to circumvent the FCPA and that the contribution does not violate local laws, rules, or regulations.

>> The U.S. Federal Sentencing Guidelines for Organizations (1991)

The U.S. Federal Sentencing Commission was established in 1984 by the Comprehensive Crime Control Act and was charged with developing uniform sentencing guidelines for offenders convicted of federal crimes. The guidelines became effective on November 1, 1987. At that time, they consisted of seven chapters and applied only to individuals convicted of federal offenses.

Federal Sentencing Guidelines for Organizations (FSGO) Chapter 8 of the guidelines that hold businesses liable for the criminal acts of their employees and agents.

In 1991, an eighth chapter was added to the guidelines. Chapter 8 is more commonly referred to as the **Federal Sentencing Guidelines for Organizations (FSGO).** It applies to organizations and holds them liable for the criminal acts of their employees and agents.

FSGO requires that organizations police themselves by preventing and detecting the criminal activity of their employees and agents.

In its mission to promote ethical organizational behavior and increase the costs of unethical behavior, the FSGO establishes a definition of an organization that is so broad as to prompt the assessment that "no business enterprise is exempt." In addition, the FSGO includes such an exhaustive list of covered business crimes that it appears frighteningly easy for an organization to run afoul of federal crime laws and become subject to FSGO penalties.

Penalties under FSGO include monetary fines, organizational probation, and the implementation of an operational program to bring the organization into compliance with FSGO standards.

MONETARY FINES UNDER THE FGSO

If an organization is sentenced under FSGO, a fine is calculated through a three-step process:

Step 1. *Determination of the "Base Fine."* The base fine will normally be the greatest of:

- The monetary gain to the organization from the offense.
- The monetary loss from the offense caused by the organization, to the extent the loss was caused knowingly, intentionally, or recklessly.
- The amount determined by a judge based upon an FSGO table.

The table factors in both the nature of the crime and the amount of the loss suffered by the victim. Fraud, for example, is a level 6 offense; a fraud causing harm in excess of $5 million is increased by 14 levels to a level 20 offense. Evidence of extensive preplanning to commit the offense can raise that two more levels to level 22. To put these levels in dollar terms, crimes at level 6 or lower involve a base fine of $5,000; offense levels of 38 or higher involve a base fine of $72.5 million.

Step 2. *The Culpability Score.* Once the base fine has been calculated, the judge will compute a corresponding degree of blame or guilt known as the **culpability score.** This score is simply a multiplier with a maximum of 4, so the worst-case scenario would be a fine of 4 times the maximum base fine of $72.5 million, for a grand total of $290 million. The culpability score can be increased (or aggravated) or decreased (or mitigated) according to predetermined factors.

Aggravating Factors

- High-level personnel were involved in or tolerated the criminal activity.
- The organization willfully obstructed justice.
- The organization had a prior history of similar misconduct.
- The current offense violated a judicial order, an injunction, or a condition of probation.

Mitigating Factors

- The organization had an effective program to prevent and detect violations of law.

- The organization self-reported the offense to appropriate governmental authorities, fully cooperated in the investigation, and accepted responsibility for the criminal conduct.

Step 3. *Determining the Total Fine Amount.* The base fine multiplied by the culpability score gives the total fine amount. In certain cases, however, the judge has the discretion to impose a so-called **death penalty,** where the fine is set high enough to match all the organization's assets. This is warranted where the organization was operating primarily for a criminal purpose.

> **Culpability Score (FSGO)** The calculation of a degree of blame or guilt that is used as a multiplier of up to 4 times the base fine. The culpability score can be adjusted according to aggravating or mitigating factors.
>
> **Death Penalty (FSGO)** A fine that is set high enough to match all the organization's assets—and basically put the organization out of business. This is warranted where the organization was operating primarily for a criminal purpose.

ORGANIZATIONAL PROBATION

In addition to monetary fines, organizations also can be sentenced to probation for up to five years. The status of probation can include the following requirements:

- Reporting the business's financial condition to the court on a periodic basis.
- Remaining subject to unannounced examinations of all financial records by a designated probation officer and/or court-appointed experts.
- Reporting progress in the implementation of a compliance program.
- Being subject to unannounced examinations to confirm that the compliance program is in place and is working.

COMPLIANCE PROGRAM

Obviously the best way to minimize your culpability score is to make sure that you have some form of program in place that can effectively detect and prevent violations of law—a compliance program. The FSGO prescribes seven steps for an effective compliance program:

1. *Management oversight.* A high-level official (such as a corporate ethics officer) must be in charge of and accountable for the compliance program.
2. *Corporate policies.* Policies and procedures designed to reduce the likelihood of criminal conduct in the organization must be in place.

3. *Communication of standards and procedures.* These ethics policies must be effectively communicated to every stakeholder of the organization.

4. *Compliance with standards and procedures.* Evidence of active implementation of these policies must be provided through appropriate monitoring and reporting (including a system for employees to report suspected criminal conduct without fear of retribution).

5. *Delegation of substantial discretionary authority.* No individuals should be granted excessive discretionary authority that would increase the risk of criminal conduct.

6. *Consistent discipline.* The organization must implement penalties for criminal conduct and for failing to address criminal misconduct in a consistent manner.

7. *Response and corrective action.* Criminal offenses, whether actual or suspected, must generate an appropriate response, analysis, and corrective action.

If all of this seems like an enormous administrative burden, consider the following example: A $25,000 bribe has been paid to a city official to ensure an award of a cable television franchise. This is a level 18 offense with a base penalty of a $350,000 fine. Due to a variety of factors (e.g., culpability, multipliers), that penalty is now increased to $1.4 million. The minimum fine with mitigating circumstances (e.g., the company has a compliance plan and there was no high-level involvement in the bribery) would have placed this fine in the $17,500 to $70,000 range instead of $1.4 million.

If that doesn't discourage you, consider the additional risk of negative publicity to your organization, which could result in a significant loss of sales, additional scrutiny from vendors, and even a drop in your stock price.[3]

PROGRESS ✓ QUESTIONS

5. What are the three steps in calculating financial penalties under FSGO?

6. What is the maximum fine that can be levied?

7. What is the maximum term of organizational probation?

8. What is the "death penalty" under FSGO?

THE BRIBERY GAP

In 1997, 35 countries signed the convention of the Organization for Economic Cooperation and Development (OECD) to make it a crime to bribe foreign officials. However, in the last half of 2004:

- Bristol-Myers Squibb revealed that the Securities and Exchange Commission launched an investigation into some of the company's German units for possible violations of the FCPA.

- Three former Lucent Corp. employees were alleged to have bribed Saudi Arabia's former telecommunications minister with cash and gifts worth up to $21 million.

- Halliburton Corp., under investigation by both the Department of Justice and the SEC, disclosed that it may have bribed Nigerian officials to secure favorable tax treatment for a liquefied natural gas facility.

- The SEC hit the U.S. unit of Swiss-based ABB Ltd. with a $16.4 million judgment reflecting information on bribery and accounting improprieties. The charges, which ABB settled without admitting or denying guilt, were that ABB's U.S. and foreign units paid $1.1 billion in bribes to officials in Nigeria, Angola, and Kazakhstan between 1998 and 2003. In one instance, the SEC alleged, ABB's country manager for Angola gave out $21,000 in a paper bag to five officials of the state-owned oil company.

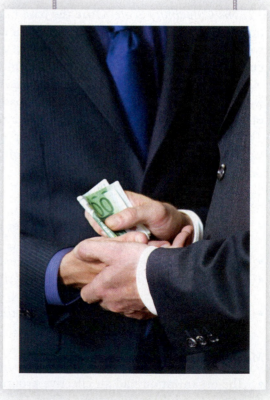

American companies operating under increasing federal and regulatory scrutiny face real consequences from trying to do business in a global business environment in which foreign business seems to function on the basis of "gifts" at every stage of the transaction:

- During the 12 months ended April 30, 2004, according to a U.S. Commerce Department report, competition for 47 contracts worth $18 billion may have been affected by bribes that foreign firms paid to foreign officials. Because U.S. companies wouldn't participate in the tainted deals, the department estimates, at least 8 of those contracts, worth $3 billion, were lost to them.

- For Lockheed Martin Corp., a $2.4 billion merger agreement with Titan Corp. eventually fell through in 2004 after what Titan [documents] described as "allegations that improper payments were made, or items of value were provided by consultants for Titan or its subsidiaries."

QUESTIONS

1. Is it ethical for U.S. regulations to put U.S. companies at an apparent disadvantage to their foreign competitors? Explain why or why not.
2. If foreign companies pay bribes, does that make it OK for U.S. companies to do the same? Explain why or why not.
3. If you could prove that new jobs, new construction, and valuable tax revenue would come to the United States if the bribe were paid, would that change your position? Explain your answer.
4. It would seem that the playing field will never be level—someone will always be looking for a bribe, and someone will always be willing to pay it if she or he wants the business badly enough. If that's true, why bother to put legislation in place at all?

Source: David M. Katz, "The Bribery Gap," *CFO* 21, no. 1 (January 2005), p. 59.

REVISED FEDERAL SENTENCING GUIDELINES FOR ORGANIZATIONS (2004)

In May 2004, the U.S. Sentencing Commission proposed to Congress that there should be modifications to the 1991 guidelines to bring about key changes in corporate compliance programs. The revised guidelines, which Congress formally adopted in November 2004, made three key changes:

- They required companies to periodically evaluate the effectiveness of their compliance programs on the assumption of a substantial risk that any program is capable of failing. They also expected the results of these risk assessments to be incorporated back into the next version of the compliance program.
- The revised guidelines required evidence of actively promoting ethical conduct rather than just complying with legal obligations. For the first time, the concept of an ethical culture was recognized as a foundational component of an effective compliance program.
- The guidelines defined accountability more clearly. Corporate officers are expected to be knowledgeable about all aspects of the compliance program, and they are required to receive formal training as it relates to their roles and responsibilities within the organization.

> **Study Alert**
>
> The multiplication of a base fine amount by a culpability score under FSGO has the potential to generate fines in the hundreds of millions of dollars. Do you think that knowledge will prompt organizations to reconsider their unethical practices? Why or why not?

PROGRESS ✓ QUESTIONS

9. Explain the seven steps of an effective compliance program.
10. What are *aggravating* and *mitigating* factors?
11. Explain the risk assessments required in the 2004 revised FSGO.
12. What were the three key components of the 2004 revised FSGO?

>> The Sarbanes-Oxley Act (2002)

The **Sarbanes-Oxley Act (SOX)** became law on July 30, 2003.[4] It was a legislative response to a series of corporate accounting scandals that had begun to dominate the financial markets and mass media since 2001.

Launched during a period of extreme investor unrest and agitation, SOX was hailed by some as "one of the most important pieces of legislation governing the behavior of accounting

Sarbanes-Oxley Act (SOX) A legislative response to the corporate accounting scandals of the early 2000s that covers the financial management of businesses.

firms and financial markets since [the SEC] legislation in the 1930s."

However, supporters of this law were equally matched by its critics, leaving no doubt that SOX may be regarded as one of the most controversial pieces of corporate legislation in recent history.

The act contains 11 sections, or titles, and almost 70 subsections covering every aspect of the financial management of businesses. Each of the 11 sections can be seen to relate directly to prominent examples of corporate wrongdoing that preceded the establishment of the legislation—the Enron scandal in particular.

TITLE I: PUBLIC COMPANY ACCOUNTING OVERSIGHT BOARD

The series of financial collapses of publicly traded companies that the financial community had previously recommended as "strong buys" or "Wall Street darlings" had the greatest negative impact on investor confidence—especially since the accounts of all these companies had supposedly been audited as accurate by established and highly regarded auditing firms.

The creation of the **Public Company Accounting Oversight Board (PCAOB)** as an independent over-

Public Company Accounting Oversight Board (PCAOB) An independent oversight body for auditing companies.

sight body was an attempt to reestablish the perceived independence of auditing companies that the conflict of interest in Arthur Andersen's auditing and consulting relationship with Enron had called into question. In addition, as an oversight board, the PCAOB was charged with maintaining compliance with established standards and enforcing rules and disciplinary procedures for those organizations that found themselves out of compliance. Any public accounting firms that audited the records of publicly traded companies were required to register with the board and to abide by any operational standards set by that board.

TITLE II: AUDITOR INDEPENDENCE

In addition to establishing the PCAOB, SOX introduced several key directives to further enforce the independence of auditors and hopefully restore public confidence in independent audit reports:

1. Prohibits specific "nonaudit" services of public accounting firms as violations of auditor independence.
2. Prohibits public accounting firms from providing audit services to any company whose senior officers (chief executive officer, chief financial

officer, controller) were employed by that accounting firm within the previous 12 months.
3. Requires senior auditors to rotate off an account every five years, and junior auditors every seven years.
4. Requires the external auditor to report to the client's audit committee on specific topics.
5. Requires auditors to disclose all other written communications between management and themselves.

TITLES III THROUGH XI

Here are some highlights of Titles III through XI.

Title III: Corporate Responsibility

- Requires audit committees to be independent and undertake specified oversight responsibilities.
- Requires CEOs and CFOs to certify quarterly and annual reports to the SEC, including making representations about the effectiveness of their control systems.
- Provides rules of conduct for companies and their officers regarding pension blackout periods—a direct response to the Enron situation where corporate executives were accused of selling their stock while employees had their company stock locked in their pension accounts.

Title IV: Enhanced Financial Disclosures

- Requires companies to provide enhanced disclosures, including a report on the effectiveness of internal controls and procedures for financial reporting (along with external auditor sign-off on that report), and disclosures covering off–balance sheet transactions—most of the debt Enron hid from analysts and investors was placed in off–balance sheet accounts and hidden in the smallest footnotes in its financial statements.

Title V: Analyst Conflicts of Interest

- Requires the SEC to adopt rules to address conflicts of interest that can arise when securities analysts recommend securities in research reports and public appearances—each of the "rogue's gallery" of companies in the 2001–2002 scandals had been highly promoted as growth stocks by analysts.

Title VI: Commission Resources and Authority

- Provides additional funding and authority to the SEC to follow through on all the new responsibilities outlined in the act.

Title VII: Studies and Reports

- Directs federal regulatory bodies to conduct studies regarding consolidation of accounting firms, credit rating agencies, and certain roles of investment banks and financial advisers.

Title VIII: Corporate and Criminal Fraud Accountability

- Provides tougher criminal penalties for altering documents, defrauding shareholders, and certain other forms of obstruction of justice and securities fraud. Arthur Andersen's activities in shredding Enron documents directly relates to this topic.
- Protects employees of companies who provide evidence of fraud. Enron and WorldCom were both exposed by the actions of individual employees (see Chapter 7, "Blowing the Whistle").

Title IX: White-Collar Crime Penalty Enhancements

- Provides that any person who attempts to commit white-collar crimes will be treated under the law as if the person had committed the crime.
- Requires CEOs and CFOs to certify their periodic reports and imposes penalties for certifying a misleading or fraudulent report.

Title X: Corporate Tax Returns

- Conveys the sense of the Senate that the CEO should sign a company's federal income tax return.

Title XI: Corporate Fraud and Accountability

- Provides additional authority to regulatory bodies and courts to take various actions, including fines or imprisonment, with regard to tampering with records, impeding official proceedings, taking extraordinary payments, retaliating against corporate whistle-blowers, and certain other matters involving corporate fraud.

Section 404 of the Sarbanes-Oxley Act (listed as Title IV in this chapter) is estimated to have generated auditing fees in the hundreds of millions of dollars—all in the hope of enforcing ethical conduct in U.S. organizations. The legislation was swift and wide-ranging and was specifically designed to restore investor confidence in what, for a brief period, appeared to be financial markets that were run with two primary goals: corruption and greed.

The danger with such a rapid response is that key issues have a tendency to be overlooked in the eagerness to demonstrate responsiveness and decisiveness. In this case, the question of whether you can really legislate ethics was never answered.

What SOX delivers is a collection of tools and penalties to punish offenders with enough severity to put others off the idea of bending or breaking the rules in the future, and enough policies and procedures to ensure that any future corporate criminals are going to have to work a lot harder to earn their money than the folks at Enron, WorldCom, and the rest—there are a lot more people watching now.

However, SOX does not help you create an ethical corporate culture or hire an effective and ethical board of directors—you still have to do that for yourself. Just be sure to remember that there are now a lot more penalties and people waiting to catch you if you don't.

PROGRESS ✓ QUESTIONS

13. Explain the role of the PCAOB.
14. Which title requires CEOs and CFOs to certify quarterly and annual reports to the SEC?
15. Which title protects employees of companies who provide evidence of fraud?
16. What are the five key requirements for auditor independence?

>> Wall Street Reform

In September and October 2008, financial markets around the world suffered a severe crash as the consequences of aggressive lending to subprime borrowers in a deregulated environment came back to haunt companies that, as recently as a few months earlier, had reported record earnings based on these questionable lending practices. Some companies, such as JPMorgan Chase (which purchased the assets of Bear Stearns and Washington Mutual at fire sale prices) and Wells Fargo (which purchased Wachovia Bank at an equally discounted price), were able to benefit from this downturn, but two companies in particular came to exemplify a new round of corporate arrogance and questionable ethics that earned them a place in the rogue's gallery previously occupied by such infamous companies as Enron, WorldCom, and HealthSouth.

American Insurance Group (AIG), formerly one of the world's largest insurance companies, received a lifeline loan of $85 billion from the U.S. government in September 2008, followed by an additional $37.8 billion in October 2008. The need for the rescue funding (which AIG was expected to repay by selling

FOXES GUARDING THE HENHOUSE?

The Sarbanes-Oxley Act, which the United States enacted in an atmosphere of extraordinary agitation in 2002, is one of the most influential—and controversial—pieces of corporate legislation ever to have hit a statute book. Its original aim, on the face of it, was modest: to improve the accountability of managers to shareholders, and [then] calm the raging crisis of confidence in American capitalism aroused by scandals at Enron, WorldCom, and other companies. The law's methods, however, were anything but modest, and its implications . . . are going to be far-reaching.

The cost of all this [new oversight] is steep. A survey by Financial Executives International, an association of top financial executives, found that companies paid an average of $2.4 million more for their audits [in 2004] than they had anticipated (and far more than the statute's designers had envisaged). . . . This result underlines a notable and unintended consequence of the legislation: it has provided a bonanza for accountants and auditors—a profession thought to be much at fault in the scandals that inspired the law, and which the statute sought to rein in and supervise.

Already reduced in number by consolidation and the demise of Arthur Andersen, the big accounting firms are now known more often as the Final Four than the Big Four, since any further reduction is thought unlikely.

WHO'S LOOKING OUT FOR THE LITTLE GUY?

Smaller companies without access to the internal resources (or funds to pay for external resources) to comply with Sarbanes-Oxley are being particularly hard-hit by the legislation, even though the transgressions that prompted the statute in the first place came from large, publicly traded organizations. This is not to suggest that smaller firms don't face their own ethical problems—it just seems that they are expected to carry an administrative burden that is equal to that of their much larger counterparts.

NOT VERY NEIGHBORLY

Sarbanes-Oxley applies to all companies that issue securities under U.S. federal securities statutes, whether headquartered within the United States or not. Thus, in addition to U.S.-based firms, approximately 1,300 foreign firms from 59 countries fall under the law's jurisdiction.

Reactions to SOX from this quarter were swift. Some foreign companies that had previously contemplated

ETHICAL ◄ DILEMMA ►

offering securities in the U.S. market reconsidered in light of the conflicts they believe SOX created. For example, in October 2002, Porsche AG announced it would not list its shares on the New York Stock Exchange. A company press release identified the passage of SOX as the "critical factor" for this decision and singled out CEO and CFO certification of financial statements for criticism. After recounting the process Porsche uses to prepare, review, and approve its financial reports, the release concluded that "any special treatment of the Chairman of the Board of Management [i.e., Porsche's CEO] and the Director of Finance would be illogical because of the intricate network within which the decision-making process exists; it would be irreconcilable with German law."

QUESTIONS

1. SOX has introduced sweeping changes in the name of enforcing corporate ethics. Is it really a "fair" piece of legislation? Explain your answer.
2. Do U.S. ethical problems give us the right to demand ethical controls from international companies based outside the United States?
3. Does the decision to increase auditing requirements seem to be an ethical solution to the problem of questionable audits? Explain your requirements.
4. If there were more than four large accounting firms in the marketplace, would that make the decision more ethical? Explain your answer.

Source: "A Price Worth Paying?" *The Economist,* May 19, 2005.

pieces of its global business) followed the company's descent into near bankruptcy after it invested extensively in complicated financial contracts used to underwrite mortgage-backed securities.

Intervening to rescue a venerable name in the finance industry could be justified on the basis of a need to restore stability at a time of extreme global instability, but when two senior executives for AIG—Chief Executive Martin J. Sullivan and Chairman Robert Willumstad—appeared before the House Oversight and Government Reform Committee, questions focused less on the company's recovery strategy and more on the lack of oversight and poor financial judgment that got them into the mess in the first place.

The decision to proceed with a celebratory sales meeting in California for the top sales agents of AIG's life insurance subsidiary, with a budget for the event of $440,000, only one week after the government came forward with the $85 billion bailout loan, drew particular criticism from members of the committee. In addition, Sullivan's positive comments, recorded in December 2007, reassuring investors of AIG's financial health only days after receiving warnings from company auditors about the company's exposure to these risky mortgage contracts drew severe criticism from the committee.

In November 2008, the Federal Reserve and the Treasury Department coordinated an even larger deal for AIG that raised the overall cost of the rescue to $152.5 billion, after the company petitioned that the sale of assets to repay the loan would take longer than originally anticipated. After announcing a $25 billion loss for the third quarter of 2008, AIG was able to negotiate a reduction in the original bailout loan from $85 billion to only $60 billion, along with a reduction in the interest rate on that loan. The additional $37.8 billion loan was replaced by an outright purchase of $40 billion of AIG stock as part of the Treasury's $700 billion bailout package—the so-called Troubled Asset Relief Program (TARP). In addition, the Federal Reserve purchased $22.5 billion of the company's mortgage-backed securities and added an additional $30 billion to underwrite the complicated financial contracts that had led to AIG's near collapse.

Lehman Brothers Holdings, an investment house that had historically been held in the same high regard as AIG, did not fare as well in this financial crisis. For reasons known only to the government, Lehman did not receive a bailout loan like AIG's and collapsed in summer 2008. When Chief Executive Richard S. Fuld Jr. appeared before the House Oversight and Government Reform Committee in

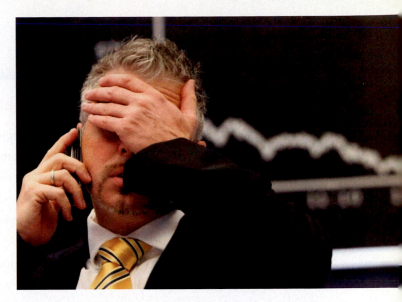

The financial crisis that began in fall 2008 had an impact that will likely affect markets for some time.

October 2008, questions focused on the same issue of reassurances of financial health in the face of audited reports indicating extreme risk exposures and, in particular, Fuld's highly lucrative compensation package with Lehman—a total of almost $500 million in salary and bonus payments over the last eight years of his employment with the company.

It is ironic and alarming that the enactment of the Sarbanes-Oxley Act, supposedly to prevent the recurrence of the type of corporate malfeasance that Enron and WorldCom came to exemplify, should be followed so quickly by evidence that the lessons from the days of Enron remained unlearned.

THE DODD-FRANK WALL STREET REFORM AND CONSUMER PROTECTION ACT

On July 21, 2010, the U.S. government's plan to ensure that the words "too big to fail" would never be applied to Wall Street again was delivered in the form of the **Dodd-Frank Wall Street Reform and Consumer Protection Act.**[5] Weighing in at an astounding 2,319 pages, Dodd-Frank survived an acrimonious journey through Congress in the face of Republican opposition and aggressive lobbying by Wall Street companies ("Big Finance"), which sought to weaken what was expected to be a tough response to a global financial crisis.

> **Dodd-Frank Wall Street Reform and Consumer Protection Act** Legislation that was promoted as the "fix" for the extreme mismanagement of risk in the financial sector that lead to a global financial crisis in 2008–2010.

Life Skills

Check List notepad with pencil

Life Skills logo

>> Governing your own ethical behavior

Does the fact that we appear to need government legislation to enforce ethical business practices both here and overseas suggest that we are unable to self-govern our individual ethical behavior? Can we be trusted to act in an ethical manner both in our personal and professional lives? Or do we need a regulatory framework and a clearly defined system of punishment to force people to act ethically or face the consequences?

As we discussed in Chapter 1, your personal value system represents the cumulative effect of a series of influences in your life—your upbringing, religious beliefs, community influences, and peer influences from your friends. As such, your ethical standards already represent a framework of influences that have made you the person you are today. However, where you take that value system in the future depends entirely on you. State and federal bodies may put punitive legislation in place to enforce an ideal model of personal and professional behavior, but whether or not you abide by that legislation comes down to the decisions you make on a daily basis. Can you stay true to your personal value system and live your life according to your own ethical standards? Or are you the type of person who is swayed by peer pressure and social norms to the point where you find yourself doing things you wouldn't normally do?

Developing a clear sense of your personal values is as much about knowing what you aren't willing to do as it is about knowing what you are willing to do. Understanding the difference allows you to remain grounded and focused while those around you sway in the wind in search of someone to help them make a decision. It's when that someone is not acting in his or her best interests that poor decisions are made and things can start to go wrong.

With midterm elections scheduled for November 2010, the expectation from critics was that the final version of the bill would be watered down with a series of compromises as politicians balanced their support for key provisions of the bill without risking any damage to their reelection hopes. A final verdict on the legislation may take a while, since many of the provisions have implementation deadlines of two years or more, but for now the primary achievements of Dodd-Frank can be summarized as follows.

The Consumer Financial Protection Bureau

Applauded as bringing a much-needed consumer focus to regulatory oversight of financial products and services, the creation of the **Consumer Financial Protection Bureau (CFPB)** generated considerable debate over the independence and power of the bureau—in other words, who would control it, and how much damage could it do. The final version placed the bureau within the Federal Reserve and assigned separate financing and an independent director to minimize the potential for aggressive lobbying practices by financial services companies.

The responsibilities granted to the bureau (at least, as they have been written in the legislation) are extensive and include authority to examine and enforce regulations for banks and credit unions with assets over $10 billion; the creation of a new Office of Financial Literacy; the creation of a national consumer complaint hotline; and, most confusingly, the consolidation of all consumer protection responsibilities currently handled by the Office of the Comptroller of the Currency, Office of Thrift Supervision, Federal Deposit Insurance Corporation (FDIC), Federal Reserve, National Credit Union Administration (NCUA), the

Consumer Financial Protection Bureau (CFPB) A government agency within the Federal Reserve that oversees financial products and services.

Department of Housing and Urban Development (HUD), and the Federal Trade Commission (FTC).

The Financial Stability Oversight Council
Promoted as the "fix" for "too big to fail," the **Financial Stability Oversight Council (FSOC)** is empowered to act if a bank with more than $50 billion in assets "poses a grave threat to the financial stability of the United States."[6] That action in response to the threat can include limiting the ability of the bank to merge with, acquire, or otherwise become affiliated with another company; restricting the ability to offer financial products or services; terminating one or more activities; imposing conditions on how the company conducts business; and selling or transferring assets to unaffiliated entities to mitigate any perceived risk.

The council will be lead by the Treasury secretary and made up of top financial regulators. With over 180 banks with assets above $50 billion, the FSOC can act on not only banks that are too big to fail but also banks that may be deemed to be "too interconnected" with other financial institutions to fail. The warning being given here, at least, is that the riskier the institution is determined to be, the more regulated it will become.

The Volcker Rule
American economist and past Federal Reserve Chairman Paul Volcker proposed that there should be a key restriction in the legislation to limit the ability of banks to trade on their own accounts (termed *proprietary trading*). The original *Volcker rule* sought to stop the trading of *derivatives* (which are financial instruments based on the performance of other financial instruments, such a mortgage-backed securities) completely, but was scaled back to a compromise that, it is hoped, will limit the ethically questionable practices of banks taking opposing positions to trades that they are simultaneously promoting to their clients.

With over 2,300 pages, the elements of the legislation go far beyond the three items listed above, but these three have been most actively promoted as

> **Financial Stability Oversight Council (FSOC)** A government agency established to prevent banks from failing and otherwise threatening the stability of the U.S. economy.

evidence of a strong response to extreme mismanagement of risk in the financial sector. However, the effectiveness of the legislation remains to be proved, and critics are concerned that there are still too many unknowns for the Dodd-Frank Act to be acknowledged as a success. For example, the "people's champion" in the CFPB can still be overruled by the FSOC if the council determines that any proposed rule change will threaten the soundness or stability of the financial system.[7] In addition, promises to simplify confusing mortgage disclosure forms (which many foreclosed homeowners blamed as contributing to their lack of understanding of the true nature of their adjustable mortgages) won't be met until 2012 at the earliest.[8]

>> Conclusion

With the ink barely dry on yet another piece of legislation seeking to enforce ethical business conduct, students of business ethics can be forgiven for wondering if corporations can ever be counted on to "do the right thing." Indeed, cynics would argue that the first order of business for the financial institutions directly affected by Dodd-Frank was to assign teams to figure out ways around the new rules and restrictions. However, if, as we discussed in Chapter 5, the internal governance mechanisms of corporations can't always be counted on to prevent unethical behavior, what other options are there to protect consumers?

In the especially complex world of financial services, where individual investors trust their hard-earned savings to mutual fund managers in the hope of providing enough for a secure and comfortable retirement, any evidence of mismanagement of those savings can result in a loss of trust that may prove very difficult to regain.

In the next chapter we consider the actions of employees on the inside of corporations who experience corporate malfeasance directly and find themselves face to face with the ethical dilemma of speaking out or looking the other way.

FRONTLINE FOCUS
Too Much Trouble—Lara Makes a Decision

Lara was beginning to realize that the Sarbanes-Oxley Act was a mixed blessing. Greater scrutiny of corporate financial reports was meant to reassure investors, and it was certainly bringing her firm plenty of business, but now she was faced with this "small favor" to her boss. On the face of it, she couldn't really understand why they just didn't tell this guy that they only worked with clients worth a dollar figure that was higher than his company's valuation and be done with it, but Bartell was so paranoid about their reputation, and he was convinced that the next big client was always just around the corner.

Lara spent a couple of hours reviewing the file. Bartell's assessment had been accurate—this was a simple audit with no real earning potential for the company. If they weren't so busy, they could probably assign a junior team—her team perhaps—and knock this out in a few days, but Bartell had bigger fish to fry.

Lara thought for a moment about asking Bartell to let her put a small team together to do this one, but then she realized that by not delivering on the small favor he had asked, she could be ruining her chances for getting assigned to some of the bigger audits down the road. So she ran the numbers, multiplied them by 4, and submitted the price quotation.

Unfortunately, the quotation was so outrageous that the small business client complained to the PCAOB, which promptly wrote a letter demanding a full explanation of Lara's company's pricing schedule.

QUESTIONS

1. What could Lara have done differently here?
2. What do you think will happen now?
3. What will be the consequences for Lara, Greg Bartell, and their auditing firm?

[For Review]

1. **Identify the five key pieces of U.S. legislation designed to discourage, if not prevent, illegal conduct within organizations.**
   - *The Foreign Corrupt Practices Act (1977):* The act was passed to more effectively control bribery payments to foreign officials and politicians by American publicly traded companies.
   - *The U.S. Federal Sentencing Guidelines for Organizations (1991):* FSGO applies to organizations and holds them liable for the criminal acts of their employees and agents.
   - *The Sarbanes-Oxley Act (2002):* SOX was a legislative response to a series of corporate accounting scandals that had begun to dominate the financial markets in 2001.
   - *The Revised Federal Sentencing Guidelines for Organizations (2004):* The revision modified the 1991 guidelines by requiring periodic evaluation of the effectiveness of corporate compliance programs and evidence of active promotion of ethical conduct rather than passive compliance.
   - *The Dodd-Frank Wall Street Reform and Consumer Protection Act (2010):* The act introduced a complex list of new rules and restrictions designed to provide greater regulatory oversight of the financial sector, along with improved protection for consumers.

2. **Understand the purpose and significance of the Foreign Corrupt Practices Act (FCPA).**

   The FCPA represented an attempt to send a clear message that the competitiveness of U.S. corporations in overseas markets should be based on price and product quality rather than the extent to which companies had paid off foreign officials and political leaders. However, the legislation was criticized for lacking any real "teeth" because of its formal recognition of "facilitation payments" for "routine governmental action" such as the provision of permits, licenses, or visas. Critics argued that since the payment of bribes was typically designed to expedite the paperwork on most projects, the recognition of these facilitation payments did nothing more than legalize the payment of bribes.

3. **Calculate monetary fines under the three-step process of the U.S. Federal Sentencing Guidelines for Organizations (FSGO).**
   - Step 1: Calculate the "base fine" based on the greatest of the monetary gain to the organization from the offense, the monetary loss from the offense caused by the organization, or an amount determined by the judge.
   - Step 2: Compute a corresponding degree of blame or guilt known as the "culpability score" that can be increased (or aggravated) or decreased (or mitigated) according to predetermined factors.
   - Step 3: Multiply the base fine by the culpability score to arrive at the total fine amount. In certain cases the judge has the discretion to impose a so-called death penalty, where the fine is set high enough to match all the organization's assets.

4. **Compare and contrast the relative advantages and disadvantages of the Sarbanes-Oxley Act (SOX).**

   The aim of SOX was to improve the accountability of managers to shareholders and to calm the raging crisis of confidence in American capitalism aroused by scandals at Enron, WorldCom, and other companies. The establishment of the PCAOB and the specific changes to auditor independence and corporate responsibility certainly helped achieve that aim. However, critics argue that the rush to restore confidence produced legislation that was too heavy-handed in its application. Smaller companies were directly affected by the additional auditing costs, even though the unethical behavior that SOX was designed to address had occurred in publicly traded companies. In addition, the legislation applied to all companies issuing securities under U.S. federal securities statutes (whether headquartered in the United States or not), which brought 1,300 foreign firms from 59 countries under the law's jurisdiction.

5. **Explain the key provisions of the Dodd-Frank Wall Street Reform and Consumer Protection Act.**

Passed into law in July 2010, Dodd-Frank was promoted as the "fix" for the extreme mismanagement of risk in the financial sector that lead to a global financial crisis in 2008–2010. At over 2,300 pages, the legislation presented a complex list of new rules and restrictions designed to provide greater regulatory oversight of the financial sector, along with improved protection for consumers. The three most actively promoted elements of Dodd-Frank were:

- *The Consumer Financial Protection Bureau (CFPB):* Designed as an independently run entity in the Federal Reserve, the CFPB promises to act upon any perceived misconduct by financial institutions in the treatment of their customers.

- *The Financial Stability Oversight Council (FSOC):* Led by the Treasury secretary and a team of senior financial regulators, the FSOC is empowered to regulate any bank with assets over $50 billion if it determines that the business practices of the bank pose "a grave threat to the financial stability of the United States." As the promised fix for "too big to fail," the FSOC has the power to intervene in any aspect of the bank's management up to and including the termination of business practices.

- *The Volcker Rule:* Proposed by former Federal Reserve Chairman Paul Volcker, this rule limits the ability of banks to trade on their own accounts (i.e., invest their own money) in any way that might threaten the financial stability of the institution (and, by definition, the financial markets as a whole).

[Key Terms]

Culpability Score (FSGO) **113**

Death Penalty (FSGO) **113**

Disclosure (FCPA) **110**

Dodd-Frank Wall Street Reform and Consumer Protection Act **119**

Facilitation Payments (FCPA) **110**

Federal Sentencing Guidelines for Organizations (FSGO) **112**

Foreign Corrupt Practices Act (FCPA) **110**

Prohibition (FCPA) **110**

Public Company Accounting Oversight Board (PCAOB) **116**

Routine Governmental Action (FCPA) **110**

Sarbanes-Oxley Act (SOX) **115**

[Review Questions]

1. Which is the most effective piece of legislation for enforcing ethical business practices: FCPA, FSGO, SOX, or Dodd-Frank? Explain your answer.

2. "The FCPA has too many exceptions to be an effective deterrent to unethical business practices." Do you agree or disagree with this statement? Explain your answer.

3. What issues prompted the revision of the Federal Sentencing Guidelines for Organizations in 2004?

4. Do you think the requirement that CEOs and CFOs sign off on their company accounts will increase investor confidence in those accounts? Why or why not?

5. Why may the Sarbanes-Oxley Act of 2002 be regarded as one of the most controversial pieces of corporate legislation in recent history?

6. Based on the information in this chapter, can the Dodd-Frank Act of 2010 prevent "too big to fail"? Explain your answer.

Review Exercise

Universal Industries. Universal Industries is in desperate need of a large contract to boost its declining U.S. revenues. The company doesn't have a lot of international exposure, despite its ambitious name, but its chief operating officer (COO) may be about to change that. By coincidence, at a recent class reunion, he ran into an old classmate who was a high-ranking federal official responsible for a lot of the bidding for large defense contracts. After several rounds of drinks, the classmate began talking about his latest projects.

Universal has done a lot of defense work as a subcontractor for the major players in the industry, and the COO was able to leverage that experience to use his insider information to get Universal added to the list for several requests for proposal (RFPs) on a large expansion of a Middle Eastern military base.

To strengthen its position in the bidding process, several key Universal operatives made unpublicized visits to the towns surrounding the base and, in return for gifts of cash and other favors to local businesspeople and politicians, managed to tie up the exclusive services of several local contractors, making it almost impossible for the other contenders to meet the requirements of the RFPs. The COO was equally generous in his gift to the daughter of his classmate in recognition of his help in getting the inside information.

Unfortunately, even though the new military contracts were going to provide more than enough money to boost Universal's performance numbers, they weren't going to go into effect until the following quarter. After a behind-closed-doors discussion, the senior management team decided that Universal would adjust some of its fourth quarter expenses in order to hit the price target that the analysts were expecting. The team fully expected that the revenue from the military contracts would allow them to make up for the adjustments in the next financial year.

However, since Universal's annual revenue exceeded $1.4 billion, the CEO and CFO were required to put their signatures on the financial reports confirming their authenticity.

After a couple of sleepless nights, and confident that the military contracts would help them fix all this in the end, they both signed.

1. Identify the ethical transgressions in this case.

2. Which piece of legislation would apply to each transgression?

3. What would be the penalties for each transgression?

4. If Universal could prove that it had a compliance program in place, how would that affect the penalties?

Internet Exercises

1. Locate the Web site for Berlin-based Transparency International (TI).

   a. What is the stated mission of TI?

   b. Explain the Corruptions Perception Index.

   c. Which are the least and most corrupt countries on the index?

   d. Explain the Global Corruption Barometer.

2. Using Internet research, review the involvement of Harvard law professor Elizabeth Warren in the Consumer Financial Protection Bureau (CFPB).

   a. What was Warren's involvement in the government response to the collapse of the financial markets?

   b. How is she connected to the CFPB?

   c. What were the objections to her involvement with the CFPB?

   d. What is Warren's declared agenda for the CFPB?

[Team Exercises]

1. **Protecting your people at all costs.**

   Your company is a major fruit processor that maintains long-term contracts with plantation owners in Central America to guarantee supplies of high-quality produce. Many of those plantations are in politically unstable areas and your U.S.-based teams travel to those regions at high personal risk. You have been contacted by a representative from one of the local groups of freedom fighters demanding that you make a "donation" to their cause in return for the guaranteed protection of the plantations with which you do business. The representative makes it very clear that failure to pay the donation could put your team on the ground at risk of being kidnapped and held for ransom. Your company is proud of its compliance with all aspects of the FCPA and the revised FSGO legislation. Divide into two groups, and argue your case *for* and *against* paying this donation.

2. **Budgeting for bribes.**

   You are a midlevel manager for the government of a small African nation that relies heavily on oil revenues to run the country's budget. The recent increase in the price of oil has improved your country's budget significantly, and, as a result, many new infrastructure projects are being funded with those oil dollars— roads, bridges, schools, and hospitals—which are generating lots of construction projects and very lucrative orders for materials and equipment. However, very little of this new wealth has made its way down to the lower levels of your administration. Historically, your government has always budgeted for very low salaries for government workers in recognition of the fact that their paychecks are often supplemented by payments to expedite the processing of applications and licensing paperwork. Your boss feels strongly that there is no need to raise the salaries of the lower-level government workers since the increase in infrastructure contracts will bring a corresponding increase in payments to those workers and, as he pointed out, "companies that want our business will be happy to make those payments." Divide into two groups, and argue *for* and *against* the continuation of this arrangement.

3. **The pros and cons of SOX.**

   Divide into two teams. One team must defend the introduction of Sarbanes-Oxley as a federal deterrent to corporate malfeasance. The other team must criticize the legislation as being ineffective and an administrative burden.

4. **The key components of SOX.**

   Divide into groups of three or four. Distribute the 11 sections of SOX reviewed in this chapter. Each group must prepare a brief presentation outlining the relative importance of its section to the overall impact of SOX and the prohibition of unethical business practices.

Thinking Critically

>> PONZI SCHEMES

The practice of providing old (or early) investors above-average returns on their investment with funds raised from new (or late) investors in the absence of any real business operation to generate profits is illegal, unethical, and, regrettably, not a new idea. It used to be referred to as "robbing Peter to pay Paul." In 1899, a New York scam artist named William Miller promised investors returns as high as 520 percent in one year based on his supposed insider information on profitable businesses. He scammed people out of almost $25 million in today's money before being exposed and jailed for 10 years.

In 1920 the practice was given a new name—Ponzi scheme—in "honor" of Charles Ponzi, an Italian immigrant who, after numerous failed business ventures, began to promote the spectacular returns to be made by buying international reply coupons (IRC)—coupons that could be used to purchase stamps in order to reply to a letter, like an international self-addressed envelope—in local currencies, and cashing them in at U.S. currency rates. For example, "a person could buy 66 International Reply Coupons in Rome for the equivalent of $1. Those same 66 coupons would cost $3.30 in Boston," where Ponzi was based. It is debatable whether or not Ponzi genuinely believed that he had stumbled across a real business opportunity—a simplified version of currency trading in a way—but his response was immediate, promising investors returns of 50 percent on their original investment in just 90 days. However, the opportunity attracted so much money so quickly—as much as $1 million poured into his office in one day—that Ponzi was either unable or unwilling to actually buy the IRCs. Had he tried to do so, he would have realized that there were not enough IRCs in existence to deliver the kinds of returns he was promising his investors. Instead, Ponzi chose to use the funds coming in from new investors to pay out the promised returns to older investors—robbing Peter to pay Paul.

It was only a matter of time before the funds coming in would be insufficient to meet the demands of older investors with their original capital and their 50 percent return. Ponzi was able to keep the scheme going by encouraging those older investors to keep "rolling over" their investment, but once rumors began to surface about the questionable nature of the Ponzi enterprise, fewer and fewer people opted to roll over, choosing instead to take their money out. At that point the whole system collapsed, and Ponzi's business enterprise was exposed as fraudulent. For his brief encounter with fame and fortune, Charles Ponzi eventually served 12 years in prison, and was deported back to Italy. He later emigrated to Brazil, still presumably in search of fame and fortune. He died in 1949 in the charity ward of a Rio de Janeiro hospital with only enough money to his name to cover his burial expenses. His name, however, lives on—the practice of robbing Peter to pay Paul was forever replaced with the name *Ponzi scheme.*

In subsequent decades, Ponzi has inspired many imitators:

- In the 1990s, a Florida church—Greater Ministries International—scammed nearly 20,000 people out of $500 million on the basis of a promise that God would double the money of truly pious investors.
- Lou Pearlman, the theatrical impresario and businessman who launched the screams of thousands of teenage girls with the boy band 'N Sync, stole over $300 million from investors over two decades.
- In January 2009, the Securities and Exchange Commission charged an 82-year-old man, Richard Piccoli, with operating a Ponzi scheme that scammed investors out of $17 million over five years by promising "safe" returns of only 7 percent based on real estate investments that were never made.
- In July 2010, Fort Lauderdale lawyer Scott Rothstein sold stakes in large fictitious legal settlements, scamming investors out of $1.2 billion, and causing considerable embarrassment to Florida Republican politicians who were recipients of large donations from Rothstein's newfound wealth.
- In April 2010, former Minnesota business tycoon Tom Petters was sentenced to 50 years in prison for orchestrating a $3.7 billion scheme to convince investors that they were buying large shipments of electronics that would then be sold to big-box retailers such as Costco and Sam's Club. Victims included retirees, church groups, and Wall Street hedge funds.

In December 2008, a formerly highly respected Wall Street money manager, Bernard Madoff, was accused of masterminding a Ponzi scheme on such a grand scale that the practice may well be replaced with the name "Madoff scheme" from this point onward. The amount of money involved in Madoff's alleged scam is staggering—an estimated total of $65 billion stolen over decades.

As a traditionally low-profile investment professional, former chairman of the NASDAQ stock exchange, and an occasional consultant to the Securities and Exchange Commission on matters of investment regulation, Madoff became a multimillionaire in the early days of computer-based stock trading before he became attracted to the more lucrative business of managing other people's money. He built a reputation of sure and steady returns for his clients, earning the affectionate nickname "T-Bill Bernie" to reflect the same security as investing in government-backed Treasury bills. Madoff's success wasn't based on spectacular returns from year to year (he averaged between 10 and 18 percent per year), but rather on consistent solid performance year after year. He didn't market his services aggressively, preferring instead to allow satisfied clients to bring in family members and friends. He generated an aura of exclusivity, often declining to accept investments, which only served to make those potential investors want to invest with him even more.

This perceived exclusivity and a strategic marketing plan that targeted wealthy investors in places like Palm Beach, Florida, allowed Madoff to build a solid reputation over decades, attracting high-profile investors and large investments from global banks in the hundreds of millions of dollars along the way. However, the financial meltdown at the end of 2008 prompted investors to start withdrawing their funds to meet other obligations, and when Madoff was faced with withdrawal requests totaling almost $7 billion, the carefully constructed scam fell apart in a matter of hours.

In the early emotional days of this exposed and still alleged scandal, one of the primary concerns is the appointment of blame. Who knew what, when, and could this have been prevented? The SEC has come under considerable scrutiny for its role in this. Madoff's operation was examined on four separate occasions since 1999, with two detailed investigations launched in 1992 and 2006. No evidence of fraud was uncovered, and Madoff received only a mild reprimand for irregularities in paperwork. Now that $65 billion appears to have disappeared, with no trading records available to track the money, there are many questions to be answered. What is known for sure is that Madoff was sentenced to 150 years in jail (the maximum sentence allowed) in June 2009. Given Madoff's age of 71, the district judge for the case, Denny Chin, acknowledged that the sentence was designed to be symbolic and to reflect the severity of the crime and the damage done to so many individual investors.

Boston-based money manager Harry Markopoulos had written an 18-page letter to the SEC in 2005 identifying 29 different red flags about Madoff's operation, basically questioning the mathematical improbability of such solid returns year after year and suggesting that the only way to achieve those returns was to either trade on insider information or create a totally fictitious trading record.

Supposedly "sophisticated" investors, who gave Madoff large sums to invest from pension funds, family trusts, and endowments, have been wiped out. Even worse, many individual investors, who entrusted their savings to other money managers who then invested that money with Madoff, have also lost substantial amounts in an investment they never even knew they had.

Much will be written about Madoff's psychological state of mind in allegedly masterminding such a complex scam over decades and, more importantly, fooling so many of the elite of Wall Street and the regulatory mechanisms that are supposed to be in place to prevent such a scam from ever happening. It remains to be seen whether this information will produce any dramatic changes in the regulatory framework of the financial markets to ensure that a Ponzi scheme on such a staggering scale never occurs again.

QUESTIONS

1. Charles Ponzi was a working-class Italian immigrant who was eager to find success in America. Bernard Madoff was already a multimillionaire before he started his scheme. Does that make one more unethical than the other? Why or why not?

2. Explain how a Ponzi scheme works.

3. Does the SEC bear any responsibility in the extent of the Madoff scheme? In what way?

4. Does the fact that Madoff offered less outrageous returns (10–18 percent per year) on investments compared to Ponzi's promise of a 50 percent return in only 90 days make Madoff any less unethical? Why or why not?

5. Can the investors who put their money in Madoff's funds without any due diligence, often on the basis of a tip from a friend or a "friend of a friend," really be considered victims in this case? Why or why not?

6. What should investors with Bernard Madoff have done differently here?

Sources: A. Altman, "Ponzi Schemes," *Time.com,* December 15, 2008; J. Gapper, "Wall Street Insiders and Fools' Gold," *Financial Times*, December 17, 2008; A. Sloan, "Commentary: The Real Lesson of the Madoff Case," CNN.com, January 9, 2009; M. Zuckoff, "What Madoff Could Learn from Ponzi," CNN.money.com, January 13, 2009; and R. Chew, "Bernie Madoff's Victims: Why Some Have No Recourse," Time.com, January 12, 2009.

>> INDIA'S ENRON

In December 2008, one of the largest players in India's out-sourcing and information technology sectors, Satyam Computer Services, fell from grace with such force and speed that the reverberations were felt around the globe. Ironically, the name *Satyam* means "truth" in Sanskrit, but the company, founded by brothers Ramalinga and Ramu Raju, now has a new nickname: India's Enron.

Founded in 1987, Satyam was positioned to take full advantage of the capabilities of satellite-based broadband communications, allowing it to serve clients across the globe from its offices in Hyderabad. The rising demand for computer programmers to fix code in software programs in advance of Y2K (the year 2000 problem) fueled an aggressive growth plan for the company. It was listed on the Bombay Stock Exchange in 1991, and achieved a listing on the New York Stock Exchange in May 2001. By 2006, Satyam had about 23,000 employees and was reporting annual revenues of $1 billion.

Growth continued as the company served expanding needs for outsourced services from U.S. companies looking to control and preferably reduce operating costs. By 2008, Satyam was reporting over $2 billion in revenue with 53,000 employees in 63 countries worldwide. This made the company the fourth-largest software services provider alongside such competitors as WiPro Technologies, Infosys, and HCL. It was serving almost 700 clients, including 185 Fortune 500 companies, generating more than half of its revenue from the United States. Satyam's client roster included such names as General Electric, Cisco, Ford Motor Company, Nestlé, and the U.S. government.

Prominence in the software services sector brought with it increased attention and a growing reputation. In 2007, Ramalinga Raju was the recipient of Ernst & Young's Entrepreneur of the Year award. In September 2008 the company received the Golden Peacock Award for Corporate Governance from the World Council for Corporate Governance, which endorsed Satyam as a leader in ethical management practices.

Signs that there were problems at Satyam first appeared in October 2008 when it was revealed that the World Bank had banned the company from pursuing any service contracts after evidence was uncovered that Satyam employees had offered "improper benefits to bank staff" and "failed to account for all fees charged" to the World Bank. WiPro Technologies had also been banned by the World Bank in 2007 for "offering shares of its 2000 initial public offering to World Bank employees," so Satyam appeared to have some company in the arena of questionable business practices in the software solutions sector.

However, the situation escalated in December 2008 after Satyam's board voted against a proposed deal for Satyam to buy two construction companies for $1.6 billion. The Raju brothers held ownership stakes in both companies, and they were run by Ramalinga Raju's sons. Four directors resigned in response to the proposed deal, and Satyam stock was punished by investors, forcing the brothers to sell their own stock as the falling share price sparked margin calls on their investment accounts. The dire financial situation prompted Ramalinga Raju to confess in a four-and-a-half-page letter to the board of Satyam Computer Services that the company had been overstating profits for several years and that $1.6 billion in assets simply did not exist. It did not take long for investors to piece the information together that the proposed $1.6 billion purchase of the construction companies would have, conveniently, filled the $1.6 billion hole in Satyam's accounts.

In his confession, Raju attempted to address accusations of a premeditated fraud by stating: "What started as a marginal gap between actual operating profit and the one reflected in the books of accounts continued to grow over the years. It has attained unmanageable proportions as the size of the company operations grew." He wrote, "It was like riding a tiger, not knowing how to get off without being eaten."

The analogy of being eaten by a tiger certainly seems appropriate. The scandal has had repercussions for the software services sector as a whole, casting shadows on Satyam's competitors and also on India's corporate governance framework. As with Enron's collapse, attention immediately turned to the role of the accounting company responsible for auditing Satyam's accounts and, allegedly, failing to notice that $1.6 billion in assets did not exist. For Enron it was Arthur Andersen, and the accounting firm did not survive. For Satyam it was PricewaterhouseCoopers, which had certified that Satyam had $1.1 billion in cash in its accounts, when the company really had only $78 million.

The response of Indian authorities was immediate—jail for the founders of Satyam, and the swift appointment of an interim board of more reputable businessmen as the country scrambled to restore its reputation and reassure investors and customers alike that Satyam was a regrettable exception rather than a common example of unethical business practices in the face of competitive pressures in a global market.

In January 2009, the Securities and Exchange Board of India made it mandatory for the controlling shareholders of companies to disclose when they were pledging shares as collateral to lenders—a direct response to the Satyam scandal. In April 2009, Tech Mahindra, the technology arm of Indian conglomerate Mahindra group, won an auction to buy the operations of Satyam at a price of less than one-third of the company's stock value before the confession of Ramalinga Raju. The justification for the bargain price lay in the loss of 46 customers, including Nissan, Sony, the United Nations, and State Farm Insurance, in the aftermath of the scandal. Analysts commented in response to the sale that the situation could have been much worse for Satyam were it not for the timing of the global recession. With so many other priorities to address, many customers elected to avoid the headaches of switching IT suppliers (with all the software and hardware changes that might entail) and give Satyam the opportunity to figure things out. It remains to be seen whether the extensive financial resources of Tech Mahindra and its parent company will be sufficient to allow Satyam to restore its tarnished reputation.

QUESTIONS

1. Does Ramalinga Raju's assertion that this fraud only "started as a marginal gap" change the ethical question here? Would the situation be different if there was evidence that there had been a deliberate intent to deceive investors from the beginning?

2. Why do you think Satyam's board of directors refused to support the proposed purchase of the construction companies?

3. Outline the similarities between the Enron scandal and Satyam Computer Services' situation.

4. PricewaterhouseCoopers (PWC) made a public commitment to cooperate with investigators. Did the Satyam situation represent the same threat for PWC as Enron did for Arthur Andersen? Why or why not?

5. Will the response of the Securities and Exchange Board of India be enough to prevent another scandal like Satyam? Explain.

6. What challenges will the new owners of Satyam be facing? Explain.

Sources: H. Timmons, "Financial Scandal at Outsourcing Company Rattles a Developing Country," *The New York Times*, January 8, 2009; E. Corcoran, "The Seeds of the Satyam Scandal," *Forbes*, January 8, 2009; S. V. Balachandran, "The Satyam Scandal," *Forbes*, January 7, 2009; J. Kahn, H. Timmons, and B. Wassener, "Board Tries to Chart Path for Outsourcer Hit by Scandal," *The New York Times*, January 13, 2009; and "Salvaging the Truth," *The Economist*, April 16, 2009.

Thinking Critically

>> MARTHA STEWART AND IMCLONE SYSTEMS

At the end of December 2001, design guru Martha Stewart, chief executive of Martha Stewart Living Omnimedia, reportedly sold 3,928 shares of stock in a drug company called ImClone Systems. The 3,928 shares represented her entire holding in ImClone, and the sale fetched over $227,000 for Stewart, based on an average selling price of around $58 per share—not a large transaction by Wall Street standards. In fact, such an average sale, out of the millions of transactions that took place that day, should not have drawn any undue attention, until it was revealed that Stewart had a long-standing relationship with the chief executive of ImClone Systems, Dr. Sam Waksal, and that within a day or two of her sale, the Food and Drug Administration (FDA) would announce an unfavorable ruling on ImClone's new cancer drug, Erbitux, which sent the stock plummeting from a high of $75 per share to an eventual low of only $5.24 per share in September 2002.

Further investigation revealed that members of Waksal's immediate family also sold blocks of shares in the two days preceding the FDA announcement. One of his daughters sold a block of shares worth $2.5 million, and his other daughter, along with her husband, sold shares worth $300,000. Waksal was unable to complete the sale of almost 80,000 of his own shares in the company. The fact that Waksal had dated Stewart's daughter for years added a further complication to what was rapidly becoming a very questionable business arrangement.

The Erbitux drug was believed to hold tremendous potential as a cancer treatment—so much so that Bristol-Myers Squibb had agreed to pay $2 billion in 2001 for the rights to the drug, prompting the increase in the share price to $70. The subsequent collapse in the share price also affected shares in Stewart's own company: After Waksal was arrested on accusations of insider trading in his own company's shares, the shares of Martha Stewart Living Omnimedia fell by 12 percent.

At the time of Waksal's arrest, Stewart, who had yet to be accused of any wrongdoing, offered a defense to the media that she had an arm's-length relationship to the sale of the stock—in other words she had an existing order with her broker to sell the stock if it went below $60 per share, and so this transaction was automatic rather than an event prompted by insider information from her friend Sam Waksal. However, further investigation revealed that even though the stock price had fallen below $60 on other occasions in the months preceding the sale, there was no automatic sale of the shares as Stewart had claimed. In addition, it was revealed that Stewart had placed a call to her broker, Peter Bacanovic, during a refueling stop on a flight to Mexico on her private jet. She made a call to Waksal during that same stop, and, by coincidence, Bacanovic was also the broker for Waksal and his two daughters. He was subsequently suspended by Merrill Lynch.

After numerous attempts by her legal team to fight on her behalf, Stewart was required to deliver more than 1,000 pages of documents—including e-mail messages from her laptop and phone records—to the congressional committee investigating the sale of her ImClone stock in August 2002. She was eventually indicted, not for the sale of the stock based on insider trading, but for obstruction of justice for lying to federal regulators under oath about the details surrounding the transaction. She served a five-month prison sentence and an additional five months under house arrest. Bacanovic also served a five-month sentence for crimes related to the sale of the stock on behalf of Stewart and members of the Waksal family; he was banned from the securities industry and paid a $75,000 fine to the Securities and Exchange Commission to settle insider-trading charges. Waksal himself received an 87-month prison sentence, and he settled the SEC insider trading case against him and his father for more than $5 million.

Ironically, Erbitux proved to be more persistent than many had imagined. After being rejected by the FDA in 2001 on the basis of "shoddy data from ImClone," the drug received formal approval in February 2004. The impact on ImClone's share price was immediate, and by July 2008, more than six years after the now infamous sale of Stewart's shares, the price of ImClone was once again back above $60 per share. The original transaction saved Stewart about $45,000 in losses by selling before the FDA rejection was announced. In retrospect, the cost to her company, her investors, and, some would argue, to her reputation was much higher.

QUESTIONS

1. Identify the ethical transgressions that took place in this case.

2. When the connection between ImClone Systems and Martha Stewart was first revealed, analysts speculated that she would emerge relatively unscathed from any investigation, "forced at worst to return any profit she made from selling ImClone." Does her subsequent jail sentence imply that she was targeted as a high-profile test case of insider trading? Why or why not?

3. Does the size of Stewart's transaction (3,928 shares for about $227,000) make her behavior any more or less ethical than that of Waksal's daughter who sold $2.5 million in ImClone shares at the same time as Stewart? Explain your answer.

4. What would prompt a highly regarded public figure such as Martha Stewart to obstruct the course of justice by failing to reveal the true nature of her sales transaction with the ImClone stock?

5. What do you think would have happened if Stewart had cooperated with federal investigators?

6. If Martha Stewart's sale of ImClone stock really was a high-profile test case, what message do you think it sent to other high-profile investors?

Sources: Andrew Pollack, "Martha Stewart Said to Sell Shares before FDA Ruling," *The New York Times,* June 7, 2002; Constance L. Hays, "ImClone Case Drags Martha Stewart Shares Down," *The New York Times,* June 13, 2002; Andrew Pollack, "ImClone Cancer Drug behind Martha Stewart Trial Approved by FDA," *The New York Times,* February 13, 2004; Jenny Anderson, "Two Are Charged over Trading in ImClone," *The New York Times,* March 10, 2005; and Landon Thomas Jr., "The Broker Who Fell to Earth," *The New York Times,* October 13, 2006.

CHAPTER 7

BLOWING THE WHISTLE

After studying this chapter, you should be able to:

1. Explain the term *whistle-blower,* and distinguish between internal and external whistle-blowing.
2. Understand the different motivations of a whistle-blower.
3. Evaluate the possible consequences of ignoring the concerns of a whistle-blower.
4. Recommend how to build internal policies to address the needs of whistle-blowers.
5. Analyze the possible risks involved in becoming a whistle-blower.

FRONTLINE FOCUS
Good Money

Ben is a sales team leader at a large chain of tire stores. The company is aggressive and is opening new stores every month. Ben is very ambitious and sees plenty of opportunities to move up in the organization—especially if he is able to make a name for himself as a star salesman.

As with any retail organization, Ben's company is driven by sales, and it is constantly experimenting with new sales campaigns and incentive programs for its salespeople. Ben didn't expect this morning's sales meeting to be any different—a new incentive tied to a new campaign, supported by a big media campaign in the local area.

Ben's boss, John, didn't waste any time in getting to the point of the meeting:

"OK guys, I have some big news. Rather than simply negotiating short-term incentives on specific brands to generate sales, the company has signed an exclusive contract with Benfield Tires to take every tire produced in the new Voyager line. That exclusive contract comes with a huge discount based on serious volume. In other words, the more tires we sell, the more money we'll make—and I'm talking about good money for the company and very good bonus money for you—so put everybody into these tires. If we do well in this first contract with Benfield, there could be other exclusives down the road. This could be the beginning of something big for us."

John then laid out the details on the sales incentive and showed Ben and his fellow team leaders how they could earn thousands of dollars in bonuses over the next couple of months if they pushed the new Benfield Voyagers.

Ben could certainly use the money, but he was concerned about pushing a new tire model so aggressively when it was an unknown in the marketplace. He decided to talk to their most experienced tire mechanic, Rick. Rick had worked for the company for over 25 years—so long that many of the younger guys joked that he either had tire rubber in his veins or had apprenticed on Henry Ford's Model T.

"So, Rick, what do you think about these new Benfield Voyagers?" asked Ben. "Are they really such a good deal for our customers, or are they just a moneymaker for us?"

Rick was very direct in his response: "I took a look at some of the specs on them, and they don't look good. I think Benfield is sacrificing quality to cut costs. By the standards of some of our other suppliers, these tires would qualify as 'seconds'—and pretty bad ones too. You couldn't pay me to put them on my car—they're good for 15,000 miles at the most. We're taking a big risk promoting these tires as our top model."

QUESTIONS

1. If Ben decides to raise concerns about the product quality of the Benfield Voyagers, he will become a whistle-blower. The difference between internal and external whistle-blowing is explained on page **134**. Which approach should Ben follow if he does decide to raise his concerns?
2. The five conditions that must exist for whistle-blowing to be ethical are outlined on page **134**. Has Rick given Ben enough information to be concerned about the Benfield Voyagers?
3. What should Ben do now?

> The word *whistle-blower* suggests that you're a tattletale or that you're somehow disloyal. . . . But I wasn't disloyal in the least bit. People were dying. I was loyal to a higher order of ethical responsibility.

Dr. Jeffrey Wigand, *The Insider*

>> What Is Whistle-Blowing?

When an employee discovers evidence of malpractice or misconduct in an organization, he or she faces an ethical dilemma. On the one hand, the employee must consider the "rightness" of his or her actions in raising concerns about this misconduct and the extent to which such actions will benefit both the organization and the public good. On the other hand, the employee must balance a public duty with a corresponding duty to his or her employer to honor the trust and loyalty placed in him or her by the organization.

So some serious choices have to be made here. First, the employee can choose to "let it slide" or "turn a blind eye"—a choice that will relate directly to the corporate culture under which the organization operates. An open and trusting culture would encourage employees to speak out for the greater good of the company and fellow employees. A closed and autocratic culture, on the other hand, would lead employees to believe that it would be wiser not to draw attention to themselves, to simply keep their mouths shut. However, if an employee's personal value system prompts him or her to speak out on the misconduct, the employee immediately takes on the role of a **whistle-blower.**

Whistle-Blower An employee who discovers corporate misconduct and chooses to bring it to the attention of others.

Internal Whistle-Blowing An employee discovering corporate misconduct and bringing it to the attention of his or her supervisor, who then follows established procedures to address the misconduct within the organization.

External Whistle-Blowing An employee discovering corporate misconduct and choosing to bring it to the attention of law enforcement agencies and/or the media.

The employee then faces a second and equally important choice. One option is to bring the misconduct to the attention of a manager or supervisor and take the complaint through appropriate channels within the organization. We refer to this option as **internal whistle-blowing.** If the employee chooses to go outside the organization and bring the misconduct to the attention of law enforcement officials or the media, we refer to this decision as **external whistle-blowing.**

PROGRESS ✓ QUESTIONS

1. What is a whistle-blower?
2. What is internal whistle-blowing?
3. What is external whistle-blowing?
4. Is whistle-blowing a good thing?

>> The Ethics of Whistle-Blowing

It may be argued that whistle-blowers provide an invaluable service to their organizations and the general public. The discovery of illegal activities before the situation is revealed in the media could potentially save organizations millions of dollars in fines and lost revenue from the inevitable damage to their corporate reputations. The discovery of potential harm to consumers (from pollution or product-safety issues, for example) offers immeasurable benefit to the general public. From this perspective, it is easy to see why the media often applaud whistle-blowers as models of honor and integrity at a time when integrity in the business world seems to be in very short supply.

However, in contrast to the general perception that whistle-blowers are brave men and women putting their careers and personal lives at risk to do the right thing, some argue that such actions are not brave at all—they are, it is argued, actions motivated by money or by the personal egos of "loose cannons" and "troublemakers" who challenge the policies and practices of their employers while claiming to act as the corporate conscience. In addition, rather than being viewed as performing a praiseworthy act, whistle-blowers are often severely criticized as informers, "sneaks," spies, or "squealers" who have in some way breached the trust and loyalty they owe to their employers.

WHEN IS WHISTLE-BLOWING ETHICAL?

Whistle-blowing is appropriate—ethical—under five conditions:[1]

1. When the company, through a product or decision, will cause serious and considerable harm to the public (as consumers or bystanders) or break existing laws, the employee should report the organization.
2. When the employee identifies a serious threat of harm, he or she should report it and state his or her moral concern.
3. When the employee's immediate supervisor does not act, the employee should exhaust the internal procedures and chain of command to the board of directors.

4. The employee must have documented evidence that is convincing to a reasonable, impartial observer that his or her view of the situation is accurate, and evidence that the firm's practice, product, or policy seriously threatens and puts in danger the public or product user.

5. The employee must have valid reasons to believe that revealing the wrongdoing to the public will result in the changes necessary to remedy the situation. The chance of succeeding must be equal to the risk and danger the employee takes to blow the whistle.

WHEN IS WHISTLE-BLOWING UNETHICAL?

If there is evidence that the employee is motivated by the opportunity for financial gain or media attention or that the employee is carrying out an individual vendetta against the company, then the legitimacy of the act of whistle-blowing must be questioned.

The potential for financial gain in some areas of corporate whistle-blowing can be considerable:

- On November 30, 2005, New York City's Beth Israel Hospital agreed to pay $72.9 million to resolve allegations from a former hospital executive that it falsified Medicare cost reports from 1992 to 2001. The case stemmed from a 2001 whistle-blower lawsuit filed in the U.S. District Court in New York City by former Beth Israel vice president of financial services, Najmuddin Pervez. Mr. Pervez is expected to receive 20 percent of the recovery amount, around $15 million.[2]

- In June 2010, Northrop Grumman Corp. agreed to pay the federal government $12.5 million to settle allegations that the company caused false claims to be submitted to the government. Allegedly, Northrop Grumman's Navigation Systems Division failed to test electronic components it supplied for military airplane, helicopter, and submarine navigation systems to ensure that the parts would function at the extreme temperatures required for military and space uses. This case was filed under the *qui tam* provisions of the federal False Claims Act by whistle-blower Allen Davis, a former quality assurance manager at Northrop Grumman's Navigation Systems Division facility in Salt Lake City. Mr. Davis will receive $2.4 million out of the settlement.[3]

- Douglas Durand, former vice president of sales for TAP Pharmaceutical Products, received a $126 million settlement from the U.S. government after filing suit against his employer and a TAP rival, the former Zeneca, Inc., accusing both companies of overcharging the federal government's Medicare program by tens of millions of dollars.[4]

Under the Federal Civil False Claims Act, also known as "Lincoln's Law," whistle-blowers (referred to as "relators") who expose fraudulent behavior against the government are entitled to between 10 and 30 percent of the amount recovered. Originally enacted during the Civil War in 1863 to protect the government against fraudulent defense contractors, the act was strengthened as recently as 1986 to make it easier and safer for whistle-blowers to come forward. The lawsuits brought under the act are referred to as *qui tam*, which is an abbreviation for a longer Latin phrase that establishes the whistle-blower as a deputized petitioner for the government in the case. Since 1986, more than 2,400 *qui tam* lawsuits have been filed, recovering over $2 billion for the government and enriching whistle-blowers by more than $350 million.

> **Qui Tam Lawsuit** A lawsuit brought on behalf of the federal government by a whistle-blower under the False Claims Act of 1863.

Whether the motivation to speak out and reveal the questionable behavior comes from a personal ethical decision or the potential for a substantial financial windfall will probably never be completely verified, but the threat of losing your job or becoming alienated from colleagues by speaking out against your employer must be diminished by the knowledge that some financial security will likely result. Whether the choice is based on ethical or financial considerations, the key point is that you had better be very sure of your facts and your evidence had better be irrefutable before crossing that line.

THE YEAR OF THE WHISTLE-BLOWER

Since examples of internal whistle-blowing rarely receive media attention, it is impossible to track the history of such actions. However, external whistle-blowing is a 20th-century phenomenon. One of the first instances of the use of the term *whistle-blower* occurred in 1963 when Otto Otopeka was dismissed from the U.S. State Department after giving classified documents on security risks to the chief counsel of the Senate Subcommittee on Internal Security. In the 1970s, the Watergate scandal broke after former Marine commander Daniel Ellsberg leaked over 7,000 pages of confidential Pentagon documents on government misconduct in the Vietnam conflict to the press, risking life imprisonment to do so; and an anonymous source named Deep Throat (only recently revealed to be Mark Felt, former assistant director of the FBI during the Nixon administration) helped *Washington Post* journalists Bob Woodward and Carl Bernstein expose the extent of government misconduct in attempting to track down Ellsberg.

Public awareness of whistle-blowers reached a peak in 2002 when *Time* magazine awarded its Person of the Year award to three women "of ordinary demeanor but exceptional guts and sense":[5]

- *Sherron Watkins,* the vice president at Enron Corporation, who, in the summer of 2001, wrote two key e-mails (quoted at the beginning of this chapter) warning Enron Chairman Ken Lay that it was only a matter of time before the company's creative "accounting treatment" would be discovered and bring the entire organization down.

- *Coleen Rowley,* an FBI staff attorney, who rose to public prominence in May 2002 when she made public a memo to Director Robert Mueller about the frustration and dismissive behavior she faced from the FBI when her Minneapolis, Minnesota, field office argued for the investigation of a suspected terrorist, Zacarias Moussaoui, who was later indicted as a co-conspirator in the September 11, 2001, attacks.

- *Cynthia Cooper,* whose internal auditing team first uncovered questionable accounting practices at WorldCom. Her team's initial estimates placed the discrepancy at $3.8 billion; the final balance was nearer to $11 billion.

>> The Duty to Respond

Whether you believe whistle-blowers to be heroes who face considerable personal hardship to bring the harsh light of media attention to unethical behavior, or you take the opposing view that they are breaking the oath of loyalty to their employer, the fact remains that employees are becoming increasingly willing to respond to any questionable behavior they observe in the workplace. The choice for an employer is to ignore them and face public embarrassment and potentially ruinous financial penalties, or to create an internal system that allows whistle-blowers to be heard and responded

Karen Silkwood

In the 1983 film Silkwood, Meryl Streep portrayed Karen Silkwood, a nuclear plant employee who blew the whistle on unsafe practices. The real Karen Silkwood died in an auto accident under mysterious circumstances.

With their classic portrayals of good guys against the corporate bad guys, movie portrayals of whistle-blowers are by no means a new idea. Films such as *The China Syndrome*, *Silkwood*, and *The Insider* have documented the risks and challenges whistle-blowers face in bringing the information they uncover to the general public.

The movie *The Insider* documents the case of Dr. Jeffrey Wigand and his decision to go public with information alleging that his employer, the tobacco company Brown & Williamson (B&W), was actively manipulating the nicotine content of its cigarettes. Wigand was portrayed by Russell Crowe, and the part of Lowell Bergman, the CBS *60 Minutes* producer who helped Wigand go public, was portrayed by Al Pacino.

The movie captures several key issues that are common to many whistle-blower cases:

- Wigand was initially reticent to speak out about the information—partly out of fear of the impact on his family if he lost his severance package and health benefits under the terms of his confidentiality agreement with B&W, and partly because of his strong sense of integrity in honoring any contracts he had signed. It was only after B&W had chosen to modify the confidentiality agreement after firing Wigand (allegedly for "poor communication skills") that Wigand, angered by B&W's apparent belief that he wouldn't honor the confidentiality agreement he had signed, chose to go public.

- B&W's response was immediate and aggressive. It won a restraining (or "gag") order against Wigand to prevent him from giving evidence as an expert witness in a case against tobacco companies brought by the state of Mississippi, but he testified anyway. B&W then proceeded to undertake a detailed disclosure of Wigand's background in order to undermine his reputation, eventually releasing a thick report titled "The Misconduct of Jeffrey S. Wigand Available in the Public Record." The extent to which the findings of this investigation were exaggerated was later documented in a *New York Times* newspaper article. The movie portrays Bergman as providing the material for a *New York Times* journalist to refute the B&W claims against Wigand.

- Wigand's testimony was extremely damaging for B&W. He not only accused the CEO of B&W, Thomas Sanderfur, of misrepresentation in stating before congressional hearings in 1994 that he believed that nicotine was not addictive, but Wigand also claimed that cigarettes were merely "a delivery system for nicotine."

- Even though Wigand's credibility as a witness had been verified, CBS initially chose not to run Wigand's interview with CBS reporter Mike Wallace in fear of a lawsuit from B&W for "tortious interference" (which

is defined as action by a third party in coming between two parties in a contractual relationship—that is, CBS would be held liable for intervening between Wigand and B&W in the confidentiality agreement Wigand had signed). The fact that CBS's parent company was in the final stages of negotiations to sell CBS to the Westinghouse Corporation was seen as evidence of CBS's highly questionable motivation in avoiding the danger of tortious interference. In reality, the fear of litigation was probably well founded. After ABC had run an equally controversial segment on its *Day One* show accusing Philip Morris of raising nicotine levels in their cigarettes, Philip Morris, along with another tobacco company, R. J. Reynolds, launched a $10 billion lawsuit against ABC, which was forced to apologize and pay the tobacco companies' legal fees (estimated at over $15 million).

- In November 1998, B&W subsequently joined with three other tobacco giants—Philip Morris, R. J. Reynolds, and Lorillard—in signing the Tobacco Master Settlement Agreement (MSA), settling state lawsuits against them in 46 states for recovery of the medical costs of treating smoking-related illnesses. The settlement totaled $206 billion and included provisions that forbade marketing directly or indirectly to children and banned or restricted the use of cartoons, billboards, product placement, or event sponsorship in the marketing of tobacco products.

- As vice president for research and development for B&W, Wigand was a corporate officer for the company and, therefore, the highest-ranking insider ever to turn whistle-blower at the time. His reward for speaking out was that he never reached the $300,000 salary level he held at B&W again. At the time his story went public, he had found employment as a teacher in Louisville, Kentucky, teaching chemistry and Japanese for $30,000 a year—a profession he proudly and happily maintains to this day. His marriage

CONTINUED >>

THE INSIDER

didn't survive the intense media scrutiny and B&W's attempts to discredit him.

- Six years later, Wigand was interviewed by *Fast Company* magazine, and he shared his unhappiness with the title of whistle-blower: "The word whistle-blower suggests that you're a tattletale or that you're somehow disloyal," he says. "But I wasn't disloyal in the least bit. People were dying. I was loyal to a higher order of ethical responsibility."

Sources: Elizabeth Gleick, "Where There's Smoke," *Time,* February 12, 1996, p. 54; Ron Scherer, "One Man's Crusade against Tobacco Firms," *Christian Science Monitor,* November 30, 1995, p. 3; and "Jeffrey Wigand: The Whistle-Blower," *Fast Company,* March 2002.

QUESTIONS

1. Wigand was initially unwilling to go public with his information. What caused him to change his mind?
2. Did CBS pursue Wigand's story because it was the right thing to do or because it was a good story?
3. Since CBS played such a large part in bringing Wigand's story to the public, do you think the network also had an obligation to support him once the story broke? Explain why or why not.
4. Was CBS's decision not to run the interview driven by any ethical concerns?

to *before* the issue escalates to an external whistle-blowing case. Obviously, responding to whistle-blowers in this context means addressing their concerns, and not, as many employers have decided, firing them.

Prior to 2002, legal protection for whistle-blowers existed only through legislation that encouraged the moral behavior of employees who felt themselves compelled to speak out, without offering any safeguards against retaliation aimed at them. As far back as the False Claims Act of 1863, designed to prevent profiteering from the Civil War, the government has been willing to split up to 50 percent of the recovered amount with the person filing the petition—a potentially lucrative bargain—but it offered no specific prohibitions against retaliatory behavior.

The Whistleblower Protection Act of 1989 finally addressed the issue of retaliation against federal employees who bring accusations of unethical behavior. The act imposed specific performance deadlines in processing whistle-blower complaints and guaranteed the anonymity of the whistle-blower unless revealing the name would prevent criminal activity or protect public safety. The act also required prompt payment of any portion of the settlement to which the whistle-blower would be entitled, even if the case were still working its way through the appeals process.

The Whistleblower Protection Act of 1989 applied only to federal employees. Not until the Sarbanes-Oxley Act of 2002 (also known as the Corporate and Criminal Fraud Accountability Act, and most commonly abbreviated to SOX) did Congress take an integrated approach to the matter of whistle-blowing by both prohibiting retaliation against whistle-blowers and encouraging the act of whistle-blowing itself:[6]

THE COLD, HARD REALITY

The media's attention to Jeffrey Wigand, Sherron Watkins, Coleen Rowley, and Cynthia Cooper could lead you to believe that doing the right thing and speaking out against the perceived wrongdoings of your employer will guarantee you public support as an honorable and ethical person, putting the needs of your fellow human beings before your own. In reality, the majority of whistle-blowers face the opposite situation. They are branded as traitors, shunned by their former colleagues, and often singled out to the extent that they never find work in their respective industries again. Consider the cases of the following two individuals who made the same tough ethical choices as their more-famous counterparts with far more negative outcomes.

Christine Casey joined the toy maker Mattel in 1994. In 1997 she was assigned to develop a system to more efficiently allocate production among Mattel's factories. Future production was based on sales forecasts, and it was these forecast figures that led to Casey's ethical crisis with her employer. She quickly discovered that the factory managers regarded the official sales forecasts as being so high that they usually ignored them and worked toward production quotas on the basis of what their fellow managers were using—often keeping two sets of figures to hide their actions. The inflation of sales figures was a key problem for Mattel's most profitable item—Barbie dolls.

In February 1999, Casey made her concerns known to a Mattel director, Ned Mansour, and proposed a new approach to sales forecasting that would address the inflated figures that the CEO of Mattel, Jill Barad, had been sharing with financial analysts through 1997, 1998, and into 1999. Casey believed that her new approach would ensure that profits could be forecasted more accurately based on more realistic sales and production figures. She documented that the initial response from Mansour was friendly, but her position and reputation within Mattel began to decline very rapidly. In August 1999, she received her first-ever negative performance review since joining Mattel. She was then stripped of most of her job duties and relocated to a cubicle next to a pile of packing boxes.

In October 1999, she expressed concerns that "misrepresentation of earnings projections has made the company vulnerable to shareholder litigation" in a letter to Mattel's former chief financial officer, Harry Pierce. Her concerns went unheeded, and after declining a monetary offer from Mattel to waive her legal rights, Casey resigned in November 1999.

After Casey filed suit against Mattel in November 2000, the company hired John Quinn, a top corporate attorney with an established winning record for his corporate clients. In September 2002, the judge ruled in favor of Mattel and against Casey, arguing that she was not eligible for protection under whistle-blower laws because she had made constructive proposals to senior management rather than filing explicit complaints. An appeal is pending.

Jill Barad, former CEO of Mattel, left the company with a severance package of $50 million in February 2000, and the company settled $122 million of shareholder lawsuits without admitting any wrongdoing in accusations of inflated sales forecasts.

David Welch became the chief financial officer at the Bank of Floyd (Virginia) in 1999 after working for the bank's outside auditing firm. The bank, a unit of Cardinal Bancshares, was just shy of 50 years old with a slow and steady growth record and six local branches. Two years into his contract, Welch began noticing financial irregularities in how the bank was being operated. Specifically, these irregularities included the following:

- Bank officials had been inflating Cardinal's reported income.

- CEO R. Leon Moore had engaged in insider trading (trading stock on the basis of access to privileged information).
- The bank had been holding cash reserves in separate accounts to manipulate earnings in future quarters.
- The bank had allowed charge-offs (i.e., bad debts written off) that exceeded their internal control policies.

Welch raised his concerns within the organization, but he was ignored, and in October 2002 he was fired. Two months later, he filed for whistle-blower protection under the Sarbanes-Oxley Act. In reviewing the case, the judge ruled that "Welch's whistle-blowing made him vulnerable to 'adverse and discriminatory employment action'" and awarded him $38,327 in back pay and $26,505 in special damages, and specified that Welch would be eligible for back pay until he was reinstated. Cardinal insisted that the judge "simply didn't understand the case" and appealed.

Legal documentation gathered in support of the appeal included a bank examiner's report that allegedly found a number of errors in Welch's work performance to the extent that Cardinal Bancshares has "concerns about the quality of his work as CFO." In addition, several Cardinal employees have allegedly threatened to quit if Welch were reinstated.

To date, it is estimated that Welch has incurred almost $125,000 in legal fees fighting the case, compared to Cardinal Bancshares' legal bill of around $500,000. The CEO of the Bank of Floyd, R. Leon Moore, remains convinced that Welch's actions were motivated solely by money and refuses to settle the case until the bank is vindicated. In the meantime, despite two legal orders to reinstate him "with the same seniority, status and benefits he would have had but for [Cardinal's] unlawful discrimination," Welch remains unemployed and is convinced that "my worst fears were realized. I can't get a job in this industry."

QUESTIONS

1. Who took the greater risk here: Christine Casey or David Welch?
2. Was the alleged behavior at Mattel more or less unethical than the behavior at the Bank of Floyd?
3. Do you think Casey and Welch regret their decisions to go public with their information? Why or why not?
4. Do you think their behavior changed anything at either company?

Sources: "Christine Casey: Whistleblower," *The Economist*, January 18–24, 2003, p. 62; Karen Krebsbach, "The Long, Lonely Battle of David E. Welch," *US Banker* 115, no. 30 (August 2005), pp. 30–34; and Duncan Adams, "Whistle-Blower's Case Blazes Trail," *Knight Ridder Tribune Business News*, September 7, 2005, p. 1.

Study Alert

The language on a whistle-blower's entitlement to "all compensatory damages to make the employee whole" is not clear in the SOX legislation. Considering the cases you have read in this chapter, what would you need to be made "whole"?

Whistle-Blower Hotline
A telephone line by which employees can leave messages to alert a company of suspected misconduct without revealing their identity.

The statute requires public companies not only to adopt a code of business ethics, but also to set up an internal apparatus to receive, review, and solicit employee reports concerning fraud and/or ethical violations. The teeth of the statute can be found in an enforcement scheme that includes administrative, civil, *and* criminal enforcement mechanisms and provides for both corporate *and* individual liability. Interestingly, SOX does not protect employee complaints to the news media. Such reports, by themselves, do not constitute whistle-blowing under SOX.

Employees who prevail in whistle-blower cases are entitled to damages, which may include:

1. Reinstatement to the same seniority status that the employee would have had but for the adverse employment action.
2. Back pay.
3. Interest.
4. All compensatory damages to make the employee whole.

5. "Special Damages," including litigation costs, reasonable attorney fees and costs, expert witness fees, and "all relief necessary to make the employee whole."

SOX does not provide for punitive damages.

>> Addressing the Needs of Whistle-Blowers

Given this new legal environment surrounding whistle-blowers, all employers would be wise to put the following mechanisms in place:

1. A well-defined process to document how such complaints are handled—a nominated contact person, clearly identified authority to respond to the complaints, firm assurances of confidentiality, and nonretaliation against the employee.
2. An employee hotline to file such complaints, again with firm assurances of confidentiality and non-retaliation to the employee.
3. A prompt and thorough investigation of all complaints.
4. A detailed report of all investigations, documenting all corporate officers involved and all action taken.

Above all, employers must have a commitment to follow through on any and all reports whether or not those reports end up being substantiated. For a **whistle-blower hotline** to work, *trust* must be established between employees and their employer—trust

PROGRESS ✓ QUESTIONS

9. If an employee blows the whistle on an organization on the basis of a rumor, is that ethical?
10. If that information turns out to be false, should the employee be liable for damages? Explain your answer.
11. Compensation to "make the employee whole" under SOX isn't as clear as a percentage of the funds recovered for a government whistle-blower. Does that make it less likely that we'll see more whistle-blowing under SOX?
12. Under SOX, complaining to the media isn't recognized as whistle-blowing. Is that ethical?

PROGRESS ✓ QUESTIONS

13. How should managers or supervisors respond to an employee who brings evidence of questionable behavior to their attention?
14. Should that employee be given any reassurances of protection for making the tough decision to come forward?
15. Do you think a hotline that guarantees the anonymity of the caller will encourage more employees to come forward?
16. Does your company have a whistle-blower hotline? How did you find out that there is (or isn't) one?

of a cover-up, then the hotline will definitely never ring again.

>> Whistle-Blowing as a Last Resort

The perceived bravery and honor in doing the right thing by speaking out against corporate wrongdoing at personal risk to your own career and financial stability adds a gloss to the act of whistle-blowing that is undeserved. The fact that an employee is left with no option but to go public with information should be seen as evidence that the organization has failed to address the situation internally for the long-term improvement of the corporation and all its stakeholders. Becoming a whistle-blower and taking your story public should be seen as the last resort rather than the first. The fallout of unceasing media attention and the often terminal damage to the reputation and long-term economic viability of the organization should be enough of a threat to force even the most stubborn executive team to the table with a commitment to fix whatever has been broken. Regrettably, the majority of executives appear to be unwilling to fix the problem internally and, where necessary, notify the appropriate authorities of the problem—they choose to either bury the information and hire the biggest legal gunslinger they can find to discredit the evidence or, as in the case of Jeffrey Wigand, tie their employees in such restrictive confidentiality agreements that speaking out exposes the employee to extreme financial risk, which managers no doubt hope will prompt the employee to "keep his mouth shut."

As Peter Rost explains:[7]

> A study of 233 whistle-blowers by Donald Soeken of St. Elizabeth's Hospital in Washington, DC, found that the average whistle-blower was a man in his forties with a strong conscience and high moral values.
>
> After blowing the whistle on fraud, 90 percent of the whistle-blowers were fired or demoted, 27 percent faced lawsuits, 26 percent had to seek psychiatric or physical care, 25 percent suffered alcohol abuse, 17 percent lost their homes, 15 percent got divorced, 10 percent attempted suicide, and 8 percent were bankrupted. But in spite of all this, only 16 percent said they wouldn't blow the whistle again.

Real World Applications

Pat Curl is the newest member of a three-person crew for the local franchise of a national moving company. The team leader is Gene Kivett, who has been with the company for a couple of years now. Pat has serious concerns about some of Gene's business practices—he has asked Pat to do some "private" cash-only moves (off the books but using the company's equipment) and has negotiated very low prices for "friends" with, Pat suspects, an agreement to receive cash under the table in return for the low price bid. Pat thinks that Gene's tactics are damaging the company's reputation and putting Pat's job security in jeopardy. The company has a hotline number for employees to share such concerns, and the company guarantees anonymity for all callers. However, with only three people on the crew, if something happens to Gene, Pat is concerned that it won't take Gene too long to figure out who placed the call. What should Pat do?

that the information can be given anonymously and without fear of retaliation, even if the identity of the whistle-blower is ultimately revealed during the investigation.

The organization can make all the promises in the world, but until that first report is investigated through to a full conclusion, the hotline may never ring again. If the investigation is perceived to be half-hearted, or there is even the remotest suggestion

Life Skills

>> Making difficult decisions

In the previous chapter we talked about using your personal value system to live your life according to your own ethical standards. As you have seen in this chapter, people like Jeffrey Wigand, Sherron Watkins, Christine Casey, and David Welch may come across situations in their business lives where the behavior they observe is in direct conflict to their ethical standards, and they find themselves unable to simply look the other way.

Ask yourself what you would do in such a situation. Would you ignore it? Could you live with that decision? If you chose to speak out, either as an internal or external whistle-blower, could you live with the consequences of that decision? What if there was a negative impact on the company as a result of your actions and people lost their jobs, as they did at Enron or WorldCom? Could you live with that responsibility?

Speaking out in response to your own ethical standards is only one part of the decision. The consequences for you, your immediate family, your co-workers, and all the other stakeholders in the organization represent an equally important part of that decision. You can see why whistle-blowers face such emotional turmoil before, during, and after what is probably one of the toughest decisions of their lives.

If you find yourself in such a situation, don't make the decision alone. Talk to people you can trust, and let them help you review all the issues and all the potential consequences of the decision you are about to make.

FRONTLINE FOCUS
Good Money—Ben Makes a Decision

Ben lost a lot of sleep that night. He trusted Rick as his most experienced tire mechanic, but he had never seen him be so negative about one particular tire model—and it wasn't as if he had anything to gain by trashing the reputation of a tire that the company wanted to sell so aggressively.

The company had sold seconds before—heck, they even sold "used" tires for those customers looking to save a few bucks. How was this any different? Plus, Rick didn't have to deal with the sales pressure that John placed on his team leaders—you had to hit your quota every week or else—and if the company was pushing Benfield Voyagers, then John expected to see him sell Benfield Voyagers by the dozen.

But what if Rick was right? What if Benfield had cut corners to save on costs? They could end up with another Firestone disaster on their hands. What was Ben supposed to do with this information? If Rick was so concerned, why wasn't he speaking up? The company advertised its employee hotline for everyone to use if they had concerns about any business practices. Why was it Ben's job to say something? He needed this job. He had bills to

pay just like the other guys in the store—in fact, the bills were getting pretty high and that bonus money would really help right now.

Ben tossed and turned for a few more hours before reaching a decision. Rick might be right to be concerned, but he was only one guy. The guys at corporate looked at the same specs as Rick did, and if they could live with them, then so could Ben. He wasn't going to put his neck on the block just on the basis of Rick's concerns. If the company was putting its faith in Benfield Voyagers, then Ben was going to sell more of them than anyone else in the company.

Two weeks later, there was a fatal crash involving a minivan with three passengers—a husband and wife and their young son. The minivan had been fitted with Benfield Voyagers at Ben's tire store just one week earlier.

QUESTIONS
1. What do you think will happen now?
2. What will be the consequences for Ben, Rick, their tire store, and Benfield?
3. Should Ben have spoken out against the Voyager tires?

[For Review]

1. **Explain the term *whistle-blower,* and distinguish between internal and external whistle-blowing.**

   When an employee discovers evidence of corporate misconduct and chooses to bring that evidence to the attention of others, he or she becomes a whistle-blower. If that employee chooses to bring the evidence to the attention of executives within the organization through appropriate channels, that option is referred to as internal whistle-blowing. If, on the other hand, the employee chooses to go outside the organization and contact law enforcement officials or the media, that option is referred to as external whistle-blowing.

2. **Understand the different motivations of a whistle-blower.**

   Whistle-blowers are generally considered to be models of honor and integrity at a time when integrity in the business world seems to be in very short supply. However, such actions can also be motivated by the desire for revenge, when an ex-employee feels maligned and tries to create trouble for her or her former employer. In addition, the potential for financial gain through the settlement of qui tam lawsuits can be seen to bring the true intent of the whistle-blower into question.

3. **Evaluate the possible consequences of ignoring the concerns of a whistle-blower.**

   The opportunity to address illegal or unethical activities before the situation is revealed in the media could potentially save an organization's corporate reputation, prevent a punitive fall in the company's stock price, and, as we saw in Chapter 6, help to minimize federal fines. Choosing to dismiss the concerns of a whistle-blower, as organizations seem to do with disheartening frequency, merely serves to escalate an already volatile situation and place the organization in an even deeper hole when the situation is made public.

4. **Recommend how to build internal policies to address the needs of whistle-blowers.**

   The greatest fear of any whistle-blower is retaliation, both within the organization and within that employee's profession. Addressing that fear requires a guarantee of anonymity in coming forward with whatever evidence has been uncovered. For that guarantee to have any credibility, there must be trust between employees and their employer. Critics argue that expecting such trust to be present in an environment where illegal/unethical behavior is taking place is unrealistic. Nevertheless, the organization can encourage whistle-blowers to come forward with a series of clearly defined initiatives:

   - *A well-defined process to document how such complaints are handled—a nominated contact person, clearly identified authority to respond to the complaints, firm assurances of confidentiality, and nonretaliation against the employee.*
   - *An employee hotline to file such complaints, again with firm assurances of confidentiality and nonretaliation to the employee.*
   - *A prompt and thorough investigation of all complaints.*
   - *A detailed report of all investigations, documenting all corporate officers involved and all action taken.*

5. **Analyze the possible risks involved in becoming a whistle-blower.**

   The media attention given to whistle-blowers as guardians of corporate conscience adds a gloss to the act of whistle-blowing that is undeserved. Jeffrey Wigand's decision cost him his marriage and his career. The media attention can be intrusive and unceasing, with harmful effects on every member of your family. Potentially lucrative settlements may offer some compensation, but those settlements can often take years to materialize and may offer little consolation to family members who have been uprooted and moved cross-country to start new lives away from the media spotlight. We may analyze the actions of a whistle-blower as a personal choice, but ultimately that choice affects many people.

[Key Terms]

External Whistle-Blowing **134**

Internal Whistle-Blowing **134**

Qui Tam Lawsuit **135**

Whistle-Blower **134**

Whistle-Blower Hotline **140**

[Review Questions]

1. Why are whistle-blowers regarded as models of honor and integrity?

2. Which whistle-blowing option is better for an organization: internal or external? Why?

3. Why would an organization decide to ignore evidence presented by a whistle-blower?

4. Is it reasonable for a whistle-blower to expect a guarantee of anonymity?

5. Why would a whistle-blower be concerned about retaliation?

6. Why is trust such an important issue in whistle-blowing?

[Review Exercises]

How would you act in the following situations?

1. You work for a meatpacking company. You have discovered credible evidence that your company's delivery drivers have been stealing cuts of meat and replacing them with ice to ensure that the delivery meets the stated weight on the delivery invoice. The company has 12 drivers, and, as far as you can tell, they are all in on this scheme. Your company has a well-advertised whistle-blower hotline. What do you do?

2. What would you do if your company did not have a whistle-blower policy?

3. You later discover that one of the drivers was not a part of the scheme but was fired anyway when the information was made public. What do you do?

4. Should the driver get his job back? Why or why not?

[Internet Exercises]

1. Visit the Government Accountability Project (GAP) at www.whistleblower.org.
   a. What is the mission of GAP?
   b. How is GAP funded?
   c. What kind of assistance is available through GAP for someone thinking about becoming a whistle-blower?

2. Visit the National Whistleblowers Center at www.whistleblowers.org.

   a. Using the interactive map, select one country and summarize the whistle-blowing activity in that country.
   b. Identify the whistle-blower protections in effect in your home state.

3. There are now two whistle-blowing Web sites separated by only one letter: Summarize their differences, and propose which one offers the greatest assistance to a potential whistle-blower.

[Team Exercises]

1. **Guilt by omission.**
   Divide into two groups, and prepare arguments *for* and *against* the following behavior: *You work for a large retail clothing company that spends a large amount of its advertising budget emphasizing that its clothes are "Made in America." You discover that only 15 percent of its garments are actually "made" in America. The other 85 percent are actually either cut from patterns overseas and assembled here in the United States or cut and assembled overseas and imported as completed garments. Your hometown depends on this clothing company as the largest local employer. Several of your friends and family work at the local garment assembly factory. Should you go public with this information?*

2. **"Tortious interference."**
   Divide into two groups, and prepare arguments *for* and *against* the following behavior: *In the case of Dr. Jeffrey Wigand and the Brown & Williamson Tobacco Company, the CBS Broadcasting Company chose not to air Dr. Wigand's 60 Minutes interview with Mike Wallace under threat of legal action for "tortious interference" between B&W and Dr. Wigand. There were suspicions that CBS was more concerned about avoiding any potential legal action that could derail its pending sale to the Westinghouse Corporation. Was CBS behaving ethically in putting the welfare of its stakeholders in the Westinghouse deal ahead of its obligation to support Dr. Wigand?*

3. **A new approach to freshness.**
   Divide into two groups, and prepare arguments *for* and *against* the following behavior: *You work in the meat department of store 2795 of a large retail grocery chain. The company recently announced a change in the meat-handling protocols from the primary supplier. Starting in January 2011, the meat will be gassed with carbon monoxide before packaging. This retains a brighter color for the meat and delays the discoloration that usually occurs as the meat begins to spoil. You understand from the memo that there will be no information on the product label to indicate this protocol change and that the company has no plans to notify customers of this new process. Should you speak out about the procedure?*

4. **California organic.**
   Divide into two groups and prepare arguments *for* and *against* the following behavior: *You work in the accounting department of a family-owned mushroom grower based in California that sells premium organic mushrooms to local restaurants and high-end retail grocery stores. The company's product range includes both fresh and dried mushrooms. Your organic certification allows you to charge top dollar for your product, but you notice from invoices that operating costs are increasing significantly without any increase in revenues. The market won't absorb a price increase, so the company has to absorb the higher costs and accept lower profits. One day you notice invoices for the purchase of dried mushrooms from a Japanese supplier. The dried mushrooms are not listed as being organic, but they are apparently being added to your company's dried mushrooms, which are labeled organic and California-grown. Should you speak out about this?*

Thinking Critically

>> QUESTIONABLE MOTIVES

Bradley Birkenfeld was born in the Boston area but spent the last decade of his professional banking career in Geneva, Switzerland, as a personal banker for wealthy American clients of Swiss banking giant UBS. He has achieved notoriety in the financial services industry as the whistle-blower of the largest tax fraud case in history. As a result of evidence he provided, his former employer, UBS, paid a $780 million fine, agreed to modify its international banking practices, and turned over the account records of 4,450 American account holders who, the IRS believed, were actively seeking to evade their U.S. tax obligations.

Birkenfeld was an average midlevel banking executive, and his motives in becoming the first banker to ever provide evidence on Swiss banking practices were initially perceived as altruistic. He offered to wear a wire transmitter to record conversations with high-level UBS executives and to provide documentation on almost 19,000 UBS accounts. In return, he asked for immunity for his past actions as a UBS employee. When we consider the nature of his work, his request for immunity appears to be a very smart move.

Birkenfeld's duties—he was a personal banker—included providing concierge-level service, under the protection of highly secretive Swiss banking laws, helping clients invest, spend, and move their money around the world. Such personal service included, for one wealthy client, the purchase of loose diamonds in Geneva and then personal delivery of those diamonds to the United States, carried through customs in a toothpaste tube. Despite a statement from Birkenfeld that the value of the diamonds was "less than $10,000" (which meant that they did not need to be declared at U.S. Customs), the choice of packaging raises questions about his desire to not draw attention to himself while traveling to the United States. Indeed, it was this practice of low-key, "under the radar" visits from UBS bankers to the United States on trips recorded in their business calendars as "vacations" that drew the attention of the FBI.

Evidence provided by Birkenfeld revealed that these "vacations" were, in fact, carefully planned trips to service UBS's wealthy American clients at luxury yacht races and art shows where, conveniently, UBS bankers could also mingle, network, and solicit new clients. Unfortunately, since those bankers were not licensed to conduct business in the United States, their actions amounted to a clear violation of U.S. banking regulations.

With such a strong case, the U.S. government was able to negotiate, for the first time, the delivery of client records of U.S. citizens who were using UBS accounts to evade their domestic tax obligations. Even though UBS sought the intervention of the Swiss government to help its case, it came down to pragmatic reality. With 30,000 employees and a large financial services business in the United States, the bank could not risk losing access to such a large market if it was to remain a global banking institution.

For Birkenfeld, the outcome was not so positive. Despite his request for immunity for past actions as a UBS banker, he elected not to fully disclose his relationship with Californian real estate billionaire Igor Olenicoff, who was indicted for trying to evade U.S. taxes on $200 million hidden in Swiss and Lichtenstein bank accounts. Birkenfeld was charged with helping Olenicoff by referring him to a UBS specialist in the creation of offshore "shell" corporations designed to hide the true ownership of UBS accounts. Olenicoff cooperated with the investigation and paid $52 million in fines and back taxes. As a result of his cooperation, Olenicoff served no jail time.

Birkenfeld, on the other hand, was charged with conspiracy to commit tax fraud, pleaded guilty, and received a sentence of 40 months in prison, beginning in January 2010. While he does not dispute his relationship with Olenicoff, Birkenfeld maintains that his involvement was only as a referral to another UBS specialist. As such, he feels strongly that his jail time is unjust given his altruistic services to the U.S. government in providing evidence against UBS that is expected to generate billions of dollars in recovered taxes for the U.S. Treasury. He is currently appealing to President Obama for clemency.

Critics are concerned that his prison sentence will discourage other tax whistle-blowers from coming forward, with the result that many more billions of lost tax revenue may never be recovered. The Justice Department officials who indicted Birkenfeld have stated that if he had fully disclosed the nature of his relationship with Olenicoff, it's unlikely that he would have been prosecuted, which brings us back to the question of Birkenfeld's true motives in coming forward as a whistle-blower—was it really altruism, or was he looking for a way to handle the mess that the Olenicoff case had created for him? In either event, there may still be a silver lining in Birkenfeld's cloud. As a key figure in the *qui tam* lawsuit between the U.S. government and UBS, he may be eligible for up to 30 percent of the money recovered from UBS—but that still has to be decided by the IRS.

QUESTIONS

1. Birkenfeld is adamant that his prison sentence is unfair when compared to the fact that no one else (e.g., Olenicoff or UBS bankers) went to jail. Does he have a point?

2. Why did UBS elect to settle with the U.S. government?

3. Given that there was an immunity agreement in place, what did the Justice Department gain from prosecuting Birkenfeld?

4. Critics are concerned that Birkenfeld's prison sentence will discourage other tax whistle-blowers from coming forward. Is that a valid concern? Why or why not?

Sources: Janet Novack, "Banker Charged with Helping Billionaire Dodge Taxes," *Forbes*, May 13, 2008; Ken Stier, "Why Is the UBS Whistle-Blower Headed to Prison?" *Time*, October 6, 2009; Stephen M. Kohn, "Whistleblowing: A Get-Rich-Quick Scheme?" *Forbes*, December 4, 2009; Haig Simonian, "The Price of a Whistleblower," *Financial Times*, February 9, 2010; Ken Stier, "U.S. vs. Swiss Tax Cheats: A Whistleblower Ignored," *Time*, February 13, 2010; David Voreacos, "Banker Who Blew Whistle over Tax Cheats Seeks Pardon," *Bloomberg*, June 24, 2010; and CBS, "A Crack in the Swiss Vault," *60 Minutes*, August 15, 2010.

Thinking Critically 7.2

>> WIKILEAKS: PRINCIPLED LEAKING?

Movies like *Silkwood* and *The Insider* have portrayed whistle-blowers as lone heroes working against corrupt organizations at great personal risk to their own well-being—secrecy is an absolute must until the story explodes in the media. But what if you took a different approach? What if there was a central site for any and all material that a concerned employee, civil servant, or military staffer could post with the promise of anonymity through encrypted software and the protection of national press secrecy laws? What would that do to the world of corporate and government secrecy? WikiLeaks has become the live experiment to answer all those questions. Though not the first document-leaking Web site ("Cryptome" was started by John Young in 1996), WikiLeaks has become the most prominent as a result of its apparent willingness to post any information, classified or otherwise, in the stated interest of public advocacy.

Cofounded by Australian Julian Assange in 2007, Wikileaks was conceived as a safe haven for whistle-blowers to reveal their secrets to the world. Its first big story documented how former Kenyan President Daniel Arap Moi had diverted millions of dollars of state funds

CONTINUED >>

to overseas accounts, a leak that led to an upset in Kenya's presidential election. Since then there has been a constant stream of government, industry, and military reports published that have brought WikiLeaks and its cofounder both fame and notoriety, including takedown threats and a temporary ban in the United States.

The site, which proudly states that it owes no allegiance to any government or group, went on to release Pentagon rules of engagement for troops in Iraq, operating manuals for the U.S. detention facility in Guantanamo Bay, lists of U.S. munitions stores in Iraq (included banned chemical weapons), and a classified operating manual for the U.S. military's guided bombs known as the *joint direct attack munitions (JDAM)*. Since the JDAM manual also included known weaknesses of the bomb system, military officials responded that WikiLeaks was acting irresponsibly in making such information public and putting the lives of American military personnel at risk.

It is this willingness to post anything under an apparent hands-off editorial policy that has brought the most criticism of the site. Assange acknowledges that the community fact-checking and editing of posted documents that he envisioned with the "wiki" title of the domain (as in "wikipedia") has not materialized, but he is committed to supporting any and all postings, even if they include such questionable items as an early script for the movie *Indiana Jones and the Kingdom of the Crystal Skull* and the tax bill for actor Wesley Snipes that included his Social Security number.

On July 25, 2010, WikiLeaks released more than 75,000 classified reports about the war in Afghanistan, allegedly provided by an Army intelligence analyst, Bradley Manning. Manning was already under suspicion for allegedly leaking a 38-minute video of a 2007 helicopter attack in Baghdad that killed 12 people, including a reporter and photographer from the news agency Reuters. Publication of the documents was coordinated with *The New York Times, The Guardian* in Britain, and *Der Speigel* in Germany to ensure maximum attention (and suitable fact-checking before publication). Professor Jonathan Zittrain of Harvard Law School described the event as, "The *Exxon Valdez* of intelligence leaks—it's crude and messy, with uncertain implications." Even with a further 15,000 documents withheld by WikiLeaks in a "harm minimization process," military leadership personnel expressed concern about the revelation of names of Afghans who had helped U.S. forces, potentially endangering them.

WikiLeaks clearly represents a new world of whistle-blowing with the potential for immediate broad distribution of potentially devastating material previously considered to be "top secret." However, there is a growing concern that the technology, while protecting the whistle-blowers, will not be sufficient to stop a more disruptive agenda than simple document leaking. For example, Assange came under direct attack for releasing an edited 17-minute version of the Baghdad helicopter attack, entitled "Collateral Murder," without clarifying that the attack happened during clashes in a Baghdad neighborhood and that one of the men fired on by the helicopter crew was carrying a rocket-propelled grenade. Critics cite this example as evidence not of whistle-blowing but "information vandalism." With a promise from Assange of "even more controversial documents in the pipeline," it remains to be seen whether the site will achieve its target of achieving transparency for the unethical behavior of governments and corporations around the world, or whether it will be dismissed for "attention-craving subversion."

QUESTIONS

1. Critics have argued that WikiLeaks is now attacking secrecy on all fronts, with no concern for the consequences of the information posted on its site. Do those actions align with the ethical principles of whistle-blowing?

2. Does WikiLeaks have an obligation to censor postings to protect innocent individuals who may be harmed by making the information public? Should the site take steps to verify the accuracy of the posted documents?

3. Would fulfilling the vision of a "wiki" community (with editors and fact-checkers) reduce the criticism directed at the site? Why or why not?

4. Does the decision to withhold 15,000 documents in a "harm minimization process" indicate that WikiLeaks is developing some sense of the potential consequences of its actions? Why or why not?

Sources: Ryan Singel, "Immune to Critics, Secret-Spilling WikiLeaks Plans to Save Journalism . . . and the World," *Wired*, July 3, 2008; "Wiki Gaga," *The Economist*, June 10, 2010; Noam Cohen, "Ex-Hacker Who Accused Leak Suspect Is Still Talking," *The New York Times*, June 27, 2010; Eric Schmitt, "In Disclosing Secret Documents, WikiLeaks Seeks 'Transparency,' " *The New York Times*, July 25, 2010; Tim Bradshaw, "WikiLeaks: Hard Facts and a Hacker Ethos," *Financial Times*, July 26, 2010; Olivia Lang, "Welcome to a New Age of Whistle-Blowing," *BBC News*, July 27, 2010; and Richard Waters, "Online Leaks: A Digital Deluge," *Financial Times*, July 30, 2010.

Thinking Critically

>> THE OLIVIERI CASE

In April 1993, Dr. Nancy Olivieri, head of the hemoglobinopathy program at the Hospital for Sick Children (HSC), the teaching hospital for the University of Toronto in Canada, signed an agreement with the Canadian drug company Apotex to undertake clinical trials on a drug called deferiprone (referred to as L1 during the study). The drug was designed to help children with thalassemia, an inherited blood disorder that can cause the fatal buildup of iron in the blood. The agreement that Olivieri signed with Apotex included a clause (later referred to as a "gag clause") that specifically prevented the unauthorized release of any findings in the trial for a period of three years:

> As you now [sic], paragraph 7 of the LA-02 Contract provides that all information whether written or not, obtained or generated by you during the term of the LA-02 Contract and for a period of three years thereafter, shall be and remain secret and confidential and shall not be disclosed in any manner to any third party except with the prior written consent of Apotex. Please be aware that Apotex will take all possible steps to ensure that these obligations of confidentiality are met and will vigorously pursue all legal remedies in the event that there is any breach of these obligations.

The existence of this clause was to prove significant to the relationship between Olivieri and Apotex. After reporting some initial positive findings in the trial in April 1995, Olivieri reported in December 1996 that long-term use of the drug appeared to result in the toxic buildup of iron in the liver of a large number of her pediatric patients—a condition known as *hepatic fibrosis*. When she reported the findings to Apotex, the company determined that her interpretation of the data was incorrect. Olivieri then contacted the hospital's Research Ethics Board (REB), which instructed her to change the consent form for participation in the trial to ensure that patients were made aware of the risks of long-term use of the drug.

After copying Apotex on the revised form, the company notified Olivieri that the Toronto trials were being terminated effective immediately and that she was being removed as chair of the steering committee of the global trial that included patients in Philadelphia and Italy. When Olivieri notified Apotex that she and her research partners, including Dr. Gary Brittenham of Case Western Reserve University in Cleveland, were planning to publish their findings in the August 1998 issue of the *New England Journal of Medicine,* Apotex Vice President Michael Spino threatened legal action for breaching the confidentiality clause in her agreement with the company.

Olivieri then asked the HSC administration for legal support in her forthcoming battle with Apotex. The administrators declined. She then approached the University of Toronto, where the dean of the Faculty of Medicine declined to get involved on the grounds that her contract with Apotex had been signed without university oversight and that the university would never have agreed to the confidentiality clause in the first place.

"Olivieri forged ahead with the publication despite this [lack of support] and instantly became celebrated as a courageous whistleblower in the face of corporate greed."

The situation was further clouded by reports that the University of Toronto and HSC were, at the time, in the process of negotiating a $20 million donation from Bernard Sherman, the CEO and founder of Apotex.

The bitter relationship with her employers was to continue for several years, during which time she was referred to the Canadian College of Physicians and Surgeons for research misconduct and dismissed from her post at HSC, only to be reinstated following the aggressive support of several of her academic colleagues, including Dr. Brenda Gallie of the division of immunology and cancer at HSC, who led a petition drive that succeeded in garnering 140 signatures in support of a formal enquiry into Dr. Olivieri's case.

That enquiry was undertaken by both the Canadian College of Physicians and Surgeons, which found her conduct to be "exemplary," and by the Canadian Association of University Teachers, whose 540-page report concluded that Dr. Olivieri's academic freedom had been violated when Apotex stopped the trials and threatened legal action against her.

The two-and-a-half-year battle ended in January 1999 when an agreement was brokered between the university, HSC, and Olivieri thanks to the efforts of two world-renowned experts in blood disorders—Dr. David Nathan of Harvard and Dr. David Weatherall of Oxford who intervened on the basis of the international importance of Dr. Olivieri's research. Working with the president of the University of Toronto, Robert Pritchard, and lawyers for both parties, a compromise settlement was reached that reinstated Olivieri as head of the hemoglobinopathy program at HSC, covered her legal expenses up to $150,000, and withdrew all letters and written complaints about her from her employment file.

As part of the agreement, a joint working group appointed by the University of Toronto and the university's Faculty Association was chartered with the task of making "recommendations on changes to university policies on the dissemination of research publications and conflict of interest and the relationship of these issues to academic freedom."

QUESTIONS

1. Was it ethical for Apotex to include a three-year gag clause in the agreement with Dr. Olivieri?

2. Even though Dr. Olivieri later admitted that she should never have signed the agreement with Apotex that included a confidentiality clause, does the fact that she *did* sign it have any bearing on her actions here? Why or why not?

3. Was Olivieri's decision to publish her findings about the trial an example of *universalism* or *utilitarianism*? Explain your answer.

4. If we identify the key players in this case as Dr. Olivieri, Apotex, the Hospital for Sick Children, and the University of Toronto, what are the conflicts of interest between them all?

5. What do you think would have happened if Dr. Olivieri's fellow academics had not supported her in her fight?

6. How could this situation have been handled differently to avoid such a lengthy and bitter battle?

Sources: Robert A. Phillips and John Hoey, "Constraints of Interest: Lessons at the Hospital for Sick Children," *Canadian Medical Association Journal* 159 (October 20, 1998), p. 8; John Hoey and Anne Marie Todkill, "The Olivieri Story, Take Three," *Canadian Medical Association Journal* 173 (October 11, 2005), p. 8; and David Hodges, "Dr. Olivieri, Sick Kids, U of T Resolve Disputes," *Medical Post* 38, no. 43 (November 26, 2002), p. 4.

>> Introduction: Ethics and Technology

Technological advances often deliver new and improved functional capabilities before we have had the chance to fully consider the implications of those improvements. Consider the dramatic changes in workplace technology over the last two decades—specifically desktop computing, the Internet, and the growth of e-mail and instant messaging (IM). These technological advances arrived with the promise of "ease of access," "ease of use," and the ever-popular "increased worker productivity."

There is some truth to this assessment of the advantages of technology in the workplace. Consider the following:

Intranet A company's internal Web site, containing information for employee access only.

Extranet A private piece of a company's Internet network that is made available to customers and/or vendor partners on the basis of secured access by unique password.

- Companies are now able to make vast amounts of information available to employees and customers on their Internet, **intranet,** and **extranet** sites. Information previously distributed in hard-copy format—handbooks, guidebooks, catalogs, and policy manuals—can now be posted to a site and made available to employees and/or customers anywhere in the world in a matter of minutes, and updating that material can be accomplished in hours rather than weeks.
- JetBlue Airlines was able to achieve significant cost savings by avoiding the expensive overhead of developing call centers for its reservations department. Using available call-routing technology with a desktop computer and dedicated phone line, JetBlue was able to hire 700 part-time workers in the Salt Lake City area to become its reservations department, working from the comfort of their dens, dining rooms, or spare bedrooms with no costly buildings to staff and maintain, and a much more flexible and satisfied workforce that can log on at a time that's convenient for them with no commute or office dress code.

However, now that these tools have become part of our everyday work environment, many of those wonderful

promises have been overshadowed by concerns over loss of privacy in two key areas:

1. Customers must be aware that companies now have the technical capability to send their personal data to any part of the world to take advantage of lower labor costs.
2. As an employee, you must be aware that employers now have the capability of monitoring every e-mail you send and Web site you visit in order to make sure that you really are delivering on the promise of increased worker productivity.

>> Do You Know Where Your Personal Information Is?

With the availability of a network of fiber-optic cable that spans the globe and an increasingly educated global workforce that is fluent in English, the potential cost savings for American corporations in shipping work overseas to countries with lower labor costs is becoming increasingly attractive. Technically, anything that can be digitized can be sent over a fiber-optic cable.

The first wave of this technological advance came with the establishment of call centers in other parts of the world (predominantly India) to answer, for example, your customer service calls to your credit card company or for tech support on your computer. Very polite young people with suitably American names but with a definite accent can now answer your call as if you were calling an office park in the Midwest. This is just the beginning, as Thomas L. Friedman points out in *The World Is Flat:*[1]

A few weeks after I spoke with [Jaithirth "Jerry"] Rao, the following e-mail arrived from Bill Brody, the president of Johns Hopkins University, whom I had just interviewed for this book:

Dear Tom, I am speaking at a Hopkins continuing education medical meeting for radiologists (I used to be a radiologist). . . . I came upon a very fascinating situation that I thought might interest you. I have just learned that in many small and some medium-size hospitals in the

US, radiologists are outsourcing reading of CAT scans to doctors in India and Australia!!! Most of this evidently occurs at night (and maybe weekends) when the radiologists do not have sufficient staffing to provide in-hospital coverage. While some radiology groups will use teleradiology to ship images from the hospital to their home (or to Vail or Cape Cod, I suppose) so that they can interpret images and provide a diagnosis 24/7, apparently the smaller hospitals are shipping CAT images to radiologists abroad. The advantage is that it is daytime in Australia or India when it is nighttime here—so after-hours coverage becomes more readily done by shipping the images across the globe. Since CAT (and MRI) images are already in digital format and available on a network with a standardized protocol, it is no problem to view the images anywhere in the world. . . . I assume that the radiologists on the other end . . . must have trained in [the] US and acquired the appropriate licenses and credentials. . . . The groups abroad that provide these after-hours readings are called "Nighthawks" by the American radiologists that employ them.

The ethical obligations of this new technical capability are just being realized. Should the customer be notified where the call center is based? Should the customer be notified that the person answering the call who introduces himself as "Ray" is really Rajesh from Mumbai? If you are referred to a radiologist for treatment, are you entitled to know that your CAT scan is being beamed across the globe for another radiologist on the opposite side of the world to read? Advocates argue that assigning patient ID numbers rather than full names or personal information can guarantee patient confidentiality, but once the information is in digital format on a network, what guarantees are there that someone else isn't tapping into that network?

>> The Promise of Increased Worker Productivity

Desktop computers, e-mail, instant messaging, and the World Wide Web have changed our work environments beyond recognition over the last two decades, but with those changes have come a new world of ethical dilemmas. With a simple click, you can check the news on CNN, e-mail a joke to a friend, check the weather forecast for your trip next weekend, check in with that friend you've been meaning to call, and spread some juicy "dirt" that you just overheard in the break room—but the question is, Should you? We can identify two distinct viewpoints on this issue: the *employer view* and the *employee view*.

THE EMPLOYER POSITION

As an employee of the organization, your productivity during your time at work represents the performance portion of the pay-for-performance contract you entered into with the company when you were hired. Therefore, your actions during that time—your allotted shift or normal work period—are at the discretion of the company. Other than lunch and any scheduled breaks, all your activity should be work-related, and any monitoring of that activity should not be regarded as an infringement of your privacy. If you want to do something in private, don't do it at work.

The organization has an obligation to its stakeholders to operate as efficiently as possible, and to do so, it must ensure that company resources are not being misused or stolen and that company data and proprietary information are being closely guarded.

THE EMPLOYEE POSITION

As an employee of the company, I recognize that my time at work represents the productivity for which I

PROGRESS ✓ QUESTIONS

1. How would you feel if you found out that someone halfway around the world from your doctor's office was reading your CAT scan?

2. Would your opinion change if you knew the cost savings from outsourcing were putting American radiologists out of a job? What if they were being read this way because there was a shortage of qualified medical personnel here? Would that change your opinion?

3. Should your doctor be obligated to tell you where your tests are being read? Why or why not?

4. Storing private information in digital format simplifies the storage and transfer of that information and offers cost savings to companies that are (hopefully) passed on to their customers. Does using ID numbers instead of names meet their obligation to maintain your privacy in this new digital world?

Telecommuting The ability to work outside of your office (from your home or anywhere else) and log in to your company network (usually via a secure gateway such as a virtual private network, or VPN).

receive an agreed amount of compensation—either an hourly rate or an annual salary. However, that agreement should not intrude upon my civil rights as an individual—I am an employee, not a servant. As such, I should be notified of any electronic surveillance and the purpose of that surveillance. The actions of a small number of employees in breaking company rules should not be used as a justification to take away everyone's civil rights. Just because the guy in the cube next to me surfs the Web all day doesn't mean that we all do. Electronic monitoring implies that we can't be trusted to do our jobs—and if you can't trust us, why are you employing us in the first place?

Arriving at a satisfactory resolution of these opposing arguments has proved to be difficult for two reasons. First, the availability of ongoing technological advancements has made it increasingly difficult to determine precisely where work ends and personal life begins. Second, the willingness to negotiate or compromise has risen and fallen in direct relation to the prevailing job market.

>> When Are You "at Work"?

The argument over privacy at work has traditionally centered on the amount of time that employees were on-site—in the office or at the factory or store or hospital or call center, and so on. With the advances in computer technology and the new capability of **telecommuting,** which allows you to work from home (or anywhere) and log in to your company's network remotely, the concept of "at work" has become blurred.

With the availability of technology has come the expectation that you can check e-mails at home or finish a presentation the night before the big meeting. The arrival of the BlackBerry (affectionately known as the "crackberry" by many users and their partners) has made many employees available to their boss at all times of the day and night—24/7 unless they turn off the message notification function!

A FAILURE TO DISCLOSE

My name is Sally Jones, and I am the office manager for Chuck Wilson, CPA, a small accounting firm in the Midwest. Life is good—it's a healthy business with a good mix of small business and individual returns, and Chuck has been a great guy to work for. He's well respected in our community as an active member of the local chamber of commerce; he does pro bono work for several local nonprofit organizations; and he's built up a loyal customer base over the years. The problem is Chuck Junior. It's always been Chuck's plan that Junior would take over the business, and with Junior having just passed his CPA exams, that time would seem to be now. The number of boating and fishing magazines that have suddenly appeared on Chuck's desk make me believe that he is thinking more seriously about retirement than ever before.

I don't begrudge Chuck his retirement—he's earned it. My job here is secure. I have done good work for Chuck, and his customers like me. However, Chuck Junior is already looking to put his mark on the business. I wouldn't be surprised if he's having some "Under New Management" signs prepared for the day when he does take over the practice. Junior likes to think of himself as "on the cutting edge of new technology" and "ready to take it to the streets" to take on the local H&R Block and Jackson Hewitt offices that handle such a large portion of the

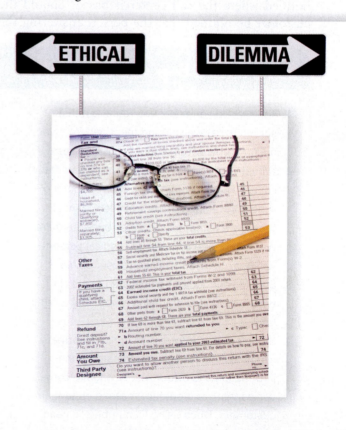

individual tax returns every year. He's all excited about an article he read in one of his business magazines that he thinks will give us an advantage over the big guys—and he's already been in contact with the company that was featured in the article.

His plan is to send all our individual tax returns to a company in India that will guarantee the return will be prepared in less than 48 hours by accountants in its offices who are U.S.-licensed CPAs. The term for this is *outsourcing*. This, says Junior, will allow us to go after the more labor-intensive but profitable corporate returns at tax time instead of having all our time taken up with the individual returns. It will also save us from hiring any additional staff for the season. He's even figured out that, with the cost of each return this company will charge us, we can undercut the big guys and take away some of their business. He's already planning a big advertising campaign in the local papers and radio stations.

I'm happy to give him the benefit of the doubt on this idea, but here's my concern—he's not planning to tell anyone how we're going to do this. He's not going to mention that someone else (whom he's never met) will be preparing the tax return or that the customers' personal information will be e-mailed to India to complete the return. He says that the customers won't care as long as the return is quick, accurate, and cheaper than the other guys. With all those ads for "immediate refunds," I can see his point, but his failure to disclose just doesn't sit right with me.

QUESTIONS

1. Is Sally right to be concerned about Chuck's plan? Explain why or why not.
2. Chuck Junior is obviously focusing on the money to be saved (and made) with this plan. What are the issues he is not considering?
3. Do you think Chuck Senior has signed off on this plan? If not, should Sally tell him? Explain why or why not.
4. Would the plan still succeed if Chuck Junior disclosed all the details?

Source: Inspired by "The Ethical Dilemmas of Outsourcing," Steven Mintz, *The CPA Journal* 74 (March 2004), p. 3.

In this new environment, the concept of being at work has become far more flexible. Availability has now become defined by accessibility. If I can reach you by phone or e-mail, I can ask you a question or assign you a task. The time of day or the day of the week is of secondary importance—it's a competitive world out there, and only the truly committed team players get ahead.

Employees, in return, have begun to expect the same flexibility in taking care of personal needs during working hours. If I stay up late working on a presentation for an important meeting the next day, shouldn't I then be allowed to call my dentist and make an appointment during my workday? What happens if I forget to send my mother some flowers for Mother's Day? If I order them online during my workday, am I still technically goofing off and therefore failing to meet my boss's expectations as a dedicated and productive employee?

If employee rights were recognized in this argument, then for those rights to have any validity, it would follow that employees should give their consent to be monitored by all this technology. However, as Adam Moore points out, the state of the job market will inevitably create a distinction between two types of consent: **thin** and **thick**.[2]

employment—and it is made clear in that notification that his or her continued employment with the company will be dependent on the employee's agreement to abide by that monitoring, then the employee may be said to have given thin consent. In other words, there are two options: agree to the monitoring or pursue other employment opportunities. You could argue that the employee has at least been notified of the policy, but the notification is based on the assumption that jobs are hard to come by and the employee is not in a position to quit on principle and risk temporary unemployment while seeking a position with another company.

Thin Consent Consent in which the employee has little choice. For example, when an employee receives formal notification that the company will be monitoring all e-mail and Web activity—either at the time of hire or during employment—and it is made clear in that notification that his or her continued employment with the company will be dependent on the employee's agreement to abide by that monitoring.

Thick Consent Consent in which the employee has an alternative to unacceptable monitoring. For example, if jobs are plentiful and the employee would have no difficulty in finding another position, then the employee has a realistic alternative for avoiding an unacceptable policy.

THIN CONSENT

If an employee receives formal notification that the company will be monitoring all e-mail and Web activity—either at the time of hire or during

THICK CONSENT

If employment conditions are at the other end of the scale—that is, jobs are plentiful and the employee would have no difficulty in finding another position—then consent to the monitoring policy could be classified as thick since the employee has a realistic alternative if he or she finds the policy to be unacceptable.

Abstract notions of notification and consent are idealistic at best. Consider the following account of life in a call center in the United Kingdom documented by "Jamie":[3]

> Back in October 1999, I started work at a call centre for a very large UK company. There were about 1,000 staff there, split into teams which would compete with each other on sales volumes. Winning teams might get a case of wine to share, or something like that. There was also a personal bonus scheme driven by sales.
>
> I was an "outbound telesales agent." This means we phoned customers at home with the aim of selling the company's services. I knew that most customers don't like to be phoned while at home, and if any customer clearly didn't want the call, I would end it, and flag their account for "no future correspondence," though we were specifically told only to do this in extreme cases.
>
> The bonus scheme encouraged some of my colleagues (mostly students) to sell aggressively—selling products that customers didn't want—for the bonus. These staff would usually have left the company by the time there were any repercussions.
>
> A lot of customers imagine telesales agents as being spotty idiots trawling phonebooks ringing people as they go through the book. But the company's call system is quite complex. A database of all customers is kept (obviously!) and the computers dial these customers (depending on flags set on their accounts). As soon as someone picks the phone up, the computer transfers it to the next available agent. The agent has no physical control over the call, the headphones beep, and there's a customer on the other end saying "Hello?" and that's it. The agent then performs the schpiel.
>
> There would probably be about 30 seconds between coming off a call, and the next one coming in (when I started, I was told there was about 90 seconds) and this continues throughout the shift.
>
> The call centre is a pretty stressful place, with most of the agents getting as stressed or more stressed than the customers.
>
> Increasingly higher sales targets started coming in, and more products were being introduced. Unfortunately, the training to go with these products was pretty poor, being in the form of glossy—but shallow—PowerPoint presentations. We knew the basics of the products, but we could not answer all questions, and this didn't go down well with some of the more knowledgeable customers. If it was something we might have an idea on, then I'm afraid we would sometimes bullsh't.
>
> I think telesales calls were targeted not to exceed about six minutes.
>
> One day, they decided to open an inbound sales channel. The idea was to try to sell products to customers who were calling in to us. I signed up, thinking maybe things would be a bit easier. What a surprise to come onto the sales floor and take incessant customer complaint calls, having completed three weeks of training for inbound sales!

We were expected to take all manner of calls. We had to use different systems for logging orders and calls, and those systems were very difficult to use—with DOS-like command-line interfaces.

There would be a command to look up a customer's address/general details. Another command would look up an order on a customer's account. Instead of having a mouse and clicking things, we had to use commands and order codes to issue products on customers' accounts. We would then have to use a different command if we wanted to enter the customer's delivery address details. Another command later, and we would then be able to confirm the dates for the order. And after another command, the order would be confirmed.

So, the customer would be waiting impatiently on the phone, thinking the agent was a slow typist. The agent may then get stressed, because they cannot find a particular order code for a certain product, or cannot remember a certain command, or might make a typing error—that sort of thing.

This all had to be done within nine minutes.

After dealing with the complaint, we then had to try to sell them extra products using our inbound sales training. And this is far from easy—nothing like ringing up a company to complain and having one of their agents try to flog you more products!

I started to question my manager as to whether there was any point in this, but got nowhere. Managers, in general, seemed uninterested in what we were doing, beyond telling us of the new products

we were to try to sell, or relaying irrelevant upper-management news. The general level of management skill seemed low to me.

Eventually, I resigned and was escorted off the premises by security.

>> The Dangers of Leaving a Paper Trail

We may resent the availability of technology that allows employers to monitor every keystroke on our computers, but it is often the documents written on the machines that do the most harm. Consider the following recent events:

- In October 2003, Microsoft contractor Michael Hanscom was fired after posting a picture on his personal blog. The picture showed some new Apple Macintosh G5 computers being delivered to Microsoft's Redmond, Washington, headquarters—presumably for a detailed "inspection."[4]
- In March 2005, Boeing CEO Harry Stonecipher was dismissed after e-mails "of a romantic nature" were brought to the attention of the board of directors, revealing Stonecipher's affair with a Boeing vice president of operations.[5]
- In November 2009, a technology consultant at Cornell Business School managed to forward a detailed and highly personal e-mail to his mistress (another Cornell Business School employee) to the entire school.[6]
- In September 2010, Facebook CEO and cofounder Mark Zuckerburg faced the embarrassment of seeing internal instant messages (IMs) that he had written made public. The IM's revealed Zuckerburg bragging about how much information he had obtained about people based on their Facebook submissions. He admitted publicly that he wrote the IMs and stated that he "absolutely' regretted writing them.[7]
- In November 2010, the Dublin, Ireland, office of accountancy firm PricewaterhouseCoopers was forced to launch an internal investigation after an e-mail ranking the "Top 10" of the new young female associates was circulated among 17 male staff members in the office. The e-mail was quickly forwarded to other businesses and proceeded to "go viral," spreading across the Internet.[8]

PROGRESS ✓ QUESTIONS

9. How would you describe the atmosphere in this call center?
10. Jamie's calls were monitored at all times by a call center supervisor. Is that ethical? Why or why not?
11. What would you say is the worst part of working in this call center?
12. When Jamie resigned, she was escorted from the building by security. Is that ethical? Why or why not?

Life Skills

>> The mixed blessing of technology

Take a moment and think about how many benefits we are able to derive from the Internet, personal computers, and cell phones. Without them, you could still call someone on a landline, but for a long-distance friend you would probably write a letter and send it by snail-mail. To do research for a homework assignment you would go to the library to use an encyclopedia rather than Google or Wikipedia, and then type your paper on a typewriter!

The world of instant access—e-mails, IM, texting on your Sidekick, Blackberry, or iPhone—has certainly made communication faster and easier, but have you ever stopped to consider the downside of that instantaneous access? You may pride yourself on your ability to multitask and do homework, e-mails, texts, shop online, and check out some YouTube videos, all at the same time, but how often do you turn everything off and really focus on the subject you are working on?

In the work environment, instant access goes both ways. To your boss, you are just an e-mail, phone call, or text message away—so what if you are at home eating dinner? She needs that information now or needs that report on her desk by 9 A.M., so why shouldn't she call you?

Recent technological advances have blurred the lines between work and home life, and while being a team player can help your long-term career prospects, you're no good to your company if you are a burned-out shell who never finds downtime to rest and recharge your batteries. So find the time to switch off, unplug and, as the saying goes, just chill!

Vicarious Liability A legal concept that means a party may be held responsible for injury or damage even when he or she was not actively involved in an incident.

Cyberliability A legal concept that employers can be held liable for the actions of their employees in their Internet communications to the same degree as if those employers had written those communications on company letterhead.

With the immediate nature of Internet communication and the potential damage that evidence gathered from the electronic trail of e-mails can do, it's easy to see why organizations have become so concerned about the activities of their employees. If the negative effect on your corporate brand and reputation weren't enough of a reason to be concerned, then the legal concept of vicarious liability should grab any employer's attention.

VICARIOUS LIABILITY

Vicarious liability is a legal concept that means a party may be held responsible for injury or damage even when he or she was not actively involved in an incident. Parties that may be charged with vicarious liability are generally in a supervisory role over the person or parties personally responsible for the injury or damage. The implications of vicarious liability are that the party charged is responsible for the actions of his or her subordinates.

There are a variety of situations in which a party may be charged with vicarious liability. Contractors may face charged [sic] of vicarious liability if their subcontractors fail to complete a job, perform the job incorrectly, or are found guilty of other contract violations. Parents have been charged with vicarious liability when the actions of their children cause harm or damage. Employers can face a number of situations involving vicarious liability issues, including sexual harassment of one employee by another, discriminatory behavior by an employee against fellow employees or customers, or any other action in which one of their employees personally causes harm, even if that employee acts against the policies of the employer.[9]

So as an employer, you could be held liable for the actions of your employees through Internet communications to the same degree as if they had written those communications on company letterhead. The new term for this is **cyberliability,** which applies the existing legal concept of liability to a new world—computers. The extent of this new liability can be seen in the top categories of litigation recorded by Elron Software:[10]

- Discrimination
- Harassment
  - Obscenity and pornography
  - Defamation and libel
  - Information leaks
  - Spam

If we acknowledge the liabilities employers face that are a direct result of the actions of their employees, does that justify employee monitoring to control (and hopefully prevent) any action that might place the company at risk? Or are employees entitled to some degree of privacy at work?

TOP 20 BLONDE JOKES

Bill Davis was really torn about the complaint that had just landed on his desk from a female employee in the accounting department. As HR director for Midland Pharmaceuticals, it was his job to address any complaints about employee behavior. Over the years, the company had invested a lot of money in training employees on the biggest employee behavior issues—sexual harassment and discrimination—probably, Bill suspected, because of the real danger of lawsuits that could cost the company tens if not hundreds of thousands of dollars to settle. However, this complaint had Bill stumped.

Midland was a midsize regional company of about 180 employees. Their rural location provided a good quality of life for their employees—no commuting headaches, good schools, and salaries that were competitive with their more metropolitan competitors. Turnover was not an issue—in fact, the last employee newsletter had featured eight members of the same family working for Midland, and the

next edition would feature one family with three generations working for the company. This was a good company to work for, and Bill enjoyed his job as HR director.

CONTINUED >>

Jane Williams was a new employee in accounting. She had moved here as part of her husband's relocation to the area with another company about three months ago. Bill's conversation with her manager had revealed that she was a model employee—punctual, reliable, and very productive. Then Steve Collins in the warehouse had decided to brighten everyone's Friday by forwarding an e-mail that one of his buddies had sent to him. The title of the e-mail was "Top 20 Blonde Jokes." Collins had used the corporate e-mail directory to send the e-mail to everyone with a simple "Happy Friday!" message, so Bill had opened it and, he confessed to himself, laughed at a couple of the jokes. He had then moved on to the quarterly report he was working on and thought nothing more of it.

Jane, who was blonde ("a natural blonde," as she had pointed out in her e-mail), did not find the e-mail funny at all—in fact, she took such offense to it that she filed a formal grievance against Collins, claiming that the e-mail created "a hostile working environment" for her (one of the key phrases the lawyers had emphasized in the harassment training). Bill had also been told that Jane was trying to get some of the other women in the department on her side by complaining that since the blonde jokes were always about females, they were discriminatory to women.

Bill had interviewed Jane personally when she was hired, and she didn't strike him as the type of employee who would try to hold the company for ransom over such a thing, so he suspected that the "hostile work environment" comment was meant more as an indication of her emotional response to the e-mail than a serious threat of legal action. However, her complaint was a formal one, and he needed to act on it. Unfortunately, Midland's policies on e-mail communication had always been fairly informal. It had never been raised as an issue before now. People were always sending jokes and silly stories, and Midland had relied upon the common sense of their employees not to send anything offensive or derogatory.

The IT folks took all the necessary precautions for network and data security, but as a family-owned company, the thought of monitoring employee e-mails had never been considered. Now, Bill feared, the issue would have to be addressed.

QUESTIONS

1. Was Steve Collins wrong to send the e-mail? Why?
2. Is Jane Williams overreacting in filing her formal complaint? Explain why or why not.
3. What impact do you think any change in the employee privacy policies would have at Midland?
4. What are Bill Davis's options here?

It was terribly dangerous to let your thoughts wander when you were in any public place or within range of a telescreen. The smallest thing could give you away. A nervous tic, an unconscious look of anxiety, a habit of muttering to yourself— anything that carried with it the suggestion of abnormality, of having something to hide. In any case, to wear an improper expression on your face . . . was itself a punishable offense. There was even a word for it in Newspeak: facecrime . . .

—George Orwell, *1984*, Book 1, Chapter 5

THE RIGHT TO PRIVACY—BIG BROTHER IS IN THE HOUSE

Listen for this generic statement the next time you call a company and navigate through the voice mail menu—this is usually the last thing you hear before you are (hopefully) connected to a live person:

Calls may be monitored for quality control and training purposes.

In his novel *1984*, George Orwell created a dark and bleak world where "Big Brother" monitored everything you did and controlled every piece of information to which you were given access. Many supporters of employee privacy rights argue that we have reached that state now that employers have the technology to monitor every keystroke on your computer, track every Web site you visit, and record every call you make. The vicarious liability argument is presented to justify these actions as being in the best interests of shareholders, but what is in the best interests of the employees?

The liability argument and the recent availability of capable technology may be driving this move toward an Orwellian work environment, but what are the long-term effects likely to be? Employee turnover costs organizations thousands of dollars in recruitment costs,

FIG. 8.1 Ten Commandments of Computer Ethics

1. Thou Shalt Not Use a Computer to Harm Other People.

2. Thou Shalt Not Interfere with Other People's Computer Work.

3. Thou Shalt Not Snoop Around in Other People's Computer Files.

4. Thou Shalt Not Use a Computer to Steal.

5. Thou Shalt Not Use a Computer to Bear False Witness.

6. Thou Shalt Not Copy or Use Proprietary Software for Which You Have Not Paid.

7. Thou Shalt Not Use Other People's Computer Resources without Authorization or Proper Compensation.

8. Thou Shalt Not Appropriate Other People's Intellectual Output.

9. Thou Shalt Think about the Social Consequences of the Program You Are Writing or the System You Are Designing.

10. Thou Shalt Always Use a Computer in Ways That Ensure Consideration and Respect for Your Fellow Humans.

Source: Computer Ethics Institute, "Ten Commandments of Computer Ethics," Computer Professionals for Social Responsibility, http://cpsr.org/issues/ethics/cei.

PROGRESS ✓ QUESTIONS

13. Which of the "Ten Commandments of Computer Ethics," in Figure 8.1, carry the strongest ethical message? Why?

14. Define the term *vicarious liability*.

15. List four of the top categories of litigation related to Internet communications.

16. Define the term *cyberliability*.

training, and lost productivity. Creating a "locked-down" place to work may protect your liability, but it may also drive away those employees who really aren't comfortable being treated like lab rats.

Critics argue that constant employee surveillance only serves to escalate the stress of an already pressure-filled work environment. What do you think?

Study Alert

>> Conclusion

The Computer Ethics Institute offers some simple guidelines on the appropriate use of technology, but the debate over whether all this technology demands a new techno-friendly school of ethics is likely to continue. However, addressing the issue in real time requires us to consider how many of the issues have really changed from the variables we have been discussing in the previous seven chapters of this book. We are still talking about the same stakeholders, conducting the same business transactions in the same fiercely competitive markets. What have changed are the platforms on which those transactions can now take place and, more importantly, the speed with which they occur.

Should the same rules that apply to recording telephone calls apply to e-mails in the same way, or should there be a different set of rules? The reality is that our working lives have changed dramatically since the arrival of all this technology. We all spend a lot more time at work, and the availability

CONTINUED >>

of instant access to our work means that the line between work life and private life is now much less clearly defined. This change should mean that the employer's ability to intrude on our personal lives with an urgent request would be balanced by an equal flexibility in our time at work—but does that really happen where you work? If you think this debate is being overhyped in the media, consider the following summary of employee surveillance capabilities.[11]

Remarkably invasive tools exist to monitor employees at the workplace. These include:

- Packet-sniffing software can intercept, analyze, and archive all communications on a network, including employee e-mail, chat sessions, file sharing, and Internet browsing. Employees who use the workplace network to access personal e-mail accounts not provided by the company are not protected. Their private accounts, as long as they are accessed on workplace network or phone lines, can be monitored.
- Keystroke loggers can be employed to capture every key pressed on a computer keyboard. These systems will even record information that is typed and then deleted.
- Phone monitoring is pervasive in the American workplace. Some companies employ systems that automatically monitor call content and breaks between receiving calls.
- Video surveillance is widely deployed in the American workplace. In a number of cases, video surveillance has been used in employee bathrooms, rest areas, and changing areas. Video surveillance, under federal law, is acceptable where the camera focuses on publicly accessible areas. However, installment in areas where employees or customers have a legitimate expectation of privacy, such as inside bathroom stalls, can give the employee a cause of action under tort law.
- "Smart" ID cards can track an employee's location while he or she moves through the workplace. By using location tracking, an employer can monitor whether employees spend enough time in front of the bathroom sink to wash their hands. New employee ID cards can even determine the direction the worker is facing at any given time.

FRONTLINE FOCUS
Problems at ComputerWorld—Steve Makes a Decision

Steve thought long and hard about what he should do now. As a new employee, he really didn't want to get a reputation as a troublemaker, and he liked working with Larry most of the time. Anyway, there was no harm done. Mr. Johnson got a new hard drive under his warranty, ComputerWorld got the replacement contract (keeping Larry and him employed!), and Larry got his perk of a slightly used hard drive to sell at the flea market next weekend. As far as ComputerWorld was concerned, the drives were destroyed—its employee manual instructed them to drill holes through the drives and throw them away. What else was the manufacturer going to do with them? Break them up and recycle them for scrap? That seemed like a waste of a perfectly good hard drive.

"Larry's a reliable guy," thought Steve. "I'm sure he'll remember to erase those drives before he sells them.

Before he knew it, Steve was "one of the guys." Larry taught him all the "tricks of the trade," and between them they built a lucrative side business of used computer parts repaired under warranty, listed as "destroyed," and then sold at the flea market on the weekends.

Unfortunately, two months later, Mr. Johnson received a telephone call from someone who had bought a used hard drive at the flea market. The seller had told him that the drive had been erased, but when he installed it, he found all Mr. Johnson's personal information still on the hard drive.

QUESTIONS

1. What could Steve have done differently here?
2. What do you think will happen now?
3. What will be the consequences for Steve, Larry, Mr. Johnson, and ComputerWorld?

[For Review]

1. **Evaluate the ethical ramifications of recent technological advances.**

   Technological advances often deliver new and improved functionality before we have had the chance to fully consider the ethical ramifications of those improvements. Having a computer at every employee's workstation enables rapid communication, but it also allows employers to monitor every e-mail sent and Web site visited. Consumers who register on a company's Web site often provide personal data with no clear understanding of what the company will do with that data or how securely they will be stored.

2. **Explain the opposing employer and employee views of privacy at work.**

   The employer view begins with the premise that other than lunch and any scheduled breaks, all your activity should be work-related. Any nonwork-related Web-surfing or personal e-mails represent a misuse of company property. Using monitoring software to track such activity is not an infringement of privacy but a standard monitoring procedure of company property.

   In contrast, the employee view resents the intrusion of monitoring practices as a clear infringement of civil rights. With the constant connectivity of laptops and smart phones now blurring the line between work hours and home life, employees argue that greater flexibility is warranted. In addition, from a trust perspective, employees raise the question that if you feel the need to monitor them constantly, why did you hire them in the first place?

3. **Distinguish between thin and thick consent.**

   In an economic climate of high unemployment, any formal notification of corporate monitoring of e-mail and Web activity with a clear "take it or leave" message, represents thin *consent, since the employees have limited options available to them if they object to the monitoring practices.*

   If employees do have options available to them, such as when jobs are plentiful or their skills are highly marketable, then consent to the monitoring practices would be considered thick, *since those employees would have realistic alternatives if they found the practices unacceptable.*

4. **Evaluate the concept of vicarious liability.**

   Vicarious liability is a legal concept that means a party may be held responsible for injury or damage even when he or she was not actively involved in an incident. The implications of vicarious liability are that the party charged is responsible for the actions of his or her subordinates. In this case, the "party" would be the corporation, and the "subordinates" would be the employees of that corporation. However, companies have always been liable for the actions of their employees in the performance of their designated work responsibilities. What has changed is the notion of cyberliability, where an employee's Internet activity (Web surfing and e-mails) can be treated in the same manner as letters written on company letterhead. Therefore, anything inappropriate, offensive, unethical, or illegal that an employee does while "on the clock" can expose the company to vicarious liability. On that basis, monitoring software is just allowing companies to do something they have always wanted to do but never had the capability until now.

5. **Analyze an organization's employee-surveillance capabilities.**

   In chronological order of arrival in our work environment, phone monitoring has been employed for decades. Before the technology existed to record calls automatically, human beings (operators or supervisors) could be called upon to "listen in" to conversations. Video surveillance has slowly expanded from the secure protection of key access points to an office or factory to a more widespread monitoring of every area of the company's physical plant.

   The rapid advancement of computer technology (and the perceived increase in cyberliability) has led to the development of keystroke-logging software to capture every key pressed on a computer keyboard. Similarly, "packet-sniffing" software (named after the practice of breaking up blocks of information into packets for distribution over the Internet) can intercept, analyze, and store all communications on a network.

   The most recent advance has been the "smart" ID card that can track an employee's location while he or she moves through the workplace. In the same manner as GPS monitoring of delivery vehicles, the company now knows where you are at all times.

[Key Terms]

[Review Questions]

1. Should you be allowed to surf the Web at work? Why or why not?

2. Are your telephone calls monitored where you work? If they are, how does that make you feel? If they aren't monitored, how would you feel if that policy were introduced?

3. What would you do if someone sent you an e-mail at work that you found offensive? Would you just delete it or say something to that person?

4. If you had the chance to work from home and telecommute, would you take it? If the opportunity meant that you had to allow your company to monitor every call on your phone and every keystroke on your computer, would you still take it? Explain why or why not.

5. You have just been issued a new company BlackBerry (to make sure you never miss an important e-mail or phone call!). Are you now obligated to answer those calls and e-mails at any time, day or night? Why or why not?

6. Would you use that new BlackBerry for personal calls and e-mails? Why or why not?

[Review Exercise]

Removing temptation. I'm the customer service director for Matrix Technologies, a manufacturer of design software. We've recently upgraded our customer service extranet service to allow our clients to download software updates (including any patches or "bug fixes") directly from our extranet site. The initial response from the majority of our customers has been very positive—the new process is convenient, quick, and reliable—they love it. Everyone, that is, except for our large local government client. The new service doesn't help it at all—and the reason for that really has me stumped. Earlier this year, this client made the decision to remove access to the Internet from all its desktop computers, so no access to the Internet means no access to our customer service site to download our upgrades. When I asked the IT director if he was pulling my leg, he got mad at me. Apparently its IT personnel installed some monitoring software on the system and found that employees were spending almost 40 percent of their time surfing the Web—mostly to news and entertainment sites, but sometimes to places that would make you blush! Its response was swift and effective. The employees came in one morning and found that they no longer had access to the Web from their desktops. Now we have to come up with a plan to mail upgrade CDs to 24 regional offices.

1. How well did Matrix's client handle this situation?

2. What kind of message does this send to the employees of Matrix's client?

3. What other options were available here?

4. On the assumption that the downloadable software patches can greatly improve updates for its client, does Matrix have an ethical obligation to get involved here? Explain your answer.

[Internet Exercises]

1. Visit the Web site for the LRN Corporation at www.lrn.com.
   a. What does the LRN Corporation do?
   b. What are the five core values of the LRN culture?
   c. What is the stated purpose of the LRN-RAND Center for Corporate Ethics, Law and Governance?

2. Visit the Web site for the Electronic Frontier Foundation (EFF) at www.eff.org.
   a. What does the EFF do?
   b. What is the EFF "Blogger's Rights" Project?
   c. Why is the EFF concerned about Google's approach to reader privacy?

[Team Exercises]

1. **When are you "at work"?**

   Divide into two teams. One team must defend the *employer* position on employee monitoring. The other team must defend the *employee* position. Draw on the policies and experiences you have gathered from your own jobs.

2. **A new billing system.**

   A new system that bills corporate clients is under development, and there is a discussion over how much to invest in error checking and control. One option has been put forward so far, and initial estimates suggest it would add about 40 percent to the overall cost of the project but would vastly improve the quality of the data in the database and the accuracy of client billing. Not spending the money would increase the risk of overcharging some midsize clients. Divide into two groups and prepare arguments *for* and *against* spending the extra money on error checking and control. Remember to include in your argument how stakeholders would be affected and how you would deal with any unhappy customers.

3. **E-mail privacy.**

   Divide into two groups and prepare arguments *for* and *against* the following behavior: *Your company has a clearly stated employee surveillance policy that stipulates that anything an employee does on a company-owned computer is subject to monitoring. You manage a regional office of 24 brokers for a company that offers lump-sum payments to people receiving installment payments—from lottery winnings or personal injury settlements—who would rather have a large amount of money now than small monthly checks for the next 5, 10, or 20 years.*

   You have just terminated one of your brokers for failing to meet his monthly targets for three consecutive months. He was extremely angry about the news, and when he went back to his cube, he was observed typing feverishly on his computer in the 10 minutes before building security arrived to escort him from the premises.

   When your IT specialist arrives to shut down the broker's computer, he notices that it is still open and logged in to his Gmail account and that there is evidence that several e-mails with large attachments had been sent from his company e-mail address to his Gmail address shortly after the time he was notified that he was being fired. The e-mails had been deleted from the folder of sent items in his company account. The IT specialist suggests that you take a look at the e-mails and specifically the information attached to those e-mails. Should you?

4. **Software piracy.**

   Divide into two groups and prepare arguments *for* and *against* the following behavior: *You run your own graphic design company as a one-person show, doing primarily small business projects and subcontracting work for larger graphic design agencies. You have just been hired as an adjunct instructor at the local community college to teach a graphic design course. You decide that it's easier to use your own laptop rather than worry about having the right software loaded on the classroom machines, and so the college IT department loads the most current version of your graphic design software on your machine. Business has been a little slow for you, and you haven't spent the money to update your own software. The version that the IT department loads is three editions ahead of your version with lots of new functionality.*

   You enjoy teaching the class, although the position doesn't pay very well. One added bonus, however, is that you can be far more productive on your company projects using the most current version of the software on your laptop, and since you use some of that work as examples in your class, you're not really doing anything unethical, right?

>> STUMBLING OVER GMAIL

In spring 2004, with business booming and Google basking in the glow of its ever-growing popularity, Larry [Page] and Sergey [Brin] prepared to dazzle Internet users with a different kind of email. Building on the strong Google brand name, they called the new service "Gmail." . . . Larry and Sergey wanted to make a big splash with Gmail. There was no reason to provide the service unless it was radically better than email services already offered by Microsoft, Yahoo, AOL, and others. They built Gmail to be smarter, easier, cheaper, and superior. Otherwise Google users wouldn't be impressed, and its creators wouldn't be living up to their own high standards . . . [Larry and Sergey] had identified email problems that Google, with its immense computing power, could address. For example, it was difficult, if not impossible, to find and retrieve old emails when users needed them. America Online automatically deleted emails after 30 days to hold down systems costs. There was no easy way to store the mountain of emails that an accumulative Internet user amassed without slowing personal computers or paying Microsoft, Yahoo, or another firm to provide additional storage.

To blow the competition away and add a Google "wow" factor, Larry and Sergey and the Gmail team inside the Googleplex addressed all these issues and then some. To make the new service an instant hit, they planned to give away one free gigabyte of storage (1,000 megabytes) on Google's own computer network with each Gmail account. That was 500 times greater than the free storage offered by Microsoft and 250 times the free storage offered by Yahoo. . . . One gigabyte was such an amazing amount of storage that Google told Gmail users they would never need to delete another email.

Finally, to inject Gmail with that Googley sense of magic, computer users would be able to find emails instantly, without ever having to think about sorting or storing them. A Gmail search would be fast, accurate, and as easy to perform as a Google search, making the service an instant hit among trusted employees who sampled it inside the Googleplex.

Unlike most of its new products, Gmail was designed to make money even during the test phase. With demand for advertising increasing, the company needed to increase the available space it could sell. It made sense to Larry and Sergey to profit from Gmail by putting the same type of small ads on the right-hand side of Gmails that Google put on the right-hand side of search results. The ads would be "contextually relevant," triggered by words contained in the emails. It was a proven business model that served advertisers and users well as part of Google's search results. By giving advertisers more space on the Google network, Gmail would provide a healthy new stream of profits for the company that would grow over time as the communications technology caught on.

Looking at the world through Google-colored lenses, this seemed like a superb idea in every respect. It didn't occur to Larry, Sergey, or any of the other engineers in senior roles at Google that serious people they respected would strenuously object to the privacy implications of having Google's computers reading emails and then placing ads in them based on the content of those messages. . . .

As word spread of Google's plans to put ads in emails, politicians and privacy groups attacked the company and its plans, kicking off a media firestorm. In Massachusetts, anti-Gmail legislation was introduced. Shocked privacy advocates urged the company to pull the product immediately and began circulating anti-Google petitions. One California lawmaker threatened the company, saying that if Google didn't dump Gmail, she would press for legislation banning it. Her bill passed the Senate's Judiciary Committee with only one opposing vote. She decried the ad-driven profiteering in emails as a gross, unwarranted invasion of privacy. For the first time, Google was being viewed with suspicion in a major way. People considered their emails private, and the notion of Google's putting ads in them based on their content seemed to cross the line. . . .

Because from their perspective this was much ado about nothing, Larry and Sergey saw no need to be defensive or respond to crazed critics. In fact, all the publicity would certainly heighten awareness of the Google search engine and its Gmail progeny. Soon enough, friendly columnists who tested Gmail and fell in love with it would begin writing about why the outcry was unjustified. Tradition-bound companies might have seriously considered pulling Gmail, at least temporarily, to quell the uprising. But this was Google, and it had clout, and confident leadership, to ride this out without flinching. The founders began to respond on-message.

"It sounded alarming, but it isn't," Sergey said. "The ads correlate to the message you're reading at the time. We're not keeping your mail and mining it or anything like that. And no information whatsoever goes out. We need to be protective of the mail and the people's privacy. Any Web service will scan your mail. It scans it in order to show it to you; it scans it for spam. All we're doing is showing ads. It's automated. No one is looking, so I don't think it's a privacy issue. I've used Gmail for a while, and I like having the ads. Our ads aren't distracting. They're helpful."

When Google tested Gmail, people bought lots of things by clicking on the ads. To Larry, this was proof that computer users, advertisers, and Google's coffers were all well served by the small ads on the right-hand side of a Gmail. "Even if it seems a little spooky at first, it's useful," he said.

QUESTIONS

1. Google sent out a press release about the Gmail service without mentioning the intention to put ads in the e-mails or how those ads would be selected. Was that ethical? Explain why or why not.

2. Sergey Brin offered the argument that all e-mail providers scan your e-mails for content to ensure that it is yours and that it isn't a spam e-mail. Does that argument justify the decision to scan e-mails for content in order to place "contextually relevant" ads? Explain why or why not.

3. Does the fact that the scanning process is done by computer, with no people reading the e-mails, make the act any less of an invasion of your privacy?

4. Could Google have launched Gmail in a way that would have avoided the media firestorm over privacy? Explain your answer.

Source: David A. Vise, *The Google Story* (New York: Delacorte Press, Random House, 2005), pp. 152–56.

Thinking Critically 8.2

>> REVERB COMMUNICATIONS • Truth in Advertising

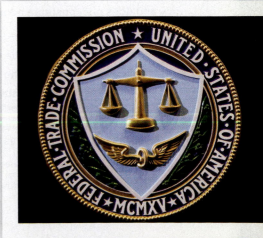

In October 2009, the Federal Trade Commission (FTC) announced its new "Guide Concerning the Use of Endorsements and Testimonials in Advertising," marking its first regulatory update since 1980. Concerned about the new trend of "official" blogs and social media sites that companies were setting up to create buzz around their products, the FTC now required all bloggers to disclose any financial relationship with the company whose products they were reviewing or face fines as high as $11,000.

Critics, while applauding the intent to ensure planted reviews were being controlled, found the guidelines to be confusing for consumer and personal Web sites where advertising content and editorial content overlap. For example, if a blogger uses Google Adwords as a revenue source on his or her blog, the selection of advertisers is automated by Google's keyword "bots," and the blogger has no control over whether or not readers choose

CONTINUED >>

to click on the ad (generating pay-per-click revenue for both the blogger and Google). Should the blogger be obligated to disclose that he or she *may* be receiving revenue from an advertiser? The guidelines are vague on that issue, leaving advertisers and bloggers alike to wait for legal precedents to establish guidance on how the guidelines will be enforced by the FTC.

In August 2010, the FTC provided the first example of such guidance by settling a complaint with video game PR firm Reverb Communications, based in Twain Harte, California. Representing clients such as MTV Games, Ignition Entertainment, and Demiurge Studios, Reverb's performance fee often included a percentage of game sales. From the FTC's perspective, this relationship should have been disclosed under the 2009 guidelines. The complaint against Reverb alleged that between November 2008 and May 2009, Reverb posted reviews about their client's games on Apple's iTunes store "using account names that gave readers the impression the reviews were written by disinterested customers." A sampling of the allegedly fraudulent reviews included: "Amazing new game" and "ONE of the BEST."

While there were no monetary penalties involved in the settlement, Reverb and its founder Tracie Snitker were required to delete any comments still on the Web and are barred from making similar review postings in the future without disclosing their affiliation with the parent company of the product they are reviewing.

As the first target of the new FTC guidelines, Reverb has received a great deal of presumably unwanted media attention over the complaint. Snitker declined most interview requests, and Reverb elected to post a statement in the comments section on every available blog and message board that covered the news of the settlement of the complaint. The statement took a very clear position on the issue:

> During discussions with the FTC, it became apparent that we would never agree on the facts of the situation. Rather than continuing to spend time and money arguing, and laying off employees to fight what we believed was a frivolous matter, we settled this case and ended the discussion because as the FTC states: "The consent agreement is for settlement purposes only and does not constitute admission by the respondents of a law violation."

This issue was specific to a handful of small, independently developed iPhone apps that several team members downloaded onto their personal iPhones in their own time using their own money and accounts, a right and privilege afforded to every iPhone and iTouch user. Any iTunes user will understand that each time a product is purchased you are allowed to post one comment per product. Seven out of our 16 employees purchased games which Reverb had been working on and to this the FTC dedicated an investigation. These posts were neither mandated by Reverb nor connected to our policies. Bottom line, these allegations are old, this situation was settled a while ago and had nothing to do with the clients that many outlets have been reporting. The FTC has continuously made statements that the reviews are "fake reviews," something we question; if a person plays the game and posts one review based on their own opinion about the game should that be constituted as "fake"? The FTC should evaluate if personal posts by these employees justifies this type of time, money and investigation. It's become apparent to Reverb that this disagreement with the FTC is being used to communicate their new posting policy. We stand by the statement from the FTC that "The consent agreement is for settlement purposes only and does not constitute admission by the respondents of a law violation."

QUESTIONS

1. Why did the FTC introduce new guidelines in 2009?

2. What was the nature of the complaint against Reverb Communications?

3. Considering Reverb's position in its widely distributed statement in response to the settlement of the complaint, was there an ethical transgression here?

4. Given that there was no admission of guilt or financial penalty applied, do you think this settlement will prompt companies such as Reverb to be more ethical in their postings in the future? Why or why not?

Sources: Maha Atal, "FTC Takes on Pay-per-Post," *Fortune*, October 5, 2009; Miguel Helft, "Charges Settled over Fake Reviews on iTunes," *The New York Times*, August 26, 2010; David Gelles, "U.S. Regulator Raps PR Group for Endorsements," *Financial Times*, August 27, 2010; Courtney Rubin, "FTC Settles First Case in New Crackdown on Fake Reviews," *Inc.*, August 27, 2010; and Jason Wilson, "Reverb Settles with FTC over iTunes Reviews," *PCWorld*, August 28, 2010.

>> THE HIPAA PRIVACY RULE

On August 21, 1996, Congress enacted the Health Insurance Portability and Accountability Act (HIPAA), a piece of legislation designed to clarify exactly what rights patients have over their own medical information and to specify what procedures are needed to be in place to enforce appropriate sharing of that information within the health care community. "This law required Congress to pass legislation within 3 years to govern privacy and confidentiality related to [a patient's] medical record. If that action did not occur, then the Department of Health and Human Services (DHHS) was to identify and publish the appropriate legislation. Because Congress did not pass required legislation, the DHHS developed and publicized a set of rules on medical record privacy and confidentiality" that required compliance from most health care providers by April 14, 2003.

Since then, the HIPAA legislation has often been referred to as a privacy rule, but in reality it is disclosure legislation that "offers a floor, rather than a ceiling, for health privacy." As such, the true purpose behind the commitment to patient privacy is to control how patient information is collected and by whom, how and where it will be stored safely for future retrieval, and how health care providers and other health care organizations will use it, ideally on a need-to-know basis only.

As Bill Trippe explains the law in an *Econtent* article, "The key . . . is to provide authorized [health care professionals] with precisely the information they need, when they need it—but only the precise information they need so that [patient] privacy is not compromised."

However, while advances in information technology—specifically database technology—appear to offer the promise of functionality to do precisely that, the sheer number of combinations of users and needs in the provision of health care would seem to exceed even those grand promises. Compare, for example, the patient records needs of a doctor prescribing a specific medication, as opposed to those of a doctor giving a full physical examination. The former might need lab results and any relevant research about the medication; the latter would prefer to have the patient's full medical history. It may be possible to retrieve that information from one comprehensive database, but if everyone has different information needs, how do you set up that database to restrict access where appropriate under the banner of need to know or to summarize information where needed to maximize patient privacy?

The logistical challenges of this scenario are further complicated when you consider that the legislation covers not only patient care but also the administrative aspects of the health care system. For example, according to Richard Sobel of the *Hastings Center Report,* HIPAA gave "six hundred thousand 'covered entities'—such as health care plans, clearing houses, and health maintenance organizations—'regulatory permission to use or disclose protected health information for treatment, payment, and health care operations' (known as TPO) without patient consent. Some of these 'routine purposes' for which disclosures are permitted are far removed from treatment . . . 'health care operations' (HCO) include most administrative and profit-generating activities, such as auditing, data analyses for plan sponsors, training of non-healthcare professionals, general administrative activities, business planning and development, cost management, payment methods improvement, premium rating, underwriting, and asset sales—all unrelated to patient care."

HIPAA was enacted to address privacy concerns in the face of increasingly sophisticated database technology that can send your most private information to the other side of the globe in a split second. Ironically, however, many violations of the privacy rule have little connection, if any, with direct patient care and treatment. Consider the following two examples:

1. Patient MW, a victim of domestic abuse, informs [her nurse] that her status as a patient in the hospital must be kept confidential. [The nurse] assures MW that she's safe and that the staff won't share information with anyone who inquires about her. [The nurse] informs the unit clerk not to release any

CONTINUED >>

information on MW, but fails to remove MW's name and room number from the assignment board [at the nurse's station]. Later in the shift, MW's husband enters the nurse's station and asks the unit clerk for his wife's number. The unit clerk, following the nurse's instructions, states that she has no information on the person named. The spouse, upon looking around the nurse's station, sees his wife's name and room number. He rushes to the room and physically abuses her. The unit clerk calls hospital security, which promptly arrives and escorts the spouse off the unit. He's subsequently jailed for spousal abuse.

2. A member of the electronic medical record (EMR) staff was conducting a training session for resident physicians and medical students at an outpatient facility. . . . The trainer used fictional patient records specifically created for EMR training purposes for the demonstrations and exercises. During the Q&A session one of the residents stated that just that morning he had had problems prescribing a specific medication in the medication module of the EMR, which had created an inaccurate entry in the patient's electronic chart. The resident asked how he could correct the mistake. Since the trainer knew that many new EMR users had had similar problems with this feature of the EMR, she thought this would be a good 'teachable moment.' She asked the resident the name of the patient. She then looked up the patient's chart and projected the patient's medication list on the screen for all the class to see. The trainer proceeded to correct the error in the EMR.

While the first example represents a clear violation of the HIPAA legislation, since the patient's room information was publicly accessible simply by visiting the nurse's station, the situation is not so straightforward in the second example. The residents and medical students being trained were employees of a covered entity, and since training falls under the heading of approved health care operations, no violation occurred. Of course, it is debatable as to whether it was appropriate to display the patient's records to the entire group rather than helping the one student after the class, since that choice calls into question the issue of using the minimum information on a need-to-know basis. What is clear, however, is that while the purpose of HIPAA may be clearly stated, the interpretation of the legislation lacks the same degree of clarity.

QUESTIONS

1. Is the term *privacy rule* accurate in describing the HIPAA legislation? Why or why not?
2. Is it ethical for covered entities to be excused from getting patient permission to use their private information for routine purposes? Why or why not?
3. Based on the limited information in this article, do you think the HIPAA legislation achieves its objective of securing patient privacy?
4. How could this issue of patient privacy have been handled in a more ethical manner?

Sources: Judith A. Erlen, "HIPAA-Clinical and Ethical Considerations for Nurses," *Orthopaedic Nursing* 23, no. 6 (November–December 2004); J. Mack, "Beyond HIPAA-Ethics in the e-Health Arena," *Healthcare Executive*, September–October 2004, pp. 32–33; Bill Trippe, "First Do No Harm: Can Privacy and Advanced Information Technology Coexist?" *Econtent* 26, no. 3 (March 2003); Richard Sobel, "The HIPAA Paradox: The Privacy Rule That's Not," *The Hastings Center Report* 37, no. 4 (July–August 2007); Patricia D. Blair, "Make Room for Patient Privacy," *Nursing Management*, June 2003, pp. 28–29; and Bob Brown, "Did They Break the Rules?" *Journal of Health Care Compliance* 10, no. 2 (March–April 2008).

THE FUTURE OF BUSINESS ETHICS

Having examined the challenges involved in developing an ethical culture within an organization, we can now consider what lies ahead for companies as they grow on an international and global scale. Crossing national boundaries to conduct business often involves crossing cultural boundaries at the same time. How do organizations address those cultural differences while staying true to their own ethical principles?

Chapter 9 examines the challenges organizations face in the pursuit of global ethics. While they may prefer to adopt their own policies as a universal standard of ethics, the reality is that the organizations and customers from other countries with whom they conduct business will bring their own moral standards and ethical principles into the relationship. What happens when there is a conflict in those standards?

Chapter 10 examines the big-picture issue of maintaining an ethical culture in the face of all these challenges. This far into the text, we have examined all the issues and the resources available to help organizations and their employees with those issues, but the challenge of maintaining and enforcing a code of ethics must be faced on a daily basis.

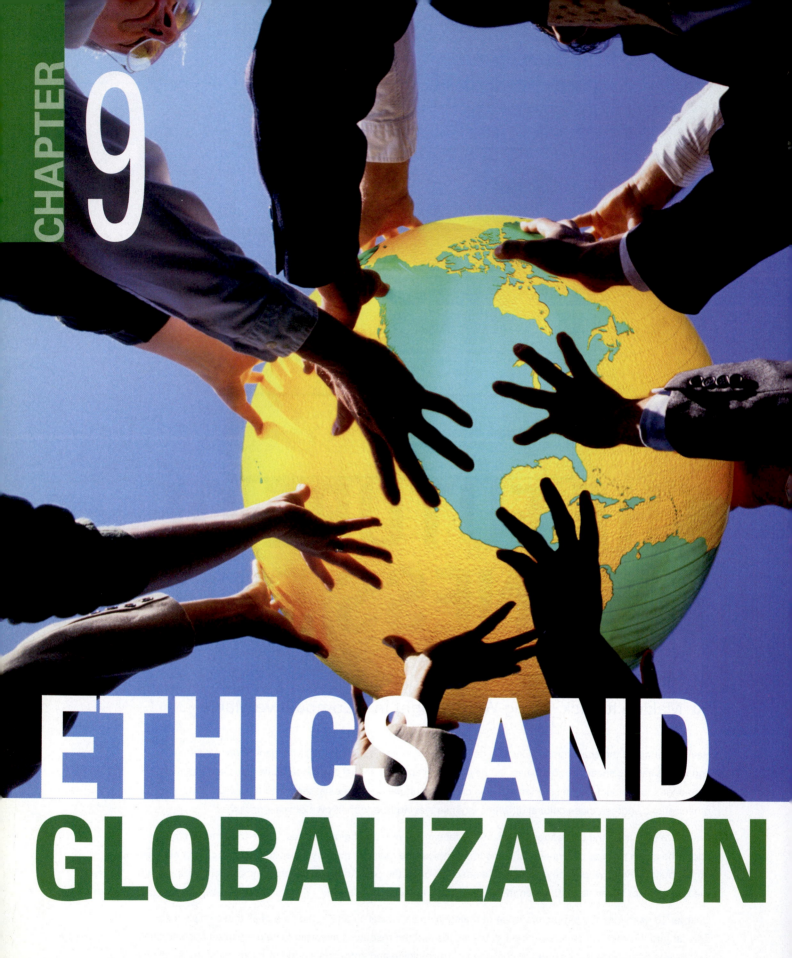

ETHICS AND
GLOBALIZATION

After studying this chapter, you should be able to:

1 Understand the ethical issues arising in global business.

2 Explain the issue of ethical relativism in a global environment.

3 Explain the challenges in developing a global code of ethics.

4 Analyze the ramifications of the UN Global Compact.

5 Explain the OECD Guidelines for Multinational Enterprises.

FRONTLINE FOCUS
A Matter of Definition

Tom DiPietropolo is a copywriter with a regional ad agency that has a very lucrative contract with the Smith's national retail chain. He likes working for a smaller agency even though he could probably make more money with a larger national organization. At least here everyone knows each other and works together as a team, and he likes the culture too. The agency does good work for good clients, and it has been known to turn down contracts for campaigns that conflicted with its corporate values. In fact, its decision to turn down a campaign for a local bourbon distillery made the trade press.

Tom has friends at a couple of the national agencies, and they describe the culture as a totally cutthroat one where it's everyone for himself and any business is good business as long as the check clears.

Landing the Smith's account was a big deal for Tom's regional agency, and they all worked hard to make it happen (and celebrated with a party that will probably go down in company history as one of the best ever!). Now the agency has to deliver on everything it promised in its bid for the work. The first big project is the new campaign for the July Fourth sales event coming up. The theme of the event is "Made in America," which the company thinks will tap into a sense of patriotism. Smith's has lined up several very low-priced "loss leaders" to get customers into the store, and it has promoting them heavily as being "made in America."

Tom has been assigned to write the copy for a series of ads featuring BBQ utensil sets featuring the American flag and red, white, and blue color combinations. As part of his prep kit, Tom receives the product specifications on the items along with the photographs that his copy will support.

As he is reading through the material, Tom notices that his contacts at Smith's included by mistake a copy of the original billing paperwork for the shipment—paperwork showing that the items were actually made in Indonesia by a company named Jakarta Enterprises.

The name seems very familiar to Tom, and he looks the company up on Google. To his dismay, he finds several articles criticizing the business practices of Jakarta Enterprises—specifically in the area of employing young children in sweatshop working conditions.

QUESTIONS

1. Ten guidelines for organizations doing business with developing nations are listed on page **179**. Do you think Smith's is following any of these?

2. Review the UN Global Compact on page **182**. How many violations has Smith's incurred by doing business with Jakarta Enterprises?

3. What are Tom's options here?

The World has become small and completely interdependent.

Wendell L. Wilkie, Republican presidential nominee defeated by Franklin D. Roosevelt in 1940

>> Ethics and Globalization

Up to now we have focused primarily on a domestic approach to business ethics—how North American organizations get their own house in order and ensure that they have a clearly defined code of ethics which all their stakeholders can relate to and understand.

Once we step outside the domestic environment and conduct business on an international or a global scale, the concept of business ethics changes dramatically. Business transactions in different countries in different languages and different cultures inevitably force North American companies to revisit the ethical principles to which they are committed and to recognize which principles and policies they are willing to negotiate in favor of the client country with which they are looking to do business.

ETHICS IN LESS-DEVELOPED NATIONS

Any discussion of business ethics in this arena must distinguish between the developed and **less-developed nations** of the world. If we follow the traditional stereotypes, companies in the **developed nations** know how the game is played. Business is typically conducted in English, and all international business travelers have read and reread their copy of *Kiss, Bow, or Shake Hands: How to Do Business in Sixty Countries*.[1]

Less-Developed Nation A country that lacks the economic, social, and technological infrastructure of a developed nation.

Developed Nation A country that enjoys a high standard of living as measured by economic, social, and technological criteria.

Utilitarianism Ethical choices that offer the greatest good for the greatest number of people.

These nations are busy playing the game of globalization—everyone is pursuing the same goal of maximum profits with minimum costs, and if individual cultures present some challenges, those can be overcome with translations and cultural adaptations. That, of course, is easier said than done. The assumption that "what works here works there" has managed to get a lot of companies into hot water over the years:[2]

- The name Coca-Cola in China was first rendered as Ke-kou-ke-la. Unfortunately, the Coke company did not discover until after thousands of signs had been printed that the phrase means, "bite the wax tadpole" or "female horse stuffed with wax," depending on the dialect. Coke then researched 40,000 Chinese characters and found a close phonetic equivalent, "ko-kou-ko-le," which can be loosely translated as "happiness in the mouth" (though a marketing "classic," this story has been denounced as an urban legend).

- In Taiwan, the translation of the Pepsi slogan "Come alive with the Pepsi Generation" came out as "Pepsi will bring your ancestors back from the dead."

- When Parker Pen marketed a ballpoint pen in Mexico, its ads were supposed to say, "It won't leak in your pocket and embarrass you." However, the company mistakenly thought the Spanish word *embarazar* meant "embarrass"; instead, the ads said, "It won't leak in your pocket and make you pregnant."

- An American T-shirt manufacturer in Miami printed shirts for the Spanish market that promoted the Pope's visit. But instead of the desired "I Saw the Pope" in Spanish, the shirts proclaimed "I Saw the Potato."

- In Italy, a campaign for Schweppes Tonic Water translated the name into Schweppes *Toilet* Water.

- Bacardi concocted a fruity drink with the name "Pavian" to suggest French chic, but "Pavian" means "baboon" in German.

- Clairol introduced the "Mist Stick," a curling iron, into Germany, only to find out that *mist* is slang for manure.

- When Gerber first started selling baby food in Africa, it used the same packaging as in the United States—jars with pictures of the cute little baby on the label. Only later did it learn that in Africa, companies routinely put pictures on the label that describe what's inside, since most people can't read.

- And, as America's favorite chicken magnate, Frank Perdue, was fond of saying, "It takes a tough man to make a tender chicken." In Spanish, however, his words took on a whole new meaning: "It takes a sexually stimulated man to make a chicken affectionate."

These are all amusing anecdotes, but the economic reality underlying them is far more serious. International markets represent growth and with profitable growth come happy shareholders and rising stock prices. In addition, international markets represent new customers as well as sources of cheaper materials and cheap labor.

From a business ethics perspective, this constant hunger for growth at any cost presents some challenges. As we recall from our discussion of **utilitarianism** in Chapter 1, any questionable behavior in overseas markets can be explained away by serving the greatest good for the greatest number of people. However, as we discussed in Chapter 1, when you focus on doing the greatest good for the greatest number of people, there is no accountability for individual actions.

So what happens if you simply transplant your "take no prisoners" aggressive business style from the United States to whatever market you happen to be in? Do the same rules apply? Or do you focus on not breaking any local laws and fall back on the old adage, "If it's legal, it must be ethical"? Are American companies bound by their domestic ethical policies when they conduct business overseas, or are they free to adopt (or completely overlook) local ethics? Is this a uniquely American phenomenon, or do French, German, Russian, or Chinese companies adopt similarly flexible attitudes to business ethics when they step outside their national boundaries?

Before we examine these questions in detail, we should clarify some terminology. The term **globalization** has applications in commercial, economic, social, and political environments. For our purposes, we are concerned with globalization as the expansion of international trade to a point where regional trade blocs (Latin America, Europe, Africa) have overtaken national markets, leading eventually to a global marketplace. As these national markets become interdependent, questions arise over the ethical behavior of economically advanced nations toward developing ones.

Operating in this increasingly globalized business world are **multinational corporations (MNCs)**— also referred to as *transnational corporations*—that pursue revenue (and hopefully profit) on the basis of operating strategies that ignore national boundaries as merely bureaucratic obstacles. Economists disagree over the correct definition of an MNC: Some argue that to be truly multinational, an organization must have owners from more than one country (such as Shell's Anglo-Dutch structure); others argue that an organization is multinational when it generates products and/ or services in multiple countries and when it implements operational policies (marketing,

As a multinational corporation, Shell must reach different markets with different needs. How might this impact local employees at a Shell Service Station?

staffing, and production) that go beyond national boundaries.

It is here that the global ethics dilemma becomes apparent: What happens when you go beyond national boundaries? If ethical standards are based on cultural and social norms and customs, what happens when you are operating in an environment that is representative of multiple cultures and societies?

Critics have argued that most MNCs have chosen to ignore all ethical standards in the pursuit of the almighty dollar on the basis of the following two arguments:

- If they didn't pursue the business, somebody else would.
- They are operating in full compliance with local laws and regulations, which conveniently happen to be far less restrictive than those they would face in their own country.

> **Globalization** The expansion of international trade to a point where national markets have been overtaken by regional trade blocs (Latin America, Europe, Africa), leading eventually to a global marketplace.
>
> **Multinational Corporation (MNC)** A company that provides and sells products and services across multiple national borders. Also known as *transnational corporations*.

PROGRESS ✓ QUESTIONS

1. Explain the term *globalization*.
2. What is an MNC?
3. When is "operating in full compliance with local laws and regulations" unethical?
4. Explain the term *utilitarianism*.

>> Ethical Relativism

For the less-developed nations, the concept of globalization has a different meaning.

Economist Lester Thurow explains:[3]

Among countries, the big losers are in Africa, south of the Sahara. They are not losing, however, because they are being crushed by globalization. . . . [T]hey are losing because they are being ignored by globalization. They are not in the global economy. No one in the business community wants anything to do with countries where illiteracy is high, where modern infrastructure (telecommunications, reliable electrical power) does not exist, and where social chaos reigns. Such countries are neither potential markets nor potential production bases.

Galaxy Mining's Indaba copper mine recently experienced its third accident in the three years that the mine has been operating. Several miners were injured but, fortunately, none seriously. However, during the accident repair process (which was accelerated to get the mine up and running as quickly as possible), one of the retaining walls for the mining blade coolant runoff was damaged, allowing several thousand gallons of chemical sludge to seep into the local river.

To manage the media response to the accident, Galaxy contracted the services of John "Monty" Montgomery, a self-proclaimed "specialist in local public relations and consulting services." Monty billed Galaxy for $1 million in advance as his standard retainer fee, which was paid without question.

Montgomery took control of the Indaba situation quickly, issuing several authoritative press releases committing Galaxy Mining to prompt and full restitution for any damage done by the leak. Thirty days later a press conference was arranged to announce the construction of a new water treatment facility (funded by Galaxy) that, to quote Montgomery, "will guarantee fresh, clean water for local residents for generations to come." The Indaba leak was never mentioned in the local press again.

When Galaxy's auditors requested more detail on the services provided by Montgomery's organization during a routine audit several months later, he responded with an e-mail confirming that the $1 million was "for services rendered in the management of the Indaba mining

incident." No further explanation or documentation was provided.

QUESTIONS

1. Was this an ethical transaction? Explain why or why not.
2. Montgomery "managed" the incident as requested. Is there any evidence to suggest that he did anything unethical?
3. Should the auditors accept his explanation of "services rendered"? Why or why not?
4. What kind of policies should Galaxy Mining put in place to make sure these kinds of "services" aren't utilized again?

Ethical Relativism Gray area in which your ethical principles are defined by the traditions of your society, your personal opinions, and the circumstances of the present moment.

In such environments, the ideal "black and white" world of ethics must give way to a gray area of **ethical relativism.** Policies and procedures can be hard to follow when your customers don't have comparable policies in their own organizations. In addition, policies that have been outlawed here in an attempt to legally enforce ethical corporate behavior may be standard operating procedure in less-developed nations. Social and political chaos can generate a bureaucracy that bears no relation to a logical reality, leaving companies with the tough decision whether to stand by their Western principles of ethical conduct or submit to the practical reality of the local market and "grease the appropriate palms" to get things done.

>> The Pursuit of Global Ethics

Globalization can be seen to have both an upside and a downside. Supporters of the upside argue that globalization is bringing unprecedented improvements in the wealth and standards of living of citizens in developing nations as they leverage their natural resources or low costs of living to attract foreign investment. For the more economically advanced nations, access to those resources enables lower production costs that equate to lower prices and higher income standards for their customers.

Advocates for the downside of globalization argue that it is merely promoting the dark side of capitalism onto the global stage—developing countries are ravaged for their raw materials with no concern for the longer-term economic viability of their national economies; workers are exploited; and corporations are free to take full advantage of less restrictive legal environments.

So how do you take advantage of the upside of globalization while maintaining your ethical standards and avoiding the downside?

As we have seen in previous chapters, any organization that commits itself to establishing and sticking with a clearly defined code of ethics will face considerable challenges, and their commitment will be tested when the quarterly numbers fall a little short of the forecast. However, moving that ethical commitment to a global stage requires a great deal more planning than simply increasing the scale of the policies and procedures. Just because it was developed here does not mean it can be applied in the same manner elsewhere in the world, and it's likely that the ethical policy will require a lot more refinement than simply translating it into the local language.

Critics have argued that the moral temptations of global expansion have simply been too strong for MNCs to ignore. Faced with constant pressure to increase revenue, cut costs, maximize profitability, and grow market share—ideally all in the next 90 days—companies find themselves tempted to take maximum advantage of the less stringent laws and regulations of local markets and (in what critics consider to be the worst transgression), if there are no clear local ethical standards, to operate in the absence of any standards rather than reverting to their own domestic ethical policies.

So what is the answer here? Is the development of a **global code of conduct** a realistic solution to this issue?

Even though we are now seeing the development of larger trading blocs as neighboring countries (such as the European Economic Community) work together to leverage their size and geographic advantage to take a bigger role on the global economic stage, the individual countries within those trading blocs are not disappearing. For this reason, the customs and norms of those individual societies are likely to prevail.

For advocates of global ethics, this means that a *flexible* solution has to be found—one that provides standards of practice to guide managers as they conduct business across national boundaries in the name of global commerce while respecting the individual customs of the countries in which they are operating.

Richard DeGeorge offers the following guidelines for organizations doing business in these situations:[4]

1. Do no intentional harm.
2. Produce more good than harm for the host country.
3. Contribute to the host country's development.
4. Respect the human rights of their employees.
5. Respect the local culture; work with it, not against it.
6. Pay their fair share of taxes.
7. Cooperate with the local government to develop and enforce just background institutions.
8. Majority control of a firm includes the ethical responsibility of attending to the actions and failures of the firm.
9. Multinationals that build hazardous plants are obliged to ensure that the plants are safe and operated safely.
10. Multinationals are responsible for redesigning the transfer of hazardous technologies so that such technologies can be safely administered in host countries.

DeGeorge's guidelines present something of an ethical ideal that can at best provide a conceptual foundation, but at worst they overlook some of the most severe transgressions that have brought such negative attention to the ethical behavior of MNCs. In the pursuit of profit and continued expansion, MNCs

Global Code of Conduct A general standard of business practice that can be applied equally to all countries over and above their local customs and social norms.

Are there differences in the ethical issues employees face at a multinational company versus a locally owned company? Which environment do you think you would prefer?

have been found guilty of bribery, pollution, false advertising, questionable product quality, and, most prominently, the abuse of human rights in the utilization of "sweatshop" production facilities that fail to meet even the minimum health and safety standards of their home countries and that utilize child labor, often at wage levels that are incomprehensible to Western consumers.

The situation becomes even more complicated when we acknowledge that many global companies have reached such a size that they have a dramatic impact on trade levels just with their own internal transactions. As economist William Greider observed in *One World, Ready or Not:*[5]

> The growth of transnational corporate investments, the steady dispersal of production elements across many nations, has nearly obliterated the traditional understanding of trade. Though many of them know better, economists and politicians continue to portray the global trading system in terms that the public can understand—that is, as a collection of nations buying and selling things to each other. However, as the volume of world trade has grown, the traditional role of national markets is increasingly eclipsed by an alternative system: trade generated within the multinational companies themselves as they export and import among their own foreign-based subsidiaries.

WHAT IS A GLOBAL BUSINESS?

On December 7, 2004, IBM announced that it was selling its whole Personal Computing Division to the Chinese computer company Lenovo to create a new worldwide PC company—the globe's third largest—with approximately $12 billion in annual revenue. Simultaneously, though, IBM said that it would be taking an 18.9 percent equity stake in Lenovo, creating a strategic alliance between IBM and Lenovo in PC sales, financing, and service worldwide. The new combined company's worldwide headquarters, it was announced, would be in New York, but its principal manufacturing operations would be in Beijing and Raleigh, North Carolina; research centers would be in China, the United States, and Japan; and sales offices would be around the world. The new Lenovo will be the preferred supplier of PCs to IBM, and IBM will also be the new Lenovo's preferred supplier of services and financing.

Are you still with me? About 10,000 people will move from IBM to Lenovo, which was created in 1984 and was the first company to introduce the home computer concept in China. Since 1997, Lenovo has been the leading PC brand in China. My favorite part of the press release is the following, which identifies the new company's senior executives.

Yang Yuanqing—Chairman of the Board. (He's currently CEO of Lenovo.) Steve Ward—Chief Executive Officer. (He's currently IBM's senior vice president and general manager of IBM's Personal Systems Group.) Fran O'Sullivan—Chief Operating Officer. (She's currently general manager of IBM's PC division.) Mary Ma—Chief Financial Officer. (She's currently CFO of Lenovo.)

Talk about horizontal value creation: This Chinese-owned computer company headquartered in New York with factories in Raleigh and Beijing will have a Chinese chairman, an American CEO, an American COO, and a Chinese CFO, and it will be listed on the Hong Kong stock exchange. Would you call this an American company? A Chinese company? To which country will Lenovo feel most attached? Or will it just see itself sort of floating above a flat earth?

The press release announcing the new company anticipated this question: "Where will Lenove be headquartered?" it asked.

Answer: "As a global business, the new Lenovo will be geographically dispersed, with people and physical assets located worldwide." Sort that out.

QUESTIONS

1. "The new Lenovo will be geographically dispersed, with people and physical assets located worldwide." Which culture will provide the greatest influence in establishing a code of ethics? Explain your answer.
2. Do you think Lenovo will have one code of ethics for the whole company or separate codes to reflect its different cultures? Explain your answer.
3. What would be the challenges in establishing one code of ethics for a global company of this size?
4. Do you think the issue of managing business ethics on a global scale was considered in this transaction?

Source: Excerpts from Thomas L. Friedman, *The World Is Flat: A Brief History of the Twenty-First Century* (New York: Farrar, Straus, and Giroux, 2005). Copyright © 2005 by Thomas L. Friedman. Reprinted by permission of Farrar, Straus, and Giroux, LLC.

With such a negative track record to begin with, how do you enforce ethical behavior in an organization that is trading with itself? Do the ethical norms of the parent company dominate the corporation's business practices in complete disregard of local customs and traditions? Or is it simply more expedient to "go with the flow" and take advantage of whatever the local market has to offer? Unfortunately, in this new environment, simply categorizing the "parent company" can prove to be a challenge.

>> Enforcing Global Ethics

While companies may be held accountable for ethical performance within their home countries (America's Foreign Corrupt Practices Act, for example), enforcing ethical behavior once they cross national boundaries becomes extremely difficult. What happens if the behavior is illegal in the company's home country, but not in the local country in which the alleged transgression took place? Would the enforcement of penalties in their home country automatically prevent any future transgressions? What if the profit margins are high enough to simply pay the fines as a cost of doing business?

Enforcing a global ethical standard would require all parties involved to agree on acceptable standards of behavior and appropriate consequences for failing to abide by those standards. Given the fact that many of the hundreds of nations in the world still experience difficulty governing their own internal politics,

it would seem that we are many years away from achieving a truly global standard.

In the meantime, organizations such as the United Nations (UN) and the Organization for Economic Cooperation and Development (OECD) have approached the issue of standardizing global ethical conduct by promoting behavior guidelines that MNCs can publicly support and endorse as a strong message to their stakeholders that they are committed to ethical corporate conduct wherever they do business in the world.

THE UN GLOBAL COMPACT

Launched in a speech to the World Economic Forum on January 31, 1999, by UN Secretary-General Kofi Annan, the **UN Global Compact** became operational in July 2000. It represents a commitment on the part of its members to promote good corporate citizenship with a focus on four key areas of concern: the environment, anticorruption, the welfare of workers around the world, and global human rights.

> **UN Global Compact** A voluntary corporate citizenship initiative endorsing 10 key principles that focus on four key areas of concern: the environment, anticorruption, the welfare of workers around the world, and global human rights.

The Global Compact is not a regulatory instrument—it does not "police," enforce, or measure the behavior or actions of companies. Rather, the Global Compact relies on public accountability, transparency, and the enlightened self-interest of companies, labor, and civil society to initiate and share

OECD Guidelines for Multinational Enterprises
Guidelines that promote principles and standards of behavior in the following areas: human rights, information disclosure, anticorruption, taxation, labor relations, environment, competition, and consumer protection; a governmental initiative endorsed by 30 members of the Organization for Economic Cooperation and Development and 9 nonmembers (Argentina, Brazil, Chile, Estonia, Israel, Latvia, Lithuania, Romania, and Slovenia).

substantive action in pursuing the principles on which the Global Compact is based.

With over 2,000 companies in more than 80 countries making a voluntary commitment to this corporate citizenship initiative, the Global Compact is widely recognized as the world's largest initiative of its kind. By endorsing and actively promoting the message of the Global Compact, companies make public commitments to a set of core values that are captured in 10 key principles that address the four areas of concern:[6]

Human Rights

1. Businesses should support and respect the protection of internationally proclaimed human rights.
2. Businesses should make sure they are not complicit in human rights abuses.

Labor Standards

3. Businesses should uphold the freedom of association and the effective recognition of the right to collective bargaining.
4. Businesses should uphold the elimination of all forms of forced and compulsory labor.
5. Businesses should uphold the effective abolition of child labor.
6. Businesses should uphold the elimination of discrimination in employment and occupation.

Environment

7. Businesses should support a precautionary approach to environmental challenges.
8. Businesses should undertake initiatives to promote greater environmental responsibility.

9. Businesses should encourage the development and diffusion of environmentally friendly technologies.

Anticorruption

10. Businesses should work against all forms of corruption, including extortion and bribery.

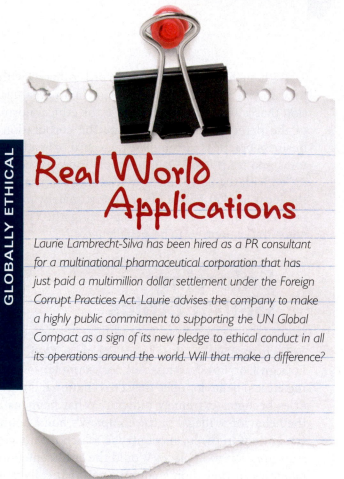

GLOBALLY ETHICAL

Real World Applications

Laurie Lambrecht-Silva has been hired as a PR consultant for a multinational pharmaceutical corporation that has just paid a multimillion dollar settlement under the Foreign Corrupt Practices Act. Laurie advises the company to make a highly public commitment to supporting the UN Global Compact as a sign of its new pledge to ethical conduct in all its operations around the world. Will that make a difference?

PROGRESS ✓ QUESTIONS

9. What is the UN Global Compact?
10. When and why was it created?
11. Explain the 10 key principles of the Global Compact.
12. What would a multinational corporation gain from signing the Global Compact?

>> The OECD Guidelines for Multinational Enterprises

Originally adopted as part of the larger Declaration on International Investments and Multinational Enterprises in 1976, the **OECD Guidelines for Multinational Enterprises** represents a more

Life Skills

>> A subtle influence

In Chapter 1 we examined the work of Lawrence Kohlberg and his argument that we develop a reasoning process (and our individual ethical standards) over time, moving through six distinct stages as we are exposed to major influences in our lives.

When we consider ethics from a global perspective and begin to recognize the impact of cultural influences on our personal value system, we come to the realization that our individual ethical standards can often be sheltered from a broader global awareness by those cultural influences.

What do you consider to be your primary cultural influences? As the child of immigrant parents, for example, your value system would be directly affected by influences from both the American culture you live in and your parents' native culture—and if your parents happen to be from two different cultures, then things can really get interesting!

Do you think those cultural influences impact your daily behavior? Much of what you learn about the world in terms of education and daily information is subject to the perspective of the country in which you live. Are you open to that, or would you describe yourself as being open to other viewpoints from other countries?

The development of a reasoning process over time allows these influences to work gradually so that you may not be fully aware of their impact until someone criticizes your viewpoint as being blinkered or, even worse, discriminatory. So if you find yourself in a situation where you are making a decision that involves different cultures or employees from different countries, consider your starting point first.

---

governmental approach to the same issues featured in the UN's nongovernmental Global Compact.

Supporters argue that the government backing adds credibility to the issues being promoted, but the guidelines carry no criminal or civil enforcement and are not regarded as legally binding. What they do offer are principles and standards of behavior that draw on the same core values as the UN Global Compact across a broader series of issues captured in 10 "chapters":[7]

I. **Concepts and Principles:** Sets out the principles which underlie the guidelines, such as their voluntary character, their application worldwide, and the fact that they reflect good practice for all enterprises.

II. **General Policies:** Contains the first specific recommendations, including provisions on human rights, sustainable development, supply chain responsibility, and local capacity building; and, more generally, calls on enterprises to take full account of established policies in the countries in which they operate.

III. **Disclosure:** Recommends disclosure on all material matters regarding the enterprise such as its performance and ownership, and encourages communication in areas where reporting standards are still emerging such as social, environmental, and risk reporting.

IV. **Employment and Industrial Relations:** Addresses major aspects of corporate behavior in this area including child and forced labor, nondiscrimination and the right to bona fide employee representation, and constructive negotiations.

V. **Environment:** Encourages enterprises to raise their performance in protecting the environment, including performance with respect to health and safety impacts. Features of this chapter include recommendations concerning environmental management systems and the desirability of precautions where there are threats of serious damage to the environment.

Study Alert

If an MNC was looking to raise its profile as an ethical organization, would it be better to support the UN Global Compact or the OECD Guidelines? Why?

VI. **Combating Bribery:** Covers both public and private bribery and addresses passive and active corruption.

VII. **Consumer Interests:** Recommends that enterprises, when dealing with consumers, act in accordance with fair business, marketing, and advertising practices; respect consumer privacy; and take all reasonable steps to ensure the safety and quality of goods or services provided.

VIII. **Science and Technology:** Aims to promote the diffusion by multinational enterprises of the fruits of research and development activities among the countries where they operate, thereby contributing to the innovative capacities of host countries.

IX. **Competition:** Emphasizes the importance of an open and competitive business climate.

X. **Taxation:** Calls on enterprises to respect both the letter and spirit of tax laws and to cooperate with tax authorities.

PROGRESS ✓ QUESTIONS

13. What is the OECD Guidelines for Multinational Enterprises?
14. How do the guidelines differ from the UN Global Compact?
15. How are they similar to the UN Global Compact?
16. Can you think of a situation in which a multinational corporation would endorse one or the other? Or should they both be endorsed? Explain your answer.

>> Conclusion

If an organization is committed to ethical business conduct, that commitment should remain constant wherever that business is conducted in the world. Unfortunately, the more evidence of ethical misconduct at home, the greater the likelihood that organizations will fall victim to the temptations offered in the less-regulated developing nations.

Carrying a reputation as a good corporate citizen may bring some positive media coverage and win the business of critical consumers who pay close attention to where the products they buy are sourced and manufactured. However, the real test comes when the quarterly numbers aren't looking as good as Wall Street would like and the need to trim costs will mean the difference between a rising stock price and a falling one.

As the Wendell Wilkie quote at the beginning of this chapter indicates, the world is now completely interdependent, and that interdependence extends to both *operations* and *information*. You may be able to save money by contracting with vendors that manufacture goods in sweatshop conditions, and you may be able to let contractors handle your hazardous waste without worrying too much about where they put it, but these will be short-lived savings and conveniences. Once those actions are made public through investigative media agencies or consumer advocacy groups, your status as a "good corporate citizen" may never be regained.

The concept of global ethics remains frustratingly complex. Advocates of a global code of conduct may rally against sweatshops and the employment of children at unspeakably low wages. However, their proposed solutions for the prohibition of these working conditions often fail to address the replacement of family income when the children are no longer allowed to work, which, in turn, can cause financial devastation to the families involved.

It can be argued that true global citizens should remain ethically involved in all their markets, rather than (as the critics maintain) taking advantage of the weak for the betterment of the strong. Supporters of Milton Friedman's *instrumental* contract may argue that corporations carry no moral obligation to the countries in which they operate beyond abiding by their laws, but when we consider the public backlash against Nike's sweatshops and Kathie Lee Gifford's child labor scandal, it would seem that there is a strong enough financial incentive to address these issues whether you accept a moral obligation or not.

FRONTLINE FOCUS
A Matter of Definition—Tom Makes a Decision

Tom considered his options very carefully. If the media found out about these sweatshops, would that negative publicity make it back to his agency? After all, the agency just wrote the ad copy and negotiated the placement of the ads. It didn't order the items, and if Tom hadn't received the billing paperwork by mistake, his agency wouldn't know where the items were made.

"Even so," thought Tom, "manufacturing any goods in sweatshop conditions is wrong, and our agency doesn't do business with customers that subscribe to the abuse of human rights."

Tom lost no time in bringing this new information about the Smith's campaign to his boss, Joanie Conaty, the founder and president of their agency:

"Ms. Conaty, this Smith's campaign could be a big problem for us. Its leading sales items weren't 'made in America' at all. This paperwork shows that the items came from a sweatshop in Indonesia. I did some research on the company that manufactures these items, and it has already been fined on several occasions for human rights violations."

Then Tom took a deep breath. "I know this is a big contract for us, Ms. Conaty, but is this the type of work we are going to do now? I didn't think our agency worked on these kinds of campaigns. Little kids working in sweatshops just so we can have cookouts on the Fourth of July doesn't seem right."

Joanie Conaty thought for several minutes before responding: "Are you sure this information is accurate, Tom?"

"Yes ma'am. This billing paperwork came with the original prep kit directly from Smith's."

"Then let's get our friends at Smith's on the phone. I'm afraid they are going to be looking for a new agency."

QUESTIONS

1. What do you think Joanie Conaty will say to her counterpart at Smith's?
2. What do you think Smith's reaction will be?
3. Is there a chance that Tom's company could save its relationship with Smith's?

[For Review]

1. **Understand the ethical issues arising in global business.**

   Managing the business ethics of a domestic corporation can be challenging enough. Once a company moves onto the international or global stage, the different languages, cultures, and business practices force North American companies to decide which of their ethical principles are nonnegotiable and which are open to discussion in favor of the client country with which they are looking to do business.

2. **Explain the issue of ethical relativism in a global environment.**

   As we learned in Chapter 1, ethical relativism can be driven by local circumstances. Ethical business practices in North America may often be enforced by laws that do not apply to other countries. In such situations, domestic corporations are often required to follow the standard operating procedures (SOPs) of the client country even if, in areas of social and political chaos, those SOPs amount to nothing more than a bureaucratic nightmare. In that scenario, business ethics can often deteriorate into "whatever it takes" to get the deal done.

3. **Explain the challenges in developing a global code of ethics.**

   The idea of developing a general standard of business practice that can be applied equally to all countries over and above their local customs and social norms is seen as the best hope for stopping the dark side of global

   capitalism. Western corporations, it is argued, have the financial strength to make extensive capital investments in developing countries, taking the natural resources of those countries as their raw materials for manufacturing plants elsewhere in the world. Without legal enforcement of ethical business practices, those corporations can conduct business without concern for employee welfare and safety. A global code of conduct, to which all international businesses would subscribe, would, it is believed, put a stop to those practices.

   However, the financial strength of the Western nations is seen as a threat to equal representation of the developing nations, and as a result, those developing nations hold onto their national identities and cultures, thereby precluding any agreement on a general standard of business practice.

4. **Analyze the ramifications of the UN Global Compact.**

   The UN Global Compact represents a voluntary commitment to corporate citizenship by the 2,000 companies which have elected to participate since the compact became operational in July 2000. Since it is not a regulatory instrument (and, by definition, not enforceable with any form of penalties for failing to comply with the standards of the compact), it is, at best, a public endorsement of the focus on the environment, anticorruption, the welfare of workers around the world, and global human rights. The credibility of the entire initiative is dependent on the public accountability, transparency, and enlightened self-interest of the member organizations in making sure that their global business practices align with the key principles of the compact.

5. **Explain the OECD Guidelines for Multinational Enterprises.**

   Originally adopted as part of the larger Declaration on International Investments and Multinational Enterprises in 1976, the **Organization for Economic Cooperation and Development (OECD) Guidelines for Multinational**

Enterprises represents a more governmental approach to the same issues featured in the UN's nongovernmental Global Compact. Supporters argue that the government backing adds credibility to the issues being promoted, but the guidelines carry no criminal or civil enforcement and are not regarded as legally binding. What they do offer are principles and standards of behavior that draw on the same core values as the UN Global Compact across a broader series of issues captured in 10 "chapters."

[Key Terms]

[Review Questions]

1. Do you think global businesses would be willing to subscribe to a global code of conduct? Explain your answer.

2. Would it be easier to just follow the business practices and customs of the country in which you're doing business? Why or why not?

3. Are there more stakeholders for an international or global company than a domestic one? Explain your answer.

4. How would the Foreign Corrupt Practices Act (FCPA) that we reviewed in Chapter 6 come into play here?

5. Which offers greater guidance to international businesses, the UN Global Compact or the OECD Guidelines? Explain your answer.

6. What is the most ethical way to do business internationally?

[Review Exercise]

Universal Training Solutions. Kathy James was Universal Training Solutions' top trainer. She had delivered client presentations, one-day open workshops on sales calls, and had led national rollouts for large training implementations. The opportunity to lead the training for Universal's new South African client, National Bank of SA, was simply too good to miss. She had met with Universal's account manager for National Bank and felt that she had a strong grasp of what the client was looking for.

National Bank of SA had recently invested $10 million (about 60 million rand) in upgrading its call center equipment, and its managers were looking for customer service

training to ensure that the call center representatives (CCRs) could provide the highest level of service in their market. Market research had shown that South Africans weren't accustomed to good service from their banks, so this initiative was seen as a good way to gain some market share.

Universal's customer service training program—First Class Service (FCS)—had a phenomenal reputation with dozens of Fortune 500 companies and several global implementations to its credit. It was designed to be delivered in three days with average class sizes of 10 to 12 employees. It was a logical choice for National, which was eager to get the program rolling.

Kathy asked to lead the cultural adaptation team, working with a translator in Johannesburg to translate FCS into Afrikaans (although she had been told by the account manager that most of National's employees spoke very good English). She anticipated that most of the group activities within the program would remain the same—that was what National's buyers had seen at the demonstration. She set up the first of what she thought would be several conference calls with the translator and looked forward to another successful project.

However, the first call brought things to a dramatic halt. As Kathy and the translator got to know each other, the translator asked how much Kathy knew about the South African culture. Kathy had been doing some extensive research on the Web after she had been assigned to the project, and she did her best to dazzle the translator with her knowledge. Then the translator asked a question that stumped Kathy: "Why are you only translating this into Afrikaans? Did you know there are 11 national languages in South Africa and that not recognizing those languages is considered to be a social blunder?"

The translator went on to describe how in many formal presentations (such as the training events Universal was planning to roll out in all National's regional offices over the next six months), it was considered rude not to recognize all the nationalities present in the room—particularly in group activities.

Kathy started to panic. How was she supposed to turn an American three-day program into a South African three-day program that allows time to recognize 11 different languages and nationalities in the group exercises?

1. What is the right thing to do here?

2. Why shouldn't National just deliver the American version of CFS? If it works here, it should work there.

3. Which stakeholders will be affected by Kathy's decision?

4. What are her options here?

[Internet Exercises]

1. Visit the Web site for the Institute for Global Ethics (IGE) at www.globalethics.org.

   a. What is IGE's stated purpose?

   b. Select one of the IGE business dilemmas and propose a resolution.

   c. How could a corporation benefit from the services of the Institute for Corporate Ethics?

2. Visit the Web site for Walmart's Global Ethics Office at http://walmartstores.com/AboutUs/280.aspx.

   a. What does Walmart have to gain from such a public commitment to global ethics?

   b. Summarize Walmart's commitment to ethical sourcing.

   c. Download Walmart's most recent "Global Sustainability Report," and provide three examples of projects that the company has undertaken that demonstrate its commitment to global ethics.

[Team Exercises]

1. **Global or local?**
   Divide into two teams. One team must prepare a presentation advocating for the development of a standardized global code of conduct. The other team must prepare a presentation arguing for the development of a more flexible local code of conduct that takes into account the cultural norms of individual nations.

2. **Restoring a reputation.**
   Divide into groups of three or four. Each group must map out its proposal for restoring the ethical reputation of a multinational corporation that has been fined for one of the following transgressions: bribery, pollution, operating sweatshops, or employing child labor. Prepare a presentation outlining your plan for restoring the reputation of the company with its stakeholders.

3. **Tamiflu.**
   Divide into two groups and prepare arguments *for* and *against* the following behavior: *Your American company operates manufacturing plants throughout Asia, with a combined staff of 20,000 employees. In 2003, after Asia was hit with the severe acute respiratory syndrome (SARS) epidemic, your company introduced a policy to stockpile drugs in locations where employees don't have access to high-quality health care.*

In 2005, SARS was replaced by avian influenza—bird flu—as the primary risk for the next pandemic. Your company responded by stockpiling quantities of the drug Tamiflu, the antiviral drug that is regarded as the best treatment for bird flu in humans.

There has been a reported outbreak of bird flu in a remote region of Vietnam, about 100 miles from where you have a manufacturing plant. The government clinic has a small supply of Tamiflu, but aware of your company's stockpile, the clinic has approached your local plant manager to share some of your supply. The plant manager contacted you for help in responding to the request. Your company policy on this is to make sure employees are taken care of first, and so you decline the request for assistance, claiming that you have insufficient quantities of Tamiflu to meet your immediate needs.

4. **Looking the other way.**

Divide into two groups and prepare arguments *for* and *against* the following behavior: *You have been sent to investigate a fraud claim made against your company by the Customs [department] in one of the countries where you do business. On arrival, an officer explains that your company is being fined for underdeclaring the number of safety boots imported into the country. You notice he is wearing a pair of the "missing" boots.*

In preparation for your trip you verified that all the shipment and customs paperwork was in order, and you are certain that the number of safety boots has not been underdeclared. Since your company's strategic plan features high growth expectations from this region, you are tempted to simply pay the fine and get the officer's name and address so you can send him some other samples of your company's products. However, your company's senior management team recently returned from a strategic planning retreat in which they made a clear commitment to enforce the organization's code of ethics in all business transactions, here and abroad, even at the risk of losing short-term business. Your CEO was quoted in the company newsletter as saying: "We should use our higher moral standards as an opportunity to win customers who want to do business with a reputable organization."

So you reach into your briefcase for your copies of the customs paperwork and begin to challenge the officer's accusation of underdeclaring.

Source: Inspired by Alison Maitland, "A Code to Export Better Practice," *Financial Times,* London (UK), January 26, 1999, p. 14.

>> TOMS SHOES: ETHICALLY GLOBAL?

The focus of most of the chapters in this text has been on companies seeking (or in many cases failing) to operate according to clearly established ethical principles that guide how they treat their stakeholders. The concept of "doing the right thing" has been presented as a natural alignment to their central business purpose, whether that's making cars, computers, or providing financial or consulting services. But what about a company that was started specifically to do the right thing? Not a consulting company to advise other companies on ethical business practices, but a company whose core purpose is "conscious capitalism"—delivering a product as a means to another end.

In 2006 Blake Mycoskie was inspired by a visit to Argentina to bring the traditional Argentine *alpargata* slip-on shoe to the U.S. market. Not an unusual decision for a serial entrepreneur like Mycoskie, but what made this idea unique was his purpose for this business. While doing community service work in Argentina, Mycoskie was struck by the country's health and poverty problems—and in particular the large numbers of children without shoes. His idea was to work with Argentinean shoemakers and vendors to produce shoes with vibrant colors and prints for the U.S. market and to offer those *genuine alpargata* shoes at a price point that would allow his company to give away one pair free for every pair sold.

Mycoskie originally intended to give 200 pairs of shoes to the children of Los Piletones in Argentina, but the buy-one-give-one-away model proved so successful that the first "shoe drop," as the donation visits have become known, delivered 10,000 pairs of shoes to match 10,000 pairs purchased by customers at such retailers as Bloomingdale's, Nordstrom's, and Urban Outfitters.

In the four years since Mycoskie's company TOMS was founded, over 600,000 pairs of shoes have been donated in Argentina, Haiti, and Ethiopia. The Ethiopian shoe drops are especially significant because of a local disease called *podoconiosis*, a form of elephantiasis. Contracted through the soil, the disease causes disfigurement and ulcers in the lower legs, and sufferers are ultimately banished from their villages like lepers. The good news is that the disease is 100 percent preventable by wearing shoes, and the last Ethiopian shoe drop delivered 37,000 pairs.

An important point to remember when learning about TOMS is that this is a for-profit company. Mycoskie was inspired by the Newman's Own company started by actor Paul Newman and writer A. E. Hotchner in 1982, which has donated over $300 million to community and health-related benefit programs in the last three decades. Newman's Own is also for profit. The pursuit of a favorable tax status as a nonprofit company was never the point; it was the ability to give away the profits to worthy causes—that's why the companies were created in the first place.

QUESTIONS

1. Does TOMS buy-one-give-one-away model make it a more ethical company than a traditional shoe manufacturer donating money to a charity? Why?

2. Why would customers pay such a high price for a simple linen shoe?

3. Mycoskie designed TOMS model from the ground up. Could an established company improve its ethical standards by launching a model like TOMS? How?

4. Select two other industries that could copy the buy-one-give-one-away model, and explain how it could be adopted.

Source: Stacy Perman, "Making a Do-Gooder's Business Model Work," *Bloomberg BusinessWeek*, January 23, 2009; Laurie Burkitt, "Companies' Good Deeds Resonate with Customers," *Forbes*, May 27, 2010; and Blake Mycoskie, "The Way I Work," *Inc.*, June 1, 2010.

>> SUICIDES AT FOXCONN

Foxconn Technology Group is a subsidiary of Taiwan's Hon Hai Precision Industry Company (reputed to be the world's largest "contract manufacturer"). Even as a subsidiary, Foxconn's numbers are impressive—the company employs about 800,000 people, half of whom work in a huge industrial park in Shenzhen, China, called Foxconn City. With 15 separate multistory buildings, each dedicated to individual customers such as Apple, Dell, Nintendo, and Hewlett Packard, Foxconn's promotional material proudly states that the company pays minimum wage (900 yuan, or $130 a month), offers free food and lodging, and extensive recreational facilities to its employees—on the face of it, not your stereotypical "sweatshop" environment.

However, in the first half of 2010, a total of 12 Foxconn employees found the working conditions so oppressive that they elected to kill themselves by jumping from the roofs of those 15-story buildings. According to reports, two other employees were seriously injured in suicide attempts, and another 20 have been saved before completing their planned attempt. This sudden spate of suicides has drawn unwelcome attention to the true state of the working conditions in factories that visitors have described as "grim." Labor activists report annual turnover of 40 percent or more as employees leave rather than face dangerously fast assembly lines, "military-style drills, verbal abuse by superiors . . . as well as occasionally being pressured to work as many as 13 consecutive days to complete a big customer order—even when it means sleeping on the factory floor."

Consider the case of 19-year-old Ma Xiangqian, a former migrant worker who leapt to his death on January 23, 2010. His family revealed that he hated his job at Foxconn: "11-hour overnight shifts, seven days a week, forging plastic and metal into electronic parts amid fumes and dust." In the month before he died, Ma worked 286 hours, including 112 overtime hours, three times the legal limit.

The negative publicity has been swift and targeted. Apple's international release of its iPad in Hong Kong was marred by the ritual burning of pictures of iPhones and calls for a global boycott of all Apple products. This negative press has prompted an equally swift response from Foxconn customers seeking to distance themselves from the story. Apple, Dell, and HP all announced investigations of the working conditions at Foxconn's plants, with the implied threat of contract termination.

Foxconn's response has been to surround the buildings with nets to prevent any further suicide attempts, to hire counselors for employees experiencing stress from the working conditions, and to assign workers to 50-person groups so that they can keep an eye on each other for signs of emotional stress. The company also announced two separate pay increases more than doubling worker pay to 2,000 yuan a month (although workers must pass a three-month review to qualify for the second pay increase). In addition, a series of "motivational rallies," entitled "Treasure Your Life, Love Your Family, Care for Each Other to Build a Wonderful Future," were scheduled for all Foxconn facilities.

While the immediate response has been targeted directly at the media criticism, there are concerns about the longer-term consequences for Foxconn and its customers. Hon Hai's reputation and dominance have been built on top quality with wafer-thin margins—margins that may prove to be too thin to absorb a 100 percent increase in labor costs. As for their customers, they may have given implied threats of contract termination, but with Hon Hai as the world leader, there are limited options for alternative suppliers.

Of greater concern is the changing demographic in China: "a generation of workers rejecting the regimented hardships their predecessors endured as the cheap labor army behind China's economic miracle." High turnover rates are leading to acute labor shortages as workers reject oppressive working conditions in favor of opportunities elsewhere in China. "Many seek positions in the service sector, or jobs closer to home." Counselors and better pay may help in the short term, but critics argue that without a dramatic shift in managerial culture, the situation at Foxconn may be just the beginning.

QUESTIONS

1. Will Foxconn's response be sufficient to stop any future suicide attempts? Why or why not?
2. If the company has operated on "wafer-thin margins," how should it deal with the increased labor cost?
3. Would you describe Foxconn's response as an example of proactive or reactive ethics? Why?
4. If China's young workers are sending a clear signal that they do not want to work in sweatshop factories, what can executives do from an ethics perspective to win them back?

Source: "Suicides at Foxconn: Light and Death," *The Economist*, May 27, 2010; Annie Huang, "Foxconn Raises Worker Pay by 30% after Suicides," Associated Press, June 2, 2010; David Barboza, "After Suicides, Scrutiny of China's Grim Factories," *The New York Times*, June 6, 2010; and Debby Wu, "iPhone Factory Suicides Spur Corporate Pep Rally," Associated Press, August 18, 2010.

Thinking Critically 9.3

>> THE ETHICS OF OFFSHORING CLINICAL TRIALS

The process of offshoring (outsourcing an organizational function overseas) is being applied to clinical drug trials with the same speed and enthusiasm as major U.S. corporations transplanting their customer service call centers to countries such as Ireland, India, and increasingly further eastern locations. In a report released in June 2010 by Daniel R. Levinson, the inspector general of the Department of Health and Human Services, 80 percent of the drugs approved for sale in 2008 had trials in foreign countries, and 78 percent of all subjects who participated in clinical trials were enrolled at foreign sites. Ten medicines approved in 2008 received no domestic testing at all.

For U.S.-based pharmaceutical companies, the rush is driven by both attractive options and practical realities:

- Pursuing the same cost advantages as other U.S. corporations, drug companies are now discovering that trials in countries in such regions as Eastern Europe, Asia, Latin America, and Africa can produce the same quality of data at a lower cost and often in a shorter time frame.
- After safety concerns over drugs like the anti-inflammatory Vioxx, which was withdrawn from sale in 2004, regulators such as the Food and Drug Administration (FDA) are now requiring even more data as a prerequisite for the approval of a new drug. That equates to more trials enrolling more people for longer periods of time—sometimes many thousands of patients over 12 months or longer.
- Patients in North America are increasingly unwilling to participate in phase 1 experimental trials, preferring instead to participate in phase 2 or 3 trials where the effectiveness of the drug has already been established and the trials are focused on identifying appropriate dosage levels or potential side effects.
- In contrast, these new overseas trial sites offer "large pools of patients who are 'treatment naive' because the relatively low standard of health care compared with Western countries means they have not had access to the latest and most expensive medicines."
- In North American trials, each doctor may only be able to offer a handful of patients who are willing and able to participate, whereas in populous nations such as India and China, a single doctor may see dozens of patients a day who would be willing trial participants, allowing faster recruitment from a smaller number of sites.

CONTINUED >>

However, pharmaceutical companies don't have everything their own way. Developing countries or not, restrictions are in place either to directly prevent trials or, at the very least, to ensure the professional and ethical management of those trials:

- Many developing countries have laws against "first in person" trials to prevent the treatment of their citizens as guinea pigs in highly experimental drug trials.
- Russia and China have both limited the export of blood and patient tissue samples in recent years, partly out of concern over illegal trafficking in human organs.
- The FDA recently set up an office in China to increase inspections of the rapidly growing number of clinical trials.
- The World Medical Association's 2004 Helsinki declaration called for stringent ethical practices in drug trials, but these remain voluntary practices.

In addition, the rush to take advantage of these cost savings and practical benefits has produced some problems ranging from questionable data to patient deaths:

- In 2003, several patients with AIDS died after an experimental drug trial in Ditan Hospital in Beijing. Viral Genetics, a California biotechnology company, was criticized for failing to explain adequately to participants that they were taking part in a drug trial rather than receiving a proven medicine.
- Further criticism was levied at Viral Genetics for an issue that has become a greater concern for clinical drug trials in general—specifically the use of a sugar pill or placebo as a comparative measure of the efficacy of the drug. In the Ditan trial questions were raised as to why an antiretroviral treatment—the most effective treatment for AIDS in the West—wasn't used as a comparative treatment.
- The lack of education and lower standards of care in these developing countries also raise questions about patient eligibility for participation in these trials. While they may qualify by diagnosis, do they really understand the concept of informed consent, and, more importantly still, do they realize that once the trial has ended, it may be months or years before they have access to the drug for a prolonged treatment regimen for their condition?

In the end, it is likely that basic economics will win out. Increasingly stringent standards in North America, driven, some would argue, by the litigious nature of our society, will only serve to increase the attractiveness of overseas trials. Without a suitable regulatory framework to oversee these trials and ensure that patients are treated in an ethical manner, the feared picture of uneducated citizens from developing countries being used as guinea pigs in experimental trials that citizens from developed nations are unwilling to participate in will become a reality.

QUESTIONS

1. Identify three factors that are driving pharmaceutical companies to host clinical drug trials overseas.
2. What regulations are in place to oversee the professional and ethical management of these trials?
3. If patients lack the language skills or education to understand the significance of informed consent or the use of a placebo, is it ethical to allow them to participate in the drug trial? Why or why not?
4. What proposals would you offer to make the offshoring of clinical drug trials a more ethical process for all the stakeholders involved?

Source: "The Next Big Thing," *The Economist*, June 16, 2005; Andrew Jack, "New Lease on Life? The Ethics of Offshoring Clinical Trials," *Financial Times*, January 29, 2008, p. 9; and Gardiner Harris, "Concern over Foreign Trials for Drugs Sold in U.S.," *The New York Times*, June 21, 2010.

MAKING IT STICK:
DOING WHAT'S RIGHT IN A COMPETITIVE MARKET

>> Making It Stick— Key Components of an Ethics Policy

Ask any CEO to describe the market she is working in, and she will probably describe the same set of characteristics:

- *Demanding customers* who want new and better products and services at lower prices.
- *Impatient stockholders* who want the stock price to rise each and every quarter.
- *Aggressive vendors* who want to sell you more of everything.
- *Demanding federal, state, and local officials* who want to burden you with more rules and regulations while encouraging you to hire more people and pay more taxes.
- *Demanding creditors* who want their loan payments on time.
- *Aggressive competitors* who want to steal your customers from you.

When you are operating a business in such a tough environment, holding on to your promise to run an ethical business and to do "the right thing" for all your stakeholders can be very challenging. It's easy to see why so many executives, after the unethical behavior of their companies has been exposed, point to the ruthless competition of the business world as their excuse for not doing the right thing.

Sustainable Ethics Ethical behavior that persists long after the latest public scandal or the latest management buzzword.

So how do you make it stick? How do you make sure your company holds on to its ethical principles even if everyone else in your marketplace doesn't? **Sustainable ethics** in a culture are those that persist within the operational policies of the organization long after the latest public scandal or the latest management buzzword.

We have seen in the previous nine chapters how a company's commitment to ethical behavior impacts every managerial level and every department of the organization. So making ethical behavior *sustainable* requires the involvement of every member of the organization in committing to a formal structure to support an ongoing

process of monitoring and enforcement. This can be summarized in the following six stages:

1. Establish a code of ethics.
2. Support the code of ethics with extensive training for every member of the organization.
3. Hire an ethics officer.
4. Celebrate and reward the ethical behavior demonstrated by your employees.
5. Promote your organization's commitment to ethical behavior.
6. Continue to monitor the behavior as you grow.

ESTABLISH A CODE OF ETHICS

In order for everyone to begin from the same starting point, the organization's commitment to ethical behavior must be documented in a code of ethics. A well-written code of ethics can do several things:

- It can capture what the organization understands ethical behavior to mean—your values statement.
- It can establish a detailed guide to acceptable behavior.
- It can state policies for behavior in specific situations.
- It can document punishments for violations of those policies.

The audience for the code of ethics would be every stakeholder of the organization. Investors, customers, and suppliers would see how serious you are about ethical performance, and employees would understand clearly the standard of behavior expected from them and the consequences for failing to meet that standard.

Review the following online material (available from www.mhhe.com/ethicsnow) for examples of codes of ethics from the following organizations:

- Society of Professional Journalists (SPJ), Online Ethics Code 1
- Association for Computing Machinery (ACM), Online Ethics Code 2
- The Institute of Internal Auditors (IIA), Online Ethics Code 3
- American Society of Civil Engineers (ASCE), Online Ethics Code 4

As you can see from those four examples featured online,

there is no perfect model for a code of ethics: Some are very specific in their commitments to their profession (consider the "Canons" of the ASCE code), and others are operational in their focus, giving very clear guidance as to the consequences if employees transgress the code.

If you are involved in creating a code of ethics from scratch, consider the following advice from the Institute of Business Ethics:[1]

1. *Find a champion.* Unless a senior person—hopefully the CEO—is prepared to drive the introduction of a business ethics policy, the chances of it being a useful tool are not high.
2. *Get endorsement from the chairperson and the board.* Corporate values and ethics are matters of governance. The board must be enthusiastic not only about having such a policy but also about receiving regular reports on its operation.
3. *Find out what bothers people.* Merely endorsing a standard code or copying that of another will not suffice. It is important to find out on what topics employees require guidance.
4. *Pick a well-tested model.* Use a framework that addresses issues as they affect different constituents or shareholders of the company. The usual ones are shareholders employees, customers, suppliers, and local/national community. Some might even include competitors.
5. *Produce a company code of conduct.* This should be distributed in booklet form or via a company intranet. Existing policies, for example on giving and receiving gifts or the private use of company software, can be incorporated. Guidance on how the code works should also be included.
6. *Try it out first.* The code needs piloting—perhaps with a sample of employees drawn from all levels and different locations. An external party such as the Institute of Business Ethics will comment on drafts.
7. *Issue the code and make it known.* Publish and send the code to all employees, suppliers, and others. State publicly that the company has a code and implementation program that covers the whole company. Put it on your Web site and send it to joint venture and other partners.
8. *Make it work.* Practical examples of the code in action should be introduced into all company internal (and external) training programs as well as induction courses. Managers should sign off on the code regularly, and a review mechanism should be established. A code "master" needs to be appointed.

SUPPORT THE CODE OF ETHICS WITH EXTENSIVE TRAINING FOR EVERY MEMBER OF THE ORGANIZATION

Writing the code of ethics is the easy part. Getting your commitment to ethical performance down on paper and specifying the standards of behavior you will accept and the punishments you will enforce is a good starting point. However, the code can only be a guide—it cannot cover every possible event. The real test of any company's ethics policy comes when one of your employees is presented with a potentially unethical situation.

Moreover, even though your code of ethics is written for employees to follow, your stakeholders aren't required to follow it.

For example, what do you do when a supplier offers one of your employees a bribe or kickback for signing an order or a customer asks for a kickback from you for giving you his business? Is that example going to be in your code? If not, what guidance are you going to offer your employees?

This is where an extensive training program to support the published code of ethics becomes so important. Since the code can't capture every possible example, each department of the organization should take the code and apply it to examples that could arise in its area. In these department or team meetings, employees can work on:

- Recognizing the ethical issue
- Discussing options for an appropriate response
- Selecting the best option for the organization

Employees in all job functions need to be familiar with their company's code of ethics. How might a code of ethics apply to these factory workers?

PROGRESS ✓ QUESTIONS

1. List six characteristics of a tough market.
2. List four key items in a code of ethics.
3. Provide three examples of unethical behavior by a customer.
4. Provide three examples of unethical behavior by a supplier.

Smaller organizations can strengthen this employee training with additional training for supervisors and managers in ethical conflict resolution. If an individual employee or team of employees is unable to resolve an ethical issue, they can then turn to their supervisor or manager for guidance and support. In

For an organization to operate ethically, senior executives must commit to developing a culture that supports ethical principles beyond minimal compliance to federal legislation. Ultimately, however, ethical conduct comes down to the actions of individual employees each and every day. "Doing the right thing" becomes an individual interpretation based on personal ethics and a series of guidelines from a company code of ethics. Can you make that work? What if you work with colleagues who don't share that perspective? If they operate from the perspective that it's a "dog-eat-dog world" with "'victory at all costs," you may find yourself as the lone voice in trying to do the right thing. How will you handle that?

larger organizations, that role is made more significant by the creation of the position of ethics officer.

HIRE AN ETHICS OFFICER

The hiring of an **ethics officer** represents a formal commitment to the management and leadership of an organization's ethics program. The role is usually developed as a separate department with the responsibility of enforcing the code of ethics and providing support to any employees who witness unethical behavior. It sends a clear message to your stakeholders and provides an appropriate person for employees and their managers to turn to when they need additional guidance and support. This person can be promoted from within the organization (selecting a familiar face who can be trusted) or hired from outside (selecting an independent face who is new to company history and office politics).

The Ethics and Compliance Officers Association (a professional group of ethics and compliance officers with over 1,000 members) documented the chief responsibilities of their members in a survey, which may be summarized as follows:

89% Oversight of hotline/guideline/internal reporting

89% Preparation and delivery of internal presentations

88% Organizationwide communications

85% Senior management and/or board briefings/communications

84% Training design

83% Assessing/reviewing vulnerabilities

83% Assessing/reviewing success/failure of initiatives

79% Overseeing investigations of wrongdoing

79% Management of program documentation

77% Direct handling of hotline/guideline/internal reporting

72% Preparation and delivery of external presentations

68% Establishing company policy and procedures

64% International program development

61% Training delivery

56% International program implementation

52% Conducting investigations of wrongdoing

Ethics Officer A senior executive responsible for monitoring the ethical performance of the organization both internally and externally.

> **Study Alert**
>
> How much authority should a chief ethics officer (CEO) have in an organization? If the company is committed to doing the right thing, should the CEO be able to challenge or even overrule the other CEO—the chief executive officer? How would you resolve a disagreement between the two positions?

CELEBRATE AND REWARD THE ETHICAL BEHAVIOR DEMONSTRATED BY YOUR EMPLOYEES

With standards of behavior specified in the code of ethics, along with the punishment served for failing to follow those standards, your ethics program can become harsh. This goes against your goal of increasing employee loyalty and customer satisfaction. So the threats of punishment must be balanced with promised rewards for successful behavior:

- Celebrate examples of good ethical behavior in your company newsletter.
- Award prizes for ethical behavior—and let the employee choose the reward.
- Award prizes for new and creative ideas—and let the employee choose the reward.
- Recognize employees who represent the standard of behavior to which you are committing.
- Declare an Ethics Day, and allow every department to share their successes.

PROMOTE YOUR ORGANIZATION'S COMMITMENT TO ETHICAL BEHAVIOR

An ethics policy commits you to doing the right thing for all your stakeholders, so that message must be shared with *all* your stakeholders—both inside and

PROGRESS ✓ QUESTIONS

5. When hiring an ethics officer, is it better to promote someone from within the company or hire someone from outside? Explain your answer.
6. List six key responsibilities of an ethics officer.
7. Give three examples of celebrating ethical behavior.
8. If you publicly celebrate ethical behavior, should you also publish punishment for unethical behavior? Why or why not?

THE PRICE OF PAST TRANSGRESSIONS

On August 6, 2010, Hewlett-Packard (HP) announced that Mark Hurd was stepping down as chairman and CEO in response to allegations of sexual harassment and improper expense violations. The announcement has sparked a fierce debate between self-proclaimed business pragmatists such as Larry Ellison, CEO of Oracle, who called it, "the worst personnel decision since the idiots on the Apple board fired Steve Jobs many years ago," and corporate governance specialists such as Jeffrey A. Sonnenfeld, senior associate dean at the Yale School of Management, who called it "a courageous call."

Ironically, the decision came at a time when HP seemed to have finally found its way again after more than a decade of "flakiness" that began with the appointment of Carly Fiorina as the first female chief executive of the company in the late 1990s. Fiorina appeared to emerge victorious from a leadership power struggle over the merger with Compaq Computer, only to see HP stock lose half its value. She was paid more than $21 million to leave in February 2005. As we saw in Chapter 5, HP then limped along to another scandal as chairwoman Patricia Dunn (who had been appointed by Fiorina when HP made a public commitment to better corporate governance by splitting the CEO and chairperson roles) authorized the use of a private security firm to spy on board members and journalists in what became known as the "pretexting" scandal. In a reversal of the separation of roles, Mark Hurd, who had been hired from National Cash Register (NCR) to replace Fiorina as CEO, then became chairman as well.

CONTINUED >>

The hiring of "numbers-guy" Hurd seemed to indicate a return to sanity for HP, and the performance delivered under his tenure seemed to endorse that choice. A few critics argued that Hurd got credit for implementing Fiorina's strategy, but under his leadership HP's stock doubled, and savvy multibillion dollar purchases of Electronic Data Systems (EDS), 3Com, and Palm propelled HP to sales of more than $100 billion, passing IBM as the world's largest IT company by revenues.

So how did things fall apart so quickly? Allegations of sexual harassment were brought by Jodie Fisher, an independent contractor working with the CEO's office as a "VIP host" at executive conferences. The exact nature of the allegations has remained confidential based on a financial settlement between Hurd and Fisher and a clarification by both parties that the relationship was not a physical one. The investigation by an outside law firm ordered by the HP board determined that the allegations were groundless. Nevertheless, the implication that Hurd falsified expense reports to conceal private dinners with Fisher was considered enough of a transgression for the board to demand Hurd's resignation. From the board's perspective, Hurd was being held to the same ethical standard as any HP employee.

Several questions remain unanswered. If the expense report transgression was serious enough to demand an immediate resignation, why was Hurd given a severance package estimated to be up to $40 million in cash and stock options? If the investigation into the sexual harassment allegations found no evidence, and Hurd stated that he didn't even fill out his own expense reports, why would the board see his departure as the only appropriate resolution? To take the conspiracy theories further, why did the board hire a public relations firm (APCO) to consult on the situation? Critics argue that the board was more concerned about revealing a third fiasco in the executive offices and therefore opted for Hurd's resignation under the guise of doing "the right thing" and enforcing HP's code of ethics. Others refer to Hurd's reputed unpopularity in the company as a cost-cutting CEO who took home over $70 million in compensation in two years while trimming the research and development budget for HP from 9 percent to only 2 percent of revenue. What better way to oust an unpopular leader than to create a scandal?

If the board really was hoping to avoid a third fiasco, it has been spectacularly unsuccessful. HP's stock value fell by more than $9 billion when the controversy broke, and shareholders are now filing a lawsuit seeking unspecified damages and changes to HP's corporate governance.

QUESTIONS

1. HP separated the roles of chairperson and CEO under Fiorina, but when Patricia Dunn was dismissed as chairwoman, the roles were combined again under Mark Hurd. Now that he has stepped down, do you think HP should keep the roles combined or separate them again? Explain your answer.

2. If the investigation over the allegations of sexual harassment found no evidence, what did the HP board gain by forcing Hurd to step down?

3. Hurd left HP with a severance package estimated to be up to $40 million in cash and stock options. Does that dilute HP's apparent commitment to strong corporate governance? Why or why not?

4. How could the HP board have handled this situation differently?

Source: Ashlee Vance and Matt Richtel, "Hewlett Took a P.R. Firm's Advice in the Hurd Case," *The New York Times,* August 9, 2010; Michael Hiltzik, "Ouster of HP Chief Hurd Has Look of Panic," *LA Times,* August 11, 2010; Joe Nocera, "Real Reason for Ousting H.P.'s Chief," *The New York Times,* August 13, 2010: Schumpeter, "The Curse of HP," *The Economist,* August 14, 2010; and Ashlee Vance, "Despite H.P.'s Efforts, Spectacle of a Chief Goes On," *The New York Times,* August 16, 2010.

outside the company. Make clear and firm promises to them, and then deliver on those promises. Offer concrete examples that your organization is committed to winning the trust (and the business) of your customers by building a reputation they can count on. For example:

- Offer a no-questions-asked refund policy like Lands' End.
- Offer a 110-percent price-match guarantee like Home Depot.
- If you overcharge clients by mistake, give them a refund *plus* interest *before* their accounting department figures out the error and asks for the money.
- Get your clients involved in the development of your ethics policies. Ask them to tell you what forms of behavior or guarantees will make them feel reassured that they are dealing with an ethical company.
- Let your employees visit client sites to talk about your code of ethics in person.
- Share your success stories with all your stakeholders, not just your employees.
- Invite your stakeholders to your Ethics Day celebration.

CONTINUE TO MONITOR THE BEHAVIOR AS YOU GROW

Any organization's commitment to ethical performance must be watched constantly. It is easy for other business issues to take priority and for the code of ethics to become taken for granted. Also, the continued growth of technology will present new situations for ethical dilemmas such as policies on e-mail monitoring and Web surfing, so your code may need to be rewritten on a regular basis. A large organization can make that one of the responsibilities of its designated ethics officer. Smaller companies need to include their code of ethics as part of any strategic planning exercise to make sure it is as up to date as possible.

JUST A SMALL FAVOR

My Tuesday morning wasn't looking good. I had a few minutes to try to catch up on my e-mails, and then a meeting with Doug Slater, the head of one of our smaller business units. Slater wasn't one of my favorite people. It's not that I'd ever had problems with him in his work performance; it was just a nagging feeling that he couldn't be trusted. He was bright enough, and he certainly knew how to work a room, but he was just too slick for my taste. He was always ready to agree at a moment's notice with anyone above him on the organizational chart, while belittling those who couldn't touch him because he was the head of a business unit. He seemed to be focused on nothing more than getting ahead, and I got the impression he would manipulate anyone and anything to get there.

Slater walked casually into my office on the stroke of 10:00 A.M., punctual as always. He was "all smiles," spending just the right amount of time on small talk and last night's triple overtime football game, before he dropped his "small favor." All he wanted, he said, was a slight delay in paying his unit's bills this month.

Our company is highly automated, and the companies we do business with operate in much the same manner. When we receive their bills and approve them for payment, they go to accounts payable, where they're matched electronically against the contracts or purchase orders for payment terms. As with all good cash flow management programs, if the terms are net 10 days, we automatically pay in 10 days. If they're 30 days, then we pay in 30. Messing with this system requires multiple signatures, in triplicate, and it's usually only possible if one of our vendors offers us a deal for early payment that's too good to pass up.

This was precisely Slater's "small favor," and I knew why he wanted it. Our monthly business-unit profitability reports are calculated on a cash basis—actual receipts against actual expenses. So if Slater could keep the expense figure artificially low by delaying payment on some bills, his margin figures would look that much better. Obviously, the figures would catch up with him in the end, but he was gambling that a few good quarters would catch the attention of the right people in the right places and he'd be promoted to another position, leaving his poor unsuspecting replacement to deal with it.

I didn't answer immediately—I needed a minute to get my temper under control. Did he really think I was so dumb that I wouldn't know what he was trying to do, or had he assumed that I didn't care enough about our code of ethics to mind? Either way, it was a poor reflection on me. The only bright side was that I figured he was in my office because no one in my IT team had been willing to help him with his "small favor." Even if he had found someone to help him, if it were to come to light, the internal auditors would be notified because it would indicate a violation of our controls. If we manually change the terms on a contract (to modify payment terms, for example), an exception report is printed that goes straight to the chief financial officer. He obviously either didn't realize how tightly we monitor such things, or he thought he would be long gone by the time it was discovered and he could blame someone else.

I told Slater that I wouldn't override the software nor would I authorize one of my team to do it. I also warned him that if anyone on the IT team did it for him, that person would be clearing out his desk by the end of the day. He replied, "It's not such a big deal! Anyway, you can't blame a guy for trying," and walked out.

QUESTIONS

1. Why is Slater's "small favor" unethical?
2. Are there any federal or legal safeguards in place to prevent this type of behavior?
3. Should Slater's request be reported to anyone? Who and why?
4. If Slater had requested his small favor from members of the IT team, they had obviously refused to do it. Why?

Source: Adapted from Herbert W. Lovelace, "But It's a Business Favor, Herb, Not Ethics," *Information Week*, August 12, 2002, p. 62.

9. List six examples of commitments that companies can make to win the trust of their stakeholders.
10. Provide four of your own examples.
11. Why would a code of ethics need to be updated?
12. Find out when your company's code of ethics was last updated.

>> Becoming a Transparent Organization

Study Alert

Many manufacturing companies in the United States have seen tremendous success from the Japanese business practice of *kaizen* (a Japanese word meaning "continuous improvement"). The constant search for ways to improve their internal processes has led these companies to significant cost reductions and sales growth. Could you apply the same practice to ethical business practices? How would an already ethical company become *more* ethical?

Many organizations have been prompted to introduce or modify their codes of ethics by the sight of CEOs pleading the Fifth Amendment in front of congressional committees. Others have been inspired by the large number of zeroes that can now be tacked onto financial penalties for corporate misconduct. Unfortunately, neither motivation is enough. These are examples of **reactive policies,** which result when organizations are driven by events and/or a fear of future events. True ethical policies are **proactive,** which occur when the company develops a clear sense of what it stands for as an ethical organization—not only what ethics means to that company and its stakeholders but also the extent of the actions it will take (and the necessary punishments it will enforce) to get there.

One characteristic that is common to such organizations is a commitment to organizational **transparency,** which means the company is open and honest in all its communications with all its stakeholders. However, the financial markets that govern stock prices (and the profits to be made as corporate executives cash in their stock options) have proved to be remarkably indifferent to "open and honest communications."

As Microsoft's 2006 white paper, "The New World of Work: Transparent Organizations," summarized:[2]

Transparency in business means that stakeholders have visibility deep into the processes and information of an organization. This is becoming

A SACRIFICIAL LAMB

Real World Applications

Randall Swift has been offered the position of chief ethics officer for an insurance company that recently settled a large lawsuit for unethical business practices (without admitting any wrongdoing) brought by several state insurance regulators. The creation of the ethics officer position was part of the agreed settlement, and the company has committed to several specific action items by agreed deadlines. However, when Randall asked detailed questions about those action items in his final round of interviews, the answers he received were very vague. The position would represent a significant promotion for Randall, with a nice salary to match, but his wife is concerned that the insurance company has no plans to change, and if the unethical behavior is caught again, the chief ethics officer would be blamed for poor leadership and he would be fired as the sacrificial lamb. Should Randall take the job?

an important focus for businesses in several ways. Important qualities of transparency include the following:

- A requirement that is being enforced on markets and companies through regulation.
- An enabler of better relationships with partners and customers (that is soon to be an expectation).
- A great opportunity to rework business processes to increase efficiency.
- A risk to confidential intellectual property.

It is the risk factor of becoming too transparent that still remains as the biggest obstacle to change in this area. Managers may be able to break through their business school teachings and start sharing cost and revenue figures with employees, and even produce honest appraisals of organizational performance in annual reports (rather than polished, vetted PR documents), but giving away too much information, from their perspective, leads to the inevitable conclusion of the loss of market advantage through corporate espionage, for if you give away your secrets, what do you have left? Ultimately, however, organizations can only build trust with their stakeholders if there are "open and honest communications."

PROGRESS ✓ QUESTIONS

13. What is a *reactive* ethical policy?

14. What is a *proactive* ethical policy?

15. Why would a company want to be transparent?

16. Would you say the company you work for is transparent? Explain your answer.

>> Organizational Integrity

The intense media coverage of the many corporate scandals that have been uncovered over the last few years has brought the subject of business ethics to the attention of a large portion of this country's population. That increased attention has proved to be something of a mixed blessing.

On the one hand, the average investor can be forgiven for thinking that the business world is full of crooks whose only purpose is to make as much money as possible. Problems with product quality, poor customer service, made-up financial reports, and out-of-court settlements with no admission of guilt paint a very negative picture.

The response to this negative picture has been new rules (Sarbanes-Oxley and others) and tighter controls that now represent a greater risk for organizations that fail to comply with the expected standard of behavior. Large financial penalties and expensive lawsuits can now place a substantial dollar figure on the cost of unethical behavior.

On the other hand, ethics has also become an issue that positively impacts the business world. Stockholders want to invest in companies with solid reputations and strong ethical programs. Employees prefer to work for companies they can trust and where they feel valued. That sense of value results in increased commitment and reduced turnover, which means greater profits for the company. Customers prefer to buy from companies with proven track records of integrity in their business dealings—even if that choice costs them a little more. So if the threat of negative publicity, ruined reputations, and million dollar legal settlements won't lead a company into developing an ethics policy, perhaps the promise of increased profits, happy stockholders, happy employees, and happy customers will!

Recognizing the concept of *business ethics* allows us to categorize behavior as unethical, but when you are looking to manage the reputation and policies of an organization, the commitment to doing the right thing becomes more about **organizational integrity** than any sense of a written ethics policy. Understanding that your company does not operate independently from its community, its customers, its employees, its stockholders, and its suppliers is vital to the long-term survival of the organization. Winning the trust and confidence of all your stakeholders would be a great achievement in today's business world, but *keeping* that trust and confidence over the long term would be an even greater one.

Reactive Ethical Policies Policies that result when organizations are driven by events and/or a fear of future events.

Proactive Ethical Policies Policies that result when the company develops a clear sense of what it stands for as an ethical organization.

Transparency A characteristic of an organization that maintains open and honest communications with all stakeholders.

Organizational Integrity A characteristic of publicly committing to the highest professional standards and sticking to that commitment.

FRONTLINE FOCUS
You Scratch My Back—Adam Makes a Decision

Dr. Green continued to stare at Adam. He was obviously looking for an answer now, and Adam knew that if he tried to stall by asking to check with his regional manager, Green would show him the door.

One small part of Adam wanted to laugh out loud at this ridiculous situation. Doctors had asked him for extra free samples before, and the industry had always been willing to underwrite lunches and tickets to sports events or shows as appropriate marketing expenses, but no one had ever asked him outright for money to decorate his office—and this guy was dead serious!

For a moment Adam wondered if he was bluffing about Zach. He knew Zach was a tough competitor, and they fought a tough battle in this region, usually managing to win clients away from each other on a couple of occasions. "Come to think of it," thought Adam, "Zach probably would go along with this deal. Winning this practice would be a real catch for his territory."

Then Adam looked at Dr. Green again. Something was bothering him about this guy. He got the feeling that this wasn't a one-time special request. If Adam gave in on this, he knew there would be other requests for "marketing funds" in the future, always with the threat of switching to the competition.

Suddenly Adam, almost as a surprise to himself, knew what he had to do: "I'm sorry Dr. Green. We value our relationships with our doctors very highly—that's how we were able to work so closely with Dr. Stevens for as long as we did. Unfortunately, that type of relationship doesn't include 'marketing funds.' I hope Zach's interior designer friend does a good job for you."

With that, Adam got up and turned to leave.

Six weeks later, the local paper featured a very unflattering picture of Dr. Green and Zach on the front page. Dr. Green had developed a very close relationship with Zach and his company—so close, in fact, that Dr. Green had been willing to massage some of his patient data to help Zach's company in a new drug trial.

QUESTIONS

1. What do you think the reaction of Adam's regional manager was to the initial news of the loss of Dr. Green's business?
2. Do you think Zach's company supported his willingness to provide Dr. Green's "marketing funds"?
3. What do you think will happen to Zach and Dr. Green now?

[For Review]

1. Develop the key components of an ethics policy.

For an organization to develop an ethical culture, and for that culture to be sustainable, an ethics policy requires the involvement of every member of the organization in committing to a formal structure to support an ongoing process of monitoring and enforcement. This can be achieved through six initiatives:

- *Establish a code of ethics that presents a common understanding of organizational values and provides clear guidance on acceptable behavior.*
- *Support the code of ethics with extensive training for every member of the organization.*
- *Hire an ethics officer to formalize the management and leadership of the organization's commitment to an ethical culture.*
- *Celebrate and reward ethical behavior so that employees come to see ethical behavior as a positive event rather than an avoidance of punishment.*
- *Promote your organization's commitment to ethical behavior so that all your stakeholders can learn what to expect from you.*
- *Continue to monitor the behavior as you grow so that ethical conduct remains ingrained in the organizational culture.*

2. Analyze the ramifications of becoming a *transparent* organization.

Organizational transparency represents a commitment to honest and open communication with all stakeholders, and can often be the hardest adjustment in any ethics policy. Trusting your employees enough to share your cost and revenue figures with them goes against most business school teachings. Similarly, presenting an honest picture of organizational performance in a detailed annual report can generate paranoia about proprietary information and the dangers of corporate espionage. However, carefully "wordsmithed" documents and carefully positioned press releases suggest you have something to hide, and if you have something to hide, how can you be trusted?

3. Understand the difference between *reactive* and *proactive* ethical policies.

A reactive ethical policy exists when organizational decisions are driven by events or the fear of future events. A proactive ethical policy is established when the company develops a clear sense of what it stands for as an ethical organization and what actions will be taken (and what punishments will be enforced, if necessary) to get there.

4. **Discuss the challenges of a commitment to *organizational integrity*.**

   Organizational integrity is very easy to commit to, but very difficult to enforce. Integrity involves winning the trust and confidence of all your stakeholders and working to keep that trust over the long term. In practice, that means understanding that the company does not operate independently from its community, its customers, its employees, its stockholders, and its suppliers. Any and all decisions should be made with those partners in mind. As such, doing the right thing has a much broader reach than just doing the right thing for the company.

[Key Terms]

Ethics Officer **198**

Organizational Integrity **203**

Proactive Ethical Policies **202**

Reactive Ethical Policies **202**

Sustainable Ethics **196**

Transparency **202**

[Review Questions]

1. You have been asked to join a team as the representative of your department. The team has been tasked with the development of an ethics training program to support the company's new code of ethics. What would your recommendations be?

2. Your company wrote its code of ethics in 1986. You have been assigned to a team that has been tasked with updating the code to make it more representative of current business ethics issues like the Internet and modern business technology. What are your recommendations?

3. Does the role of an ethics officer bring real value to an organization, or is it just "window dressing" to make the company look good?

4. Do you think you could be an ethics officer? Why or why not?

5. When you go shopping, do you pay attention to how *transparent* the company is in its business practices? Why or why not?

6. Would *organizational integrity* make a difference in your loyalty to a company? Why or why not?

[Review Exercises]

Gus Bouchard runs a shrimp boat out of Jefferson Parish in Louisiana. After the Deep Horizon oil well explosion in the Gulf of Mexico, all shrimp fishing was banned until the well was capped and the surface oil collected. As his family's sole breadwinner, Gus went to work for BP, using his boat to deliver thousands of feet of oil-collecting booms to protect the marshlands and barrier islands from the oil. BP announced the creation of a compensation fund of at least $20 billion to help businesses and homeowners in the affected areas recover from the damage of the Deep Horizon disaster. However, Gus has just been notified that since he earned an income from BP as a contractor during disaster recovery, that amount will be deducted from any compensation he receives. Gus is extremely upset about this. When interviewed by a local newspaper journalist, he pointed out that "I could have stayed home and made just as much money! Instead, I put my boat to work and did what I could to help protect the Louisiana coastline and our fragile fishing grounds—it's not fair!"

1. Which ethical theories could be applied here?

2. The administrator of the BP compensation fund argues that everyone should be compensated according to his or her loss in the disaster. Those with an opportunity to make money (such as Gus) were at an advantage and should not, therefore, receive the same amount. Is that an ethical argument? Why or why not?

3. If you were a business owner who didn't have the chance to work for BP and you heard that people like Gus were getting the same compensation as you, how would you react?

4. How would you resolve the situation?

stakeholder relations than they typically do at present. But even here, as we shall explain in a moment, there is nothing distinctive to the 3BL approach to the call to audit and report social and environment performance. If there are good justifications for firms to report such data, these will be independent of the distinctive feature of the 3BL: namely the Aggregation Claim, the idea that it is possible in some sense to quantify a firm's social performance in a way that arrives at some kind of "bottom line" result.

WHAT IS NOVEL ABOUT 3BL IS NOT SOUND

The keenest supporters of the 3BL movement tend to insist, if only in passing, that firms have social and environmental bottom lines *in just the same way* that they have "financial" or "economic" bottom lines. We submit that the only way to make sense of such a claim is by formulating it (roughly) in the way we have with the Aggregation Claim, above. That is, we cannot see how it could make sense to talk about a bottom line analogous to the bottom line of the income statement unless there is an agreed-upon methodology that allows us, at least in principle, to add and subtract various data until we arrive at a net sum.

Probably the most curious fact about the 3BL movement—certainly the one that surprised us most as we researched it—is that none of the advocates of so-called 3BL accounting ever actually proposes, presents or even sketches a methodology of the sort implied by the Aggregation Claim. In other words, for all the talk of the novelty of the 3BL idea, and for the importance of taking all three "bottom lines" seriously, nobody (as far as we know) has actually proposed a way to use the data on social performance to calculate some kind of a net social bottom line.[18] The charitable interpretation of this stunning omission is that advocates of the concept see these as early days for the idea of real social and environmental bottom lines, and hope that progress on a methodology will come once the general desirability of the idea has gained acceptance.[19] In this section we will suggest that this is probably a vain hope. We will first try to give some indication of how disanalogous the evaluations of financial and social performance are. Then we will argue that in fact there is good reason to think that it would be *impossible* to formulate a sound and relatively uncontroversial methodology to calculate a social bottom line.

If it makes sense to say that there is a bottom line for performance in some domain, x, that is directly analogous to the financial bottom line, then it makes sense to ask what a given firm's x-bottom line is. And there should be a relatively straightforward answer to this question, even if we do not yet know what that answer is. So we might reasonably ask of firms like The Body Shop, or British Telecom, or Dow Chemical—all companies that have claimed to believe in the 3BL—what their social bottom line actually was last year. But just posing this question conjures up visions of Douglas Adams's comic tour de force, *The Hitchhiker's Guide to the Galaxy,* in which the greatest of all computers is asked to come up with an answer to "the great question of Life, the Universe and Everything." That answer, which takes seven-and-a-half million years to calculate, is "42."

At least part of the charm in this *Hitchhiker* shtick is that "42" seems wrong not because it arrives at the wrong number, but because it is ridiculous to think that the answer to such a question could be expressed numerically or even just with one word (especially a dangling adjective—42 *what?*). We do not know exactly what the answer should look like—indeed we may not really know what that question means—but we are pretty sure such a "great question" cannot be solved that succinctly.

Perhaps this is how you would feel if you asked what the social or environmental "bottom line" of a firm was, and someone told you it was 42, or 42-thousand, or 42-million. We may not be sure what the right answer should look like, but this kind of answer, even (or especially?) if it were expressed in monetary units, just does not seem right. So it is worth reflecting for a moment about what *would* look like a plausible answer to the question of what some particular firm's social bottom line is. We can have good grounds for thinking that one firm's social performance (say, BP's) is better than another's (say, Enron's); or that a given firm's social/ethical performance improved (Shell) or declined (Andersen) over a five-year period. And indeed, our judgments in these cases would be at least partly based

18 We limit our claim here to the current generation of writers, consultants and activists who are explicitly endorsing a 3BL paradigm. There are surely some very valuable lessons for this generation in the generally unsuccessful attempts of a previous generation—largely from within the accounting profession—to develop a calculus of social accounting that could attach values to social benefits and losses. In addition to the articles cited in the preceding note, see Rob Gray, Dave Owen, Carol Adams, *Accounting and Accountability: Changes and Challenges in Corporate Social and Environmental Accounting,* Prentice Hall, 1996. We are grateful to Christopher Cowton and Jim Gaa for drawing our attention to these earlier debates.

19 Elkington (p. 72) writes that "the metrics are still evolving." AccountAbility describes social and environmental accounting as "embryonic." See AccountAbility's "Triple Bottom Line in Action," www.sustainability.com/people/clients/tbl-in-action4.asp.

on, or reflected in, the kind of indicators that various proposed social standards highlight—including, for example, charitable donations, various measures of employee satisfaction and loyalty, perceptions in the community, and so on. But this is still a long way from saying that we have any kind of systematic way of totting up the social pros and cons, or of arriving at some global figure for a firm's social performance.

The problem with alleged analogy between the "traditional" bottom line and social or environmental bottom lines runs deeper still. The traditional bottom line, of course, is the last line of the income statement indicating net income (positive or negative). Net income is arrived at by subtracting the expenses incurred by the organisation from the income earned by it within a given period.[20] We have just suggested that we are not sure what the social version of this "line" should look like, or in what sort of units it should be expressed. But we are also puzzled when we look for conceptual analogies *above* the bottom line, so to speak. What are the ethical/social equivalents or analogues of, say, revenue, expenses, gains, losses, assets, liabilities, equity, and so on? The kinds of raw data that 3BL and other SEAAR advocates propose to collect as indications of social performance do not seem to fit into general categories, analogous to these, that will allow for a straightforward subtraction of "bads" from "goods" in order to get some kind of net social sum.

With reference to typical SEAAR criteria we could imagine a firm reporting that:

a. 20% of its directors were women,

b. 7% of its senior management were members of "visible" minorities,

c. it donated 1.2% of its profits to charity,

d. the annual turnover rate among its hourly workers was 4%, and

e. it had been fined twice this year for toxic emissions.

Now, out of context—e.g., without knowing how large the firm is, where it is operating, and what the averages are in its industrial sector—it is difficult to say how good or bad these figures are. Of course, in the case of each indicator we often have a sense of whether a higher or lower number would generally be better, from the perspective of social/ethical performance. The conceptual point, however, is that these are quite simply not the sort of data that can be fed into an income-statement-like calculation to produce a final net sum. For one thing, most of these figures are given in percentages, and one obviously cannot add or subtract percentages attached to different figures—for example, (a) and (b), above, do not add up to 27% of *anything*. But even when there are cardinal numbers involved (e.g., ". . . 8 employees of Shell companies . . . lost their lives in 1997. . . ,"[21] it is not at all clear where on a given sliding scale we treat a figure as a "good" mark to raise the "social bottom line" and where we treat it as a "bad" mark that takes away from the bottom line. (Is eight a high number or a low number for fatalities from the worldwide operations of a firm like Shell? Something to be proud of or ashamed of?) Again, we are not disputing that these are relevant considerations in the evaluation of a firm's level of social responsibility; but it does not seem at all helpful to think of this evaluation as in any way analogous to the methodology of adding and subtracting used in financial accounting.[22]

---

20 It really should be noted that the income statement, with its famous "bottom line," is but one of the principal financial statements used to evaluate the health of a firm. The others include the balance sheet, the statement of cash flows and the statement of owners' equity. For the sake of charity, we are assuming that when 3BL advocates speak of traditional management preoccupations with "the bottom line" they are using this as shorthand for the use of all of the major financial statements—including the details revealed in the footnotes to these statements.

21 Reported in *The Shell Report 1999: People, Planet and Profits,* p. 18.

22 Another kind of methodology for evaluating performance would be a *rating scheme* that assigned scores to various levels of performance on certain key indicators. For example, a rating organisation might score firms out of 100 with, say, 10 of those points derived from data about charitable contributions as a percentage of the firm's profits. Perhaps a firm would get 2 points for each half-percent of its profits donated to charity up to a maximum of 10 points. Similar scores could be assigned on the basis of the percentage of women and minorities in senior positions, and so on. Schemes like these are sometimes used by firms that screen investment funds on ethical grounds, and one is described in detail and employed in a book produced by the ethics consultancy EthicScan, *Shopping with a Conscience,* Toronto: John Wiley & Sons, 1996. Now any such scheme will be loaded with inherently controversial value judgments about how morally worthy these various factors are; and for this reason, such schemes are unlikely ever to receive the kind of widespread support and legitimacy that is enjoyed, say, by most of the basic accounting standards. Our point here, however, is simply that ratings schemes like this constitute a very different paradigm for evaluation than the one used in financial accounting; and not simply because they are more controversial. Not surprisingly, none of the major organisations that has tried to develop international, cross-sector standards for reporting and auditing social performance has gone this route of trying to develop an overall rating scheme. Nor have the major ("Final Four") accounting firms who are lining up to sell 3BL auditing services.

AN IMPOSSIBILITY ARGUMENT

Ultimately, we argue, there are fundamental philosophical grounds for thinking that it is impossible to develop a sound methodology for arriving at a meaningful social bottom line for a firm. There is a strong and a weak version of the argument: the strong version says that it is in principle impossible to find a common scale to weigh all of the social "goods" and "bads" caused by the firm; and the weak version says, from a practical point of view, that we will never be able to get broad agreement (analogous, say, to the level of agreement about accounting standards) for any such proposed common scale.[23] We would not pretend to be able to demonstrate the strong version here, since it would require a significant detour into the realm of moral epistemology. But we do think we can give a glimpse at why the weaker version of our critique is plausible, and that should be enough to cast doubt on the prospects of Triple Bottom Line accounting.

We can begin by expressing this "impossibility" argument in the decidedly less metaphysical terminology of accountancy. One of the three basic assumptions underlying the methodologies of the standard financial statements, including the income statement, is the so-called "unit of measure" assumption—that all measures for revenue, expenses, assets, and so on, are reducible to a common unit of currency.[24] What is lacking in the ethical/social realm is an obvious, and obviously measurable, common "currency" (whether in a monetary or non-monetary sense) for expressing the magnitude of all good and bad produced by the firm's operations and affecting individuals in different stakeholder groups.

Part of the problem is that it is difficult to make *quantitative* assessments of how good or bad some action or event is; and partly it is that we seem to be dealing with *qualitative* as well as quantitative distinctions when we evaluate the social impact of corporate activities. Again, let us start with the "objective" indicators of social performance that are now being used in corporate social reports and in the leading social-auditing standards. Let us consider the comparatively simple task of merely trying to determine whether some particular "good" score outweighs another particular "bad" score. Imagine a firm with any one of the following pairs of scores in its record:

- Pair 1: a generous family-friendly policy that includes extended maternity-leave as well as part-time and job-sharing provisions for women returning to the firm after maternity leave, but also three sexual-harassment suits against it in the past year.

- Pair 2: an "ethical sourcing" policy for its overseas contractors that is audited by an international human-rights NGO, but also a spotty record of industrial relations at home, including a bitter three-month strike by members of one union.

- Pair 3: a charitable donation equal to 2% of gross profits, but also a conviction for price-fixing in one of its markets.

Other things equal, is there any obvious way to judge whether any one of these pairs of data would result in a net gain or loss on the firm's social bottom line? We could also consider the challenge of comparing good to good and bad to bad. For example, would a firm do more social good by donating one million dollars to send underprivileged local youths to college, or by donating the same amount to the local opera company? How should we evaluate the charitable donation by a firm to a not-for-profit abortion clinic, or to a small fundamentalist Christian church? Examples like these make it clear that although there are many relevant and objective facts that can be reported and audited, any attempt to "weigh" them, or tot them up, will necessarily involve subjective value judgments, about which reasonable people can and will legitimately disagree. (And of course this task can only get more difficult when there are hundreds of data points, rather than just two, to tot up.)

The power of this illustration does not rest on acceptance of any deep philosophical view about whether all value judgments are ultimately subjective or objective; it rests only on a realistic assessment of the open-ended nature of any attempt to make a global assessment of a firm's social impact given the kind of data that would go into such an evaluation. In the language of moral philosophers, the various values involved in evaluations of corporate behaviour are "incommensurable"; and reasonable and informed people, even reasonable and informed moral philosophers, will weigh them and trade

---

23 We do not wish to imply that setting "ordinary" accounting standards is an uncontroversial process; but simply that inherently moralistic social accounting will be significantly more controversial.

24 Two of the other basic assumptions are the "separate entity" assumption (the assumption that the economic events measured can be identified as happening to the entity in question, an entity separable from other individuals or organizations for accounting purposes), and the "time period" assumption (the assumption that the economic events measured occur within a well-defined period of time). For these assumptions, see Thomas Beechy and Joan Conrod, *Intermediate Accounting, Volume 1,* Toronto: McGraw-Hill/Ryerson, 1998, among other sources. These three assumptions sometimes go by different names, and are often accompanied by other assumptions not named here.

them off in different ways. To say they are incommensurable is to say that there is no overarching formula that can be appealed to in order to justify all of these trade-offs (e.g., to decide definitively what the net social impact is for any of the pairs listed in the preceding paragraph).[25] In short, whatever is going on in this sort of normative evaluation, it would seem to be about as far as you could get from the paradigm of the accountant performing calculations on the basis of verifiable figures and widely accepted accounting principles.

One suspects that numerous problems with the aggregative assumptions underlying 3BL have gone unnoticed in part because they are also implicit in many discussions of CSR. It is common for advocates of 3BL and CSR to talk of the "social performance" or "social impact" of a firm, as if this captured everything that was relevant for an ethical evaluation of the firm. (Indeed, in articulating these theories throughout this paper we have had to use these expressions.) On this view, what is morally relevant is how the firm improves its positive impact on individuals or communities (or reduces its negative impact). Presumably "social impact" here must be closely related to "impact on well-being" (including the well-being of non-human organisms). In the language of moral philosophy, this is to locate all of business ethics and social responsibility within the *theory of the good*: asking, roughly, how does the firm add value to the world? Obviously, this is a very important question when evaluating a corporation. But much of what is ethically relevant about corporate activities concerns issues in what moral philosophers call the *theory of right*: e.g., concerning whether rights are respected and obligations are fulfilled. Now clearly there are important links between our views about rights and obligations, on the one hand, and the question of what actions make the world better or worse, on the other. But unless we are the most simple-minded act-utilitarians, we recognize that the link is never direct: that is, we do not simply have one obligation, namely, to maximise well-being.[26] Sometimes fulfilling a particular obligation or respecting a particular person's rights (e.g., by honouring a binding contract that ends up hurting the firm or others) might not have a net positive "social impact"—but it should be done anyway. More importantly, for our purposes here, obligation-fulfillment and rights respecting are not what we might call "aggregative" concepts. They are not things that a good individual or firm should necessarily be trying to increase or *maximise.* If you have an obligation, then you should try to fulfill it. But there is no special value in obligation fulfillment per se. If you promised to pay someone back in the future then you must do your best to pay them back. And if you do, that is something that improves our ethical evaluation of you, so to speak. But you do not become more ethical by maximising the number of promises you can make in order to maximise your social performance as promise fulfiller. Put another way, for a firm and its managers to keep their promises is a good thing, an ethical thing, a socially responsible thing. But other things equal, you are not more ethical or responsible by making and keeping ten promises than you are by making and keeping one promise. To conceive of ethics and social responsibility as necessarily aggregative is to confuse very different ethical categories; and yet that is what happens in the logic of 3BL (and much of CSR) when we treat all ethically relevant aspects of a firm as if they can be measured in terms of social impact.[27]

---

25 Utilitarians might object in principle to these claims that there is (a) no common "currency" for evaluating the impact of corporate activities, and (b) no overarching formula to justify trade-offs involving different values affecting different individuals. In its most straightforward, classical formulations, utilitarians believe that "utility" is this currency, and that anything of value can ultimately be judged in terms of its impact on the amount of utility. We will ignore the fact that utilitarianism is no longer especially popular among academic moral philosophers. Even if it were in some sense the best moral theory, it would hardly rescue the 3BL model of social accounting. The theory itself does not provide any objective formula for extrapolating "utility impact" from the kinds of data that are typically reported in social reports (again, see Appendix 1 for examples of typical social indicators). Any two reasonable and well informed utilitarians would be just as likely to disagree about the net social impact of a firm's many operations as would two non-utilitarians.

26 In a longer critique of 3BL and CSR it would be worth trying to identify just how much of the basic logic of these views is a reiteration of act utilitarianism. For a good summary of some of the stock criticisms of utilitarianism—particularly in the context of measuring social development—see Amartya Sen, *Development as Freedom*, Oxford University Press, 1999, pp. 54–61.

27 It must be said that the brute notion of "social performance" or "social impact" also seems to flatten out the concept of *responsibility*. In effect, for advocates of CSR, the most socially responsible corporation is the one that has the greatest net social impact. But this erases many important "deontic" categories that are relevant for determining the nature of specific obligations. We are not always obliged to maximise "social impact." There are good and noble actions that we are not obliged to do (sometimes called supererogatory duties); other things that we are permitted to do but not obliged to do; other things that we are obliged to do even if they do not improve welfare; and so on. For a much richer notion of responsibility than the one implied in most writings on 3BL and CSR, see Enderle and Tavis, op. cit., pp. 1131–1137.

CONCLUSION: WHAT USE BOTTOM LINES WITHOUT A BOTTOM LINE?

We cannot help but conclude that there is no meaningful sense in which 3BL advocates can claim there is a social bottom line. (Again, we believe that analogous arguments would undermine the idea of an environmental bottom line; but that argument deserves more space than we could devote to it here.) This piece of jargon is, in short, *inherently misleading:* the very term itself promises or implies something it cannot deliver. This raises two issues worth reflecting upon. First, why has the idea spread so quickly, not just among Green and CSR activists, but also among the top tier of multinational corporations? And secondly, should we be concerned about the use, and propagation of the use, of jargon that is inherently misleading?

There is no simple answer to the first question, and certainly no general explanation for why so many different kinds of individuals and groups have found the language of 3BL so attractive. There are no doubt many conflicting motivations at play here, and by and large we can do no more than speculate about the mental states of different key actors. For many grassroots activists it is likely that the metaphor of bottom lines captured perfectly their long-held sense that social responsibility and environmental sustainability are at least as important as profitability when evaluating the performance and reputations of firms. After all, in ordinary discourse, when one announces that one's "bottom line" on a given subject is *P,* it rarely means more than that the speaker wants to convey that *P* is something worth noting, perhaps as a way of summing up.[28] For some of the initiators and early adopters of the concept within activist circles (including Elkington himself), it is likely that there were also perceived rhetorical advantages to borrowing from the "hard-headed" language and legitimacy of accountancy.[29] Perhaps senior executives would find it easier to take seriously the fuzzy notions of CSR and sustainability if they could be fit into more familiar paradigms with objective measures and standards. Many of these early movers (including Elkington himself)[30] were also offering large corporations consulting and auditing services that were built, at least in part, around the 3BL paradigm; and they would soon be joined, as we noted at the outset, by some of the most powerful "mainstream" accounting and consulting firms. Paid consultants have, of course, mixed motives for promoting and legitimising something like the 3BL paradigm: on the one hand, they can be committed to the utility for the clients of collecting, auditing, and reporting social and environmental data (for reasons given in list B, above (pp. 217–218)); but on the other, they cannot be blind to the fact that this opens up a market niche that might not otherwise have existed. Corporations are almost certainly paying more for SEAAR-related services now than they were previously paying for ethics and CSR consultants.

More fanciful leaps of speculation are necessary for explaining the motivations of some of the early adopters of 3BL rhetoric and principles among multinational corporations. As we have noted already, there are a number of corporations that have long prided themselves on their traditions of social responsibility and good corporate citizenship. Having succeeded despite putting principles ahead of short-term profits is part of the lore in the cultures of companies like Johnson & Johnson, Levis Strauss, Cadbury's, and IKEA. And in the cultures of many smaller or more recent firms, from The Body Shop to your local organic grocer, CSR and green principles have often served as the organisation's very raison d'être.[31] For many of these firms, social and environmental reporting provides an opportunity to display their clean laundry in public, so to speak. They have long sought to improve their social and environmental performance, so they can be confident that reporting these achievements publicly will cause little embarrassment. Indeed, insofar as many of these firms make social responsibility part of their corporate image (hoping to woo the increasingly large pool of consumers and investors who claim to be willing to pay more to support ethical firms), the adoption of 3BL principles and the production of social reports is *consistent with* other strategies of brand management. (This observation is not meant in any way to reduce these efforts to a simple marketing strategy, but just to show why they are a logical step in a direction in which the firm was already traveling.)

The adoption of 3BL rhetoric by a number of very prominent multinationals *without* traditions of support for green and CSR principles is a more curious phenomenon. Perhaps it should not be wholly surprising that prominent on this list are some firms trying to shake off recent reputations for decidedly *irresponsible* business practices or aloof

---

28 For example, a hockey broadcaster summed up a game in which team A defeated team B with the remark, "the bottom line is that team A out-hustled team B tonight." But surely in sports if there's a literal bottom line, it is reflected in the final score, not in the explanation for the score!

29 Of course, post-Andersen, accountancy looks rather less hard-headed and legitimate than it did in 1997.

30 Elkington is co-founder of the consultancy SustainAbility, and played a key role in the production of Shell's 3BL report, "Profits and Principles—does there have to be a choice?" (1998).

31 Business for Social Responsibility in the USA has many hundreds of corporate members, most of which are small- to medium-sized enterprises.

management structures—firms like Shell and BP, British Telecom, AT&T and Dow Chemical. Now we certainly do not wish to cast aspersions on the principled convictions that have been expressed repeatedly in reasoned, and sometimes almost evangelical, fashion by corporate leaders such as BP's Sir John Browne and Shell's Sir Mark Moody-Stuart.[32] Any impartial observer must be impressed with the way these two have been able to make real changes in the cultures of their organisations and to achieve real improvements in terms of human-rights issues and emissions reductions. At the same time, some critics have noted how useful it can be to multinational companies to adopt some of the rhetoric and principles of their critics from the world of the increasingly influential NGOs. David Henderson refers to this as a strategy of "sleeping with the enemy," and Robert Halfon's take is revealed in the two-part, Churchillian title of his report, *Corporate Irresponsibility: Is Business Appeasing Anti-business Activists?*[33] Without similarly casting any aspersions on the integrity of John Elkington, a longstanding critic of capitalism and globalisation, it is noteworthy that he seems to have had nothing but good to say about Shell since he was contracted by them to help prepare their first 3BL report.[34]

And this leads us to the second question we posed at the start of this section: should we be concerned about the use, and propagation of the use, of 3BL jargon that is inherently misleading? From an abstract normative point of view the answer clearly has to be Yes. If the jargon of 3BL implies that there exists a sound methodology for calculating a meaningful and comparable social bottom line, the way there is for the statement of net income, then it is misleading; it is a kind of lie. Even if advocates of 3BL were to issue explicit disclaimers to this effect, and to admit that it was little more than a slogan or shorthand for taking social and environmental concerns seriously, there are still reasons for concern. For one thing, words and expressions continue to carry connotations despite official renunciations—including, for new jargon, the misleading connotation that there is something novel about the new concept. But there is another more serious concern that should trouble the most committed supporters of CSR and sustainability principles who have embraced the 3BL.

The concept of a Triple Bottom Line in fact turns out to be a "Good Old-fashioned Single Bottom Line plus Vague Commitments to Social and Environmental Concerns." And it so happens that this is exceedingly easy for almost any firm to embrace. By committing themselves to the principles of the 3BL it sounds like companies are making a *more* concrete, verifiable commitment to CSR and sustainability. And no doubt many are. But it also allows them to make almost no commitment whatsoever. Without any real social or environmental bottom lines to have to calculate, firms do not have to worry about having these "bottom lines" compared to other firms inside or outside of their sector; nor is there likely to be any great worry about the firm being seen to have declining social and environmental "bottom lines" over the years or under the direction of the current CEO. At best, a commitment to 3BL requires merely that the firm report a number of data points of its own choosing that are potentially relevant to different stakeholder groups—typically in the form of a glossy 3BL report full of platitudinous text and soft-focus photos of happy people and colourful flora.[35] From year to year, some of these results will probably improve, and some will probably decline. Comparability over time for one firm is likely to be difficult and time-consuming for anybody without a complete collection of these reports and handy filing system. The firm can also change the indicators it chooses to report on over time, perhaps because it believes the new indicators are more relevant (. . . or perhaps to thwart comparability). And comparability across firms and sectors will often be impossible. At any rate, such comparisons will be on dozens or hundreds of data points, not on any kind of global figure like profit/loss, cash flow, return-on-investment, or earnings-per-share. (For example, company A might have more female directors and fewer industrial accidents than company B; but company B might have more female executives and fewer fatalities than company A; and so on across the various data points, many of which will not even be common to both reports.) In short, because of its inherent emptiness and vagueness, the 3BL paradigm makes it as easy as possible for a cynical firm to appear to be committed to social responsibility and ecological sustainability. Being vague about this commitment hardly seems risky when the principal propagators of the idea are themselves just as vague.

---

32 See, e.g., John Brown, "International Relations: The New Agenda for Business," Elliott Lecture, St Anthony's College, Oxford, 1998; or Mark Moody-Stuart, "Forward" in *Responsible Business,* London: Financial Times, 2000.

33 David Henderson, *Misguided Virtue: False Notions of Corporate Social Responsibility,* Wellington, NZ: New Zealand Business Roundtable, 2001; Robert Halfon, *Corporate Irresponsibility: Is Business Appeasing Anti-business Activists?* Social Affairs Unit, Research Report 26, 1998.

34 See, e.g., Elkington, pp. 10, 48, 125, 176.

35 It is a bad sign when a report begins with an entirely glossy page used to announce that "This BP Australia Triple Bottom Line Report is printed on environmentally conscious paper." What exactly is "environmentally conscious paper," and how much of it is being used to make this announcement? Fortunately, the report, which was published in November 2001, is rather more specific when it comes to data on social and environmental performance.

Once again, we do not wish by these remarks to be casting aspersions on any particular firm that has adopted 3BL rhetoric and issued some form of 3BL report. We have tried to emphasize that there can be many non-cynical motivations for doing this. A careful reading of these reports is often sufficient to judge a firm's real level of commitment to the principles.[36] If activists interested in propagating the rhetoric of Triple Bottom Line are not troubled by its inherently misleading nature (perhaps because they feel the ends justify the means), they should at the very least be concerned with the fact that it is potentially counterproductive (that is, a means to ends they do not think are justifiable).

We think it likely that the *future* of firms deciding voluntarily to report on their social performance will end up looking very much like the *history* of firms deciding to bind themselves to a corporate code of ethics. On the one hand, the mere fact that it has produced a social report or a code of ethics tells us very little about a firm's actual commitment to the principles expressed in the documents.[37] It is relatively costless to produce these documents, and—especially if they are relatively vague—they do not generally open up any serious risks for a corporation. On the other hand, both types of documents can play a critical role in a firm's serious strategy to improve its ethical and social performance and to integrate this goal into its corporate culture. It is our belief that clear and meaningful principles are most likely to serve firms of the latter type; and that vague and literally meaningless principles like those implied by the Triple Bottom Line are best only for facilitating hypocrisy.

APPENDIX 1: SOCIAL PERFORMANCE INDICATORS[†]

Here is a small sample of the kinds of data that are included in social reports. Such reports typically report dozens of different data points, and often give future targets and comparisons with past performance.

Diversity

- Existence of equal opportunity policies or programmes;
- Percentage of senior executives who are women;
- Percentage of staff who are members of visible minorities;
- Percentage of staff with disabilities.

Unions/Industrial Relations

- Percentage of employees represented by independent trade union organizations or other bona fide employee representatives;
- Percentage of employees covered by collective bargaining agreements;
- Number of grievances from unionized employees.

Health and Safety

- Evidence of substantial compliance with International Labor Organization Guidelines for Occupational Health Management Systems;
- Number of workplace deaths per year;
- Existence of well-being programmes to encourage employees to adopt healthy lifestyles.
- Percentage of employees surveyed who agree that their workplace is safe and comfortable.

---

36 Some, but not all, are available on the home pages of 3BL-friendly firms mentioned throughout this article.

37 We now have a couple of decades worth of experience with the widespread use of corporate ethics codes, and a number of studies suggest that most are neglected by corporations and have very little impact on their culture or operations. See, e.g., P. E. Murphy, "Corporate Ethics Statements: Current Status and Future Prospects," *Journal of Business Ethics* 14, 1995: 727–40; and P. M. Lencioni, "Make Your Values Mean Something," *Harvard Business Review*, July 2002.

† These representative indicators have been drawn from three sources: *Guided by Values: The VanCity Social Report (1998/99)*, www.vancity.com/downloads/2592_1998socialreport.pdf; Global Reporting Initiative's *Draft 2002 Sustainability Reporting Guidelines*, April 2002; *People, Planet and Profits, The Shell Report 2001* (www.shell.com/shellreport).

Child Labour

- Number of children working.
- Whether contractors are screened (or percentage screened) for use of child labour.

Community

- Percentage of pre-tax earnings donated to the community;
- Involvement and/or contributions to projects with value to the greater community (e.g., support of education and training programs, and humanitarian programs, etc.);
- Existence of a policy encouraging use of local contractors and suppliers.

A

Accounting Function The function that keeps track of all the company's financial transactions by documenting the money coming in (credits) and money going out (debits) and balancing the accounts at the end of the period (daily, weekly, monthly, quarterly, annually).

Altruistic CSR Philanthropic approach to CSR in which organizations underwrite specific initiatives to give back to the company's local community or to designated national or international programs.

Applied Ethics The study of how ethical theories are put into practice.

Audit Committee An operating committee staffed by members of the board of directors plus independent or outside directors. The committee is responsible for monitoring the financial policies and procedures of the organization—specifically the accounting policies, internal controls, and the hiring of external auditors.

Auditing Function The certification of an organization's financial statements, or "books," as being accurate by an impartial third-party professional. An organization can be large enough to have internal auditors on staff as well as using external professionals—typically certified professional accountants and/or auditing specialists.

B

Board of Directors A group of individuals who oversee governance of an organization. Elected by vote of the shareholders at the annual general meeting (AGM), the true power of the board can vary from institution to institution from a powerful unit that closely monitors the management of the organization to a body that merely rubber-stamps the decisions of the chief executive officer (CEO) and executive team.

Business Ethics The application of ethical standards to business behavior.

C

Code of Ethics A company's written standards of ethical behavior that are designed to guide managers and employees in making the decisions and choices they face every day.

Compensation Committee An operating committee staffed by members of the board of directors plus independent or outside directors. The committee is responsible for setting the compensation for the CEO and other senior executives. Typically, this compensation will consist of a base salary, performance bonus, stock options, and other perks.

"Comply or Else" A set of guidelines that require companies to abide by a set of operating standards or face stiff financial penalties.

"Comply or Explain" A set of guidelines that require companies to abide by a set of operating standards or explain why they choose not to.

Conflict of Interest A situation in which one relationship or obligation places you in direct conflict with an existing relationship or obligation.

Consumer Financial Protection Bureau (CFPB) A government agency within the Federal Reserve that oversees financial products and services.

Corporate Citizenship *See* Corporate Social Responsibility.

Corporate Conscience *See* Corporate Social Responsibility.

Corporate Governance The system by which business corporations are directed and controlled.

Corporate Governance Committee Committee (staffed by board members and specialists) that monitors the ethical performance of the corporation and oversees compliance with the company's internal code of ethics as well as any federal and state regulations on corporate conduct.

Corporate Social Responsibility (CSR) The actions of an organization that are targeted toward achieving a social benefit over and above maximizing profits for its shareholders and meeting all its legal obligations. Also known as *corporate citizenship* and *corporate conscience*.

Culpability Score (FSGO) The calculation of a degree of blame or guilt that is used as a multiplier of up to 4 times the base fine. The culpability score can be adjusted according to aggravating or mitigating factors.

Culture A particular set of attitudes, beliefs, and practices that characterize a group of individuals.

Cyberliability A legal concept that employers can be held liable for the actions of their employees in their Internet communications to the same degree as if those employers had written those communications on company letterhead.

D

Death Penalty (FSGO) A fine that is set high enough to match all the organization's assets—and basically put the organization out of business. This is warranted where the organization was operating primarily for a criminal purpose.

Developed Nation A country that enjoys a high standard of living as measured by economic, social, and technological criteria.

Disclosure (FCPA) The FCPA requirement that corporations fully disclose any and all transactions conducted with foreign officials and politicians.

Dodd-Frank Wall Street Reform and Consumer Protection Act Legislation that was promoted as the "fix" for the extreme mismanagement of risk in the financial sector that lead to a global financial crisis in 2008–2010.

E

Ethical CSR Purest or most legitimate type of CSR in which organizations pursue a clearly defined sense of social conscience in managing their financial responsibilities to shareholders, their legal responsibilities to their local community and society as a whole, and their ethical responsibilities to do the right thing for all their stakeholders.

Ethical Dilemma A situation in which there is no obvious right or wrong decision, but rather a right or right answer.

Ethical Reasoning Looking at the information available to us in resolving an ethical dilemma, and drawing conclusions based on that information in relation to our own ethical standards.

Ethical Relativism Gray area in which your ethical principles are defined by the traditions of your society, your personal opinions, and the circumstances of the present moment.

Ethics The manner by which we try to live our lives according to a standard of "right" or "wrong" behavior—in both how we think and behave toward others and how we would like them to think and behave toward us.

Ethics Officer A senior executive responsible for monitoring the ethical performance of the organization both internally and externally.

External Whistle-Blowing An employee discovering corporate misconduct and choosing to bring it to the attention of law enforcement agencies and/or the media.

Extranet A private piece of a company's Internet network that is made available to customers and/or vendor partners on the basis of secured access by unique password.

F

Facilitation Payments (FCPA) Payments that are acceptable (legal) provided they expedite or secure the performance of a routine governmental action.

Federal Sentencing Guidelines for Organizations (FSGO) Chapter 8 of the guidelines that hold businesses liable for the criminal acts of their employees and agents.

Financial Stability Oversight Council (FSOC) A government agency established to prevent banks from failing and otherwise threatening the stability of the U.S. economy.

Foreign Corrupt Practices Act (FCPA) Legislation introduced to control bribery and other less obvious forms of payment to foreign officials and politicians by American publicly traded companies.

G

GAAP The generally accepted accounting principles that govern the accounting profession—not a set of laws and established legal precedents but a set of standard operating procedures within the profession.

Global Code of Conduct A general standard of business practice that can be applied equally to all countries over and above their local customs and social norms.

Globalization The expansion of international trade to a point where national markets have been overtaken by regional trade blocs (Latin America, Europe, Africa), leading eventually to a global marketplace.

Golden Rule Do unto others as you would have them do unto you.

I

Instrumental Approach The perspective that the only obligation of a corporation is to maximize profits for its shareholders in providing goods and services that meet the needs of its customers.

Instrumental Value The quality by which the pursuit of one value is a good way to reach another value. For example, money is valued for what it can buy rather than for itself.

Internal Whistle-Blowing An employee discovering corporate misconduct and bringing it to the attention of his or her supervisor, who then follows established procedures to address the misconduct within the organization.

Intranet A company's internal Web site, containing information for employee access only.

Intrinsic Value The quality by which a value is a good thing in itself and is pursued for its own sake, whether anything comes from that pursuit or not.

L

Less-Developed Nation A country that lacks the economic, social, and technological infrastructure of a developed nation.

M

Multinational Corporation (MNC) A company that provides and sells products and services across multiple national borders. Also known as *transnational corporations*.

O

OECD Guidelines for Multinational Enterprises Guidelines that promote principles and standards of behavior in the following areas: human rights, information disclosure, anticorruption, taxation, labor relations, environment, competition, and consumer protection; a governmental initiative endorsed by 30 members of the Organization for Economic Cooperation and Development and 9 nonmembers (Argentina, Brazil, Chile, Estonia, Israel, Latvia, Lithuania, Romania, and Slovenia)

Organizational Culture The values, beliefs, and norms that all the employees of that organization share.

Organizational Integrity A characteristic of publicly committing to the highest professional standards and sticking to that commitment.

Oxymoron The combination of two contradictory terms, such as "deafening silence" or "jumbo shrimp."

P

Proactive Ethical Policies Policies that result when the company develops a clear sense of what it stands for as an ethical organization.

p. 32; Richard C. Warren, "Whistleblowing: Subversion or Corporate Citizenship?" (review), *Journal of Occupational and Organizational Psychology* 71, no. 4 (December 1998), p. 372; Ann Hayes Peterson, "Inside the WorldCom Fraud," *Credit Union Magazine* 71, no. 8 (August 2005), p. 15.

6 Laura M. Franze, "Corporate Compliance: The Whistleblower Provisions of the Sarbanes-Oxley Act of 2002," *Insights: The Corporate & Securities Law Advisor* 16 (December 2002), p. 12.

7 Peter Rost, *The Whistleblower: Confessions of a Healthcare Hitman* (Brooklyn, NY: Soft Skull Press, 2006).

Chapter 8

1 Thomas L. Friedman, *The World Is Flat: A Brief History of the Twenty-First Century* (New York: Farrar, Straus, and Giroux, 2005). Copyright © 2005 by Thomas L. Friedman. Reprinted by permission of Farrar, Straus, and Giroux, LLC.

2 A. Moore, "Employee Monitoring and Computer Technology Evaluative Surveillance v. Privacy," *Business Ethics Quarterly* 10, no. 3 (2000), pp. 697–709.

3 "Life inside a Call Centre," www.letsfixbritain.com/callcentres .htm.

4 Michael Hanscom, www.michaelhanscom.com.

5 Stanley Holmes, "The Affair That Grounded Stonecipher," *BusinessWeek,* March 7, 2005.

6 Amar Toor, "Employees' Extramarital E-Mails Creep Out Entire Cornell Campus," www.switched.com/2009/11/09/employees-extramarital-e-mails-creep-out-entire-cornell-campus/.

7 Jose Antonio Vargas, "The Face of Facebook," *The New Yorker,* September 20, 2010, www.newyorker.com/ reporting/2010/09/20/100920fa_fact_vargas?currentPage=all.

8 Shane Hickey and Fiona Ellis, "PricewaterhouseCoopers Staff Brought to Book over Raunchy Emails," *Belfast Telegraph,* November 10, 2010.

9 Online Lawyer Source, www.onlinelawyersource.com.

10 "Cyberliability: An Enterprise White Paper," Elron Software, 2001.

11 Electronic Privacy Information Center, www.epic.org/privacy /workplace/.

Chapter 9

1 Terri Morrison and Wayne A. Conaway, *Kiss, Bow, or Shake Hands: The Bestselling Guide to Doing Business in More Than 60 Countries,* 2d ed. (Holbrook, MA: Adams Media, 2006).

2 "Unfortunate Translations That Harmed Brand Reputations," www.thethinkingblog.com/2007/09/13-unfortunate-translations-that-harmed.html.

3 Lester Thurow, "Third World Must Help Itself," *Boston Globe,* August 7, 2001, p. F4.

4 R. DeGeorge, "Ethics in Personal Business—A Contradiction in Terms?" *Business Credit* 102, no. 8, 1993, pp. 45–46.

5 William Greider, *One World, Ready or Not: The Manic Logic of Global Capitalism* (New York: Touchstone, 1998), p. 22.

6 "Overview of the UN Global Compact," www.unglobalcompact .org/AboutTheGC/index.html.

7 OECD Guidelines for Multinational Enterprises, June 2001, www .oecd.org.

Chapter 10

1 Simon Webley, "Eight Steps for a Company Wishing to Develop Its Own Corporate Ethics Program," www.ibe.org.uk/developing .html.

2 Dan Rasmus, "The New World of Work: Transparent Organizations," White Paper, Microsoft Business Division, February 2006.

Recurring design images: "Ethical Dilemma" by Thomas Northcut/Life-size/Getty Images and "Checklist" by thesuperph/iStockphoto

Part 1

1 Corbis Premium RF/Alamy

Chapter 1

2–3 Corbis/PictureQuest; **4** BananaStock/PunchStock; **5** Swim Ink 2, LLC/CORBIS; **6** Peter Coombs/Alamy; **8** © PunchStock/Brand X Pictures; **9** Stockbyte/PunchStock; **11** © Hulton-Deutsch Collection/CORBIS; **17** John Brecher/Corbis; **18** Hulton Archive/Getty Images; **19** Keith Brofsky/Getty Images

Chapter 2

20–21 Veer; **24** (l) Custom Medical Stock Photo/Alamy, (r) BananaStock/PunchStock; **25** © AP Photo; **28** PNC/The Image Bank/Getty Images; **30** © Stockbyte/Getty Images; **36** MAX NASH/AFP/Getty Images; **37** Thinkstock Images/Comstock/Getty Images; **39** Siede Preis/Getty Images

Part 2

41 Fancy/Veer/Corbis

Chapter 3

42–43 BananaStock Ltd.; **45** © Radius Images/Alamy; **47** The McGraw-Hill Companies, Inc./Jill Braaten, photographer; **49** Digital Vision; **51** © 2009 Jupiterimages Corporation; **53** TRBfoto/Getty Images; **54** Tanya Constantine/Digital Vision/Getty Images; **60** AP Photo/Joe Raymond; **61** The McGraw-Hill Companies, Inc./Andrew Resek, photographer; **62** The McGraw-Hill Companies, Inc./Photo by Eric Misko, EliteImages Photography

Chapter 4

64–65 U.S. Coast Guard photo by Petty Officer 3rd Class Patrick Kelley; **67** Steven Mark Needham/Envision/Corbis; **69** Reuters/CORBIS; **70** © Brand X Pictures/PunchStock; **72** © The McGraw-Hill Companies, Inc./Mark Dierker, photographer; **73** Brand X Pictures; **75** Jocelyn Augustino/FEMA; **82** The McGraw-Hill Companies, Inc./John Flournoy, photographer; **83** Photodisc/Getty Images; **85** Digital Vision/PunchStock

Chapter 5

86–87 Royalty-Free/Corbis; **89** Photodisc Collection/Getty Images; **90** Simon Dawson/Bloomberg via Getty Images; **92** © AARON M. SPRECHER/epa/Corbis; **95** © Royalty-Free/CORBIS; **97** (b)Tetra Images/Corbis; **102** Tony Avelar/Bloomberg via Getty Images; **103** Photodisc/Getty Images; **105** Siede Preis/Getty Images

Chapter 6

108–109 Royalty-Free/CORBIS; **111** Stockdisc/PunchStock; **114** © Charles Gullung/zefa/Corbis; **118** © PhotoAlto/PunchStock; **119** Frank Rumpenhorst/epa/Corbis; **121** Eyewire (Photodisc)/PunchStock; **126, 128** Photodisc/Getty Images; **130** Photo by Janette Pellegrini/WireImage

Chapter 7

132–133 OJO Images Ltd/Alamy; **134** Radlund & Associates/Getty Images; **136** (l) Christian Simonpietri/Sygma/Corbis, (r) Mark Peterson/Corbis; **137** © Photodisc/Getty Images; **138** © BEEPstock/RobinBeckham/Creative/Alamy; **146** Stockbyte/PunchStock; **147** Joe Raedle/Getty Images; **149** Royalty-Free/CORBIS

Chapter 8

152–153 Royalty-Free/CORBIS; **154** BananaStock/Jupiterimages; **156** © INSADCO Photography/Alamy; **158** Tony Baker/Brand X/Corbis; **161** © Radius Images/Corbis; **168** Randy Allbritton/Getty Images; **169** Andrew Harrer/Bloomberg via Getty Images; **171** ColorBlind Images/Blend Images/Corbis

Part 3

173 Sean Gladwell/Alamy

Chapter 9

174–175 Ryan McVay/Getty Images; **177** Copyright 1997 IMS Communications Ltd/Capstone Design. All Rights Reserved; **178** © Comstock/PunchStock; **179** Ingram Publishing/Alamy; **180** © Photodisc/Getty Images; **182** Brand X Pictures; **189** Courtesy TOMS Shoe Company; **190** iPhone product photo courtesy of Apple; **191** Getty Images/Jon Feingersh Photography Inc.

Chapter 10

194–195 moodboard/Corbis; **196** Stockbyte/PunchStock; **199** (t) © Digital Vision, (b) © Adam Gault/Getty Images; **201** © Terry Vine/Getty Images; **207** C Squared Studios/Getty Images; **208** U.S. Navy photo by Mass Communication Specialist 2nd Justin E. Stumberg; **209** Science Photo Library/Getty Images.

U.S. Federal Sentencing Guidelines for Organizations
     (FSCO) (1991)
  compliance program recommendations of, 113–114
  function of, 112, 122
  monetary fines under, 113, 122
  organizational probation under, 113
  revision of, 115
Universal ethics, 6–7, 47
University of Michigan, 72–74
Utilitarianism, 6, 47, 176–177

V

Value chain, 44–45, 53, 54
Values
  conflict in, 5, 29
  explanation of, 4–5, 14
Value system
  business ethics and, 29
  conflict in, 54
  cultural differences and, 183
  explanation of, 4
  role of, 7
Vance, Ashlee, 200
VanCity, 218
Vargas, Jose Antonio, 232
Vendor Code of Conduct (University of Michigan), 72
Verschoor, Curtis C., 231
Vicarious liability, 160–161, 165
Vickers, M. R., 231
Vietnam War, 136
Virgin Group, 74
Virtue ethics, 6
Vise, David A., 169
Volcker, Paul, 121
Volcker Rule, 121, 123

W

Wachovia Bank, 117
Wakefield, Andrew, 209–210
Waksal, Sam, 130
Walmart, 23, 37, 38, 78, 82–83
Walton, Sam, 82
Ward, Steve, 180
Warren, Richard C., 232
Washington Mutual, 117
Wassener, B., 129
Watergate scandal, 136
Waters, Richard, 148
Watkins, Sherron, 136
Weatherall, David, 150
Webley, Simon, 232

Weeden, Curt, 83, 84
Weinberg, Neil, 231
Weintraub, Arlene, 39
Welch, David, 139
Wells Fargo, 117
Whistle-blower hotline, 140–141
Whistleblower Protection Act of 1989, 138, 140
Whistle-blowers
  addressing needs of, 140–141, 143
  examples of, 136, 138–139, 146–150
  explanation of, 134, 143
  legal protections for, 138–139
  movie portrayals of, 137–138, 147
Whistle-blowing
  duty to respond and, 136, 138, 140
  ethics of, 134–136
  explanation of, 134
  external, 134
  internal, 134
  as last resort, 141
White-collar crime, 117
Wigand, Jeffrey, 132, 137–138, 143
WikiLeaks, 147–148
Wilkie, Wendell L., 175, 184
Willard, Bob, 216
Willumstad, Robert, 119
Wilson, Jason, 170
WiPro Technologies, 128
Woellert, Lorraine, 103
Woodward, Bob, 136
Workplace
  employee monitoring in, 157–159, 164
  privacy issues in, 153, 154, 159, 162–163
World Bank, 128
WorldCom, 23, 24, 38, 97, 98, 117–119, 136
The World Is Flat (Friedman), 154–155
Wu, Debby, 191

Y

Young, Andrew, 30
Young, Larry, 207
Yuanquig, Yang, 180

Z

Zadek, Simon, 219
Zarrella, Ronald, 60
Zeneca, Inc., 135
Zimmer Holdings, 39
Zittrain, Jonathan, 148
Zuckerberg, Mark, 159
Zuckoff, M., 127